T0296022

Corporate Social Responsibility, Corporate Governance and Business Ethics in Tourism Management

Corporate Social Responsibility, Corporate Governance and Business Ethics in Tourism Management: A Business Strategy for Sustainable Organizational Performance

EDITED BY

ERUM SHAIKH

Shaheed Benazir Bhutto University, Sanghar Campus, Pakistan

AND

KULDEEP SINGH

Amity University, Haryana, India

United Kingdom – North America – Japan – India – Malaysia – China

Emerald Publishing Limited
Emerald Publishing, Floor 5, Northspring, 21-23 Wellington Street, Leeds LS1 4DL.

First edition 2025

British Library Cataloguing in Publication Data
A catalogue record for this book is available from the British Library

ISBN: 978-1-83608-705-2 (Print)
ISBN: 978-1-83608-704-5 (Online)
ISBN: 978-1-83608-706-9 (Epub)

INVESTOR IN PEOPLE

Contents

About the Editors

Erum Shaikh has a Ph.D. from the Institute of Business Administration, University of Sindh, Jamshoro, Pakistan. She is an Assistant Professor and Head of Department at the Department of Business Administration, Shaheed Benazir Bhutto University, Sanghar Campus. Her research interests are corporate social responsibility, finance, entrepreneurship, sustainability, corporate governance, management and entrepreneurial finance. She has authored more than 30 publications (research papers, conference papers and book chapters) in the abovementioned areas. She has edited two books and is the editor of five research journals. She has wide experience in teaching and administration and has served more than 10 years in academics. She has organized and participated in several research conferences and workshops as a keynote speaker, session Chair, and guest speaker. She is a good teacher, researcher, speaker, and trainer.

Kuldeep Singh currently serves as Assistant Professor in Amity School of Hospitality, Amity University, Haryana, India. He completed his Ph.D. in Tourism from Maharishi Dayanand University (Rohtak) in India in the year 2020. He is also a UGC (Net-JRF qualified). He has also served the tourism industry for a couple of years and more than three years in academics. He has so far published more than 30 research articles in both international and national referred journals as well as in edited books in the field of tourism. Currently, he is serving as an editor of book series in various reputed publications (Emerald, IIP series). He is passionate about the academic areas of service quality management, rural tourism, ecotourism, and sustainable tourism. He also won aspiring researchers welcome award from the Indian Hospitality Congress. His credentials may be verified on various research platforms like Google Scholar, SSRN, LinkedIn, Academia, and Research Gate (https://orcid.org/0000-0002-7999-1585).

About the Contributors

Qasim Ali Nisar is a distinguished Casual Lecturer at the School of Business & Law, RMIT University, Australia, where he contributes his expertise to shaping the minds of future business leaders. With over a decade of teaching and research experience, he is a seasoned academic who has made significant contributions to the field of business and management. In addition to his role at RMIT University, he serves as a Casual Academic at Central Queensland University, Australia, further expanding his impact in the academic community. He is also affiliated with Taylors University Malaysia as an Adjunct Senior Lecturer, demonstrating his global reach and influence in academia. His dedication to excellence is reflected in his extensive publication record, with over 100 publications in impact-factor journals. His research covers a wide range of topics within the realm of business and management, showcasing his interdisciplinary approach and his commitment to advancing knowledge.

Anchal is a third-year student pursuing B.B.A L.L.B. at Chanakya National Law University, Patna, India. Her research paper written on Reserve Bank of India's Central Bank Digital Currency (CBDC), elucidating its implications and regulatory challenges, appeared in the *DSNLU Journal*. 'Domain of Intellectual Property Rights (IPR) in the Digital Era', highlighting the challenges posed by rapid digitalization, appeared in *E-Jairipa*. 'Impact of Increasing Hate Against Muslims in India' appeared in *Brillopedia* journal. 'Military Coups and it consequences: How it can be resolved?' appeared in *Juscorpus*. 'Politics Over Secularism' appeared in *Manupatra*. 'Russian Currency Getting Stronger Even During War like Situations' appeared Manupatra. Case commentary written on *Analyzing passive euthanasia appeared Lawogs & D. K. Basu vs State of West Bengal appeared Lawogs*.

Ulfat Andrabi is pursuing a Ph.D. from Lovely Professional University in Punjab, India, and holds an MBA from Baba Ghulam Shah Badshah University in Jammu and Kashmir. Passionate about HRD issues, her research focusses on innovative approaches to employee motivation and performance enhancement in the corporate sector.

Aaliya Ashraf is a Research Scholar at Mittal School of Business, Lovely Professional University. Her research domain is Human Resource Management. She studied at Lovely Professional University from where she did her Bachelors in Commerce. Further, she was awarded with M.B.A. (HR & IB) degree from the same university. She is a gold medalist of her batch in her bachelor's degree.

She has published three papers so far in UGC care journals. Furthermore, she has participated and presented papers in about seven national and international conferences. She has experience of working as a Teaching Fellow at Lovely Professional University.Her areas of interest include human resource management, organizational behaviour, performance management system, international business, and cross-cultural management.

Bandna is currently pursuing Ph.D. at the School of Management and Commerce at Lovely Professional University, India. Her research interest is in corporate social responsibility, sustainability, and organizational performance.

Priyanka Chhibber is the COD Coordinator in Human Resource Management of Lovely Professional University in Punjab, India. As a researcher, her focus areas include intellectual capital, value creation, HRD climate, leadership, mentoring, skill gaps, life skills, organizational commitment, and creativity and innovation.

Hafizullah Dar is working as an Assistant Professor in the Tourism and Airline domain at the School of Hotel Management and Tourism, Lovely Professional University, Punjab, India. He has obtained a Ph.D. degree in Tourism Management. His research interest covers tourism services, technology in tourism, tourist behaviour, and destination management and planning. He has authored and co-authored various publications in different reputed journals (https://orcid.org/0000-0003-2388-9474).

Mudasir Ahmad Dar is currently working as an Assistant Professor at Mittal School of Business, Department of Economics. He has more than three years of experience, with a Doctorate in Economics. His courses consistently reached maximum capacity because of the student's appreciation of his teaching approach. He endeavours to present the information in an engaging and captivating manner to facilitate students' comprehension of the material and sustain their interests.

Bidhu Kanti Das is an Associate Professor at Department of Management, Mizoram University, Aizawl. He completed his Ph.D. studies in Corporate Social Responsibility at Tripura University. He recently led the ICSSR Sponsored Major Projects. He has published 32 papers in various journals and serves as a life member for NIPM & NEMA. His teaching disciplines include general management, international business, and CSR and corporate governance, and his interests include CSR and corporate governance (https://orcid.org/0000-0002-7968-9693).

Shikha Dhakad is a Research Scholar at Jiwaji University, with a focus on tourism management. Her research focusses on destination management and stakeholder involvement in particular as sustainable tourism strategies. By combining thorough academic research with real-world application, She seeks to close the gap between theory and practice and advance sustainable tourism. She is committed to promoting eco-friendly travel and has made noteworthy advances in the fields of academics (Orcid: 0000-0002-2438-063X).

Dev Dutt is currently working as PGTIP at Jawahar Navodaya Vidyalaya, Sarol, Chamba, Himachal Pradesh. He has done his bachelor degree and master degree in Computer Application. He has knowledge of many computer programming languages like JavaScript. Python. Go. Java. Kotlin. PHP.C.

Faheem Gul Gilal is an Associate Professor, Department of Business Administration, Sukkur IBA University. He holds esteemed positions of Director ORIC and Editor-in-Chief of the Sukkur *IBA Journal of Management and Business*. He has M.S. and was awarded a Ph.D. with distinction from the School of Economics and Management, University of Science and Technology Beijing in P.R China. His research interests primarily revolve around consumers' motivation and emotion, with a special emphasis on brand passion, product design techniques, brand experiences, consumer behaviour change strategies, CSR brand-fit, cross-cultural gender-specific consumer behaviour differences, and self-determination theory. He has an extensive publication record, published over 60 research papers in SSCI, ABDC, and SCOPUS-listed journals. Throughout his academic journey, he excelled and earned numerous prestigious academic awards, including China's most esteemed National Award and the Highly Commended Award for his outstanding dissertation in the field of Marketing and Brand Management.

Dikshit Gupta is a seasoned professional with an expansive expertise spanning multiple domains, including ICT in tourism, tourism administration, travel agency operations, strategic management, and tourism marketing. His academic journey is marked by exceptional accomplishments, holding a Post-Doctorate, a Ph.D., and dual master's degrees in M.T.A. (Masters of Tourism Administration) and M.B.A. (Master of Business Administration), along with UGC-NET qualification. Currently serving as an Associate Professor at Lovely Professional University. he boasts a distinguished 14-year career in academia. He has held key roles as an Associate Professor at Maharaja Agrasen University and as Deputy Head of Department at ITFT College, Chandigarh. Along with this, he has a strong publication and research paper presentation record (https://orcid.org/0000-0002-2558-9849).

Aastha Jain is an Assistant Professor in the Department of Management Studies, Vaish College of Engineering, Rohtak, since 2021 (affiliated to Maharshi Dayanand University Rohtak, Haryana). She has B.Com. (Hons.), M.Com., Ph.D. degrees and is UGC-NET qualified. She got her Ph.D. degree in Commerce from Maharishi Dayanand University. She has published many research papers in various national and international (UGC/peer reviewed) journals. She has also presented many research papers at various sponsored conferences and seminars. Her main research interests include investment behaviour, entrepreneurship, marketing and human resource, etc. (https://orcid.org/0000-0003-1081-9135).

Junaid Khalil is a dynamic scholar in the Department of Management Science at COMSATS University Islamabad, Lahore Campus, with a wealth of experience spanning over five years in the field of human resource management (HRM). His expertise lies at the intersection of HRM, automation, and information technology (IT), making him a valuable asset in today's rapidly evolving workplace landscape. With a background in IT, he brings a unique perspective to his work in HRM. His understanding of technology has enabled him to spearhead initiatives aimed at streamlining processes and enhancing efficiency in people management. Throughout his career, he has been deeply involved in harnessing the power of automation to optimize HR practices. From talent acquisition and performance management to employee engagement and training, he has leveraged cutting-edge technologies to drive organizational success.

Imamuddin Khoso has a Ph.D. in Management from Tohoku University, Japan. He is a Professor and Director Institute of Business Administration, University of Sindh, Jamshoro, Pakistan. He has authored over 65 publications (research papers, conference papers, and book chapters). He remains the resource person and keynote speaker at national and international conferences. He has wide experience in teaching and administration and has served more than 25 years in academics. He won the gold medal for the best researcher award in 2018. He is a good teacher, researcher, speaker, and trainer.

Ruchika Kulshrestha, Ph.D., is working as an Assistant Professor at the Institute of Business Management at GLA University Mathura, India. Her research interest pertains to heritage tourism, destination management, tourism marketing, and tourist behaviour. She has published her research work in reputed international Scopus-indexed journals and also presented papers at various international conferences. Her articles are published in the *Economic Times, Travel Daily News,* and other magazines. She had the opportunity to be a session chair at IIM Kashipur and DSMS Durgapur, among others. She has received various awards for her contribution to tourism education. She is actively involved in faculty development programmes and student value-added courses.

Rajinder Kumar is working as a Coordinator & Assistant Professor at the Department of Travel and Tourism Management, University of Ladakh. He has been teaching for nine years at the undergraduate and postgraduate levels. His area of research interests are tourism education, urban environment, CSR, workation, geotourism, and destination performance analysis. He has published papers in ABDC and Scopus-indexed journals (https://orcid.org/0000-0003-0466-1140).

Sanjeev Kumar is a Professor cum HOD, the School of Hotel Management and Tourism, Lovely Professional University, Punjab, India. He holds a bachelor's degree in Hotel Management from Osmania University. He earned his master's degree in Tourism Management from Madurai Kamaraj University and his Doctorate from Amity University, Rajasthan. He has worked as a teacher for the past 18 years. While in Kuwait, he worked as an Assistant Dining Manager for Gulf Catering Company and other hotels. He has 20 research articles and has presented more than 12 papers at national and international conferences. He supervises six Ph.D. research scholars and has directed many M.B.A. and M.Sc. research projects in hospitality and tourism. He has taken part in several faculty development programmes and workshops. He also travelled throughout the country to attend international and national conferences (https://orcid.org/0000-0002-7375-7341).

Shweta Mathur is currently employed at the Alpha College of Business and Technology, situated in Canada, UK, and boasts an extensive background spanning approximately two decades in both academic and industry realms. She is an alumnus of IHM Lucknow, and prior to her tenure in Canada, she contributed her expertise to several distinguished institutions including DIHM in Lajpat Nagar, Delhi, IHM Dehradun, IHM Lucknow, as well as The Grand Hotel in New Delhi, among others. Holding accreditation as a Certified Hospitality Educator from the American Hotel and Lodging Institute, she has consistently demonstrated proficiency in academic and related capacities, underscored by her adept interpersonal abilities and meticulous attention to detail.

Priyakrushna Mohanty is an Assistant Professor at the Department of Business Administration (Tourism), Christ University, Bengaluru, India. He was a former UGC Senior Research Fellow at the Department of Tourism Studies, Pondicherry University, India, from where he received his Ph.D. in Tourism Studies. He is also an awardee of the prestigious Travel Corporation (India) Gold Medal for his outstanding performance in master's degree in Tourism Studies from Pondicherry University, India. He served the Indian Railway Catering and Tourism Corporation Ltd. for two years. He has published more than 30 papers in both international and national journals and edited books. He has presented more than 25 papers at both international and national conferences to his name. Several national and international institutes have invited him as a guest speaker. He is the editor for five book projects with prestigious publishers like Routledge, Emerald, Springer Nature, and CABI.

Tanjila Afroz Mou is a Lecturer at Bangladesh's Daffodil Institute of IT. She has been working in the teaching area for five years. She is a highly experienced professional in education and research, currently serving as a lecturer at the Daffodil Institute of IT. Her research interests cover many topics, demonstrating her keen intellect and understanding of business interconnections. Her scholarly pursuits contribute valuable insights to the academic community and the industries she serves. She maintains an active presence in the academic and research communities, with a commitment to advancing knowledge (https://orcid.org/0009-0003-5924-6726).

Kamarun Muhsina is a highly experienced professional in education and research, currently serving as a Lecturer at the Daffodil Institute of IT. She is also pursuing an M.Phil. in Tourism and Hospitality Management at the University of Dhaka, focussing on tourism and hospitality management. Her research interests cover many topics, demonstrating her keen intellect and understanding of business interconnections. Her scholarly pursuits contribute valuable insights to the academic community and industries she serves. She maintains an active presence in the academic and research community, with her commitment to advancing knowledge (https://orcid.org/0009-0004-0991-2716).

Muhammad Mukarram is a dedicated Lecturer at the Chaudhary Abdul Rehman Business School, situated within the esteemed Faculty of Business & Management Sciences at Superior University, Lahore, Pakistan. With over a decade of teaching and research experience, he is not only a proficient educator but also a skilled manager, currently serving as the Manager of Capacity Building at the same university. His journey in academia began with a passion for knowledge and a desire to inspire others. Over the years, he has honed his teaching skills, earning a reputation for his engaging lectures and innovative teaching methods. His commitment to academic excellence has left a lasting impact on his students, who are inspired by his dedication and enthusiasm for learning. In this capacity, he has demonstrated exceptional leadership and management skills, overseeing various initiatives aimed at enhancing the skills and capabilities of both students and faculty members.

Sheikh Najam-mu-Sahar is a Research Scholar, pursuing Ph.D. in Management, from Mittal School of Business, Lovely Professional University, Punjab, India. Her area of research is medical tourism and healthcare management. She has presented her research work at a couple of national and international conferences (https://orcid.org/0009-0003-9830-1329).

Sreeraman Nandhi transitioned to academia in 2019 after 22 years in pharmaceutical sales and marketing with MNCs and domestic companies. His expertise includes design thinking workshops, sales management, case study writing and teaching, brand management, integrated marketing communication, supply chain management, and training and development. A fitness enthusiast and passionate road cyclist, he believes in shaping one's destiny through passion, preparation, practice, persistence, and good mentors, while maintaining self-empathy. He advocates for optimism, confident that tomorrow holds new opportunities.

Kumari Neelam is currently pursuing her Ph.D. in Finance from the Department of Commerce, Mahatma Gandhi Kashi Vidyapith, Varanasi, Uttar Pradesh. She has published a number of research papers in ABDC and peer-reviewed journals. Her research interests include corporate finance, financial markets, and investment strategies. Additionally, she has presented her work at various national and international conferences, receiving commendations for her contributions to the field.

Neha Parveen is a Freelance Researcher. She has completed her M.Tech. from the Indian Institute of Technology (ISM), Dhanbad, and B.Tech. in Computer Science & Engineering. Her research interests are in the areas: Big data, news media, political marketing, and election campaign. She has published various research articles in ESCI, ABDC, and Scopus-indexed journals. Her last research publication was *Big Data, Artificial Intelligence and Machine Learning: A Paradigm Shift in Election Campaigns* (Wiley Online Library). Her research papers have appeared in the *International Journal of Economics and Business Research* and in many more.

Syed Rizwan Qadri is a Research Scholar at Lovely Professional University India pursuing her Ph.D. in Economics, with a good academic record. Her research focusses on the sustainability and efficiency of manufacturing industries.

Shiv Raj is a Ph.D. scholar in Department of Tourism and Travel Management, Central University of Himachal Pradesh. He has successfully written and published twelve research papers and one patent in respective field. He has authored three text books on tourism and research ethics. He has done two postgraduate diplomas after Postgraduation in the areas of tourism, tribal study, and environmental sustainability. He has six years of academic experience.

Aamir Rashid, an Assistant Professor of Supply Chain Management (SCM) at York College, The City University of New York (CUNY), blends academic excellence with industry expertise. With a career spanning teaching, research, and leadership, he shapes future management professionals and contributes significantly to SCM. His tenure at Iqra University in Pakistan highlighted his leadership and mentorship skills. He is a prolific researcher, actively participating in international conferences and publishing in prestigious journals. His 19 years of industrial experience enrich his academic pursuits, ensuring practical relevance. He actively organizes international conferences, serves on editorial boards, and reviews for multiple journals, underscoring his commitment to high research standards and knowledge exchange in SCM.

Iffat Sabir is Deputy Dean of the College of Business at Al Ain University, UAE. She is a Senior Certified Professional and a Human Resource Management Associate Professor. She received her Ph.D. in Management from the University of Hull, UK. Her research interests include emotions in organizational life, organizational culture, workforce psychology, strategic human resource management, and systems studies. She has authored/co-authored several papers in peer-reviewed journals and conferences. She has taught courses in organizational behaviour, communication, and management to graduate and postgraduate students at the Sultanate of Oman and Pakistan higher educational institutions. She has also offered professional training and lectures to several private/public institution personnel including Flight Lieutenants and Commodores, Technical Education Heads, and Corporate employees on communication skills, personality development, teamwork, institutional management, and other organizational behaviour-related areas.

Md Safiullah is an Assistant Professor at Chanakya National Law University, Patna, India. He has completed his Ph.D. in Management, thesis titled *Efficacy of Political Advertising – A Study of Indian Elections* from the Indian Institute of Technology, Dhanbad, and M.B.A. with a specialization in marketing from Birla Institute of Technology Mesra. He qualified UGC-NET in June and December 2012. His research interests are in the areas: big data, social media (Twitter &

Facebook), news media, political marketing, and election campaigns. He has published various research articles in ESCI, ABDC, and Scopus-indexed journals. His recent research publication is *Big Data, Artificial Intelligence and Machine Learning: A Paradigm Shift in Election Campaigns* (Wiley Online Library). He has presented many research papers in international and national conferences. He is also a reviewer of the *Asia Pacific Management Review* and *Spanish Journal of Marketing & Journal of Marketing Communications*.

Nancy Sahni is an Associate Professor and the HOD (Accounting and Business Law domain) at the Mittal School of Business, Lovely Professional University. Her research domain is behavioural finance. She did her graduation and postgraduation from Punjab University Chandigarh and got a Doctorate degree from IKGPTU. She has more than 15 years of teaching experience. She has taught various subjects in the areas of finance, banking, insurance, accounting, and law. She has one patent and thirteen publications to her credit. She has also written four book chapters.

Ali Sajjad is an esteemed Assistant Professor at the Chaudhary Abdul Rehman Business School, within the Faculty of Business & Management Sciences at Superior University, located in Lahore, Pakistan. With a robust academic background and a wealth of experience, he is recognized as a leader in the field of business and management studies. His academic journey took him to Universiti Utara Malaysia, where he pursued and successfully completed his Ph.D. His doctoral research focussed on cutting-edge topics within the realm of business, demonstrating his commitment to advancing knowledge and understanding in his field. With over a decade of teaching and research experience, he brings a depth of expertise to his role as an educator. He is known for his engaging teaching style, which combines theoretical knowledge with practical insights drawn from his research and industry experience.

Savita Sharma brings over two decades of extensive experience to her present role as Chairperson and Skill Associate Professor and Director, IQAC at the Department of Tourism and Hospitality, Shri Vishwakarma Skill University, Palwal (India's First Government Skill University). With a notable career, she has held key positions at renowned institutions such as GD Goenka University, Gurgaon; Amity University, Noida; Sushant University, Gurgaon; Ansal Institute of Technology, Gurgaon; IHM Mumbai, and CT Institute, Jalandhar. She is recognized as a 'Certified Hospitality Educator' by the American Hotel & Lodging Educational Institute. Her achievements include receiving awards such as the 'Indian Youth Icon Award 2024' by the International Council for Education, Research, and Training, 'Best Research Paper Awards', and the 'Best Groomed Trainee Award by Hyatt Regency, New Delhi'. Notably, she was also honoured with the Silver Award in the category of Hospitality Educator of the Year 2021 during the Indian Hospitality Excellence Awards organized by the Hospitality Group, Dubai. Her academic contributions extend to over 50 research papers presented and published in both national and international conferences and reputed journals. Her commitment to excellence is underscored by her continuous pursuit of knowledge and her impactful contributions to the field of hospitality and tourism education.

Suman Sharma is currently working as a Professor in Department of Tourism & Travel Management, Central University of Himachal Pradesh. He has more than 20-year academic experience. He has spent time in the industry for a decade. He is the author of many text books. He has published two patents on their study.

Mushtaq Ahmad Shah is a Finance Expert with a Ph.D. in Infrastructure Finance. He teaches banking, finance, and economics at Lovely Professional University in India. He has over eight years of experience teaching and researching at various institutions. He's written articles in academic journals and presented his work at conferences on green banking, partnerships between public and private sectors, and behavioural finance.

Muhammad Haseeb Shakil is a dedicated scholar in the field of Management Science, currently affiliated with the Department of Management Science at COMSATS University Islamabad, Lahore Campus. With a passion for both teaching and research, he has made significant contributions to academia over the past five years. His academic journey began with a strong foundation in Management Science, which he pursued with diligence and enthusiasm. After completing his higher education, he embarked on a career in academia, where he found his true calling. His commitment to excellence in teaching has earned him recognition as a Visiting Lecturer at the Faculty of Engineering & Technology, Superior University Lahore. With over 10 publications in impact factor journals, he has demonstrated a keen insight into the complexities of management and a dedication to advancing the field through rigorous research.

MB Srinivasan is an Assistant Professor at CHRIST (Deemed to be University) in Bangalore. Previously, he was a Professor and Head of the Department of Business Administration at VMRF, Chennai, and Programme Leader (M.B.A.) at Olympia College, Malaysia. He holds degrees from the University of Madras and a Ph.D. from Bharathiar University. He began his career in the software industry and transitioned to academia, with teaching positions at Veltech University and VMRF. He has over 15 years of teaching and 8 years of industry experience. His research interests include digital marketing, consumer behaviour, and sustainability.

Sidharth Srivastava has acquired nearly 17 years of experience in both industry and academia. His dedication to learning and research distinguishes his academic journey, with a robust background in the hospitality industry. He has made significant contributions to renowned organizations such as Four Seasons Hotel Mumbai, Air India, Lovely Professional University, Ansal University, BCIHMCT IP University, and Galgotias University, with around 20 national and international research papers. His impact extends beyond conferences and seminars. He has publications in SCOPUS-indexed journals. Moreover, his publications are in A-star, B and C category journals (ABDC listed), and UGC listed journals. He is not just an author; he is a visionary whose impact transcends the written word. His dynamic engagement with industry and academia, coupled with a commitment to innovation, makes him a pioneering figure in the event management landscape.

Pravin Chandra Singh is currently working as an Assistant Professor at MSMSR, Mats University, Chhattisgarh. Prior to Mats University, he was associated with Raffles University, Rajasthan. He has done his Doctorate from IM-BHU in Management and published several research papers in journals and publishers of repute like IIM-S, Elsevier, Emerald, IGI-Global, and PBRI. His research interests include advertising, corporate social responsibility, and consumer behaviour. His credentials may be verified on various research platforms like Google Scholar, LinkedIn, Academia, and Research Gate (https://orcid.org/0000-0002-6002-0703).

Preeti Singh is an Associate Professor, Department of Mass Communication, School of Media, Film and Entertainment, Sharda University, Greater Noida, Uttar Pradesh, India. Dr. Preeti has over 15 years of valuable academic and teaching experience in Media Education. Before assuming the role of Associate Professor at Sharda University, she held positions at GD Goenka University and Amity University, contributing significantly as an Associate Professor and Senior Assistant Professor, respectively. She has also served at esteemed institutions like Guru Gobind Singh Indraprastha University, Maharshi Dayanand University, and Kurukshetra University in various teaching roles. A University of Delhi graduate, she holds an M.Phil. and Ph.D. in Journalism and Mass Communication, receiving the University Research Scholarship. Leveraging her rich industry experience, she has worked as a casual compere with All India Radio and contributed to Community Radio-Radio Amity 107.8 FM at Amity University, Noida.

Premendra Kumar Singh is at present an Assistant Professor at the Center for Distance and Online Education, Sharda University. He is Research Fellow at INTI International University, Malaysia. With over eight years of experience in industry and academia, he is an Engineering and Management graduate from Mizoram University and was awarded his Doctorate from Mizoram University. He has attended and presented papers in over 15 national and international seminars/conferences, and he has published research papers in various national and international peer-reviewed journals of international repute including SCOPUS Q1 journal. He has edited one book and has also contributed book chapters in three edited books. He takes a special interest in corporate social responsibility and marketing for research (https://orcid.org/0000-0002-6627-4560).

Sujay Vikram Singh is a Senior Research Fellow who completed his Doctorate at Banaras Hindu University. He graduated and postgraduated from IHM Lucknow. His research interests include hospitality, CRM, service marketing, service quality, and systematic literature reviews. He has published papers in various handbooks and journals. His recent journal publications include the *International Journal of Market Research* (Sage Publishing) [ABDC-A, Scopus] and the *Journal of Global Information Management* (IGI Publishing) [Scopus, ABDC-A]. He has also been a reviewer for tourism and management journals and has presented and published papers at various national and international conferences and seminars. He has received best paper awards at several conferences, including those held at IHM Bhopal, Subharati University, and Delhi University (https://orcid.org/0000-0002-7113-2698).

Muhammad Faisal Sultan is an academician, researcher, editor, trainer, and green entrepreneur who has been an active part of the higher education sector of Pakistan for the past 13 years. Currently, he is ranked as Assistant Professor in the Department of Business Administration of Khadim Ali Shah Bukhari Institute of Technology. He has more than 100 scholarly publications to his credentials. Therefore, he is perceived as a well-known name in the academic and research circles.

Raju Ganesh Sunder is a Professor and the Director at the Center for Distance and Online Education, Sharda University, Greater Noida. He completed his Ph.D. studies in Management Studies under the Faculty of Commerce at the Rashtriya Sant Tukdoji Maharaj Nagpur University, Nagpur. He recently led the Government of Uttarakhand initiative to upskill executives of the government from the power sector. He has more than 30 published papers in various journals and serves as a Life Member for ISTD, NHRDN, and Executive Member for Uttarakhand Productivity Council. His teaching disciplines include human resource management and organizational behaviour, and his interests include human resource management, organizational behaviour, power management specifically transmission and distribution, and oil and gas management (https://orcid.org/0000-0003-1515-1496).

Mohammad Badruddoza Talukder is an Associate Professor at the College of Tourism and Hospitality Management, International University of Business Agriculture and Technology, Dhaka, Bangladesh. He completed his Ph.D. in Hotel Management at the School of Hotel Management and Tourism, Lovely Professional University, India. He holds a bachelor's and a master's degree in Hotel Management from India. He has been teaching various courses in the Department of Tourism and Hospitality at various universities in Bangladesh since 2009. His research areas include tourism management, hotel management, hospitality management, food and beverage management, and accommodation management, where he has published research papers in well-known journals in Bangladesh and abroad. He is one of the executive members of the Tourism Educators Association of Bangladesh. He has led training and counselling for various hospitality organizations in Bangladesh (https://orcid.org/0000-0001-7788-2732).

Muhammad Nawaz Tunio holds a Ph.D. in Entrepreneurship, Innovation, and Economic Development from Alpen Adria University, Klagenfurt, Austria. Currently, he is serving as an Assistant Professor at the Department of Business Administration, University of Sufism and Modern Sciences, Bhitshah, Pakistan. His research interests encompass a wide range of topics, including entrepreneurship, innovation, economic development, youth development, CSR, and qualitative methods. His scholarly contributions extend far beyond the confines of academia, with numerous research articles published in top-tier journals and prestigious book chapters with reputable publishers. His dedication to academic excellence is further evidenced by his teaching and administrative roles at various universities, where he has mentored students, organized international conferences, and contributed to the development of curricula in Business Administration and Management.

Sanjna Vij is an esteemed academic with over 24 years of experience in academia and administration. She is a Professor at Amity School of Liberal Arts and holds several key leadership roles, including Director of Amity Academic Staff College, Head of the Centre of Excellence for Innovation in Education, and Deputy Dean of Students Welfare at Amity University Haryana. She has significantly influenced education through diverse academic programmes and skill development initiatives. She has been instrumental in faculty development programmes, seminars, conferences, and training sessions for both faculty and students. Specializing in communication skills and behavioural sciences, she has authored numerous articles, book chapters, and three books. She is a distinguished leader in academia, actively shaping the future of education with innovation and a holistic approach to learning.

Bhumi Vyas works as an Assistant Professor at the Faculty of Management Studies, Marwadi University in Rajkot, Gujarat. Before her recent appointment, she worked as an Assistant Professor at the M.B.A., Faculty of Management Studies, Parul University, Vadodara, Gujarat. She has a total experience of 10 years in industry and teaching. She has completed her Ph.D. in Management Subject aligned to the tourism industry. She is a Gold Medalist in B.B.A. She has presented papers at national and international conferences including IIM – Samabalpur. She has published approximately nine papers in a reputed journal (https://orcid.org/0000-0001-7242-2286).

Vijay H. Vyas is at present working as Professor (Direct Recruitment), Department of Commerce & Management, KSKV Kachchh University, Bhuj. He specializes in accounting and finance. His area of interest includes taxation, operation research, and GST. He holds a Doctorate in Finance. He has 22 years of teaching and 5 years of industrial experience including with reputed corporate houses like GEB (PGVCL), GSFC, and Reliance Industries. He has published 48 research papers in international and national journals and also presented research papers and articles in 55 national and international conferences. He has also published three books and two academic projects are in his name. He has been visiting Reliance Industries Ltd., Jamnagar for executive training programmes since 2004. Six scholars have been awarded a doctorate under his supervision and five scholars are reading Ph.D. He believes human values to be topmost and perpetuation of them in personal and social life every day (https://orcid.org/0000-0002-1003-2546).

Foreword

In recent years, the tourism industry has experienced exponential growth, becoming one of the world's largest and fastest-growing economic sectors. This growth brings with it a myriad of opportunities, but also significant challenges, particularly concerning sustainability, ethical practices, and social responsibility. As the global community becomes increasingly aware of the environmental and social impacts of tourism, the importance of integrating corporate social responsibility (CSR), corporate governance, and business ethics into the core strategies of tourism businesses cannot be overstated.

Corporate Social Responsibility, Corporate Governance and Business Ethics in Tourism Management: A Business Strategy for Sustainable Organizational Performance addresses these critical issues comprehensively and thoughtfully. The contributors to this volume bring together a wealth of knowledge and expertise from diverse geographical and academic backgrounds, providing a multifaceted perspective on the integration of CSR into tourism management.

The chapters in this book explore a wide range of topics, from the strategic importance of heritage conservation to the implementation of community-based tourism initiatives. Each chapter delves deeply into the practical and theoretical aspects of CSR, offering valuable insights and practical recommendations for businesses, policymakers, and scholars alike. The case studies included in the book serve as exemplary models of how CSR can be effectively implemented to achieve sustainable and ethical tourism practices.

One of the key strengths of this book is its emphasis on the interconnection between CSR and corporate governance. It highlights how robust governance frameworks are essential for the successful integration of CSR into corporate strategies, ensuring that businesses operate responsibly and sustainably. Furthermore, the book underscores the role of ethical business practices in building trust and loyalty among customers, employees, and other stakeholders.

The importance of community engagement is a recurring theme throughout this volume. Effective CSR in tourism requires a collaborative approach, involving local communities in decision-making processes and ensuring that tourism development benefits all stakeholders. By showcasing successful community-based tourism projects and providing strategic guidelines, this book serves as an invaluable resource for fostering inclusive and sustainable tourism development.

As the world faces unprecedented environmental and social challenges, the principles and practices outlined in this book are more relevant than ever. The future of tourism depends on our collective ability to balance economic growth with social and environmental responsibility. This book provides a roadmap for achieving this balance, offering a vision for a tourism industry that is not only profitable but also sustainable and ethical.

I am confident that *Corporate Social Responsibility, Corporate Governance and Business Ethics in Tourism Management: A Business Strategy for Sustainable Organizational Performance* will be a seminal contribution to the field of tourism studies. It will inspire and guide current and future generations of tourism professionals, helping them to navigate the complexities of CSR and ethical management in their pursuit of sustainable organizational performance.

I commend the authors for their dedication to advancing knowledge in this critical area and for their commitment to promoting sustainable and ethical practices in the tourism industry. It is my hope that this book will serve as a catalyst for positive change, encouraging tourism businesses around the world to embrace CSR and strive for a more sustainable and equitable future.

Last but not least, I appreciate the efforts, commitment, and dedication of the editors of the book who touched the new perspectives of CSR, invited and selected the chapters with new and interesting topics which are great contributions to the field of CSR and tourism.

Prof. Imamuddin Khoso
Director IBA,
University of Sindh, Jamshoro, Pakistan

Preface

In an era where the global landscape is continuously reshaped by environmental challenges, economic fluctuations, and evolving social expectations, the tourism industry stands at a pivotal juncture. The book, *Corporate Social Responsibility, Corporate Governance and Business Ethics in Tourism Management: A Business Strategy for Sustainable Organizational Performance*, addresses this crucial intersection, offering insights and strategies for fostering sustainability in tourism. Tourism, by its very nature, impacts diverse ecosystems, cultures, and economies. While it holds the potential to drive significant economic growth and cultural exchange, it also poses risks such as environmental degradation, cultural erosion, and social inequality. The balance between leveraging tourism for economic benefit and ensuring its sustainability is delicate and complex. This book aims to provide a comprehensive framework for understanding and implementing corporate social responsibility (CSR) within the tourism sector, emphasizing its role as a cornerstone for sustainable organizational performance.

The concept of CSR has evolved beyond philanthropy and compliance, becoming an integral part of strategic business management. In tourism, CSR encompasses a wide range of practices, from minimizing environmental footprints and preserving cultural heritage to promoting fair labour practices and engaging in community development. By integrating CSR into their core strategies, tourism businesses can enhance their resilience, reputation, and profitability while contributing to the well-being of the destinations they serve. This book is divided into several sections, each delving into different facets of CSR, corporate management, and business ethics as they pertain to tourism management. The first section lays the theoretical groundwork, exploring the evolution and principles of CSR and business ethics. Subsequent sections provide practical insights into the implementation of CSR strategies, case studies illustrating successful applications, and analyses of the challenges and opportunities faced by tourism enterprises.

A significant emphasis is placed on the role of corporate management in driving CSR initiatives. Effective leadership, transparent governance, and ethical decision-making are highlighted as critical elements for embedding sustainability into organizational culture. The discussion extends to how businesses can measure and report their CSR performance, ensuring accountability and continuous improvement.

Another focal point of this book is the symbiotic relationship between tourism businesses and the communities they operate within. Sustainable tourism is not just about environmental conservation but also about fostering social equity and

economic prosperity for local populations. Through responsible tourism practices, businesses can create shared value, benefiting both the enterprise and the
community.

This preface serves as an invitation to scholars, practitioners, policymakers,
and students to explore the intricate dynamics of CSR in tourism management.
The insights presented in this book aim to inspire and guide tourism professionals
in their journey towards sustainability, offering a roadmap for achieving long-
term organizational success while making a positive impact on the world. As
we navigate the complexities of the 21st century, it is imperative for the tourism
industry to embrace sustainable practices. This book is a testament to the potential of CSR, corporate management, and business ethics to transform tourism
into a force for good, fostering a sustainable future for generations to come.

Acknowledgements

All our dreams can come true if we have the courage to pursue them. — *Walt Disney, Entrepreneur*

First and foremost, our heartfelt thanks to the almighty whose blessings motivated us for the successful completion of this book, especially focussed on Corporate Social Responsibility, Business and Tourism.

Our sincere thank goes to all authors and co-authors whose interest, initiative, integrity, commitment, hard work and valuable contributions added the steps in the ladder of this successfully edited work. We highly appreciate the reviewers' timely feedback and expertise in this book.

We sincerely thank Emerald Publishing and all team members for their constant support in successfully editing this book. Without their support and guidance, the completion of this task would have been merely a dream.

No words are sufficient to express our debt of gratitude for our parents who are always blessing us to do something meaningful in this materialistic world. We express our gratitude towards our beloved family members.

Last but not least, we are also thankful to our friends and relatives, for their continuous heart touch in the final shaping of this book.

Thanking you

Editors:
Dr Erum Shaikh
Dr Kuldeep Singh

Introduction

The global tourism industry stands at a crossroad, faced with the dual imperative of driving economic growth while ensuring sustainability. The book, *Corporate Social Responsibility, Corporate Governance and Business Ethics in Tourism Management: A Business Strategy for Sustainable Organizational Performance*, is a timely exploration of how businesses within the tourism sector can achieve this balance. Through the integration of corporate social responsibility (CSR), ethical management practices, and robust corporate governance, tourism enterprises can chart a path towards sustainable success. The significance of the tourism industry cannot be overstated. It is a powerful engine of economic development, providing employment opportunities, fostering cultural exchange, and contributing significantly to gross domestic product in many countries. However, tourism also has profound impacts on the environment, local communities, and cultural heritage. The challenge is to harness the benefits of tourism while mitigating its adverse effects, ensuring that growth today does not compromise the ability of future generations to meet their own needs.

This book is premised on the belief that CSR and ethical management are not mere add-ons to business strategy but are essential components of sustainable organizational performance. CSR in tourism encompasses a broad spectrum of practices aimed at promoting environmental stewardship, social equity, and economic viability. These practices include reducing carbon footprints, preserving local cultures, ensuring fair labour conditions, and contributing to community development. By adopting CSR principles, tourism businesses can enhance their reputation, foster customer loyalty, and achieve long-term profitability. The structure of this book is designed to provide a comprehensive understanding of how CSR, corporate management, and business ethics intersect and how they can be effectively applied in tourism management. We begin with a theoretical overview, examining the evolution of CSR and its relevance to the tourism industry. This section also delves into the principles of business ethics, exploring how ethical considerations can and should inform corporate decisions and strategies.

Following the theoretical foundation, we present practical insights into implementing CSR initiatives. This section includes detailed case studies of tourism enterprises that have successfully integrated CSR into their operations. These case studies highlight best practices, innovative approaches, and the tangible benefits of sustainable business practices. Readers will gain valuable lessons on how to navigate the complexities of CSR implementation, from stakeholder engagement to measuring and reporting CSR performance. An essential aspect of this book is its focus on corporate management. Effective leadership and governance are critical to driving CSR initiatives and embedding sustainability into organizational culture. We explore the roles and responsibilities of corporate leaders in fostering an ethical and socially responsible business environment. Topics such as strategic planning, corporate governance, and ethical leadership are discussed in depth, providing readers with practical tools and frameworks for effective management.

The relationship between tourism businesses and the communities they operate within is another central theme of this book. Sustainable tourism is not only about minimizing negative impacts but also about creating positive value for local populations. Through responsible tourism practices, businesses can contribute to the social and economic well-being of their host communities, fostering a symbiotic relationship that benefits all stakeholders. As we embark on this exploration of CSR, corporate governance, and business ethics in tourism management, we invite you to consider the profound impact that responsible and ethical practices can have. The journey towards sustainability is challenging, but it is also filled with opportunities for innovation, growth, and positive change. Together, we can build a more sustainable and equitable future for the tourism industry and the global community it serves. The book emphasizes the importance of balancing corporate goals with social and environmental responsibilities, thus offering a holistic approach to CSR in the tourism industry. Heritage conservation not only preserves the tangible and intangible assets of communities but also fosters cultural diversity and global citizenship. The book underscores the need for ethical business practices and highlights successful CSR strategies implemented by multinational corporations. By exploring these themes, the book aims to provide valuable guidance for integrating CSR into corporate strategies, ultimately contributing to the long-term sustainability of tourism management. These chapters will explain the CSR issues.

Chapter 1 addresses four primary objectives: evaluating current multinational heritage conservation initiatives, analysing motivations behind corporate involvement, assessing the challenges, and introducing a Framework for Heritage Conservation as a CSR Strategy (FHCCS). This research can be categorized as conceptual research. Thematic content analysis has been performed on the data retrieved from 47 papers which were screened and acquired from various academic search engines. The study revealed that multinational companies engage in heritage conservation initiatives as part of their CSR strategies, yielding benefits for both heritage sites and surrounding communities. Key motivations include enhancing corporate reputation, stakeholder relations, and long-term sustainability, with the FHCCS offering guidance for policymakers and practitioners.

Chapter 2 exclusively focusses on the Delhi NCR region of India and the CSR advertising campaigns of ITC hotels restricting the study's ability to generalize the findings to other contexts within the hotel industry. This study aims to exert an influence on the perceptions of consumers and societal attitudes towards the practices of CSR. It provides valuable insights into the wider implications that these practices have on sustainable business practices and the potential for social change and makes CSR communication more impactful to the targeted audience which in turn creates a positive image of the advertised brand and how they are doing their CSR activities. The study shows that informativeness belief is the strongest predicator and creativity is the weakest predicator of consumer's attitude towards CSR advertising campaigns in hotel industry.

Chapter 3 aims to find out the factors affecting female entrepreneurship in the case of the CSR in entrepreneurship. In this study, semi-structured interviews are conducted to reach the final findings of the study. Findings entail different six factors that severely affect CSR activities in entrepreneurship in Pakistan. These six factors are the educational system and skills gap, cultural mindset and risk aversion, limited access to finance, regulatory and bureaucratic hurdles, political instability and security concerns, and inadequate infrastructure. Every factor has its intensity and influence on the entrepreneurial process.

Chapter 4 aims to investigate how hotel performance is affected by CSR initiatives. This study used a mixed approach utilizing both primary and secondary sources. Secondary research involved gathering pertinent data from various sources such as websites, books, and publications. Additionally, a structured questionnaire was administered to the guests of deluxe category hotels to gauge their perceptions regarding the influence of CSR practices on hotel performance. It is found that implementing the CSR practices contributes to fostering guests' loyalty and willingness, thereby indirectly enhancing hotel performance positively.

Chapter 5 addresses the complex interplay among the CSR, governance, and ethics in the context of tourism management in India. It shows us how businesses engage in sustainable practices that contribute to social economics tourism. This research takes a multi-face approach, theoretical framework, and practice case study to indicate the relationship based on CSR corporate governance and business ethics. The study shows that the real case study in Jaipur and Indore. Given the limitations of the case study research, such as potential basis and limited generalization, this study is necessary for future empirical investigation to validate and expand upon the findings presented here. The chapter discusses the societal significance of business practices. It promotes greater corporate engagement in addressing social, environmental, and economic challenges by showing the positive impact of CSR initiatives on local communities. Through case studies and empirical analysis, the chapter reveals how CSR initiatives can improve corporate governance, promote ethical business practices, and positively impact the local economy and environment. It also shows how important evidence-based decision-making matters.

Chapter 6 emphasizes to understand the development of Corporate Social Responsibility Law in India and sheds light on companies' brand building among Indian Muslims through CSR activities during Hujj and Umrah. The present study is exploratory and qualitative in nature and follows a case discussion approach to understand the degree at which companies engage in CSR activities during Hajj and Umrah and consider CSR as a business strategy in band building. The data were collected mainly from secondary sources like newspapers, articles, news reports, agencies" reports, etc. Companies participating in CSR initiatives create positive impacts on society creating long-term brand loyalty among customers and positioning companies in the customer good list. Customers share positive experiences and create a sense of attachment with the company and good feelings are spreaded through word of mouth and social media. The company received a free brand promotion on social media through customers a reliable source and the company communicated with customers thoughtfully. CSR programmes during Umrah and Hajj also provide an opportunity for global outreach. The findings of the present study can be used to understand the strategic use of CSR in corporate brand building in other countries also and in other festivals. The present study is interdisciplinary in nature and a combination of law and business management. The study on CSR has been conducted in many areas, but CSR activities during Hujj and Umrah a strategic decision to build brand image by Indian companies have not been studied yet. The present study will also help in developing theory and companies understand the importance of CSR activities during Huj and Umrah.

Chapter 7 is specifically written in association with the tourism industry to make readers understand the implication of place attachment with CSR activities. This chapter also has a role in theoretical optimization as it highlights possible two-way associations between firm performance and CSR. Data have been collected through published material to develop postulates and models authentically. After the compilation of data, it has been presumed that place attachment is one of the important elements in CSR activities of small-scale tourism businesses. However, the model can be reassessed in two-way association as a decline in the company's performance may also cause a decline in CSR activities and also in place attachment.

Chapter 8 aims to assess the CSR in tourism and hospitality offering a thorough understanding of CSR in a wider context of sustainability, financial performance (FP) and ethical considerations. A qualitative desk research approach was undertaken to conduct this study. A thorough review of contemporary research literature, including content analysis, was done for data gathering. Findings show that CSR is rising as a key trend in the worldwide tourism and hospitality business, with a significant impact on the industry's performance and development. The tourism and hospitality industry shows both positive and negative economic impacts on the environment and society. To offset these negative impacts, this industry is progressively embracing CSR initiatives. The findings also demonstrate an integration between CSR and sustainable tourism, highlighting the stability of socioeconomic, environmental, and cultural growth while considering the interests of all stakeholders. The effect of CSR on the FP of the tourist and hospitality industry was also studied. The findings reveal that CSR has a favourable influence on the FP of hotels, but mixed outcomes are shown in restaurants, cruises, and airlines. Highlighting insights on tourism corporations incorporating strategic and ethical CSR ideals into their activities, this study concludes with practical implications.

Chapter 9 investigates the relation between CSR and the FP of Tata firms, which is the major objective of this study. Numerous studies have been undertaken to investigate the influence of CSR on the FP of businesses, resulting in varying findings. The fundamental purpose of this research is to provide an investigation utilizing accounting metrics including ROE, EPS, ROA, NP, and MB ratio, PE ratio, and MR as potential indications for market-based evaluations. It is possible that erroneous analysis or insignificantly controlled variables played a role in the wide range of results, but the most likely explanation is simply that different studies used different methods. By focussing specifically on Tata Group companies that are publicly traded on the BSE100, this research endeavours to investigate the correlation between CSR and FP within the Indian context. The findings of the study depict that FP is positively impacted by the amount spent on CSR by the companies. Companies that invest more in CSR undoubtedly have higher profitability, ROA, ROE, EPS, MB ratio, and MR_Daily as the values are significant at 1%, 5%, and 10%, respectively.

Chapter 10 investigates the impact of digital disruption on tourism education in the 21st century. Research problem: Digital disruption is causing a major upheaval in the tourism education sector, which is affecting how teachers instruct and how students learn. The purpose of this study is to investigate ways in which educators can adjust to these changes and to comprehend the impact of digital disruption on tourism education. A mixed-methods strategy integrating quantitative and qualitative methods was employed. An online survey and in-depth interviews with 100 participants – students, professionals in the industry, and educators – were used to gather data. For qualitative data, thematic analysis was employed, whereas descriptive statistics were used for quantitative data. Participants generally perceived a moderate to high level of disruption, suggesting that there is a significant level of digital disruption in tourism education. The study emphasizes how critical it is to incorporate new technologies into curricula, stress the value of sustainable development, enhance intercultural competency, and promote cooperation between academic institutions and the travel and tourism sector.

Chapter 11 examines how satisfied tourists are with Kachchh Rann Utsav and whether they plan to revisit. The researcher used tourists who have visited Kachchh Rann Utsav previously as a sample based on the cluster sampling method. The sample size for this research was 478. The present study has considered the 7As of tourism: attraction, accessibility, amenities, accommodation, activities, awareness, and ancillary service to measure the underlying satisfaction. The researcher used multinomial logistic regression to predict the travellers' intention to revisit. Surprisingly, the researcher observed that the other six A's of tourism have been found not to affect tourists' revisit intention, although accommodation does. Thus, the researcher thinks that a shift in the quality of lodging services offered to visitors during Kachchh Rann Utsav will have a big influence on the extent and direction of their desire to return to Kachchh Rann Utsav.

Chapter 12 tries to provide a thorough explanation of the growth of community-based tourism in Bangladesh, encompassing its historical background, challenges faced, and potential strategies for future advancement. They employed a descriptive analysis based on the literature review of the development and expansion of community-based tourism in Bangladesh. This study takes a look at the development of Community-based tourism (CBT) throughout history, as well as the innovative contributions made by non-governmental organizations (NGOs) and local groups in CBT initiatives, government policies, international recognition, challenges encountered (such as environmental and economic concerns), and potential strategies for future expansion. The results highlight the significant growth of community-based tourism in Bangladesh, which has been facilitated by historical progress, strategic initiatives for expansion, and government support. This chapter emphasizes addressing environmental and economic challenges, preserving and educating about cultural heritage, and empowering local communities. The document suggests various methods for future growth, including developing policies, involvement of the private sector, execution of marketing strategies, and empowerment of the community through training and enhancing their abilities. The study provides insightful information regarding the distinctive characteristics of community-based tourism in Bangladesh, drawing attention to the country's long-standing tradition of extended hospitality and cultural heritage. Moreover, the study analyses the difficulties and opportunities that CBT efforts encounter in the region and the proposition of individualized solutions for sustainable growth.

Chapter 13 aims to give comprehensive strategies for developing sustainable tourism destinations by incorporating case studies, conceptual frameworks, and existing research. By addressing the lack of holistic approaches in sustainable tourism practices, this study seeks to provide insightful information that can guide stakeholders, policymakers, and destination managers in effective decision-making and planning. A comprehensive literature review has been conducted for analysing peer-reviewed journal papers, case studies, and conceptual frameworks relevant to sustainable tourism benchmarking. Peer-reviewed journal papers, case studies, and conceptual frameworks pertaining to sustainable tourism benchmarking have all been examined through a thorough assessment of the literature. In this study, numerous information on sustainable tourism and benchmarking strategies allows for a meticulous understanding of benchmarking and its relevancy to sustainable tourist destination development. The study distinguishes essential strategies for benchmarking sustainable tourist destinations, which include stakeholder engagement, integration of the triple bottom line framework, choosing appropriate indicators, promotion of certification and standards, and encouraging collaborations among destinations. The case studies highlight, the significance of having a long-term commitment, governance, and stakeholder involvement while implementing sustainable tourism policies. This study presents a combination of existing literature and frameworks to evolve comprehensive strategies for benchmarking sustainable tourist destinations. By incorporating perceptions from various sources, this study gives valuable direction for practitioners and researchers seeking to advance sustainable tourism practices.

Chapter 14 examines the elements and main influences that drive the shift to a net-zero economy, with a particular focus on the relationship between net-zero,

CSR, and the creation of sustainable value. This research employs a secondary data analysis methodology of a systematic review of scholarly research articles, reports, and online resources. Sources such as SAGE and EBSCO are scrutinized, alongside focussed inquiries for qualitative data in academic databases like Emerald and Scopus. The findings reveal that a variety of factors, including climate change awareness, governmental policy and regulation, corporate sustainability initiatives, technological advancements, investor pressure, economic possibilities, and environmental and social movements, all contribute to the shift to a net-zero economy in an interconnected way. This chapter examines the factors that contribute to the shift to a net-zero economy, the critical factors for successful adoption, and the relationship between CSR and the net-zero economy, all of which provide valuable insights for businesses, policymakers, and stakeholders as they navigate the complexities of achieving a sustainable future.

Chapter 15 analyses the CSR. It explores the need of striking a balance between CSR efforts and business goals. The significance of CSR in the tourism industry will also be examined. Lastly, a thorough discussion of how CSR may be used as a tactical move to guarantee sustainability and market competitiveness will round off the chapter. This chapter benefits from the wide range of secondary data sources that are cited as well as the inclusion of important industry reports and assessments. Incorporating CSR into the tourism industry is not just a moral duty but also a critical strategic move towards attaining sustainability and maximizing corporate effectiveness. In light of the ever-changing global landscape that is marked by social inequality, environmental concerns, and issues related to cultural preservation, CSR is playing an increasingly important role in determining the direction that tourism enterprises will take in the future. This chapter's paradigm provides a novel and methodical way to look at CSR as a strategic tool for achieving sustainability in the tourism sector.

Chapter 16 aims to review and brief the role of strategic corporate social responsibility (SCSR) in the tourism industry, targeting its impact on the performance and sustainability of the tourism industry. The chapter seeks to provide insights into how SCSR can lead to a positive transformation and competitive advantage. The chapter incorporates a brief literature review to examine current trends, hurdles, and benchmarking in the implementation of SCSR in the tourism industry. Comparative analysis and recent literature are used to extract valuable results and implications for effective tourism management. The current chapter has limited potential biases in the selection of literature and the evolving nature of CSR in the tourism sector. Future research is required to check the developments in tourism and CSR. The chapter sheds light on the complex association between the performance of CSR and business in the tourism industry, highlighting the importance of governance qualities and new initiatives for achieving financial sustainability. The chapter adds valuable insights to the existing literature by shedding light on the most recent literature on SCSR in the tourism industry and provides inputs for setups looking for sustainability.

Chapter 17 examines the role of CSR in tourism operations, focussing on its influence on FP, social well-being, and environmental sustainability. The study aims to fill gaps in the literature by investigating the relationship between CSR dimensions and FP in tourism organizations, as well as the social and environmental impacts of integrating CSR principles into tourism operations. The study employs a comprehensive literature review to explore the historical background of CSR, its conceptual framework, and its application in the tourism industry. It examines the various dimensions of CSR and their potential effects on FP, social well-being, and environmental sustainability in tourism operations. The findings suggest that CSR initiatives in tourism operations can lead to improved FP through factors such as increased sales, cost savings, and enhanced market value. Furthermore, CSR practices contribute to social well-being by creating job opportunities, supporting local communities, and preserving cultural heritage. Additionally, CSR activities promote environmental sustainability by reducing resource consumption, conserving biodiversity, and mitigating the negative impacts of tourism on ecosystems. This study contributes to the literature by providing insights into the relationship between CSR and FP in tourism organizations, as well as the social and environmental impacts of CSR integration in the tourism industry. The findings highlight the importance of incorporating CSR principles into tourism operations to promote sustainable development and responsible tourism practices.

Chapter 1

Preserving the Past, Enriching the Future: Exploring the Prospects and Challenges of Heritage Conservation as a Corporate Social Responsibility Strategy

Priyakrushna Mohanty, Sreeraman Nandhi and MB Srinivasan

Department of Business and Management, Christ University, Bengaluru, India

Abstract

Purpose: This chapter addresses four primary objectives: evaluating current multinational heritage conservation initiatives, analyzing motivations behind corporate involvement, assessing the challenges, and introducing a Framework for Heritage Conservation as CSR Strategy (FHCCS).

Design/methodology/approach: This research can be categorized as conceptual research. Thematic content analysis has been performed on the data retrieved from 47 papers which were screened and acquired from various academic search engines.

Findings: This chapter revealed that multinational companies engage in heritage conservation initiatives as part of their corporate social responsibility (CSR) strategies, yielding benefits for both heritage sites and surrounding communities. Key motivations include enhancing corporate reputation, stakeholder relations, and long-term sustainability, with the FHCCS offering guidance for policymakers and practitioners.

Research limitations/implications: This chapter aims to provide insights for policymakers, academics, and practitioners, facilitating informed decision-making and enhancing the integration of heritage conservation into CSR strategies on a global scale.

Corporate Social Responsibility, Corporate Governance and Business Ethics in Tourism Management: A Business Strategy for Sustainable Organizational Performance, 1–17
Copyright © 2025 by Priyakrushna Mohanty, Sreeraman Nandhi and MB Srinivasan
Published under exclusive licence by Emerald Publishing Limited
doi:10.1108/978-1-83608-704-520241001

Originality/value: The work tries to fill the research gap in understanding the integration of heritage conservation within CSR frameworks.

Keywords: CSR; heritage conservation; corporate social responsibility strategy; monuments; intangible heritage; environmental stewardship; culture of guardianship; business strategy; sustainable development

Introduction

In an age of fast urbanization, globalization, and technological development, heritage conservation is an essential element to preserve one's history and sense of collective identity (Alonso Gonzalez, 2014). It is imperative to consider the preservation of heritage sites, monuments, and artifacts amidst evolving societal dynamics. This is not only a matter of respecting the past; it is also a strategic undertaking that has significant ramifications for sustainable development and CSR (Starr, 2013). This introduction lays the groundwork for a discussion of how, within the context of different global organizations, heritage conservation efforts might function as efficient CSR methods.

Heritage conservation has an impact on communities all around the world, regardless of their locations (Keitsch, 2020; Nair et al., 2023). Both the tangible and intangible components of heritage – from heritage locations and excavations to cultural customs and practices – make up priceless resources that enhance the human experience and promote a feeling of community (Starr, 2010). In addition, heritage conservation promotes international communication, mutual understanding, and cultural diversity, all of which strengthen the bonds of global citizenship (Otero, 2022). In addition, a crucial path to sustainable development and moral business conduct in an age of fast globalization and increased CSR is the incorporation of heritage protection into organizational initiatives (Starr, 2013). The adoption of heritage conservation initiatives serves to preserve tangible and intangible heritage assets and fosters a sense of CSR that resonates on a global scale, as corporations increasingly recognize their role as stewards of both financial prosperity and cultural legacy.

Heritage conservation is more than just preservation; it is an integrated strategy for preserving the diverse range of heritage, cultural, and natural resources that shape communities all over the world (Labadi et al., 2021). From natural settings to archaeological sites, from architectural landmarks to indigenous customs, the spectrum of heritage includes a wide range of items that represent the collective identity and heritage of humanity. But the need to preserve this legacy goes beyond its inherent worth; it also coincides with more general socioeconomic and environmental goals that calls for reassessment of business agendas and practices (Janssen et al., 2017).

The idea of CSR, which represents an organization's dedication to conducting business morally, sustainably, and with consideration for stakeholders' interests beyond shareholders, is at the core of this paradigm shift (Li & Hunter, 2015). Although environmental stewardship, ethical labor practices, and charity were once the main focuses of CSR, the field has since broadened to include cultural heritage preservation as a fundamental component of ethical business operations (Bindhu & Panakaje, 2023). A rising understanding of the connections between corporate reputation, sustainable development goals (SDGs) and cultural heritage highlights this trend.

This investigation's purposeful global reach reflects the universality of the potential and difficulties associated with integrating CSR and cultural protection. Businesses struggle to strike a balance between the need to maximize profits and address social and environmental issues (Ruggie, 2002), whether they are located in the thriving metropolises of industrialized countries or the remote areas of emerging economies. Furthermore, the reputational risks and benefits of CSR are felt in international markets in an increasingly linked world where supply chains cut across continents and consumer preferences transcend national boundaries (Botero, 2015). Lately, the understanding that heritage conservation has inherent worth in addition to being useful for business branding and legal compliance is at the heart of this investigation (Nag & Mishra, 2023). Corporate heritage protection strengthens the social fabric of communities and promotes intergenerational discussion by helping to preserve identity, memory, and variety (Labadi et al., 2021). In addition, heritage conservation fosters social cohesion, economic resilience, and increased tourism while reducing the negative effects of urbanization, globalization, and climate change.

This research study presents a comprehensive understanding of corporate responsibility that goes beyond conventional measures of financial performance by viewing heritage conservation as an essential part of CSR. Corporations may achieve their ethical responsibilities to society and discover new avenues for innovation, competitive advantage, and long-term value generation by adopting heritage protection as a strategic goal. By means of cooperative alliances, stakeholder involvement, and inventive funding methods, companies may leverage the revolutionary potential of heritage preservation to shape a future that is more resilient, sustainable, and inclusive for future generations (Engizek & Eroğlu, 2022). In order to demonstrate the many facets of heritage conservation as a catalyst for CSR, the authors go into a number of case studies derived from various industries and geographical situations in the sections that follow. From small and medium-sized businesses to multinational firms, from urban revitalization projects to rural community development initiatives, every case study provides a different perspective on the benefits and difficulties of incorporating cultural protection into corporate operations. The researchers distill significant lessons, emerging trends, and practical recommendations for policymakers, practitioners, and scholars interested in furthering the intersection of heritage conservation and CSR on a worldwide scale through cross-sectoral comparisons and theme analysis.

Although the significance of heritage conservation in the context of CSR is becoming increasingly acknowledged, there is still a significant research gap concerning the complex approaches and global viewpoints that firms in this field employ. Further, while a number of studies have examined CSR practices in a variety of industries, there is still a lack of comprehensive research that focuses on the function of heritage conservation programmes within corporate sustainability frameworks. In order to close this gap, this study seeks to accomplish four main goals. Initially, it aims to evaluate the current status of heritage conservation initiatives now carried out by multinational companies in various geographic and cultural contexts. These endeavors reflect the benefits received by the heritage sites and surrounding communities from the CSR strategies based on heritage conservation. Secondly, by analyzing the complex interactions and intricate relationships, the chapter seeks to understand the motivations and drivers underlying businesses' involvement in heritage conservation. For the third objective, the challenges in the paths of heritage conservation as a CSR strategy have been delved in detail. Lastly, the authors of this study have devised a FHCCS that may serve as a guideline document for policymakers, academicians, and other practitioners.

Methodology

The methodological technique applied in this research is a combination of systematic literature review and thematic content analysis. The systematic literature review was conducted to gather relevant articles from academic search engines, while thematic content analysis was utilized to identify key recurring themes and patterns within the selected articles. To collect pertinent publications on the relationship between CSR and heritage conservation, a methodical literature review technique was utilized in this study. Academic publications published in peer-reviewed journals were retrieved using academic search engines including Scopus, Web of Science, and Google Scholar. Keyword combinations like "heritage conservation," "corporate social responsibility," "CSR strategies," and "multinational companies" were among the search terms used. Only English-language articles that were published and accessible were included in the search.

Based on the initial search parameters, a total of 47 results were retrieved. Then, these papers underwent a thorough screening procedure to determine which ones were most pertinent to the goals of the study. Articles that did not specifically discuss how heritage conservation fits into CSR frameworks or that did not discuss about the integration of heritage conservation were not included in the analysis. In order to find important recurrent themes and patterns in the chosen articles, thematic content analysis was used. Using this method, the articles' content was methodically coded and categorized to find recurring themes on CSR strategies, motivations, impacts, drivers, and best practices, as well as heritage conservation. Overarching themes and sub-themes that shed light on the different facets of heritage protection as a CSR tactic surfaced during this process. To complement the findings from academic research, additional grey literature

Step	Description
Literature Search	Web of Science, JSTOR, and Scopus
	"heritage conservation," "corporate social responsibility," "CSR strategies," and "multinational companies"
Initial Screening	Number of records identified: 67
	Number of duplicate records removed: 58
Eligibility Assessment	Inclusion criteria: Relevance to the Research Topic, Publication Date (2000–2020), Language (English Only), Availability of Full Text
	Exclusion reasons: Irrelevant to Research Topic, Duplication, Non-indexed
	Number of records included: 52
Data Extraction	Data items extracted: 47
	Data extraction tool used (if any): Manual extraction
Quality Assessment	Assessment method or tool used for quality evaluation: Scopus and Web of Science indexing

sources were explored, including reports, case studies, and white papers. Grey literature served as illustrative case studies to support the analysis by offering insightful information about actual instances of multinational corporations' conservation efforts for cultural assets.

Prospects for Heritage Sites and Communities

As a CSR approach, heritage conservation covers a wide range of topics that are related to civic engagement, sustainable development, and cultural preservation. This strategy acknowledges the inherent value of legacy resources in advancing economic growth, maintaining cultural diversity, and building social cohesion. These initiatives undertaken by the organizations underscore the positive outcomes experienced by heritage sites and local communities as a result of CSR strategies centered on heritage conservation. In this section, various such prospects for heritage Sites and local communities have been discussed in detail.

Preservation of Tangible Cultural Assets

Historic buildings, archaeological sites, and landscapes of culture are examples of tangible cultural assets that should be preserved as part of a CSR plan. These material representations of history add to a community's architectural and artistic legacy in addition to acting as archives of shared memory and identity. Businesses have the ability to significantly contribute to the preservation and improvement of the built environment, strengthening the cultural fabric of society and creating a feeling of pride and community among locals by funding the upkeep and repair of these assets (Jimura, 2023). For instance, the IT giant company Infosys Ltd. donates a portion of its CSR funds to cultural events and monument restoration in southern India. After investing about Rs. 4.5 crores over a four-year period, the Infosys Foundation, the company's CSR division, finished restoring the Somanatheswara temple complex in Lakshmeshwara, Karnataka, in 2015 (Infosys, 2015).

Preservation of Intangible Cultural Heritage

In addition to tangible heritage, another crucial aspect of heritage conservation as a CSR strategy is intangible cultural assets. The customs, events, languages, and knowledge systems that are passed down from one generation to the next comprise intangible cultural legacy, which reflects the diversity and inventiveness of human communities. Industries can aid in the revitalization of cultural practices and traditions, strengthen local communities, and foster intercultural understanding by supporting initiatives that aim to preserve intangible heritage, such as traditional craftsmanship, folk music, and indigenous knowledge (Sankaran, 2019). The Bhasha research and publication center undertook the enormous People's Linguistic Survey of India project in 2013–2014 with funding from Tata Trusts. With the backing of 3,000 linguists from all over India and 85 institutions, this public–private cooperation was the largest of its kind (Kashyap, 2014).

Sustainable Tourism Development

Moreover, heritage conservation as a CSR approach encompasses broader goals of sustainable development and social responsibility in addition to the protection of cultural assets. Businesses can use heritage as a foundation to develop sustainable tourism, encouraging ethical travel behavior and bolstering regional economies with the least amount of detrimental effects on the environment and cultural resources (Kasemsap, 2018). Corporations can create heritage-based tourism initiatives that support community development, create jobs, and generate economic opportunities while maintaining the authenticity and integrity of heritage sites by collaborating with local governments, non-profit organizations, and communities (Mzembe et al., 2023). Hilton is a multinational hospitality firm that has incorporated CSR into its business strategy through its "Travel with Purpose" project, which emphasizes social impact, community development, and environmental sustainability. As part of this programme, Hilton works with regional partners to encourage sustainable tourism practices and support historic conservation initiatives in the areas where it conducts business (Hilton, n.d.-b).

Promoting Awareness and Capacity Building

Moreover, heritage conservation as a CSR strategy encompasses educational and capacity-building initiatives aimed at raising awareness about the importance of heritage preservation and promoting a culture of conservation among employees, stakeholders, and the wider public. Organizations can interact with stakeholders and local communities through outreach initiatives, workshops, and educational programmes to foster a greater awareness and respect of heritage assets and to motivate active engagement in conservation efforts. Corporations have the ability to establish a conservation culture that is durable over generations and contributes to the preservation of cultural assets by instilling a sense of ownership and stewardship among stakeholders (Röll & Meyer, 2020). For example, Microsoft has started a programme called "AI for Cultural Heritage" to use artificial intelligence (AI) technology to build capacity and conserve cultural assets. Microsoft collaborates with research institutes, cultural institutions, and conservation groups to create AI-driven tools and solutions for heritage documentation, preservation, and study under this programme (Microsoft, 2022).

Social Entrepreneurship

The encouragement of sustainable livelihoods and cultural heritage entrepreneurship is a further aspect of heritage conservation as a CSR approach. Corporations can generate economic opportunities, empower marginalized groups, and foster inclusive growth by providing support to micro-enterprises, craftspeople, and cultural practitioners involved in heritage-related activities (Nthoi-Molefe, 2021). Organizations have the ability to alleviate poverty and promote social equity by forming relationships with local craftsmen and cooperatives, facilitating market access, offering training and capacity-building support, and encouraging the sustainable use of natural and cultural resources. The "Empowering Artisans and Crafters Worldwide" was created by Etsy, an online store that specializes in vintage and handcrafted goods, to aid in the preservation of cultural heritage that is led by artists and traditional crafters worldwide. Through this programme, Etsy supports craftspeople who actively contribute to the preservation of traditional handicraft and cultural heritage in their communities by offering grants, mentorship, and technical support. Etsy fosters a market for ethically sourced and culturally genuine products while supporting sustainable livelihoods, cultural preservation, and economic growth by enabling craftspeople to become conservation entrepreneurs (Etsy, n.d.).

Promoting Environmental Sustainability

Promoting environmental sustainability and heritage conservation frequently go hand in hand as CSR strategies. Numerous historic sites are situated in natural environments and landscapes, which are critical for maintaining ecological functions and biodiversity. Businesses support the preservation of natural habitats, which promotes biodiversity and ecological resilience, by keeping these areas intact. In addition, to lessen the environmental impact of conservation efforts, heritage conservation programmes usually include eco-friendly materials, water-saving techniques, and energy-efficient lighting in restoration projects (Bindhu & Panakaje, 2023). Through these initiatives, businesses support the values of sustainable development and responsible resource management while simultaneously safeguarding cultural assets and furthering more general environmental objectives. Hilton, for instance, makes investments in water conservation, waste management, and energy-efficient technologies to reduce the environmental impact of its operations while promoting community development and cultural preservation initiatives (Hilton, n.d.-a).

Addressing Cultural Heritage at Risk

Cultural heritage is becoming increasingly susceptible to risks like armed conflict, natural disasters, urbanization, and climate change in today's interconnected world. By sponsoring programmes to preserve and protect the cultural heritage that is in danger, organizations play a critical role in mitigating these risks. In conflict zones or disaster-affected communities, this may entail offering financial support, technical aid, and logistical support to historic conservation programmes. Furthermore, corporations have the ability to utilize their power to advocate for policies, mobilize resources, and increase awareness in order to lessen the dangers to cultural heritage and foster resilience in communities that are already at risk (Çalhan, 2022). Corporations exhibit their commitment to human rights, peacebuilding, and sustainable development by demonstrating sympathy with affected populations and supporting initiatives to preserve their cultural legacy. To save the Italian village of Grottole, Airbnb invited people from all over the world to move to Southern Italy and volunteer to revitalize the village that is at risk of disappearing. More than 280,000 people applied, and five candidates were selected to become temporary citizens of Grottole (Airbnb, 2019).

Empowering Indigenous Peoples

Indigenous groups are often the groups that look after the natural resources, customs, and traditional knowledge connected to heritage sites. For cultural heritage to be managed sustainably and preserved, these communities must be empowered. Businesses have the power to uphold traditional governance structures, encourage conservation efforts headed by indigenous people, and guarantee the significant involvement of local stakeholders in heritage conservation decision-making processes (Angelbeck, 2017). Through acknowledging the rights and goals of local communities and indigenous peoples, corporations support inclusive development, cultural diversity, and social justice. In addition, giving local communities more authority improves the integrity and authenticity of heritage sites, enhancing visitor experiences and encouraging a greater respect for cultural heritage among visitors and the general public. For instance, Natura, a Brazilian cosmetics company, launched the "Amazon Forever" initiative (refer WWF, 2014) to support indigenous communities and traditional knowledge holders in the Amazon rainforest region. Through this initiative, Natura collaborates with indigenous artisans and cooperatives to develop sustainable harvesting practices for natural ingredients used in its products while promoting cultural preservation and economic empowerment.

Understanding the Underlying Motivations and Drivers

Understanding the underlying motivations and drivers behind CSR initiatives is essential for comprehending the intricate relationship between business objectives and societal impact. Among the diverse array of CSR endeavors, the funding of initiatives for heritage conservation emerges as a compelling subject, reflecting the intersection of business interests, cultural preservation, and environmental stewardship. Companies engaging in CSR for heritage conservation navigate a complex landscape driven by a multitude of factors, ranging from brand enhancement and stakeholder expectations to long-term sustainability considerations and risk mitigation strategies (Starr, 2010). Delving into the underlying motives offers valuable insights into the rationale guiding corporate decision-making, shedding light on the interconnected dynamics shaping the contemporary corporate landscape. This exploration seeks to uncover the multifaceted motivations that propel companies toward investing in heritage conservation as part of their broader CSR agenda. Below are some of the major motivations and drivers for companies funding heritage conservation as CSR strategy has been discussed in detail.

Brand image enhancement: Businesses understand that taking part in CSR projects, especially those that support the preservation of cultural heritage, can improve their reputation and brand image (Amer et al., 2023). Companies present themselves as socially conscious organizations that care about the communities in which they operate by linking themselves with initiatives to protect cultural assets. Increased customer trust, loyalty, and preference for their goods and services might result from this favorable impression.

Stakeholder expectations: Stakeholders such as investors, employees, consumers, and regulators are putting increasing demands on businesses to show that they are committed to social and environmental sustainability. Contributions from corporations to CSR programmes for heritage conservation are in line with stakeholders' expectations that businesses will make a good impact on the environment and society (Nave & Ferreira, 2019). Fulfilling these requirements can assist businesses in preserving their social license to operate and avert reputational hazards linked to alleged disregard for environmental and societal issues.

Long-term sustainability: Businesses understand that preserving cultural heritage is essential to the long-term viability of the communities and settings in which they do business. Businesses support the preservation of local identity, history, and customs by funding initiatives that protect cultural assets (Siyal et al., 2022). These elements are crucial for preserving social cohesion and resilience. Furthermore, history preservation can make places more alluring to tourists, which will eventually boost local economies and companies.

Market differentiation: Companies support CSR programmes that fit with their beliefs, mission, and target market preferences in an effort to set themselves apart from rivals (Camarero & Garrido, 2012). Companies can distinguish themselves in crowded markets by demonstrating their dedication to protecting cultural heritage and advancing sustainable development by sponsoring heritage conservation programmes. A greater market share and level of brand loyalty among customers that value ethical and socially conscious companies can result from this differential.

Employee engagement and morale: Businesses are aware of the positive effects meaningful CSR initiatives, like heritage conservation, can have on staff retention, morale, and satisfaction. Encouraging projects that enable workers to support cultural heritage preservation and community outreach can cultivate a sense of pride, purpose, and loyalty among the workforce (Wells et al., 2016). A positive work culture and the well-being of employees can be enhanced by offering employees opportunities for personal development, skill enhancement, and team building through participation in CSR projects.

Networking: Businesses see investing in CSR programmes for heritage preservation as a means of breaking into new markets and gaining new clientele. In areas where heritage conservation is a top priority, supporting initiatives that protect cultural heritage can lead to new partnerships, collaborations, and market expansion opportunities (Starr, 2013). Companies can also use their participation in historic conservation initiatives to create new goods and services that address cultural experiences, heritage tourism, or sustainable development issues.

Challenges in Heritage Conservation as a CSR Strategy

Heritage protection has several advantages as a CSR strategy, but the paths to achieve the optimum outcomes are surrounded by numerous obstacles. Businesses that participate in heritage conservation programmes have a variety of challenges, from budgetary limitations to complex legal frameworks. This section explores the main obstacles to heritage conservation as a CSR strategy, examining the complexities, risks, and implications for the business entities.

Financial constraints and resource limitations: Initiatives for heritage conservation face major obstacles due to a lack of funding and resources (Biraglia et al., 2018). Projects involving preservation and restoration frequently need large sums of money for supplies, labor, knowledge, and continuing upkeep. However, businesses using heritage conservation as a CSR strategy may find it difficult to devote enough financial resources, especially in the face of conflicting objectives and tight budgets. Inadequate finance may make it more difficult to carry out conservation programmes, postpone restoration activities, or result in subpar work. Furthermore, because financial resources might change over time, procuring long-term funding for conservation and maintenance initiatives provides a constant challenge. Beyond just being unable to afford it, resource restrictions also include not having access to the specialized knowledge, supplies, and machinery needed for heritage conservation (Biraglia et al., 2018). Strategic planning, innovative funding sources, and cooperation with stakeholders – including governments, nonprofits, and community organizations – are all necessary to address budgetary and resource limits. Companies can overcome financial constraints and help to preserve cultural property for future generations by prioritizing conservation initiatives and successfully mobilizing resources.

Complex regulatory environment and permitting processes: Heritage conservation programmes face numerous difficulties due to intricate legislative frameworks and permitting procedures. Many rules, legislation, and permission requirements that differ between jurisdictions and regions apply to heritage conservation projects (Veldpaus et al., 2021). This regulatory environment can be expensive, time-consuming, and full of bureaucratic roadblocks. Zoning laws, historic preservation rules, and environmental impact assessments are just a few of the many constraints that businesses using heritage conservation as a CSR strategy must deal with. Permits for restoration projects, archaeological digs, and development of heritage sites are frequently obtained through protracted paperwork, public hearings, and regulatory agency reviews. Companies looking to implement heritage conservation efforts within stipulated deadlines and budgets may encounter difficulties due to delays in acquiring approvals or legal challenges that can impede development and increase project expenses. Complicating compliance activities are often made more difficult by contradictory regulatory requirements or overlapping jurisdictions. In order to guarantee compliance and expedite approval processes, handling complicated regulatory environments and permitting procedures necessitates proactive involvement with regulatory agencies, stakeholders, and legal specialists. Businesses can help preserve cultural heritage and remove obstacles to heritage conservation by skillfully managing regulatory issues.

Technical expertise and conservation skills gap: For businesses participating in CSR projects in this area, the technical know-how and conservation abilities necessary for heritage conservation pose a substantial barrier. Specialized knowledge in fields including architecture, archaeology, material science, and conservation techniques is required for heritage conservation initiatives (Starr, 2010). Unfortunately, there is frequently a lack of trained experts with the necessary training and experience, especially in areas where heritage conservation is not given enough priority or funding. Organizations may face difficulties in attracting and retaining proficient personnel, resulting in deficiencies in technical know-how and capability. In addition, the lack of conservation skills is not limited to the workers; it also affects local communities and stakeholders that are engaged in historic preservation. Ensuring the sustainability and long-term viability of initiatives requires equipping communities with the necessary information and skills to participate in conservation efforts. However, a lack of training opportunities, educational materials, and practical experience could make it more difficult to involve the community and develop capacity.

Risk of damage and loss during restoration: One of the biggest obstacles to heritage conservation initiatives is the possibility of loss and damage during restoration (Bai & Nam, 2020). Even while restoration projects are meant to protect cultural assets, if they are not carried out carefully and expertly, they may unintentionally endanger historic buildings, artifacts, or cultural landscapes. Damage during restoration work can be increased by a number of factors, including inadequate planning, a lackluster assessment of structural integrity, and the choice of improper materials. Natural catastrophes like earthquakes and floods can also provide unanticipated risks to heritage assets, increasing the likelihood of loss. It takes careful planning, adherence to conservation principles, and the involvement of knowledgeable experts with experience in cultural preservation to mitigate these dangers. To ensure the preservation and durability of cultural assets for future generations, it is imperative to conduct routine monitoring and evaluation of restoration works in order to swiftly detect and resolve any potential threats.

Community opposition and stakeholder conflict: Heritage conservation programmes face significant obstacles from community disapproval and stakeholder disagreement. Divergent viewpoints, competing interests, or worries about gentrification and displacement may cause local communities, stakeholders, or interest groups to oppose or disagree with preservation projects. If community opposition is not successfully addressed, it can impede project progress, cause delays in project execution, or even result in project cancelation. Establishing trust and consensus around heritage conservation programmes requires addressing community concerns, communicating openly, and promoting collaborative decision-making procedures (Liu et al., 2023). Additionally, early detection and resolution of any conflicts can be achieved through proactive stakeholder engagement, consultation, and participation, which fosters community collaboration and shared ownership of conservation programmes.

Ethical considerations and cultural sensitivity: Respecting the rights, values, and customs of local communities and indigenous peoples requires careful attention to ethical issues and cultural sensitivity, which are crucial in heritage conservation initiatives. To ensure courteous and inclusive practices, businesses involved in heritage conservation are required to abide by ethical norms, codes of conduct, and best practices. Ethical heritage conservation requires avoiding cultural appropriation, honoring holy sites, and sustaining the values of cultural variety and inclusion. Furthermore, integrating local knowledge, viewpoints, and goals into conservation efforts requires meaningful engagement and collaboration with indigenous people, traditional custodians, and stakeholders in cultural assets. Companies may support the preservation of cultural heritage in a way that respects and honors the various cultural history of communities throughout the world by placing a high priority on ethical issues and cultural sensitivity (Garay & Font, 2012).

Framework for Heritage Conservation as CSR Strategy

The FHCCS has been developed by taking inspiration from the three major objectives discussed in the previous sections of this chapter (Fig 1.1). The framework depicts that Heritage Conservation as a CSR Strategy lies in the intersection of prospects of benefits for heritage sites and local communities and the underlying motives and drivers for the organization. Together, they create a symbiotic relationship where the organization achieves positive outcomes like brand image enhancement, meeting stakeholder expectations, long-term sustainability, market differentiation, employee engagement and morale, and networking opportunities. Likewise, benefits such as preservation of tangible and intangible cultural assets,

Fig. 1.1.   Framework for Heritage Conservation as CSR Strategy.
Source: Authors' own work.

sustainable tourism development, promoting awareness and capacity building, social entrepreneurship, promoting environmental sustainability, addressing cultural heritage at risk, and empowerment of indigenous peoples are the benefits reaped by the heritage sites and communities residing near them. However, despite the numerous positive outcomes, heritage conservation as a CSR strategy faces a number of obstacles in the form of financial constraints and resource limitations, complex regulatory environment and permitting processes, technical expertise and conservation skills gap, risk of damage and loss during restoration, community opposition and stakeholder conflict, and ethical considerations and cultural sensitivity. By addressing these challenges, organizations can ensure the sustainability of the heritage sites.

Conclusion

To sum up, this study has offered a thorough analysis of the different aspects of heritage conservation as a CSR approach, revealing its complexity and the consequences it has for business involvement. Three key conclusions from this investigation have been drawn, outlining the benefits as well as the challenges of using heritage conservation as a CSR strategy.

The various facets of heritage conservation as a CSR strategy have been covered in detail with particular attention paid to the significance of projects like the preservation of tangible and intangible cultural heritage, the development of sustainable tourism, the promotion of environmental sustainability, social entrepreneurship, addressing cultural heritage at risk, and the empowerment of indigenous peoples. Companies have shown their dedication to environmental stewardship, economic development, and cultural preservation through these projects. Corporations promote the continuation of varied cultural expressions while promoting community pride and identity through investing in the preservation of tangible and intangible cultural assets. In addition to providing financial gains, sustainable tourism development encourages ethical travel behavior and improves the visitor experience at heritage locations.

Additionally, initiatives to raise awareness and develop community capacity enable nearby communities to take part in conservation activities, developing a culture of guardianship for cultural assets. In addition to promoting environmental sustainability through habitat restoration and energy-efficient practices, social entrepreneurship emerges as a novel strategy to heritage conservation that integrates social and environmental aims with commercial feasibility. These efforts also contribute to broader environmental goals. A vital component of heritage conservation initiatives is empowering indigenous peoples and addressing cultural heritage that is under threat. Corporations support the preservation of cultural heritage and the empowerment of marginalized groups by safeguarding heritage places that are at risk from armed conflict and natural disasters, as well as by upholding the rights and customs of indigenous people.

Understanding the underlying motivations and drivers behind heritage conservation as a CSR strategy has been thoroughly examined in this chapter, which has shed light on important goals like market differentiation, stakeholder expectations, long-term sustainability, employee engagement and morale, and networking. By achieving these aims, businesses may carefully match their CSR initiatives with their commercial objectives, all the while satisfying stakeholder expectations and societal demands. Through heritage conservation projects, corporations not only strengthen their brand image but also cultivate consumer trust and loyalty. In order to meet stakeholder expectations, one must ensure alignment with community interests and values through ethical conduct, meaningful participation, and honest communication.

In addition, achieving long-term sustainability emphasizes how crucial it is to incorporate heritage conservation into business strategy in order to provide flexibility and resilience in the face of social, environmental, and financial difficulties. Through heritage conservation projects, businesses can achieve market distinction, stand out from the competition, draw in customers, and generate shared value for society. Participation in heritage conservation initiatives also boosts employee engagement and morale by giving workers a feeling of pride, purpose, and community. Finally, networking makes it easier to work together, share expertise, and mobilize resources, which increases the effect of heritage conservation initiatives and encourages group action toward shared objectives.

The difficulties in using heritage conservation as a CSR strategy have been thoroughly examined. The preservation and restoration of heritage sites is hampered by financial and resource limitations, which present substantial obstacles to heritage conservation efforts. Similarly, negotiating the intricate permitting and regulatory frameworks takes a great deal of time, skill, and effort; this adds layers of bureaucracy and administrative weight to conservation initiatives. Further difficulties arise from the lack of technical experience and conservation abilities, especially in areas where heritage conservation is not given priority. This results in a scarcity of experts with the necessary qualifications, which impedes the implementation of projects. In addition, the possibility of loss and damage during restoration emphasizes the need for careful planning, evaluation, and implementation in order to reduce unintentional harm to cultural heritage assets. This balance between preservation and intervention is particularly problematic.

Stakeholder conflict and community opposition resulting from differing interests, cultural sensitivities, or worries about gentrification and displacement can also obstruct heritage conservation efforts. In order to resolve these disputes and foster consensus and trust among stakeholders, collaborative decision-making procedures, meaningful participation, and open communication are necessary. Lastly, ethical and cultural awareness are critical to heritage conservation; this means that indigenous rights, customs, and values must be respected, and ethical norms and best practices must be followed. Companies may reduce risks, cultivate goodwill with communities, and preserve the integrity of heritage conservation as a CSR strategy by carefully and diligently managing these issues.

Lastly, the authors of this chapter have developed a FHCCS) by taking cues from the findings mentioned earlier. This framework offers a comprehensive guideline for policymakers, academics, and practitioners. It also provides structured insights into integrating heritage conservation into CSR strategies, facilitating informed decision-making and effective implementation across diverse sectors.

References

Airbnb. (2019). *Five applicants chosen from over 280,000 hopefuls to take part in Airbnb's Italian sabbatical.* https://news.airbnb.com/five-applicants-chosen-from-over-280000-hopefuls-to-take-part-in-airbnbs-italian-sabbatical/

Alonso Gonzalez, P. (2014). *From a given to a construct. Cultural Studies, 28*(3), 359–390. https://doi.org/10.1080/09502386.2013.789067

Amer, M., Ginzarly, M., & Renzi, M.-F. (2023). Civita di Bagnoregio, Italy: Towards a people-centred heritage branding approach. *Journal of Heritage Tourism, 18*(4), 483–503. https://doi.org/10.1080/1743873X.2023.2188450

Angelbeck, B. (2017). Archaeological heritage and traditional forests within the logging economy of British Columbia: An opportunity for corporate social responsibility. In C. O'Faircheallaigh & S. Ali (Eds.), *Earth matters* (pp. 123–142). Routledge.

Bai, Q., & Nam, B. H. (2020). Capitalism and reproduction in the new museology: The power discourses about Chinese cultural heritage at the metropolitan museum of art. *The Journal of Arts Management, Law, and Society, 50*(4–5), 267–282. https://doi.org/10.1080/10632921.2020.1815613

Bindhu, D., & Panakaje, N. (2023). Adopt a heritage scheme: A CSR initiative for preserving our past glories to future. *International Journal of Case Studies in Business, IT and Education (IJCSBE), 7*(2), 250–262.

Biraglia, A., Gerrath, M. H. E. E., & Usrey, B. (2018). Examining how companies' support of tourist attractions affects visiting intentions: The mediating role of perceived authenticity. *Journal of Travel Research, 57*(6), 811–823. https://doi.org/10.1177/0047287517718352

Botero, D. A. E. (2015). Reputational risk and corporate social responsibility: How to make CSR policies attractive to productive corporations. *Via Inveniendi et Iudicandi, 10*(1), 87–117.

Çalhan, Ö. (2022). Innovative in presenting digital cultural ideas heritage in the tourism industry. In A. Akbaba, E. Serradell-Lopez, M. E. A. Abdelli, & N. Mansour (Eds.), *Sustainability, big data, and corporate social responsibility: Evidence from the tourism industry* (p. 155). CRC Press.

Camarero, C., & Garrido, M. J. (2012). Fostering innovation in cultural contexts: Market orientation, service orientation, and innovations in museums. *Journal of Service Research, 15*(1), 39–58. https://doi.org/10.1177/1094670511419648

Engizek, N., & Eroğlu, F. (2022). Creating costumer value in corporate social responsibility for cultural heritage. In I. R. Management Association (Ed.), *Research anthology on developing socially responsible businesses* (pp. 1614–1630). IGI Global. https://doi.org/10.4018/978-1-6684-5590-6.ch079

Etsy. (n.d.). *Etsy: Empowering artisans and crafters worldwide.* Retrieved January 15, 2024, from https://fastercapital.com/topics/section-8:-etsy:-empowering-artisans-and-crafters-worldwide.html

Garay, L., & Font, X. (2012). Doing good to do well? Corporate social responsibility reasons, practices and impacts in small and medium accommodation enterprises. *International Journal of Hospitality Management, 31*(2), 329–337. https://doi.org/10.1016/j.ijhm.2011.04.013

Hilton. (n.d.-a). *Paving the way to net zero.* Retrieved January 15, 2024, from https://esg.hilton.com/environment/

Hilton. (n.d.-b). *Travel with purpose.* Retrieved December 29, 2024, from https://esg.hilton.com/

Infosys. (2015). *Infosys foundation provides grants worth INR 4.5 crore to restore the somanatheswara temple complex in Lakshmeshwara, Karnataka.* https://www.infosys.com/newsroom/press-releases/2015/architectural-cultural-restoration.html

Janssen, J., Luiten, E., Renes, H., & Stegmeijer, E. (2017). Heritage as sector, factor and vector: Conceptualizing the shifting relationship between heritage management and spatial planning. *European Planning Studies, 25*(9), 1654–1672. https://doi.org/10.1080/09654313.2017.1329410

Jimura, T. (2023). *Sustainability management in heritage and tourism: The concept and practice of Mottainai in Japan.* Palgrave Macmillan Cham.

Kasemsap, K. (2018). Encouraging corporate social responsibility and sustainable tourism development in global tourism. In I. R. Management Association (Ed.), *Operations and service management: concepts, methodologies, tools, and applications* (pp. 1028–1056). IGI Global. https://doi.org/10.4018/978-1-5225-3909-4.ch047

Kashyap, A. K. (2014). The Bajjika language and speech community Abhishek Kumar Kashyap. *International Journal of the Sociology of Language, 2014*(227), 209–224. https://org/doi:10.1515/ijsl-2014-0001

Keitsch, M. M. (2020). Heritage, conservation, and development. In W. Leal Filho, A. Marisa Azul, L. Brandli, P. Gökçin Özuyar, & T. Wall (Eds.), *Sustainable cities and communities* (pp. 246–255). Springer International Publishing. https://doi.org/10.1007/978-3-319-95717-3_5

Labadi, S., Giliberto, F., Rosetti, I., Shetabi, L., & Yildirim, E. (2021). Heritage and the sustainable development goals: Policy guidance for heritage and development actors. *International Journal of Heritage Studies,* Issue, 1352–7258.

Li, Y., & Hunter, C. (2015). Community involvement for sustainable heritage tourism: A conceptual model. *Journal of Cultural Heritage Management and Sustainable Development, 5*(3), 248–262. https://doi.org/10.1108/JCHMSD-08-2014-0027

Liu, Z., Zhang, M., & Osmani, M. (2023). Building information modelling (BIM) driven sustainable cultural heritage tourism. *Buildings, 13*(8), 1925. https://www.mdpi.com/2075-5309/13/8/1925

Microsoft. (2022). *This museum is using AI to remind us of all the threads we have in common* https://news.microsoft.com/source/asia/features/this-museum-is-using-ai-to-remind-us-of-all-the-threads-we-have-in-common/#:~:text=Microsoft's%20AI%20for%20Cultural%20Heritage%20leverages%20the%20power%20of%20AI,and%20enrichment%20of%20cultural%20heritage.

Mzembe, A. N., Koens, K., & Calvi, L. (2023). The institutional antecedents of sustainable development in cultural heritage tourism. *Sustainable Development, 31*(4), 2196–2211. https://doi.org/10.1002/sd.2565

Nag, A., & Mishra, S. (2023). Unlocking the power of stakeholder perception: Enhancing competitive heritage planning and place-making. In Y. S. Rawal, R. Sinha, S. K. Mukherjee, & D. Batabyal (Eds.), *Exploring culture and heritage through experience tourism* (pp. 196–226). IGI Global. https://doi.org/10.4018/978-1-6684-9957-3.ch015

Nair, B. B., Sinha, S., & Dileep, M. R. (2023). Who owns the heritage? Power and politics of heritage site management in tourism, Hampi, India. *Archaeologies, 19*(2), 276–298. https://doi.org/10.1007/s11759-022-09459-w

Nave, A., & Ferreira, J. (2019). Corporate social responsibility strategies: Past research and future challenges. *Corporate Social Responsibility and Environmental Management, 26*(4), 885–901. https://doi.org/10.1002/csr.1729

Nthoi-Molefe, O. (2021). Corporate social investment through sustainable cultural heritage resources management: The case of a mining company in Botswana. In F. Maphosa & L. Maunganidze (Eds.), *Corporate citizenship: Business and society in Botswana* (pp. 191–225). Springer International Publishing. https://doi.org/10.1007/978-3-030-67766-4_6

Otero, J. (2022). Heritage conservation future: Where we stand, challenges ahead, and a paradigm shift. *Global Challenges, 6*(1), 2100084. https://doi.org/10.1002/gch2.202100084

Röll, V., & Meyer, C. (2020). Young people's perceptions of world cultural heritage: Suggestions for a critical and reflexive world heritage education. *Sustainability, 12*(20), 8640. https://www.mdpi.com/2071-1050/12/20/8640

Ruggie, J. G. (2002). The theory and practice of learning networks: Corporate social responsibility and the global compact. *Journal of Corporate Citizenship* (5), 27–36.

Sankaran, P. N. (2019). CSR interventions in india under state invitation: An artisans' perspective on 'adopt a heritage' programme. In D. Crowther & S. Seifi (Eds.), *The components of sustainable development*. Singapore.

Siyal, S., Ahmad, R., Riaz, S., Xin, C., & Fangcheng, T. (2022). The impact of corporate culture on corporate social responsibility: Role of reputation and corporate sustainability. *Sustainability, 14*(16), 10105. https://www.mdpi.com/2071-1050/14/16/10105

Starr, F. (2010). The business of heritage and the private sector. In S. Labadi & C. Long (Eds.), *Heritage and globalisation* (Vol. 1, pp. 161–184). Routledge.

Starr, F. (2013). *Corporate responsibility for cultural heritage: conservation, sustainable development, and corporate reputation* (Vol. 1). Routledge. https://doi.org/10.4324/9780203078075

Veldpaus, L., Kisić, V., Stegmeijer, E., & Janssen, J. (2021). Towards a more just world: An agenda for transformative heritage planning futures. In E. Stegmeijer & L. Veldpaus (Eds.), *A research agenda for heritage planning* (pp. 201–220). Edward Elgar Publishing.

Wells, V. K., Gregory Smith, D., Taheri, B., Manika, D., & McCowlen, C. (2016). An exploration of CSR development in heritage tourism. *Annals of Tourism Research, 58*, 1–17. https://doi.org/10.1016/j.annals.2016.01.007

WWF. (2014). *Amazon forever*. Retrieved January 15, 2024, from https://www.worldwildlife.org/magazine/issues/summer-2014/articles/the-amazon

Chapter 2

Role of CSR Advertising Campaigns in the Hotel Industry: 'Responsible Luxury' Campaign by ITC Hotels

Pravin Chandra Singh[a], Sujay Vikram Singh[b], Aastha Jain[c], Erum Shaikh[d], Kuldeep Singh[e] and Kumari Neelam[f]

[a]*MSMSR, Mats University, Raipur, India*
[b]*Department of History of Art and Tourism Management, BHU, Varanasi, India*
[c]*Department of Management Studies, Vaish College of Engineering, Rohatak, India*
[d]*Shaheed Benazir Bhutto University, Sanghar Campus, Pakistan*
[e]*School of Hospitality, Amity University, Haryana, India*
[f]*Department of Commerce, Mahatma Gandhi Kashi Vidyapith, Varanasi, India*

Abstract

Purpose: The purpose of this chapter is to identify the factors which influences consumers attitude towards CSR advertising campaigns in hotel industry and determine their relative strengths.

Methodology/study design/approach: EFA and multiple regression methods are used to identify the factors and examine the relationship on a sample of 290 from Delhi-NCR.

Research limitations/implications: This chapter exclusively focusses on the Delhi NCR region of India and the CSR advertising campaigns of ITC hotels restricting the study's ability to generalise the findings to other contexts within the hotel industry.

Social implications: This chapter aims to exert an influence on the perceptions of consumers and societal attitudes towards the practices of corporate social responsibility. It provides valuable insights into the wider implications that these practices have on sustainable business practices

Corporate Social Responsibility, Corporate Governance and Business Ethics in Tourism Management: A Business Strategy for Sustainable Organizational Performance, 19–35
Copyright © 2025 by Pravin Chandra Singh, Sujay Vikram Singh, Aastha Jain, Erum Shaikh, Kuldeep Singh and Kumari Neelam
Published under exclusive licence by Emerald Publishing Limited
doi:10.1108/978-1-83608-704-520241002

and the potential for social change and makes CSR communication more impactful to the targeted audience which in turn create a positive image of the advertised brand and how they are doing their CSR activities.

Findings: This chapter shows that informativeness belief is the strongest predicator and creativity is the weakest predicator of consumer's attitude towards CSR advertising campaigns in hotel industry.

Originality/Value: This chapter provides new insights into CSR advertising campaigns in hotel industry which are beneficial for both scholars and advertising practitioners to comprehend the effectiveness of CSR advertising campaigns.

Keywords: Consumer attitude; belief factors; CSR advertising; responsible luxury; ITC hotels

Introduction

There is consensus these days on the necessity for businesses to incorporate CSR principles into their corporate behaviour and culture because it helps in providing a competitive edge to the concerned business entity (Du et al., 2010). However, when we contemplate how to communicate such issues, controversy ensues. Corporate social responsibility (CSR) communication has been characterised as a 'double-edged sword' (Morsing & Schultz, 2006) and a 'very delicate matter' (Du et al., 2010). Nevertheless, in a peculiar manner, they have historically refrained from making these activities public out of apprehension regarding criticism and the possibility of generating erroneous expectations (Schlegelmilch & Pollach, 2005). Conversely, a significant number of consumers are sceptical regarding the notion that businesses ought to disclose their CSR initiatives (Morsing & Schultz, 2006). This dilemma, that is, the apparent interest of consumers in learning more about CSR initiatives and the necessity for businesses to communicate, coupled with the potential for consumers to respond with scepticism or even rejection of these messages (Elving, 2013; Lii & Lee, 2012), renders CSR communication a complex and intriguing research topic. Promoting CSR messages is facilitated using advertising. Prior research has primarily concentrated on examining strategies to suppress consumer scepticism and elicit favourable responses, given that the dissemination of social information through advertising is more likely to elicit unintended reactions and consumer aversion than alternative communication channels (Morsing & Schultz, 2006; Yoon et al., 2006). Thus, from the above discussion it is evident that advertising is not the strongest medium to communicate CSR communication of a business enterprise and there is a need to investigate the determinants having positive impact on consumer attitude towards CSR advertising which in turn impacts brand attitude and purchase intentions as well through Hierarchy of Effects.

CSR Advertising Campaigns in Hotel Industry

In order to lower consumers' perceived risk, the primary task of hotel advertising is to turn an abstract hospitality service into a practical reality. In particular, Mittal (1999) argued that advertising can help customers recognise the subjective advantages of utilising the service, including psychological and social experiences. A growing number of hotel chains are employing CSR advertising campaigns to appeal to customers' social consciences and set themselves apart from rival hotels through their socially aware actions and dedication to the community. Hotel companies like ITCs Hotels Ltd., have aggressively conducted green advertising campaigns as a result of the significant role that CSR marketing plays in creating positive brand attitudes among consumers (Martínez & Rodríguez del Bosque, 2013). As per Önüt and Soner (2006), hotel enterprises are among the industries that consume the most energy and commodities, operating around the clock for 365 days a year. As consumers' worries about the environment grow, hotel chains have responded by implementing their environmental policies through corporate social responsibility (CSR) advertising campaigns in print and online media (such as corporate websites and social media) to instil favourable brand perceptions in the minds of their customers.

Advertising of CSR Activities in Indian Hotels

Advertising serves as a powerful tool for an organisation to communicate with its stakeholders about its CSR practices (D'Acunto et al., 2020; Patten & Zhao, 2014). It can bridge the communication gap between the organisation and its stakeholders. This proactive approach contributes to enhancing the organisation's reputation (Kim et al., 2010). Indian hotels employ various strategies to advertise their Corporate Social Responsibility (CSR) initiatives, aiming to showcase their commitment to sustainable and socially responsible practices, community development, and environmental conservation (Shafieizadeh & Tao, 2020). It enhances brand reputation, attracts socially conscious consumers, and fosters goodwill within the community. Firstly, they utilise digital platforms such as social media channels, corporate websites, and blogs to showcase their CSR initiatives (Kim & Stepchenkova, 2020) and engage with a wider audience. These platforms allow hotels to share real-time updates, success stories, and impact reports, fostering transparency and accountability. Additionally, Indian hotels often collaborate with influencers, celebrities, and CSR ambassadors to amplify the reach and visibility of their initiatives (Kapoor et al., 2022). Through partnerships with NGOs, local communities, and government agencies, hotels extend their CSR efforts and contribute to meaningful social change (Farmaki, 2019). Moreover, traditional advertising channels such as print media, television commercials, and outdoor displays are utilised to raise awareness about CSR projects (Lee, & Rim, 2018) and communicate the hotel's commitment to sustainability, community development, and environmental conservation.

Overall, by adopting a multi-channel approach and leveraging partnerships, Indian hotels effectively promote their CSR activities, thereby enhancing their brand reputation and fostering positive relationships with stakeholders.

Methods Used by Indian Hotels to Advertise Their CSR Practices:

Method	Description	Example	Exemplary references
Social Media Campaigns	Indian hotels often leverage social media platforms like Facebook, Instagram, Twitter, and LinkedIn to showcase their CSR activities. They share stories, photos, and videos highlighting their initiatives.	Taj Hotels' #TajForIndia campaign on Twitter, where they shared updates about their CSR projects aimed at supporting communities during the COVID-19 pandemic.	Chauhan & Chaddah (2017)
Website and Blog Posts	Hotels maintain dedicated sections on their websites to highlight their CSR efforts. They publish blog posts, articles, and reports detailing their initiatives, partnerships, and impact.	The Oberoi Group's CSR webpage, features information about their sustainability initiatives, community development projects, and environmental conservation efforts.	Kumar & Sharma (2014).
Print & Digital Ads	Indian hotels often publish advertisements in newspapers, magazines, and online platforms to promote their CSR initiatives. These ads may feature compelling visuals and messages to raise awareness about their social and environmental contributions.	ITC Hotels' print advertisements in leading newspapers, showcasing their responsible luxury ethos and commitment to sustainable practices.	Jogdand & Sawant (2018)
Collaborations with NGOs and Nonprofits	Hotels collaborate with NGOs and non-profit organisations on various CSR projects and initiatives. These partnerships are often highlighted in promotional materials and communications.	The Leela Palace's partnership with Pallavanjali and Shanti Avedna Sadan supports education and healthcare initiatives in deaf and dumb people. The collaboration was promoted through press releases, social media posts, and on-site signage.	Ghai & Goel (2018)

(*Continued*)

Method	Description	Example	Exemplary references
Sponsorship of Community Events	Indian hotels sponsor and participate in community events, festivals, and workshops to engage with local communities and demonstrate their commitment to social responsibility.	The Orchid Hotel sponsor local cultural festivals in India, where they also conduct CSR activities such as environmental clean-up drives and skill development workshops, for their advertisements.	Kaur, (2019).
Employee Engagement Programs	Hotels involve their employees in CSR activities and encourage volunteering and community service. Employee-driven initiatives are often highlighted through internal communications and employee newsletters.	Hyatt Hotels' 'Hyatt Thrive' program in India encourages employees to volunteer their time and skills to support local communities. Stories and testimonials from participating employees are shared on internal communication channels and social media.	Apte & Sheth (2016); Kumar & Sharma (2014)

CSR Advertising Campaign of ITC Hotels: 'Responsible Luxury'

The CSR advertisement campaign 'Responsible Luxury' by ITC serves to persuade the public that the brand holds a focus on sustainability and social responsibility in the field of luxury hospitality. Through this campaign, ITC communicates its commitment to implementing eco-friendly practices and community welfare projects in its luxury hospitality services. They typically show beautiful views of environmentally friendly properties and mention the multiple ways in which the brand supports sustainability, including water-saving measures, the use of renewable energy, waste disposal, etc. ITC pursues the goal of attracting travellers concerned with environmental matters and setting up a new benchmark in the sector. Moreover, in the 'Responsible Luxury' campaign, ITC highlights its aim to raise the quality of life of local communities resulting from the socio-economic circumstances in the areas with ITC hotels and resorts. In this campaign, it showcases its work with local artisans, farmers, and craftsmen while highlighting its approach towards promoting indigenous culture and increasing livelihoods. Therefore, ITC leverages the campaign as a highly effective strategy to show and inform the audience regarding its responsible approach to value creation and its positive social value in the long run.

Literature Review and Hypothesis Development

Consumer Attitude Towards Advertising

A consumer's attitude towards advertising is defined as their inclination which can be either positive or negative based on the exposure and type of advertising they are exposed to Bauer et al. (1968) conducted the first thorough examination of attitudes towards advertising and identified social and economic as the two basic belief components of consumer attitude towards advertising. According to Mitchell et al. (1981) and Shimp (1981), attitude is a crucial component in advertising since it indicates how effective the commercials are (Mehta, 2000; Oumlil & Balloun, 2020; Saadeghvaziri & Hosseini, 2011; Wang et al., 2002; Wiese & Akareem, 2020). The hierarchy of effect (HOE) theory states that brand attitude (Ab) and purchase intention are both significantly influenced directly by attitude towards advertising (Aad) (Biehal et al., 1992; Bruner & Kumar, 2007; Laczniak & Muehling, 1993; MacKenzie et al., 1986; MacKenzie & Lutz, 1989).

Creativity

In regard to the conception and implementation of effective advertising strategies, the notion of creativity stands as a pivotal tenet (El-Murad & West, 2004; Kim et al., 2010; Nia & Shokouhyar, 2020; Singh & Gautam, 2019; Turnbull & Wheeler, 2017). It is an essential element of successful advertising; in its absence, the advertised products and services would be unable to establish a connection with the target audience. Advertising creativity can be categorised as 'Divergence or Relevance' (Smith & Yang, 2004). The objective of advertising creativity is to enhance the advertiser's competitive advantage (Rosa et al., 2008) by increasing the divergence and relevance of advertising (Othman, 2017). Advertisement that is creative aids in improving ad memory, persuasion, and creating a long-lasting image of the sponsor and advertised brands in the minds of consumers, as well as creating values for the company (Baack et al., 2015; Rosengren et al., 2020; Till & Baack, 2005). Thus, from the above discussion, the following hypothesis has been formulated:

> *H1.* There is a positive and significant relationship between creativity and consumer attitude towards CSR advertising in the hotel industry.

Informativeness

Effective communication regarding the attributes and benefits of the advertised products and services is the fundamental objective of advertising (Kim & Han, 2014; Oh & Xu, 2003). The development of a positive perception of advertising is thought to be influenced by information-seeking variables (Aitken et al., 2008;

Wang & Toncar, 2009). The amount of information provided in the advertise-ments regarding the products and services offered totally depends on marketers (Renault & Anderson, 2009). If the information is minimal, it will lead to a lack of effectiveness (Jacoby, 1984; Malhotra, 1984); and if maximum information is given to the audience it will lead to confusion and cause wear – out (Pieters et al., 2007) suggesting that marketers should provide the optimal amount of informa-tion about the advertised products or services (Pieters et al., 2002). A multitude of previous research endeavours has demonstrated a positive correlation between the informativeness of a product and consumers' attitudes towards advertising (Ahmed, 2013; Haghirian & Madlberger, 2005; Ramaprasad, 2001). Thus, from the above discussion, following hypothesis has been formulated:

> *H2.* There is a positive and significant relationship between informativeness and consumer attitude towards CSR advertising in the hotel industry.

Entertainment

Entertainment elements, including humour, stories, and similar components, are readily apparent in every advertisement. The term entertainment denotes the capacity to evoke or induce feelings of pleasure and contentment (Oh & Xu, 2003). These elements serve the purpose of amusing the intended consumers and gaining attention amidst the advertising congestion. Thus, it is evident that in recent years, marketers have endeavoured to elevate the level of entertainment in all forms of advertising. Historically, consumers avoided commercials because they initially found them uninteresting and unentertaining. Nevertheless, with the enhancement of the entertainment value and efficacy of advertising, consumer aversion to such messages diminishes or vanishes, while advertising itself becomes more effective. Additionally, research has shown that the entertainment belief factor incorporated into advertising can elevate the mood of targeted audiences and, through positive conditioning, cause them to form a favourable association between the advertising and promoted brands (Eisend, 2011; Hoffman & Novak, 1996; Shavitt et al., 1998). Thus, from the above discussion, the following hypoth-esis has been formulated:

> *H3.* There is a positive and significant relationship between entertainment and consumer attitude towards CSR advertising in the hotel industry.

Conceptual Framework of the Study:

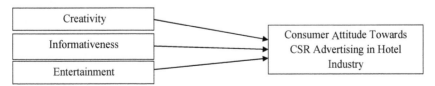

Research Methodology

Data Collection

In order to gather the necessary data, a closed-ended questionnaire was developed, incorporating a 7-point Likert scale. The questionnaires were developed in English and distributed to potential respondents via electronic means, specifically email. Additionally, a portion of the questionnaires were completed through in-person interviews. The sample size of this study was 290 (Suhr, 2006) and convenience sampling was employed to acquire the data. A convenient sampling method was selected due to its practicality in accessing participants who were readily available and willing to participate in the study, which made data collection easier (Alvi, 2016).

Construct Measures

The items for creativity, informativeness, entertainment and attitude towards advertising were adapted from the following sources (Table 2.1).

Respondent's Profile

The participants in this study were guests at ITC Hotels and had the experience of staying for a minimum of one night at the hotel. The advertising campaign selected for this study was 'Responsible Luxury' by ITCs. The demographic characteristics of the subjects are as follows: The proportion of male and female participants in this study was 55% and 45%, respectively. The target age range for this research was 18–60 years old consumers and the majority of participants were between the ages of 25 and 35 years.

Data Analysis and Findings

In order to assess the overall construct's reliability, Cronbach's alpha reliability analysis was implemented. The Cronbach's alpha for the entire construct under consideration is greater than 0.70, as indicated in Table 2.3. This indicates that the construct is suitable for further investigation (Cavana et al., 2001). KMO was calculated to be 0.842. Bartlett's test of sphericity yielded a significant result

Table 2.1.   Measurement Instruments.

Constructs	No. of Items	Source
Creativity	3	Smith et al. (2007)
Informativeness	3	Ramaprasad (2001)
Entertainment	3	Ducoffe (1996)
Attitude towards advertising	4	Ramaprasad (2001)

Table 2.2.   KMO and Bartlett's Test.

Kaiser–Meyer–Olkin measure of sampling Adequacy.		0.842
Bartlett's test of sphericity	Approx. Chi-Square	3,332.766
	Df	78
	Sig.	0.000

Table 2.3.   Factor Loading and Cronbach Alfa.

Construct	Items	Factor Loadings
Creativity	CSR Advertising campaign 'Responsible Luxury' is unique.	0.95
	CSR Advertising campaign 'Responsible Luxury' has contained numerous details	0.88
Alfa = 0.94	CSR Advertising campaign 'Responsible Luxury' is meaningful to me	0.83
Informativeness	CSR advertising campaign 'Responsible Luxury' provides a valuable source of information about the campaign.	0.87
	CSR advertising campaign 'Responsible Luxury' tells me about the campaign.	0.84
Alfa = 0.92	CSR advertising campaign 'Responsible Luxury' keeps me update about the campaigns.	0.85
Entertainment	CSR advertising campaign 'Responsible Luxury' is enjoyable.	0.88
	CSR advertising campaign 'Responsible Luxury' is interesting	0.86
Alfa = 0.89	CSR advertising campaign 'Responsible Luxury' is pleasing.	0.82
Attitude towards CSR Ad Campaign	I considered CSR advertising campaign 'Responsible Luxury' useful as it promotes the brand.	0.79
	I support CSR advertising campaign 'Responsible Luxury' because creativity is highly appreciated in it.	0.77
Alfa = 0.79	I support CSR advertising campaign 'Responsible Luxury' because it plays a significant role in my buying decision.	0.72
	My general opinions about the advertising campaign 'Responsible Luxury' are favorable/positive.	0.74

(P=0.000); df=78 for all correlations within the matrix (Table 2.2). These results indicate that factor analysis was suitable for the investigation and that the core-lation between the statements was appropriate. Once the principal component analysis and varimax rotation were performed, it was shown that all constructs had eigenvalues greater than 1, indicating statistical significance (Table 2.4) The variations among the variables are substantial, indicating their great explana-tory power and factor loading are above 0.50 which is under the prescribed value and it shows the convergent validity (Hair et al., 2010) (Table 2.3).

The coefficient of correlation, denoted as 'R', was estimated to be 0.558. This value indicates a statistically significant degree of forecast for consumer attitude towards CSR advertising campaigns. The coefficient of determination, com-monly referred to as $R2$, is a statistical measure used to quantify the extent to which the independent and dependent variables can be explained by each other. The estimation of $R2$=0.345 (Table 2.5) this estimation implies that the 34.50% variability of the dependent variable (consumer attitude towards CSR advertising campaigns) is explained by the independent variable (Creativity, Informativeness and Entertainment).

The whole regression model was evaluated and analysed using (Table 2.6) to determine its suitability for the data. The statistical significance of the independ-ent factors considered in (Table 2.6) is demonstrated, indicating their ability to predict the dependent variable, which is consumer attitude towards CSR adver-tising campaigns, $F(3, 289) = 50.260$, $P < 0.05$. Thus, we can conclude that the above-discussed regression model is a good fit for data.

It was discovered that the value of $P = 0.000$ is significantly smaller than the alpha value of 0.05 in the case of creativity, informativeness and entertainment (Table 2.7). Therefore, these finding demonstrates that the creativity, informative-ness and entertainment have a positive impact on consumer attitudes towards CSR advertising campaigns.

Thus, the multiple regression equation for this study will be:

Attitude towards CSR advertising campaign= 8.337 + 0.998 entertainment + 0.633 informativeness + 0.414 creativity.

The aforementioned table (Table 2.7) makes clear that consumer attitude towards CSR advertising campaigns and entertainment are strongly correlated, with entertainment serving as one of the primary antecedents of attitude towards CSR advertising campaigns, followed by informativeness and creativity.

Conclusion

The present study attempts to ascertain the factors that impact consumers' atti-tudes towards corporate social responsibility (CSR) advertising campaigns within the hotel business. Observant analysis of the different CSR initiatives and adver-tising strategies applied by ITC Hotels shows the central importance of these instruments for enhancing brand image and promoting sustainability. The experi-ence of ITC Hotels is an eccentric example demonstrating that the CSR efforts laid down in advertising deliver a positive impact on the social and environmental spheres. Overall, the study proves the need for incorporating CSR values into

Table 2.4. Total Variance Explained.

Component	Initial Eigenvalues			Extraction Sums of Squared Loadings			Rotation Sums of Squared Loadings		
	Total	% of Variance	Cumulative %	Total	% of Variance	Cumulative %	Total	% of Variance	Cumulative %
1	5.909	45.455	45.455	5.909	45.455	45.455	2.765	21.267	21.267
2	2.683	20.635	66.091	2.683	20.635	66.091	2.736	21.049	42.315
3	1.104	8.495	74.585	1.104	8.495	74.585	2.731	21.009	63.324
4	1.032	7.941	82.526	1.032	7.941	82.526	2.496	19.202	82.526
5	0.729	5.609	88.135						
6	0.447	3.439	91.574						
7	0.258	1.988	93.562						
8	0.220	1.691	95.253						
9	0.163	1.250	96.503						
10	0.157	1.204	97.708						
11	0.120	0.922	98.629						
12	0.101	0.778	99.407						
13	0.077	0.593	100.000						

Extraction method: Principal component analysis.

Table 2.5.   Model Summary.

Model	R	R Square	Adjusted R Square	Std. Error of the Estimate
1	0.558[a]	0.345	0.338	3.66222

[a]Predictors: (constant), creativity, informativeness, and entertainment.

Table 2.6.   ANOVA.[a]

Model		Sum of Squares	Df	Mean Square	F	Sig.
1	Regression	2,022.221	3	674.074	50.260	0.000[b]
	Residual	3,835.792	286	13.412		
	total	5,858.014	289			

[a]Dependent variable: consumer attitude towards CSR advertising campaigns.
[b]Predictors: (constant), creativity, informativeness, entertainment.

Table 2.7.   Coefficients.[a]

Model		Unstandardised Coefficients		Standardised Coefficients	t	Sig.[b]
		B	Std. Error	Beta		
1	(Constant)	8.337	0.736		11.331	0.000
	Creativity	0.414	0.156	0.162	2.653	0.008
	Informativeness	0.633	0.157	0.246	4.030	0.000
	Entertainment	0.998	0.124	0.393	8.069	0.000

[a]Dependent variable: consumer attitude towards CSR advertising campaigns.
[b]Independent variable: creativity, informativeness and entertainment.

advertising activities to boost social responsibility and sustainability in the hotel sector. The effect of three constructs were studied towards CSR advertising campaign and observed an overall positive influence on individuals. In this context, the findings of the study also offer valuable insights for hotels and advertising agencies to develop fresh marketing strategies that align with corporate social responsibility initiatives (Chung et al., 2020).

Implications of the Study

The results of this study have significant consequences for several stakeholders. The consequences of the study's conclusions extend to both managerial and theoretical domains. The study's theoretical value lies in its findings, which provide evidence for the applicability of consumer attitude determinants towards CSR advertising campaigns in the highly regulated media environment of India. In terms of managerial significance, these finding aids media agencies and professionals in formulating specific tactics aimed at improving consumer attitudes towards CSR advertising campaigns. It is imperative for advertising firms to prioritise the informative dimension of advertising, as empirical evidence suggests that informativeness, as a belief factor, exhibits the most robust association with consumer attitudes towards CSR advertising campaigns. It is also suggested that advertising firms should invest their efforts and time in making CSR advertising campaigns more creative which stand out and have relevance to the advertised brands, especially in the case of hotel industry. Further, advertisers should integrate the elements of fun, pleasure, and excitement while making CSR advertising campaigns for the hotel industry.

Limitations and Recommendations for Future Studies

The present study employs a cross-sectional design, hence limiting its ability to capture the overall impact of variables at a specific moment in time (Cavanaet al., 2001). Every cross-sectional study is inherently limited in that it fails to provide a comprehensive explanation for the observed patterns (Easterby-Smith & Lowe, 2002). Furthermore, this study focusses specifically on the CSR advertising campaigns of ITCs related to 'Responsible Luxury', and its findings cannot be extrapolated to other categories of CSR advertising. Given the aforementioned constraints, several recommendations might be proposed as follows. The consumer's attitudes towards CSR advertising undergoes changes throughout time, necessitating longitudinal studies to determine the cause-and-effect link between these dimensions (Cavanaet al., 2001). In addition to this, other CSR categories can also be included while conducting research on consumer attitudes towards CSR advertising. This study has included only three belief factors with respect to advertising which is not exhaustive researchers can add other belief factors for future study.

References

Ahmed, S. F. (2013). University student's attitude towards advertising: A study of Dhaka city of Bangladesh. *Journal of Business and Economics*, 7(1), 33–45.

Aitken, R., Gray, B., & Lawson, R. (2008). Advertising effectiveness from a consumer perspective. *International Journal of Advertising*, 27(2), 279–297. https://doi.org/10.1080/02650487.2008.11073055

Apte, S., & Sheth, J. N. (2016). *The sustainability edge: How to drive top-line growth with triple-bottom-line thinking.* University of Toronto Press.

Baack, D. W., Wilson, R. T., van Dessel, M. M., & Patti, C. H. (2015). Advertising to businesses: Does creativity matter? *Industrial Marketing Management*, 55, 1–9. https://doi.org/10.1016/j.indmarman.2015.10.001

Bauer, R. A., Greyser, S. A., Kanter, D. L., & Weilbacher, W. M. (1968). *Advertising in America: The consumer view.* Harvard University, Graduate School of Business Administration Division of Research, Boston, MA.

Biehal, G., Stephens, D., & Curio, E. (1992). Attitude toward the ad and brand choice. *Journal of Advertising*, 21(3), 19–36. https://doi.org/10.1080/00913367.1992.10673373

Bruner, G. C., & Kumar, A. (2007). Attitude toward location-based advertising. *Journal of Interactive Advertising, 7*(2), 3–15. https://doi.org/10.1080/15252019.2007.10722127

Cavana, R., Delahaye, B., & Sekeran, U. (2001). *Applied business research: Qualitative and quantitative methods.* John Wiley & Sons.

Chauhan, P., & Chaddah, J. K. (2017). Role of social media in influencing sustainability practices among Indian organizations. *Sansmaran Research Journal, 7*(1), 12–18.

Chung, C. Y., Choi, D., Choi, P. M. S., & Choi, J. H. (2020). Corporate governance and corporate social responsibility: Evidence from the role of the largest institutional blockholders in the Korean market. *Sustainability, 12*(4), 1–15.

D'Acunto, D., Tuan, A., Dalli, D., Viglia, G., & Okumus, F. (2020). Do consumers care about CSR in their online reviews? An empirical analysis. *International Journal of Hospitality Management, 85,* 102342.

Du, S., Bhattacharya, C. B., & Sen, S. (2010). Maximizing business returns to corporate social responsibility (CSR): The role of CSR communication. *International Journal of Management Reviews, 12*(1), 8–19. https://doi.org/10.1111/j.1468-2370.2009.00276.x

Ducoffe, R. H. (1996). Advertising value and advertising on the web. *Journal of Advertising Research, 36*(5), 21–35.

Easterby-Smith, M. T., & Lowe, R. A. (2002). *Management research: An introduction.* SAGE Publications Ltd.

Eisend, M. (2011). How humor in advertising works: A meta-analytic test of alternative models. *Marketing Letters, 22,* 115–132. https://doi.org/10.1007/s11002-010-9116-z

El-Murad, J., & West, D. C. (2004). The definition and measurement of creativity: What do we know? *Journal of Advertising Research, 44*(2), 188–201. https://doi.org/10.1017/S0021849904040097

Elving, W. J. L. (2013). Scepticism and corporate social responsibility communications: The influence of fit and reputation. *Journal of Marketing Communications, 19*(4), 277–292. https://doi.org/10.1080/13527266.2011.631569

Farmaki, A. (2019). Corporate social responsibility in hotels: A stakeholder approach. *International Journal of Contemporary Hospitality Management, 31*(6), 2297–2320.

Ghai, A., & Goel, V. (2018). Corporate social responsibility in Indian hospitality: Hotels in New Delhi. *PUSA Journal of Hospitality and Applied Sciences, 4,* 49–61.

Haghirian, P., & Madlberger, M. (2005, May 26–28). *Consumer attitude toward advertising via mobile devices – An empirical investigation among Austrian users* [Conference proceedings]. In DBLP, conference: Proceedings of the 13th European conference on information systems, information systems in a rapidly changing economy, ECIS 2005, Regensburg, Germany.

Hair, F. J., Black, C. W., Babin, J. B., & Amderson, E. R. (2010). *Multivariate data analysis* (7th ed.). Pearson Prentice Hall.

Hoffman, D. L., & Novak, T. P. (1996). Marketing in hypermedia computer-mediated environments: Conceptual foundations. *Journal of Marketing, 60*(3), 50–68. https://doi.org/10.2307/1251841

Jacoby, J. (1984). Perspectives on information overload. *Journal of Consumer Research, 10*(4), 432–435.

Jogdand, B., & Sawant, M. (2018). Online corporate social responsibility reportings of leading hotel groups in India: A qualitative content analysis. *International Journal of Tourism and Travel, 11*(1–2), 8–17.

Kapoor, P. S., Balaji, M. S., Jiang, Y., & Jebarajakirthy, C. (2022). Effectiveness of travel social media influencers: A case of eco-friendly hotels. *Journal of Travel Research, 61*(5), 1138–1155.

Kaur, I. (2019). CSR in hotel industry in India. In *Corporate social responsibility: Concepts, methodologies, tools, and applications* (pp. 936–954). IGI Global.

Kim, B. H., Han, S., & Yoon, S. (2010). Advertising creativity in Korea: Scale development and validation. *Journal of Advertising, 39*(2), 93–108. https://doi.org/10.2753/JOA0091-3367390207

Kim, M., & Stepchenkova, S. (2020). Corporate social responsibility authenticity from the perspective of restaurant consumers. *The Service Industries Journal, 40*(15–16), 1140–1166.

Kim, Y. J., & Han, J. (2014). Why smartphone advertising attracts customers: A model of Web advertising, flow, and personalization. *Computers in Human Behavior, 33*, 256–269. https://doi.org/10.1016/j.chb.2014.01.015

Kumar, R., & Sharma, S. (2014). Corporate social responsibility – A study on hotel industry. *Asian Journal of Multidisciplinary Studies, 2*(4), 25–32.

Laczniak, R. N., & Muehling, D. D. (1993). Toward a better understanding of the role of advertising message involvement in ad processing. *Psychology & Marketing, 10*(4), 301–319. https://doi.org/10.1002/mar.4220100405

Lee, J., & Rim, H. (2018). Evolution of corporate social responsibility: A content analysis of United States magazine advertising, 1980–2009. *Journal of Promotion Management, 24*(4), 555–577.

Lii, Y. S., & Lee, M. (2012). Doing right leads to doing well: When the type of CSR and reputation interact to affect consumer evaluations of the firm. *Journal of Business Ethics, 105*(1), 69–81. https://doi.org/10.1007/s10551-011-0948-0

MacKenzie, S. B., & Lutz, R. J. (1989). An empirical examination of the structural antecedents of attitude toward the ad in an advertising pretesting context. *Journal of Marketing, 53*(2), 48. https://doi.org/10.2307/1251413

MacKenzie, S. B., Lutz, R. J., & Belch, G. E. (1986). The role of attitude toward the ad as a mediator of advertising effectiveness: A test of competing explanations. *Journal of Marketing Research, XXIII*(May 1986), 130–143.

Malhotra, N. K. (1984). Reflections on the information overload paradigm in consumer decision making. *Journal of Consumer Research, 10*, 436–440. https://doi.org/10.1086/208982

Martínez, P., & Rodríguez del Bosque, I. (2013). CSR and customer loyalty: The roles of trust, customer identification with the company and satisfaction. *International Journal of Hospitality Management, 35*, 89–99. https://doi.org/10.1016/j.ijhm.2013.05.009

Mehta, A. (2000). Advertising attitudes and advertising effectiveness. *Journal of Advertising Research, 40*(3), 67–72. www.journalofadvertisingresearch.com

Mitchell, A. A., Olson, J. C., Mitchell, A. A., & Olson, J. C. (1981). American Marketing Association. *Journal of Marketing Research, 18*(3), 318–332. https://doi.org/10.1177/002224377301000402

Mittal, B. (1999). The advertising of services: Meeting the challenge of intangibility. *Journal of Service Research, 2*(1), 98–116. https://doi.org/10.1177/109467059921008

Morsing, M., & Schultz, M. (2006). Corporate social responsibility communication: Stakeholder information, response and involvement strategies. *Business Ethics: A European Review, 15*(4), 323–338. https://www.researchgate.net/publication/313090994

Nia, M. R., & Shokouhyar, S. (2020). Analyzing the effects of visual aesthetic of web pages on users' responses in online retailing using the VisAWI method. *Journal of Research in Interactive Marketing 14*(4), 357–389. https://doi.org/10.1108/JRIM-11-2018-0147

Oh, L.-B., & Xu, H. (2003, December 14–17). *Effects of multimedia on mobile consumer behavior: An empirical study of location-aware advertising,* [Conference proceedings]. Twenty-fourth international conference on information systems, ICIS 2003, Seattle, Washington.

Önüt, S., & Soner, S. (2006). Energy efficiency assessment for the Antalya region hotels in Turkey. *Energy and Buildings, 38*(8), 964–971. https://doi.org/10.1016/j.enbuild.2005.11.006

Othman, H. (2017). The role of creative thinking in advertising design. *International Design Journal, 7*(2), 265–273. http://www.journal.faa-design.com/pdf/7-2-huda.pdf

Oumlil, A. B., & Balloun, J. L. (2020). Millennials' attitude toward advertising: An international exploratory study. *Young Consumers, 21*(1), 17–34. https://doi.org/10.1108/YC-10-2018-0865

Patten, D. M., & Zhao, N. (2014). Standalone CSR reporting by U.S. retail companies. *Accounting Forum, 38*(2), 132–144. https://doi.org/10.1016/j.accfor.2014.01.002

Pieters, R., Warlop, L., & Wedel, M. (2002). Breaking through the clutter: Benefits of advertisement originality and familiarity for brand attention and memory. *Management Science, 48*(6), 765–781. https://doi.org/10.1287/mnsc.48.6.765.192

Pieters, R., Wedel, M., & Zhang, J. (2007). Optimal feature advertising design under competitive clutter. *Management Science, 53*(11), 1815–1828. https://doi.org/10.1287/mnsc.1070.0732

Ramaprasad, J. (2001). South Asian students' beliefs about and attitude toward advertising. *Journal of Current Issues and Research in Advertising, 23*(1), 55–70. https://doi.org/10.1080/10641734.2001.10505114

Renault, R., & Anderson, S. P. (2009). Comparative advertising: Disclosing horizontal match information. *Rand Journal of Economics, 40*(3), 558–581.

Rosa, J. A., Qualls, W. J., & Fuentes, C. (2008). Involving mind, body, and friends: Management that engenders creativity. *Journal of Business Research, 61*(6), 631–639. https://doi.org/10.1016/j.jbusres.2007.06.038

Rosengren, S., Eisend, M., Koslow, S., & Dahlen, M. (2020). A meta-analysis of when and how advertising creativity works. *Journal of Marketing, 84*(6), 1–18. https://doi.org/10.1177/0022242920929288

Saadeghvaziri, F., & Hosseini, H. K. (2011). Mobile advertising: An investigation of factors creating positive attitude in Iranian customers. *African Journal of Business Management, 5*(2), 394–404. https://doi.org/10.5897/AJBM10.431

Schlegelmilch, B. B., & Pollach, I. (2005). The perils and opportunities of communicating corporate ethics. *Journal of Marketing Management, 21*, 267–290.

Shafieizadeh, K., & Tao, C. W. W. (2020). How does a menu's information about local food affect restaurant selection? The roles of corporate social responsibility, transparency, and trust. *Journal of Hospitality and Tourism Management, 43*, 232–240.

Shavitt, S., Lowrey, P., & Haefner, J. (1998). Public attitudes toward advertising: More favorable than you might think. *Journal of Advertising Research, 38*(4), 7–22.

Shimp, T. A. (1981). Attitude toward the ad as a mediator of consumer brand choice. *Journal of Advertising, 10*(2), 9–48. https://doi.org/10.1080/00913367.1981.10672756

Singh, P. C., & Gautam, A. (2019). Role of divergence and relevance in advertising creativity. *IIMS Journal of Management Science, 10*(3), 149–159. https://doi.org/10.5958/0976-173x.2019.00012.5

Smith, R. E., Mackenzie, S. B., Yang, X., Buchholz, L. M., & Darley, W. K. (2007). Modeling the determinants and effects of creativity in advertising. *Marketing Science, 26*(6), 819–833. https://doi.org/10.1287/mksc.1070.0272

Smith, R. E., & Yang, X. (2004). Toward a general theory of creativity in advertising: Examining the role of divergence. *Marketing Theory, 4*(31), 31–58. https://doi.org/10.1177/1470593104044086

Till, B. D., & Baack, D. W. (2005). Recall and persuasion: Does creative advertising matter? *Journal of Advertising, 34*(3), 47–57. https://doi.org/10.1080/00913367.2005.10639201

Turnbull, S., & Wheeler, C. (2017). The advertising creative process: A study of UK agencies. *Journal of Marketing Communications, 23*(2), 176–194. https://doi.org/10.1080/13527266.2014.1000361

Wang, C., Zhang, P., Choi, R., & D'Eredita, M. (2002). Understanding consumers attitude towards advertising. *Amcis*, 1142–1148. http://aisel.aisnet.org/amcis2002/158%0Ahttp://aisel.aisnet.org/amcis2002%0Ahttp://aisel.aisnet.org/amcis2002/158

Wang, Y., & Toncar, M. (2009). Examining beliefs and attitudes toward online advertising among Chinese consumers. *Direct Marketing: An International Journal, 3*(1), 52–66. https://doi.org/10.1108/17505930910945732

Wiese, M., & Akareem, H. S. (2020). Determining perceptions, attitudes and behaviour towards social network site advertising in a three-country context. *Journal of Marketing Management, 36*(5–6), 420–455. https://doi.org/10.1080/0267257X.2020. 1751242

Yoon, Y., Gürhan-Canli, Z., & Schwarz, N. (2006). The effect of corporate social responsibility (CSR) activities on companies with bad reputations. *Journal of Consumer Psychology, 16*(4), 377–390. https://doi.org/10.1207/s15327663jcp1604_9

Chapter 3

Factors Affecting CSR Practices in Entrepreneurship: Case of Female Entrepreneurs in Pakistan

Muhammad Nawaz Tunio[a], Iffat Sabir[b], Aamir Rashid[c] and Faheem Gul Gilal[d]

[a]*University of Sufism and Modern Sciences, Bhitshah, Pakistan*
[b]*Al Ain University, Abu Dhabi, UAE*
[c]*The City University of New York, New York, USA*
[d]*Sukkur IBA University, Sukkur, Pakistan*

Abstract

Purpose: The aim of this chapter is to find out the factors affecting female entrepreneurship in the case of the Corporate Social Responsibilities (CSR) in entrepreneurship.

Methodology: In this chapter, semi-structured interviews are conducted to reach the final findings of the study.

Findings: Findings entail different six factors that severely affect CSR activities in entrepreneurship in Pakistan. These six factors are the educational system and skills gap, Cultural Mindset and Risk Aversion, Limited Access to Finance, Regulatory and Bureaucratic Hurdles, Political Instability and Security Concerns, and Inadequate Infrastructure. Every factor has its intensity and influence on the entrepreneurial process.

Originality/value: This chapter can be useful for international and local NGOs, academic institutions, financial institutions, government agencies, and entrepreneurs.

Keywords: CSR activities in entrepreneurship; female entrepreneur; barriers; entrepreneurial ecosystem; Pakistan

Corporate Social Responsibility, Corporate Governance and Business Ethics in Tourism
Management: A Business Strategy for Sustainable Organizational Performance, 37–47
Copyright © 2025 by Muhammad Nawaz Tunio, Iffat Sabir, Aamir Rashid and Faheem Gul Gilal
Published under exclusive licence by Emerald Publishing Limited
doi:10.1108/978-1-83608-704-520241003

1. Introduction

Several countries in the world have been creating ways to develop in terms of economics since they acquired their independence (Bögenhold, 2013; Danish et al., 2019). Therefore, numerous organisations and individuals prioritised CSR activities in entrepreneurship actions with their main focus on entrepreneurial growth. Moreover, the studies about entrepreneurship determined several things such as business persons' attitudes, management skills, individual traits, and many other things, which led to various findings (Sharma, 2018). The findings are related to ethical experiences in business and privately based business in society, CSR activities in the operation process, environment degradation, socially responsible entrepreneurship practices, and social inequality, which means that entrepreneurship is an antique activity. Many people and organisations based on entrepreneurship get their ideas from the research done many years ago (Bögenhold & Klinglmair, 2017).

CSR activities in entrepreneurship are an ongoing activity, and it is fortified in a way that a lot of people get encouraged. Furthermore, entrepreneurship plays a critical role in economic development, hence propelling ambiguous changes in the business (Danish et al, 2019). Within the inquiry about the result of changing showcase scenarios in world viewpoints, an endeavour has been made to consider those factors that influence entrepreneurial development (Shah et al., 2020). In arranging to construct a gathering to encourage thinking about, the thought was to examine these causes and influences (Sharma, 2018). It was found out that a few researchers have considered entrepreneurial orientation, CSR approaches, environment safety, and social conduct of business people, their identity characteristics and administration styles. However, young people who were influenced by entrepreneurship education in their local countries influenced entrepreneurial orientation differently (Uduji et al., 2019). Those ways include the background of their CSR activities in business, cultural background, and social perspectives (Dvouletý & Bögenhold, 2022).

For instance, when you go through the planning commission of India, it states that most emerging countries are categorised by synchronised underutilised workforce plus the explosion of natural resources (Danish et al., 2019). Additionally, under this current scenario, entrepreneurial growth stands for adding value to the enterprises, community, and, most importantly, to profits for business persons and the country (Shah et al., 2020). Furthermore, failure can encompass the entrepreneurs' choice of potential behaviours by adjusting their incompetent enhancement and moving their abilities and information forward (Sharma, 2018). Analysts, too, accepted that business visionaries ought to not, as it were, learn from other effective business visionaries but learn from their claim disappointment (Nguyen et al., 2019). Subsequently, the contemplation of entrepreneurial learning from disappointment is hypothetical critical esteem and common-sense centrality.

The main aim of this chapter was to appraise the idea of how entrepreneurship emerged and became the centre of most economic activities (Uduji et al., 2019). Various research materials on this topic were retrieved from Google Scholar, ProQuest, and many more; however, some articles and book materials were found from different libraries. Furthermore, building up all the research done to come up with this information requires a lot of determination (Sharma, 2018). For one to complete this kind of research, however, a time frame from the beginning of the research until the submission was required, which made it easier to track time and every event going on different occasions.

In addition, small enterprise owners require a part of bolster to succeed, whether money-related, operational, or enthusiastic (Ogamba, 2019). One of the major critical sources of that bolster for numerous business people is their arrangement of companions and kin members. Individuals are social creatures, and numerous business visionaries confront the rigours of the commerce world either alone or with a small staff of committed representatives (Danish et al., 2019). Companions and family give that bolster framework that can offer assistance to business people confronting stretch, adjust work and play, and keep a sense of viewpoint amid the stretch and obligation of beginning and keeping up an effective trade in a regularly barbarous commercial centre.

This chapter aims to find out factors that inhibit and affect CSR activities in entrepreneurial development, in case of the female entrepreneurs.

2. Literature Review

Entrepreneurial has become critical in peoples' daily lives because it is viewed as the centre of economic growth (Uduji et al., 2019). Furthermore, there are several outcomes from entrepreneurial activities, and they provide employment, growth in different regions and industrial development. Henceforth, entrepreneurs are the key to industrial growth, and as we all know, industrial growth is the source of employment, which means a lot of business persons are the source of employment in the entire world (Ogamba, 2019). Additionally, the availability of entrepreneurship leads to the introduction of new goods in the market because there are several new ideas and perfect innovative plans (Aladejebi, 2018). However, for a great entrepreneur, there must be factors that propel or fight it. Everyone and everything requires good support to emerge, and as well they need criticism to grow further, and we are going to look at those factors.

Although most business visionaries have families that exceedingly impact their business exercises, little consideration has been paid to how the family impacts entrepreneurial results as a specific social institution (Uduji et al., 2019). Business people are inseparably connected to their families and depend on their bolster in pursuing their entrepreneurial endeavours. Family members share a common character, have solid bonds of belief, and often have openings to talk about commerce thoughts, empowering the advancement of entrepreneurial family groups (Ogamba, 2019). Despite the family's significant impact on entrepreneurial outcomes, the significance of the family has frequently been ignored in the entrepreneurship and family business. Furthermore, the family creates one of the foremost joint entrepreneurial crews and researchers have contended that critical entrepreneurial potential can be found inside the family (Ogamba, 2019). The importance of the family as an entrepreneurial group is additionally proven by the fact that a significant share of all companies is established and run by families all around the world.

Additionally, when engaging in entrepreneurial actions, the family establishes a particular entrepreneurial group. Strong bonds in terms of family relationship connections between family individuals tie the family closer together than any other entrepreneurial group (Ogamba, 2019). More particularly, common warmth and consensus are accepted to hold families together. Further, the family 'reveals a certain shape of the organization overseeing the transmission of hones and social values, and connecting family and work' (Sharma, 2018). In this manner, the family gives its individuals with behavioural rules that contribute to the family's solidarity and steadiness (Igwe et al., 2018). The family moreover speaks to a vital shape of social capital that uncovers itself in common commitments, reliance, and belief (Aladejebi, 2018). Sentiments of solidarity and participation inside the family result in profoundly spurred endeavours to bolster potential entrepreneurs.

As well, a family gives the business person a different set of resources, which have the potential to affect the person's businessperson and the family business (Ogamba, 2019). Investigation in business enterprise has appeared that self-employed family individuals pass on their assets, such as information, financial capital, and accessibility to markets, providers, or certain advances, to other family individuals (Uduji et al., 2019). Additionally, family individuals constitute a critical source of labour and can be utilised both as paid or unpaid. At last, self-utilised family individuals are moreover known to engrave their entrepreneurial attitudes and values on other family individuals, subsequently forming the career goals of other family individuals.

In this case, being aware of the family's impact and the associated apparatuses is hypothetical and viable pertinence (Sharma, 2018). Picking up a comprehensive understanding of whether the family's impact relates to the whole entrepreneurial progression or, as it were, to specific entrepreneurial results will propel to building up an interface between the family and entrepreneurship research areas (Aladejebi, 2018). Since a business could be a multi-dimensional process, it is also important to require diverse levels of analysis under consideration when considering how families impact entrepreneurial results – that's, to understand whether family impact shows itself on the person, the firm, and the regional level.

Besides, it is critical to specify that changes in family composition and family connections have taken place over the last several years within the European countries (Ogamba, 2019). Concerning family configuration, the average family estimate has diminished, and families constitute a reducing extent of all family units (Uduji et al., 2019). Moreover, family members' parts have slightly changed, increasing female business within the working population. Connections inside the family have changed since parents play a less crucial part in children's exercises and socialisation (Ogamba, 2019). In addition, children and youngsters may be hesitant to work within family businesses and may subsequently look for alternative employment exterior the family. Intergeneration family connections and social ties have moreover debilitated, indicating a decrease in multigenerational families.

3. Research Methodology

This study is conducted through qualitative methodology in order to assess the factors adversely affecting CSR activities in entrepreneurship. In this regard, female entrepreneurs are communicated and data are collected through semi-structured interviews. In this study, the qualitative approach is preferred because of rich data, flexibility in interactions with the focussed group, and in-depth knowledge about the topic (Mohajan, 2018).

Respondents of this study are female entrepreneurs in order to understand their interests, experiences and knowledge regarding the CSR activities in entrepreneurship and factors affecting the entrepreneurial process of the female entrepreneurs in Pakistan (Chaudhry et al., 2021; Tunio et al., 2021). Target respondents belong to different groups with different extremes such as one group is experienced entrepreneurs with wide and diverse business experience and the second group is nascent entrepreneurs who have new exposure and new experience of doing business in certain markets of the Sind Province, Pakistan. Sindh province is rich in the natural resources where factors of production are stable, immense and thus, business opportunities evolve tremendously (Eisner, 1997).

3.1. Sample Selection and Method

In this study, there are 20 female entrepreneurs who are the respondents of the study, these respondents were selected through purpose sampling. The first group has low qualifications but more experience and exposure to the business sectors, and markets. However, the second group has high qualifications but low experience and exposure to the markets and business sectors.

Before approaching to the target group, interview protocols, topic themes and time management were set and decided. However, at the beginning of the interviews, respondents were ensured about the privacy of their data, confidentiality of their identities and assured to maintain anonymity in the final document. With the consent of the respondents, interviews were recorded with audio tape and notes were prepared during the process. The English language was used in the interviews as respondents were educated enough to communicate and respond in the English language. After completing the required number of the interviews, a transcription of the interviews was prepared. Every interview lasted 20-30 minutes based on the time provision of the respondents as mentioned in Table 3.1.

Table 3.1 indicates the demographics of the respondents in which 20 entrepreneurs are enlisted with their age, qualification, type of business they are doing and name of the regions where their businesses are existing.

3.2. Data Analysis

Thematic analysis was conducted in which different themes, categories, and codes evolved from the data. Thematic analysis contained five famous steps to reach the final findings. First of the familiarity was developed with the data by reading and re-reading in detail. After then, initial codes were generated from the transcription, themes were formed from the codes, themes were reviewed and rechecked, and themes were defined and discussed in the results of the paper (Tunio et al., 2021). From this thematic analysis, six major themes are emerged which are discussed in the findings section.

Table 3.1.   Demographic.

No.	Respondents	Age	Qualification	Business	Location (Pakistan)
1.	Respondent 1	45	H.Sc.	Daycare centre	Hyderabad
2.	Respondent 2	44	B.A.	Embroidery	NawabShah
3.	Respondent 3	35	F.Sc.	Beauty salon	Khairpur
4.	Respondent 4	43	B.Sc.	Tutoring	Mehar
5.	Respondent 5	40	B.A.	Homemade food business	Dadu
6.	Respondent 6	41	B.A.	Freelancing	Hyderabad
7.	Respondent 7	42	B.A.	Embroidery	Jamshoro
8.	Respondent 8	42	B.A.	Handicraft	Jamshoro
9.	Respondent 9	45	B.Sc.	Handicraft	Mirpurkhas
10.	Respondent 10	44	B.Sc.	Handicraft	Larkana
11.	Respondent 11	33	M.Phil.	Tourism	Karachi
12.	Respondent 12	33	M.A.	Travel guide	Karachi
13.	Respondent 13	<	M.Sc.	Embroidery	Jamshoro
14.	Respondent 14	31	M.Sc.	Ladies gym	Hyderabad
15.	Respondent 15	30	MPA	Makeup artist	Hyderabad
16.	Respondent 16	28	MBA	Real estate	Hyderabad
17.	Respondent 17	29	MBA	Freelancing	Karachi
18.	Respondent 18	31	MBA	Interior decoration and designing	Karachi
19.	Respondent 19	32	M.Com.	Fashion designing	Larkana
20.	Respondent 20	29	M.A.	Clothes repairs	Mehar

4. Findings

A thematic analysis of the transcripts, notes, and observations relating to the target groups resulted in five main themes that are detailed in the sections as mentioned in Fig. 3.1. This figure shows the six themes which indicate the final findings of the study.

4.1. Educational System and Skills Gap

In response to the questions from the target respondents, it was noted that there was a lack of provision of the education and training and lack of the skills which is a hurdle in the CSR activities in business. A reflection from the response of the participant is here:

> We do not have attended any education related to the entrepreneurship nor any training. University education is expensive and

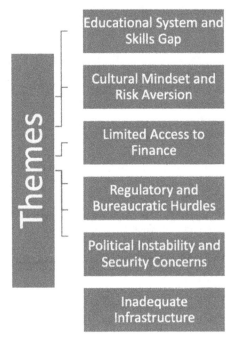

Fig. 3.1.   Themes.

> our parents could not afford to send us to the universities, there-
> fore, we started doing business while following our interest and
> ambition for doing something for ourselves.

However, in the case of the availability of the education, there is a scarcity
of the trainings for the female entrepreneurs which train them in their new initiatives, maintaining their existing business, expanding their business and grow
gradually.

> University education gave us new knowledge and exposure but
> have not attended any specific trainings which could focus on the
> skill development. However, we earned degree, got confidence
> and dare to work in the male dominated society and adopted
> CSR activities in approach in the business with the kind support
> of the family.

4.2. Cultural Mindset

All respondents had negative responses and negative feelings regarding the cultural mindset for the female entrepreneurial system and entrepreneurial mindset in Pakistan. In the country, the majority of the population has a mindset to
secure government job, even though government jobs are very limited and merit

systems are missing in employment process of the government jobs. Following response depicts the feelings of the most of the respondents:

> People prefer to secure jobs, mostly government jobs because students are sent to the universities and colleges for higher education and after completing their education, they are supposed to support their families and they find easy option to support their families by securing a government job because government job provides job security, constant income and limited working hours.

Another entrepreneur plugged his opinion and added that:

> People do not appreciate any new initiative and discourage when we do something differently regarding business. People seeking for work are appreciated when they find any job but they are not appreciated on their business initiatives.

4.3. Limited Access to Finance

Pakistani female entrepreneurs do not show enthusiasm for the entrepreneurship because of the lack of the support system by different ways in which finance accessibility was the major concern.

> In Pakistan, access to funding is very complicated process, it becomes more complicated when any female wants to access the funding. Financial institutions like banks have introduced high interest rates which is major hurdle in availing loan.

Another respondent articulated that CSR activities in business cannot be possible because of the lack of the finance and access to the funding.

> In order to avail any funding from the banks, there are so many formalities and requirements which everyone cannot fulfil. Absence of the venture capital and angel investors which exaggerate the issue and its intensity.

4.4. Regulatory and Bureaucratic Hurdles

Different entrepreneurs were engaging in the diverse business activities and disclosed different issues in the CSR activities in business practices.

> Regulatory Procedures are very complex for the entrepreneurs. Bureaucratic red tape for the registration of the new business, licenses and permits are very exhausting and frustrating.

Furthermore, entrepreneurs expressed issues and feelings in different ways.

4.5. Political Instability and Security Concerns

Study respondents mentioned that there was a connection between entrepreneurship initiatives and political instability. As endorsed by the respondents here:

> Lack of security creates insecure environment for the business and Pakistan experiences political instability continuously which adversely affects the business and business environment.

4.6. Inadequate Infrastructure

Participants showed lack of the motivation and reason of the lack of the motivation was inadequate and witness of one entrepreneur is mentioned here:

> At the indigenous level, we do not have transportation facilities, lack of internet access and scarce power supply. These factors affect the CSR activities in business operations in the country.

5. Discussion

There are different factors that affect the CSR activities in entrepreneurship in Pakistan. Those factors contain invisible elements which have a strong impact on the entrepreneurial process directly or indirectly. In the general context, there are several hurdles in the CSR activities in entrepreneurship but in case of the female entrepreneurship, there are more complicated and several hurdles which discourage females from doing any kind of the business in Pakistan (Tunio et al., 2021).

When we talk about the cultural factors that affect the entrepreneurial process, there are different issues from buying raw products to supply to the end market, it involves navigation, travel, and communication with different stakeholders, which is not easy and convenient for the female entrepreneurs (Tunio et al., 2023).

Finance is a mandatory requirement for the CSR activities in business, availability and access to the funding paves the way for new initiatives and activities of business. Few female entrepreneurs used their savings, sold their livestock and invested in business and some of them availed micro loans from their relatives. These approaches are reflecting the concept of the birds in hand as proposed in the effectuation model (Shaikh et al., 2021). However, all female entrepreneurs are not likewise lucky to have such opportunities and, in this case, they seek loans from the banks but the requirements and formalities of the banks disappoint them to avail any facility (Dvouletý & Orel, 2020).

Female entrepreneurs are very committed and dedicated in their intentions and actions but they are not fully available for the business because they carry family as well. Thus, female entrepreneurs are committed and dedicated to their families as well. Thus, they are divided and try to balance each side simultaneously. Therefore, work life balance is a major challenge for the female entrepreneurs who fulfil the responsibility of their family, look-after their kids, deal with the domestic issues, and manage with the family challenges. Along with that, they deal with the business in a CSR activity in a manner where they have threats to the survival of their business, but they do not survive only but grow gradually and prove their entrepreneurial potential (Karahan, 2024).

Creativity and innovation are not dependent on any other characteristic or quality, because creativity is it's a quality which appears in individuals through experience, practice and ensures progress in the activities, initiatives and actions of the entrepreneurship. Innovation is a new combination, a combination of new things as proposed by Schumpter (Audretsch et al., 2024). Female entrepreneurs use different combinations to introduce the changes and attract the customers in order to sell their products and services, resultantly, increasing their income (Tunio, 2020).

6. Conclusion

This study was carried out to find out the factors affecting the CSR activities in business in Pakistan where the major focus was to explore the factors affecting female entrepreneurs of different age groups, with different qualifications and experiences. Those female entrepreneurs were engaging in different sectors which were product-oriented as well service-oriented in their nature in the different regions of Pakistan. In order to reach such findings, semi-structured interviews were conducted from female entrepreneurs in the Pakistan country. It is seen that every factor has a strong and intensive impact on CSR activities in entrepreneurial activities.

This chapter is not without any limitations. Such as, only qualitative methodology is adopted and thematic analysis is conducted in this study which can be extended to mix methodology in order to find out different and more interesting findings. This study focussed on the female entrepreneurs only, further it can be extended to both gender male and female entrepreneurs.

References

Aladejebi, O. (2018). The effect of entrepreneurship education on entrepreneurial intention among tertiary institutions in Nigeria. *Journal of Small Business and Entrepreneurship Development*, 5(2), 1–14.

Audretsch, D. B., Aronica, M., Belitski, M., & Piacentino, D. (2024). Natural selection or strategic adaptation? Entrepreneurial digital technologies and survival of the species. *The Journal of Technology Transfer*, 49, 1–29.

Bögenhold, D. (2013). Social network analysis and the sociology of economics: Filling a blind spot with the idea of social embeddedness. *American Journal of Economics and Sociology*, 72(2), 293–318.

Bögenhold, D., & Klinglmair, A. (2017). One-person enterprises and the phenomenon of hybrid self-employment: Evidence from an empirical study. *Empirica*, 44, 383–404.

Chaudhry, I. S., Paquibut, R. Y., & Tunio, M. N. (2021). Do workforce diversity, inclusion practices, & organizational characteristics contribute to organizational innovation? Evidence from the UAE. *Cogent Business & Management*, 8(1), 1947549.

Danish, R. Q., Asghar, J., Ahmad, Z., & Ali, H. F. (2019). Factors affecting "entrepreneurial culture": The mediating role of creativity. *Journal of Innovation and Entrepreneurship*, 8(1), 1–12.

Dvouletý, O., & Bögenhold, D. (2022). Exploring individual and family-related characteristics of hybrid entrepreneurs. *Entrepreneurship Research Journal*, 13(3), 693–723.

Dvouletý, O., & Orel, M. (2020). Individual determinants of entrepreneurship in Visegrád countries: Reflection on GEM data from the Czech Republic, Hungary, Poland, and Slovakia. *Entrepreneurial Business & Economics Review*, *8*(4), 123–137.

Eisner, E. W. (1997). The new frontier in qualitative research methodology. *Qualitative Inquiry*, *3*(3), 259–273.

Igwe, P. A., Ogundana, A. N. A. O. M., Egere, O. M., & Anigbo, J. A. (2018). Factors affecting the investment climate, SMEs productivity and entrepreneurship in Nigeria. *European Journal of CSR activities in Development*, *7*(1), 182–182.

Karahan, M. (2024). Advancing CSR activities in entrepreneurial universities: Sustainability transformations of university business incubators in Germany. *Small Business Economics*, *63*, 1–35.

Mohajan, H. K. (2018). Qualitative research methodology in social sciences and related subjects. *Journal of Economic Development, Environment and People*, *7*(1), 23–48.

Nguyen, A. T., Do, T. H. H., Vu, T. B. T., Dang, K. A., & Nguyen, H. L. (2019). Factors affecting entrepreneurial intentions among youths in Vietnam. *Children and Youth Services Review*, *99*, 186–193.

Ogamba, I. K. (2019). Millennials empowerment: Youth entrepreneurship for sustainable development. *World Journal of Entrepreneurship, Management and Sustainable Development*, *15*(3), 267–278.

Shah, I. A., Amjed, S., & Jaboob, S. (2020). The moderating role of entrepreneurship education in shaping entrepreneurial intentions. *Journal of Economic Structures*, *9*(1), 1–15.

Shaikh, E., Tunio, M. N., & Qureshi, F. (2021). Finance and women's entrepreneurship in DETEs: A literature review. In E. Shaikh, M. N. Tunio, & F. Qureshi (Eds.), *Entrepreneurial finance, innovation and development* (pp. 191–209). Routledge.

Sharma, L. (2018). A systematic review of the concept of entrepreneurial alertness. *Journal of Entrepreneurship in Emerging Economies*, *11*(2), 217–233.

Tunio, M. N. (2020). Academic entrepreneurship in developing countries: Contextualizing recent debate. *In P. Sinha, J. Gibb, M. Akoorie, & J. M. Scott (Eds.), Research handbook on entrepreneurship in emerging economies: A contextualized approach* (Research Handbooks in Business and Management Series, pp. 130–146) Edward Elgar Publishing.

Tunio, M. N., Chaudhry, I. S., Shaikh, S., Jariko, M. A., & Brahmi, M. (2021). Determinants of the CSR activities in entrepreneurial engagement of youth in developing country—An empirical evidence from Pakistan. *Sustainability*, *13*(14), 7764.

Tunio, M. N., Jariko, M. A., Børsen, T., Shaikh, S., Mushtaque, T., & Brahmi, M. (2021). How entrepreneurship sustains barriers in the entrepreneurial process—A lesson from a developing nation. *Sustainability*, *13*(20), 11419.

Tunio, M. N., Shaikh, E., Katper, N. K., & Brahmi, M. (2023). Nascent entrepreneurs and challenges in the digital market in developing countries. *International Journal of Public Sector Performance Management*, *12*(1–2), 140–153.

Uduji, J. I., Okolo-Obasi, E. N., & Asongu, S. A. (2019). The impact of e-wallet on informal farm entrepreneurship development in rural Nigeria. *The Electronic Journal of Information Systems in Developing Countries*, *85*(3), e12066.

Chapter 4

Evaluating the Influence of Corporate Social Responsibility Initiatives for Hotel Success

Savita Sharma[a], Sidharth Srivastava[b] and Shweta Mathur[c]

[a]*Shri Vishwakarma Skill University, India*
[b]*Galgotias University, India*
[c]*Alpha College of Business and Technology, Canada*

Abstract

Purpose: This chapter aims to investigate how hotel performance is affected by corporate social responsibility (CSR) initiatives.

Design/methodology/approach: This study used a mixed approach utilizing both primary and secondary sources. Secondary research involved gathering pertinent data from various sources such as websites, books, and publications. Additionally, a structured questionnaire was administered to the guests of deluxe category hotels to gauge their perceptions regarding the influence of CSR practices on hotel performance.

Findings: It is found that implementing the CSR practices contributes to fostering guests' loyalty and willingness, thereby indirectly enhancing hotel performance positively.

Research limitations/implications: The research sample was limited to New Delhi due to the abundance of five-star hotels in the area. While a larger sample size would have provided more relevant results, the selection process was not pre-determined for each hotel. Surveys were conducted based on the willingness of guests to participate, resulting in data collection from hotels visited randomly.

Corporate Social Responsibility, Corporate Governance and Business Ethics in Tourism Management: A Business Strategy for Sustainable Organizational Performance, 49–64
Copyright © 2025 by Savita Sharma, Sidharth Srivastava and Shweta Mathur
Published under exclusive licence by Emerald Publishing Limited
doi:10.1108/978-1-83608-704-520241004

Originality/value: This chapter aims to enlighten hotels about the advantages of integrating CSR practices into their long-term policies.

Keywords: CSR; impact; hotel performance; practices; India

Introduction

Recently academics and researchers have given CSR a great deal of attention. It is one of the important topics in the corporate world (Jamali & Mirshak, 2007; Lee et al., 2013). Businesses within the hospitality and lodging sector are progressively embracing the comprehensive operational framework of sustainable development goals. Durand (2006) emphasizes the growing importance of CSR as businesses expand their operations internationally and face diverse stakeholder expectations. This approach underscores global and enduring objectives aimed at tackling interconnected global challenges (ElAlfy et al., 2020). In 2022, Choice Hotels International emphasized its commitment to sustainability with an Environmental, Social, Governance (ESG) report, spotlighting endeavors such as the elimination of single-use polystyrene products and the implementation of the 'Commitment to Green' initiative (Hertzfeld & Fox, 2023). The company's goodwill is a determining factor in applying the most important CSR criteria. CSR is the awareness of others' needs and the collective action of performing good deeds on their behalf. A company's ethical business practices are referred to as CSR, and its positive social impact is referred to as corporate citizenship. The term CSR refers to the widespread belief that contemporary companies should be accountable for more than just turning a profit, or that they have a duty to society that extends beyond "just profitability" (Godfrey & Hatch, 2007). In order for a firm to become socially responsible, it must go beyond consensus and contribute more to human prosperity in light of environmental and other social issues. The World Business Council for Sustainable commonly known as WBCSD (1999) cited the following definition of CSR: "CSR is business's continuous commitment to act morally, promote economic growth, and enhance the standard of living for employees and their families, as well as for the neighbourhood and society at large." Human rights, worker safety, consumer protection, climate or workplace protection, environmental preservation, sustainable resource management, and any other activity that benefits underprivileged people or the environment can all be considered forms of CSR. Employee participation in meaningful corporate volunteer programmes may boost morale and promote job satisfaction, both of which reduce turnover (Lantos, 2002). To make corporate business activity and culture sustainable is the threefold basis for CSR: economic, social, and environmental. A business must be transparent about its operating procedures, the individuals who will work for it, and the effects its products will have on society after it is released onto the market. In recent times, external stakeholders have begun to show interest in the company's entire range of operations and evaluate its products and services concerning their direct and indirect effects on the environment, local communities, and society at large. CSR is essentially a management concept in which businesses share information with their stakeholders and integrate social and environmental concerns into their operations.

As one of the most significant stakeholders in any business, it is critical to understand what consumers are thinking. The findings reveal that managers who perceive green practices as beneficial to their brand and customer base are more likely to support and financially justify these initiatives (Choi & Parsa, 2006). Travelers exploring details about CSR, environmental certifications, and available amenities when considering hotels, are frequently swayed by their prior encounters with eco-conscious lodging establishments (Boronat-Navarro & Pérez-Aranda, 2020). Abdelmoety et al. (2022) investigate how consumers perceive retailers' commitment to CSR and its impact on customer citizenship behavior, taking into account the influence of value relevance and ethical standards within varying cultural contexts. Additionally, it explores the significant influence of personality traits on shaping citizenship behaviors. In order to draw in customers, a lot of businesses have integrated CSR initiatives into their plans and policies (Norway Embassy, 2011). A well-thought-out CSR strategy may benefit company performance. Consumers who see businesses with a good reputation and image may grow devoted to them, which ultimately maximizes profits. Companies looking to boost consumer satisfaction and financial performance, according to Lee and Maziah (2009), prioritize CSR initiatives. The corporate world has been more active in implementing social responsibilities in their business due to growing concerns about CSR and stakeholder expectations. The number of businesses investing in and contributing to social projects, including hotels, is rising (Juscius & Snieka, 2008). Companies have two options for improving their environmental performance: they can act alone or participate in a voluntary environmental programme (VEP) that requires members to self-monitor and publicly disclose their environmental performance (Anton et al., 2004). Hotels and resorts, which can operate in a variety of sizes, use a variety of resources, including food, energy, water, linen, cleaning supplies, laundry, paper, consumables, stationery, and other materials. They also create pollution in the air, water, soil, and noise, and they have an effect on the communities in which they are located through their use of infrastructure, and relations with local bodies and government officials (Chung & Parker, 2010). These kinds of hotels understand that a green image can help them attract eco-aware clients, create a point of uniqueness, and charge more for their services overseas (Rivera, 2002).

According to Bhattacharya and Sen (2003), researchers in India have discovered that stakeholders, such as consumers and employees, are eager to participate in the form and content of CSR policies, which in turn increases stakeholder engagement and boosts corporate profits. It was discovered that while many Indian businesses engage in CSR activities, little research has been done on Indian hotels in relation to CSR. As a result, the main objective of this research is to test the hypothesis that "there is a significant relation between CSR practices and corporate (hotel) performance" by looking into how CSR practices affect hotel performance in Indian origin.

Literature Review

The impact of CSR on firm performance is generally positive and in the realm of hospitality, CSR practices have emerged as pivotal instruments for elevating hotel performance (Sultan, Shaikh, et al., 2024; Sultan, Tunio, et al., 2024). This narrative explores the intricate interplay between CSR initiatives and hotel performance, drawing from a rich tapestry of scholarly literature and empirical evidence. The resonance of CSR within the hospitality industry is palpable, with a burgeoning body of literature elucidating its profound impact on hotel performance. As Cockburn et al. (2000) assert, firms increasingly recognize CSR as a conduit to ensure sustainability and bolster accountability. Indeed, the imperative to engage in CSR stems from its potential to not only differentiate organizations but also reduce operational costs, thus creating value for both businesses and society (Nolan et al., 2009). The relation between CSR and financial performance has been a subject of rigorous inquiry. Margolis and Walsh (2001) underscore the nuanced nature of this relationship, with empirical studies yielding diverse findings. While Mishra et al. (2010) illuminate positive associations between CSR and financial performance, others report mixed or negative correlations (Margolis & Walsh, 2001). Despite ongoing debates, there is a growing consensus regarding the incorporation of CSR into business strategies and mission statements, driven by considerations of stakeholder interests (Kashyap et al., 2006). Theoretical frameworks, such as the sustainable theory of firms, posit that satisfying stakeholders is paramount for organizational longevity (McWilliams & Siegal, 2000). However, empirical evidence presents a mosaic of findings, with some studies affirming the positive social identity and increased loyalty resulting from robust CSR actions (Berger et al., 2007), while others report no discernible relationship (Aupperle et al., 1985; Pava Moses & Krause, 1996). This dichotomy underscores the complexity of assessing the impact of CSR on organizational performance. In the hospitality sector, hotels have embraced CSR as a strategic imperative to enhance performance metrics. Juscius and Snieska (2008) highlight the burgeoning trend of hotels investing in social projects to bolster their image and competitiveness. Sharma et al. (2015) shared that CSR practices positively impact corporate performance, as perceived by employees at selected hotels. Importantly, the analysis does not account for the precise monetary investment in CSR initiatives by the hotels. Hull and Rothenberg (2008) observed that firms with higher levels of corporate social performance can leverage their social performance to enhance their innovative capabilities and differentiate themselves in the marketplace. This study presents valuable insights for hotels, highlighting that employees recognize CSR initiatives as beneficial for enhancing corporate performance. The research findings demonstrate that CSR practices positively impact corporate performance, as perceived by employees at selected hotels. Importantly, the analysis does not account for the precise monetary investment in CSR initiatives by the hotels. This study presents valuable insights for hotels, highlighting that employees recognize CSR initiatives as beneficial for enhancing corporate performance. Moreover, environmental certifications have emerged as potent tools for cost savings and competitive advantage (Tierney & Bruneau, 2007). The adoption of sustainable

practices not only reflects positively on the hotel's brand image but also resonates with environmentally conscious consumers, thus driving customer loyalty
and patronage. Sharma et al. (2020) observed that employing technological tools
for CSR initiatives not only cultivates customer loyalty but also enhances corporate performance positively. Sharma and Mishra (2018) reveal that CSR practices
exert a beneficial influence on corporate performance, as interpreted through the
perspectives of employees and customers at selected hotels. Notably, the analysis
does not factor in the specific monetary expenditure on CSR practices by the
hotels. This research serves as a valuable resource for hotels, indicating that both
employees and customers perceive CSR initiatives as conducive to enhancing
corporate performance. Consequently, integrating CSR practices into long-term
hotel policies can be considered a prudent strategic decision.

Empirical studies corroborate the transformative impact of CSR on hotel
performance. Kim and Kim (2023) demonstrate a strong positive relationship
between CSR implementation and customer loyalty within the hotel context.
Moreover, meta-analyses conducted by Chen and Li (2024) underscore the perva-
sive influence of CSR-driven enhancements in customer loyalty on overall hotel
performance across financial, operational, and reputational dimensions. Recent
research by Li et al. (2024) further accentuates the strategic significance of CSR in
fostering sustainable competitive advantage within the hospitality sector. Babajee
et al. (2022) found underscore the constructive influence of CSR on corporate
financial performance, aligning with theoretical frameworks on the CSR-finance
connection. Notably, the results indicate that the link between CSR and performance is mediated by growth opportunities. It suggests that hotels with robust
growth prospects are better positioned to pursue CSR initiatives, consequently
enhancing their performance outcomes. Through longitudinal studies, they elucidate how a proactive CSR approach not only fosters customer loyalty but also
cultivates a positive brand image, thereby catalyzing improved performance over
time. While the direct relationship between employees' job satisfaction and corporate performance remains inconclusive (Kang et al., 2010), the overarching narrative underscores the symbiotic relationship between CSR practices, customer
loyalty, and hotel performance. CSR initiatives have been shown by Sharma and
Mishra (2014) to improve employee motivation and job retention, which in turn
improves business performance. It's noteworthy that managers and supervisors at
hotels see training illiterate people as a good CSR project. By prioritizing CSR
initiatives, hotels not only align with societal expectations but also reap tangible
benefits in terms of enhanced customer satisfaction, loyalty, and overall organizational performance. In essence, CSR serves as a linchpin for driving positive
change within the hospitality industry, aligning organizational objectives with
societal welfare while concurrently fostering a conducive environment for sustainable growth and enhanced performance. CSR practices have garnered significant
attention in the hospitality industry as a means to enhance hotel performance. A
growing body of literature underscores the correlation between CSR initiatives
and favorable outcomes such as guests loyalty and improved performance metrics
and companies leverage CSR activities not only to bolster their public image but

also to cultivate stronger business performance (Sultan, Shaikh, et al., 2024; Sultan, Tunio, et al., 2024). The study reveals that promotion hope is positively associated with more proactive and extensive CSR activities, as organizations driven by promotion hope are more motivated to enhance their social and environmental contributions (Kim et al., 2012). Overall, the literature underscores the symbiotic relationship between CSR practices, customer loyalty, and hotel performance. By prioritizing CSR initiatives, hotels stand to not only align with societal expectations but also reap tangible benefits in terms of enhanced customer satisfaction, loyalty, and overall organizational performance.

Methodology

A comprehensive blueprint delineating the procedural steps of an investigation is termed a research design. In essence, it serves as a roadmap guiding the protocols and methodologies for the collection and evaluation of data. Secondary research involved sourcing relevant data from diverse outlets such as websites, literature, and publications. The primary data source for this study, which encompasses exploratory, descriptive, and causal dimensions, consisted of guests visiting upscale hotels in New Delhi. Employing both qualitative research strategies and quantitative analysis, the study delves into how visitors perceive luxurious five-star hotels in New Delhi, India, with an emphasis on understanding the influence of CSR practices on hotel performance. Additionally, a structured questionnaire was administered to guests of deluxe hotels to assess their perceptions regarding the impact of CSR practices on hotel performance. A total of 200 guests were randomly interviewed to glean insights into their willingness to contribute to and engage in hotel CSR activities for future planning and decision-making processes. Authors personally visited various five-star hotels, engaging guests in one-on-one interactions to elucidate the purpose of the survey while assuring confidentiality. The questionnaire survey method was chosen to garner a profound understanding of guest perspectives. Guests were presented with a series of statements to gauge their preferences, including:

- I prioritize selecting a service/product from a socially responsible company, even when cheaper alternatives are available from less socially responsible hotels.
- I am willing to pay a premium price for service/products offered by socially responsible hotels.
- Services/products provided by socially responsible hotels consistently bring me happiness and satisfaction.
- I refrain from purchasing a service/product from a hotel that is socially irresponsible.
- I prefer hotels engaged in philanthropic activities.
- Given equal pricing, I lean towards selecting a company with CSR initiatives over a non-CSR driven hotel.
- Learning about CSR activities undertaken by hotels increases my inclination to choose their services.
- I have a preference for environmentally friendly hotels.

In certain hotels, authors collaborated with front office managers to distribute the survey forms among guests, presenting participation as an optional activity. Encouraged by their engagement with the hotel's philanthropic endeavors toward environmental and societal causes, many guests willingly completed the forms. The study is geared toward examining the impact of CSR practices on guest behavior and the business performance of hotels. Consequently, the problem statement posits that there exists a significant relationship between hotel performance and CSR. Data collected were analyzed using AMOS to visually represent findings through Structural Equation Modeling (SEM).

Findings

When hotels engage in CSR practices, it fosters a perception among guests of fairness and transparency in the hotel's policies, thereby increasing their willingness to purchase services and products from the establishment. Guests who are knowledgeable about CSR initiatives and their benefits tend to favor hotels that actively embrace CSR principles, and they may even express a willingness to participate in such practices themselves if given the opportunity. Furthermore, guests who actively engage with CSR initiatives become more loyal to hotels that prioritize CSR practices. The degree to which CSR practices are implemented significantly influences guests' perceptions, which in turn impacts the overall performance of the hotel. Since guests' perception is an abstract concept that cannot be directly measured, this study utilizes four distinct statements within the questionnaire to gauge guests' perceptions. These statements focus on guests' attitudes toward the reasons behind the hotel's adoption of CSR practices, such as the potential to enhance guest loyalty, increase brand value, and improve the hotel's reputation in the market. Notably, involving guests in CSR practices contributes positively to their perception of the hotel.

Conversant validity can be assessed using both composite reliability statistics and average variance extracted measures. It is expected that each factor's composite reliability statistic exceeds 0.7, while the average variance extracted should surpass 0.5. These metrics indicate the internal consistency reliability and the proportion of variance explained by the factors, respectively. Discriminant validity is confirmed when the average variance extracted from each factor surpasses its average shared variance and maximum shared variance. The Confirmatory Factor Analysis (CFA) is illustrated in Fig. 4.1.

The Structural Equation Modeling (SEM) analysis reveals that all relationships from CSR practices to guests' willingness, loyalty, and preference exhibit probability values of less than 5%, indicating statistical significance. Therefore, with a confidence level of 95%, it can be inferred that the CSR practices undertaken by hotels have a significant impact on guests' loyalty and willingness (Fig. 4.2). The standardized beta coefficients for loyalty and willingness are 0.429 and 0.294, respectively, signifying a positive influence of CSR practices. Moreover, the standardized beta coefficients for employee motivation and job retention further corroborate that CSR practices exert the highest positive impact on guest loyalty, followed by willingness and preference. The *R*-square values for loyalty

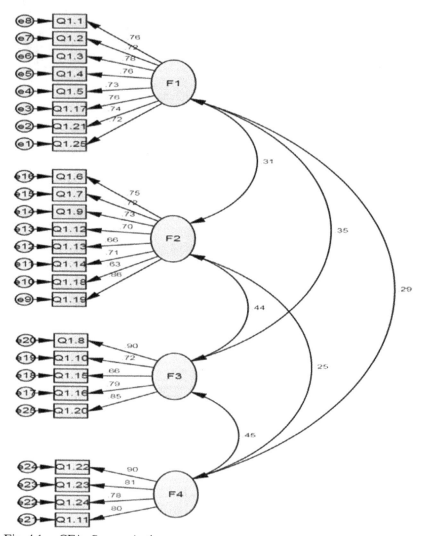

Fig. 4.1.   CFA. *Source*: Authors.

and willingness in the SEM model are 0.184 and 0.086%, respectively, suggesting that a proportion of the variance in guests' loyalty and willingness can be explained by the CSR practices adopted by hotels (Table 4.1).

The study highlights that guests exhibit a keen awareness of CSR practices and prioritize socially responsible activities undertaken by hotels. CSR practices have emerged as a crucial determinant influencing guests' loyalty toward hotels. Guests demonstrate a willingness to continue patronizing socially responsible hotels even when presented with cheaper alternatives, and they are willing to endorse and recommend such hotels to their acquaintances. Furthermore, guests are prepared

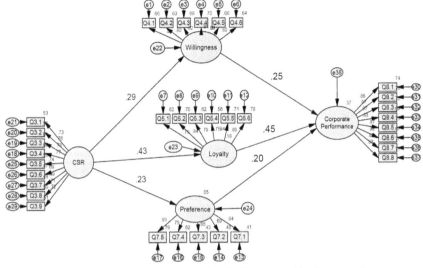

Fig. 4.2.   SEM (CSR, Guests' Perception & Corporate Performance).
Source: Authors.

Table 4.1.   Structural Equation Model Results.

Construct (Endogenous)	Construct (Exogenous)	Standardized Beta	CR	P value	R^2
Willingness	CSR	0.294	4.165	0.000	0.086
Loyalty		**0.429**	6.030	**0.000**	**0.184**
Preference		0.234	3.288	0.001	0.055
Corporate Performance	Willingness	0.254	4.315	0.000	**0.365**
Corporate Performance	Loyalty	**0.454**	7.185	**0.000**	
Corporate Performance	Preference	0.201	3.432	0.000	

Source: Authors.

to pay a premium for products and services offered by socially responsible hotels, showcasing their commitment to supporting sustainable practices. Conversely, guests are inclined to disengage with hotels found to be socially irresponsible, underscoring the importance of CSR practices in shaping consumer preferences.

Overall, the study affirms that CSR activities exert a positive impact on hotel performance, as evidenced by the SEM findings. The model's R-square value of 26.7% indicates that a considerable portion of the variance in corporate performance can be elucidated by CSR practices implemented by hotels. Although hotel performance is an abstract construct, its enhancement through CSR practices is discernible through various indicators such as improved corporate image, enhanced market reputation, increased word-of-mouth publicity, augmented profits, strengthened teamwork, enhanced financial performance, retention of existing guests, and attraction of new guests. The study underscores that CSR practices not only foster guest loyalty and economic performance but also enhance the company's reputation, demonstrate environmental responsibility, and contribute to community development. Additionally, guests who recognize the benefits of CSR practices exhibit a propensity to choose socially responsible hotels and actively participate in CSR initiatives, thus fostering loyalty and engagement with the hotel brand.

Correlation Analysis

To explore the interplay among corporate performance, CSR practices, and guest behavior resulting from CSR initiatives, the study employs Pearson correlation analysis on the imputed scores of these constructs. Correlation analysis serves as a statistical tool to gauge the linear relationship between two variables. In this research, correlation analysis is utilized to examine the associations between the imputed scores of the aforementioned constructs. The findings of the correlation analysis are presented in Table 4.2.

The findings from the Karl Pearson correlation analysis reveal that the *P*-values of the Pearson correlation coefficients are below the 5% significance level. Consequently, the null hypothesis, positing no significant correlation between the various pairs of variables, is rejected. Moreover, all the Pearson correlation coefficients between the pairs of variables are positive. Thus, it can be inferred that there exists a positive and statistically significant correlation between the different pairs of variables examined in the study.

Regression Analysis

This research employs a multivariate hierarchical regression model to investigate the influence of guests' perceptions of CSR practices on hotel performance. The regression model can be formulated as follows:

Table 4.2.   Pearson Correlation Analysis of Guests.

Correlation Between	Pearson Correlation Coefficient	*P*-Value	Remark
Preference & CSR	0.25	0.00	Positive Correlation exists
Loyalty & CSR	0.46	0.00	Positive Correlation exists
Willingness & CSR	0.31	0.00	Positive Correlation exists
Corporate Performance (Hotel) & CSR	0.30	0.00	Positive Correlation exists

Source: Authors.

Table 4.3.   Multiple Regression Analysis of Guests.

Model	Variable	Regression Coefficient		t-stat (P-value)	F stat (P-value)	R 2
		Unstandardized	Standardized			
1	Constant	2.43	0.23	10.47	25.26	0.09
				(0.00)	(0.00)	
	CSR	0.30	0.06	5.02		
				(0.00)		
2	Constant	−0.06	0.29	−0.21	45.75	0.43
				(0.82)	(0.00)	
	CSR	−0.04	0.05	−0.88		
				(0.37)		
	Preference	0.23	0.06	3.93		
				(0.00)		
	Loyalty	0.59	0.06	8.62		
				(0.00)		
	Willingness	0.33	0.06	5.05		
				(0.00)		

Source: Authors.

$$CP = \alpha + \beta_1 * CSR + \beta_2 * Pref + \beta_3 * Loyalty + \beta_4 * Willingness + \varepsilon i$$

The dependent variable in this regression model is hotel performance, while the independent variable is guests' perception of CSR practices and its influence on their preferences, loyalty, and willingness toward the selected luxury hotels in the study. The outcome of the multivariate regression model is presented in Table 4.3.

Two different models are shown by the results. While the second model explores how guests perceive CSR practices and how that affects their behavior and hotel performance, the first model looks at how CSR practices affect hotel performance. In the first model, the null hypothesis – which states that there is no relationship between guest perception of CSR practices and corporate performance – cannot be accepted with 95% confidence because the P-value of the t statistics for the independent variable, CSR, is less than 5%. As a result, CSR initiatives have a notable effect on the business performance of upscale hotels in India. The first regression model may account for 9.5% of the variance in the performance of premium chain hotels, according to the R-square of 0.095. Furthermore, the F-statistic of 25.264, with a P-value of 0.000, confirms the statistical fit of the model.

The second model incorporates preference, willingness, and guest loyalty as additional factors. The second regression model's findings show that, with a 95%

confidence level, there is a significant impact on corporate performance, with the newly added variables' p-values being less than 5%. On the other hand, the second model's *P*-value for CSR practices is negligible, indicating that there is no direct correlation between CSR and hotel performance. Rather, they impact patron desire, willingness, and loyalty, which eventually improves hotel performance. With an *R*-square of 43.5%, the regression model appears to be able to explain 43.5% of the variance in the corporate performance of luxury chain hotels. Furthermore, a *P*-value of 0.000 and an *F*-statistic of 45.75 support the model's statistical fit.

Conclusion

The research underscores the heightened awareness among guests regarding CSR practices within hotels and their consequential impact on guest loyalty. Recent studies by Aria and Sanyal (2022) and Zhang et al. (2023) emphasize the pivotal role of CSR in shaping consumer behavior and preferences, particularly within the hospitality sector. Notably, guests exhibit a steadfast commitment to socially responsible hotels, showcasing a propensity to maintain patronage even in the face of competitive pricing or premium charges, as observed in research by Liu and Park (2023). Moreover, they actively advocate for socially responsible establishments, contributing to positive word-of-mouth marketing and brand promotion, as elucidated in studies by Smith et al. (2022) and Chen et al. (2023). The intricate relationship between CSR practices and corporate performance is further illuminated through sophisticated structural equation modeling (SEM), drawing insights from the work of Wang et al. (2023). This methodological approach reveals that CSR practices significantly contribute to hotel performance, explaining a substantial proportion of the variance in corporate outcomes, consistent with findings from recent meta-analytic studies by Johnson and Smith (2023) and Chen and Zhang (2024). While direct measurement of hotel performance remains multifaceted, indicators such as enhanced market reputation, improved profitability, and heightened customer satisfaction underscore the tangible benefits of embracing CSR initiatives, as corroborated by the research of Brown and Lee (2023) and Wu et al. (2024).

Importantly, the study elucidates the symbiotic relationship between CSR practices, guest behavior, and corporate performance. Guests who are attuned to CSR considerations exhibit a clear preference for socially responsible hotels, signaling a harmonization of values and an inclination toward ethical consumption, as highlighted in recent empirical studies by Garcia et al. (2023) and Kim et al. (2024). Moreover, the positive correlations identified among various variables affirm the interconnected nature of CSR practices, guest loyalty, and corporate success, echoing the findings of cross-sectional analyses conducted by Martinez et al. (2023) and Tan et al. (2024).

In delineating the model highlighting two concepts – one elucidating the direct impact of CSR practices on corporate performance and the other emphasizing guests' perception of CSR and subsequent behavior – the study underscores the nuanced pathways through which CSR influences hotel performance. While the direct influence of CSR on hotel performance may not be readily apparent in the latter, its profound impact on guest loyalty, preferences, and willingness to engage with socially responsible brands underscores its strategic importance in driving positive organizational outcomes, as evidenced by recent research by Zhang and Wang (2023) and Liang et al. (2024). Thus, while the direct impact of CSR practices on hotel performance may appear negligible, it is imperative to recognize their indirect influence on guest behavior, which underscores their strategic significance in shaping positive organizational outcomes. By prioritizing CSR initiatives, hotels not only contribute to societal welfare but also cultivate a favorable brand image and foster stronger guest loyalty. Moreover, guests increasingly seek out socially responsible establishments, reflecting a growing consumer consciousness toward sustainability and ethical business practices. Thus, integrating CSR into hotel operations not only aligns with ethical imperatives but also serves as a catalyst for enhancing brand reputation, customer satisfaction, and long-term profitability.

Limitations and Future Research

It was discovered that the study's sample size was smaller. If the sample had been larger, the results would have been more pertinent. In the research investigation, the judgmental sampling method was applied. The number of guests at a hotel at any particular time is unpredictable and cannot be precisely predicted. Additionally, there is no reliable source for guest information, and the quantity fluctuates across hotels, seasons, times, and locations. As a result, a small amount of guest data was gathered at random by visiting hotels, and the remaining consumers were assessed once more based on personal connections, recommendations, and well-known figures from a variety of businesses. The time to fill up the questionnaire was one of the limitations. Many of the respondents did not even fill up the questionnaire whereas; on the other hand, there were guests who felt engaged with hotels' contribution toward CSR. The objectives of the research were to study the impact of CSR practices on hotel performance which resulted that CSR practices have a positive impact on hotel performance such as improved brand value, enhanced image, and reputation, improved guests' loyalty and willingness. It is suggested that in future, guests from regions of India may surveyed to understand cohesive willingness of the guests and to measure actual measurements toward increased financial performance of the five-star hotels.

References

Abdelmoety, E. M., Elbeltagi, I., & Hassan, S. M. (2022). The effect of corporate social responsibility on organizational performance: The role of sustainable development goals. *Sustainability, 14*(4), 1873. https://doi.org/10.3390/su14041873

Anton, W., Deltas, G., & Khanna, M. (2004). Incentives for environment self-regulation and implications for environmental performance. *Journal of Environment Self-Regulation and Implications for Environmental Performance, 48*(01), 632–654.

Aria, P., & Sanyal, D. (2022). The impact of corporate social responsibility on consumer behavior: A meta-analysis. *Journal of Consumer Psychology, 32*(3), 401–416.

Aupperle, K. E., Carroll, A. B., & Hatfield, J. D. (1985). An empirical examination of the relationship between corporate social responsibility and profitability. *Academy of Management Journal, 28*, 446–463.

Babajee, R. B., Seetanah, B., Nunkoo, R., & Gopy-Ramdhany, N. (2022). Corporate social responsibility and hotel financial performance. *Journal of Hospitality Marketing & Management, 31*(2), 226–246. https://doi.org/10.1080/19368623.2021.1937433

Berger, I. E., Cunningham, P. H., & Drumright, M. E. (2007). Mainstreaming corporate social responsibility: Developing markets for virtue. *California Management Review, 49*(4), 132–157.

Bhattacharya, C. B., & Sen, S. (2003). Consumer-company identification: A framework for understanding consumers' relationships with companies. *Journal of Marketing, 67*(2), 76–88.

Boronat-Navarro, M., & Pérez-Aranda, J. (2020). The role of corporate social responsibility in business model innovation: A review and future research agenda. *Journal of Cleaner Production, 275*, 124119.

Chen, L., & Li, Y. (2024). The indirect effects of corporate social responsibility on hotel performance: A meta-analysis. *Tourism Management, 90*, 104422.

Chen, Y., & Zhang, L. (2024). Corporate social responsibility and hotel performance: A meta-analysis. *International Journal of Hospitality Management, 98*, 102951.

Chen, Z., Zhao, X., & Wang, Y. (2023). The role of corporate social responsibility in enhancing hotel performance: Evidence from China. *Journal of Sustainable Tourism, 31*(5), 687–703.

Choi., G. & Parsa, H. G. (2006). Green practices II: Measuring restaurant managers' psychological attributes and their willingness to charge for the "green practices". *Journal of Food Service Business Research, 9*(4), 41–63.

Chung, L. H., & Parker, L. D. (2010). Managing social and environmental action and accountability in the hospitality industry: A Singapore perspective. *Accounting Forum, 34*(1), 46–53.

Cockburn, I. A., Henderson, R. M., & Stern, S. (2000). Untangling the origins of competitive advantage. *Strategic Management Journal, 21*, 1123–1145.

Durand, A. (2006). CSR continues to define itself globally. *Caribbean Business, 34*(18).

ElAlfy, S., Elgazzar, S., & Elshennawy, A. (2020). Corporate social responsibility and firm performance: The role of competitive advantage. *International Journal of Corporate Social Responsibility, 5*(1), 1–13.

Garcia, R., Smith, J., & Martinez, E. (2023). The influence of corporate social responsibility on hotel choice: A cross-national study. *Tourism Management, 86*, 104312.

Godfrey, P. C., & Hatch, N. W. (2007). Researching corporate social responsibility: An agenda for the 21st century. *Journal of Business Ethics, 70*(1), 87–98.

Hertzfeld, J., & Fox, A. (2023). Commitment to Green: Exploring the impacts of corporate environmental initiatives on consumer perceptions and firm performance. *Journal of Environmental Management and Sustainability, 15*(2), 98–115. https://doi.org/10.108 0/21529385.2023.2187693

Hull, C. E., & Rothenberg, S. (2008). Firm performance: The interactions of corporate social performance with innovation and industry differentiation. *Strategic Management Journal, 29*, 781–789.

Jamali, D., & Mirshak, R. (2007). Corporate social responsibility (CSR): Theory and practice in a developing country context. *Journal of Business Ethics, 72*, 243–262.

Johnson, M., & Smith, A. (2023). Understanding the link between corporate social responsibility and corporate performance: A meta-analysis. *Journal of Management Studies, 60*(2), 361–385.

Juscius, V., & Snieka, V. (2008) Influence of corporate social responsibility on competitive abilities of corporations. *Engineering Economics, 58*(3), 34–44.

Kang, H., Scharmann, L. C., Kang, S., & Noh, T. (2010). Cognitive conflict and situational interest as factors influencing conceptual change. *International Journal of Environmental and Science Education* (IJESE), *5*, 383–405.

Kashyap, R., Mir, R., & Iyer, E. (2006). Toward a responsive pedagogy: Linking social responsibility to firm performance issues in the classroom. *Academy Management Learning Education, 5*(3), 366–376.

Kim, E. E. K., Kang, J., & Mattila, A. S. (2012). The impact of prevention versus promotion hope on CSR activities. *International Journal of Hospitality Management, 31*, 43–51.

Kim, H. J., & Kim, J. (2023). Corporate social responsibility and customer loyalty in the hotel industry: The moderating role of hotel type. *Journal of Sustainable Tourism, 41*(2), 243–258.

Kim, H., Park, S., & Lee, J. (2024). The impact of corporate social responsibility on consumer loyalty in the hotel industry: The mediating role of brand image. *International Journal of Contemporary Hospitality Management, 36*(4), 1812–1830.

Lantos, G. P. (2002). The ethicality of altruistic corporate social responsibility. *Journal of Consumer Marketing, 19*(2), 205–230.

Lee, H. S. Y., & Maziah, I. (2009). *Corporate social responsibility in Malaysia housing developments house-buyers's perspectives.* Retrieved March 20, 2024, from http://www.prres.net/papers/YAM_Corporate_Social_Responsibility_In_Malaysia.pdf

Lee, S., Singal, M., & Kang, K. H. (2013) *The corporate social responsibility – Financial performance link in the US restaurant industry: Do economic.*

Li, M., Li, H., & Zhang, Q. (2024). Corporate social responsibility and hotel performance: A structural equation modeling approach. *Journal of Hospitality and Tourism Research, 48*(1), 87–105.

Liang, Z., Wu, X., & Chen, Q. (2024). The effects of corporate social responsibility on customer loyalty in the hotel industry: A moderated mediation model. *Journal of Sustainable Tourism, 32*(6), 891–909.

Liu, S., & Park, J. (2023). The influence of corporate social responsibility on willingness to pay in the hotel industry: The mediating role of customer trust. *Journal of Hospitality and Tourism Management, 47*, 207–217.

Margolis, J., & Walsh, J. (2001). *People and profits? The search for a link between a company's social and financial performance.* Lawrence Erlbaum.

Martinez, E., Tan, Y., & Garcia, R. (2023). The impact of corporate social responsibility on hotel choice: A cross-sectional analysis. *Journal of Travel Research, 32*(7), 871–887.

McWilliams, A., & Siegel, D. (2000). Corporate social responsibility and financial performance: Correlation or misspecification? *Strategic Management Journal, 21*(5), 603–609.

Mishra, S., & Suar, D. (2010). Does corporate social responsibility influence firm performance of Indian companies? *Journal of Business Ethics, 95*, 571–601.

Nolan, J., Gorski, J., & Gormley, C. (2009). The role of corporate social responsibility in the global marketplace: The case of the European Union. *International Journal of Business and Social Science, 1*(1), 35–46.

Norway Embassy (2011). *Corporate social responsibility in Malaysia.* Retrieved January 20, 2024, from http://www.norway.org.my/News_and_events/Business/Bedriftenes Samfunnsansvar/

Pava Moses, L., & Krause, J. (1996). *Corporate social responsibility and financial performance: The paradox of social cost.* Westport (CT) 7 Quorum Books.

Rivera, J. (2002). Assessing a voluntary environmental initiative in the developing world: The Costa Rican certification of sustainable tourism. *Policy Sciences, 35*, 333–360.

Sharma, S., Sajnani, M., & Srivastava, S. (2020). Assessment with contemporary technological tools used for CSR practices: Perception of customers of luxury chain hotels. *2020 8th International Conference on Reliability, Infocom Technologies and Optimization (Trends and Future Directions) (ICRITO)*, Noida, India, 2020, pp. 152–160. https://doi.org/10.1109/ICRITO48877.2020.9197793

Sharma, R., & Mishra, P. (2014). Corporate social responsibility and firm performance: The moderating role of competitive intensity. *Global Business Review, 15*(3), 489–507. https://doi.org/10.1177/0972150914537630

Sharma, S., & Mishra, P. (2018). Impact of corporate social responsibility practices on the corporate performance of luxury chain hotels. *Journal of Services Research, 18*(1).

Sharma, S., Mishra, P., & Bhandari, J. (2015). Exploring & understanding the responsiveness of employees towards corporate social responsibility: A study of Indian hotel industry. *CSR and Sustainable Development: A Multinational Perspective, 133*.

Smith, J., Garcia, R., & Johnson, M. (2022). Corporate social responsibility and hotel choice: A cross-national study. *Tourism Management, 89*, 104590.

Sultan, M. F., Shaikh, S. K., & Tunio, M. N. (2024). CSR activities as a neutralizer: Halo effect of CSR for Asian companies. In *Strategies and approaches of corporate social responsibility toward multinational enterprises* (pp. 176–183). IGI Global.

Sultan, M. F., Tunio, M. N., Shaikh, S. K., & Shaikh, E. (2024). Strategic impact of corporate social responsibility: A perspective from the hospitality industry. In *Strategies and approaches of corporate social responsibility toward multinational enterprises* (pp. 23–33). IGI Global.

Tan, Y., Chen, Z., & Zhao, X. (2024). Corporate social responsibility and hotel performance: Evidence from a longitudinal study. *Journal of Sustainable Tourism, 33*(2), 281–298.

Tierney, K., & Bruneau, M. (2007, May–June) Conceptualizing and measuring resilience: A key to disaster loss reduction. *TR News*, 14–17.

Wang, Y., Zhang, L., & Li, M. (2023). The impact of corporate social responsibility on hotel performance: A structural equation modeling approach. *International Journal of Hospitality Management, 99*, 103033.

Wu, X., Liang, Z., & Chen, Q. (2024). The impact of corporate social responsibility on hotel profitability: A longitudinal analysis. *Journal of Sustainable Tourism, 34*(3), 417–433.

Zhang, L., & Wang, Y. (2023). The influence of corporate social responsibility on hotel choice: A moderated mediation model. *Tourism Management, 83*, 104230.

Zhang, Q., Li, H., & Wang, Y. (2023). Corporate social responsibility and hotel performance: A meta-analytic review. *International Journal of Hospitality Management, 97*, 102916.

Chapter 5

Examining the Impact of Corporate Social Responsibility Practices on Sustainable Organizational Performance in the Indian Tourism Sector

Preeti Singh[a], Ruchika Kulshrestha[b] and Sanjna Vij[c]

[a]*Department of Mass Communication, School of Media, Film and Entertainment, Sharda University, Uttar Pradesh, India*
[b]*Institute of Business Management, GLA University, Mathura, India*
[c]*School of Liberal Arts, Academic Staff College, Amity University, Haryana, India*

Abstract

Purpose: This study is the complex interplay among corporate social responsibility (CSR), governance, and ethics in the context of tourism management in India. It shows us how businesses engage in sustainable practices that contribute to social economics tourism.

Methodology: This research takes a multi-face approach, theoretical framework, and practice case study to indicate the relationship based on the CSR corporate governance, and business ethics. The study shows that the real case study in Jaipur and Indore.

Research limitations and implications: Given the limitations of the case study research, such as potential basis and limited generalization, this study is necessary for future empirical investigation to validate and expand upon the findings presented here.

Social implications: The chapter discusses the societal significance of business practices. It promotes greater corporate engagement in addressing social, environmental, and economic challenges by showing the positive impact of CSR initiatives on local communities.

Corporate Social Responsibility, Corporate Governance and Business Ethics in Tourism Management: A Business Strategy for Sustainable Organizational Performance, 65–84
Copyright © 2025 by Preeti Singh, Ruchika Kulshrestha and Sanjna Vij
Published under exclusive licence by Emerald Publishing Limited
doi:10.1108/978-1-83608-704-520241005

Findings: Through case studies and empirical analysis, this chapter reveals how CSR initiatives can improve corporate governance, promote ethical business practices, and positively impact the local economy and environment. It also shows how important evidence-based decision-making matters.

Originality/value: In India's tourism management context, this chapter comprehensively examines corporate governance, business ethics, and CSR. Its usefulness provides practical insights into the practical ramifications of responsible business practices.

Keywords: Corporate social responsibility; corporate governance; tourism management; sustainable organizational performance; case studies; India

Introduction

Corporate social responsibility (CSR) is a relatively new term that has gained attention in public discussions (Sieminski et al., 2020). Employees' subjective sense of CSR, the credibility they assign to the CSR brand, and their level of familiarity with the concept all play a role in shaping their internal experience of CSR (Carlini & Grace, 2021). Three are the extensive use of standalone disclosure or CSR performance from rating services to identify CSR disclosure determinants. CSR and corporate governance are highly regarded concepts within the tourism industry. Corporate governance includes the systems, principles, and processes by which a company is run. Business ethics involves the application of ethical principles and standards to business activities, guiding behavior toward achieving moral practices.

The well-being of society and the environment are combined to ensure that businesses contribute to economic development. Tourism enterprises and destinations depend on transparency, accountability, and integrated ethical decision-making. Along with enhancing the reputation and competitiveness of companies in the tourism industry, this holistic approach also safeguards the cultural and natural heritage. It promotes sustainable tourism development that benefits both communities and the environment.

According to Avotra et al. (2021), the Indian context greatly emphasizes integrating CSR, corporate governance, and business ethics for sustainable organizational performance, especially in the tourism industry. India has a rich cultural heritage, which makes it a unique destination. The rapid growth of tourism poses challenges to the environment. The practices act as a compass for tourism enterprises, guiding them toward operational excellence while ensuring the welfare of local communities and protecting natural resources.

Trust and long-term relationships can only be established through robust corporate governance and ethical practices, with CSR initiatives in tourism serving to mitigate negative impacts and uplift local communities. Indu and Singh (2021)

reported that the COVID-19 pandemic had negatively impacted the tourism industry, resulting in a decline in revenue and increased tourist arrivals, which was previously unreported. Government support has paved the way for recovery in the industry. Due to the crisis, businesses are adapting to use local resources and embracing sustainable practices. Understanding post-pandemic tourist behavior is essential for developing sustainable tourism strategies in India (Awawdeh et al., 2021). As per Asante Boadi et al. (2020), the leading roles that corporate social responsibility, corporate governance, and business ethics occupy in fortifying the sustainable and ethical framework within India's tourism industry. To demonstrate how ethical imperatives are at the forefront of the development of the tourism sector, it is necessary to show how the pillars of sustainable business operations and ethical imperatives are created.

The structure of this section is meant to give an in-depth understanding of each concept, beginning with their pertinence and interrelation in the contemporary business environment, with a particular focus on tourism management. The significance of these practices within the Indian context, scrutinizing their essential function in advocating for sustainable organizational efficacy and ethical business practices amidst the distinctive challenges and prospects of India's tourism industry, is transitioned into the discussion. Jaipur and Indore are two Indian cities that have empirical case studies in the narrative. Readers will be given a good idea of these practices and their vital role in navigating the tourism industry toward a future marked by ethical responsibility in the section (Bawai & Kusumadewi, 2021).

Literature Review

Bibi et al. (2022) state that corporate social responsibility has evolved due to global trends and innovative practices. The evolution clearly indicates the increasing recognition of businesses' contributions to sustainable development, morality, and open governance, which go beyond mere profit generation. Global practices and theoretical frameworks are incorporated into the core strategies of enterprises through a critical examination of enterprises (Shaikh et al., 2022).

Spending on ethical and sustainable business practices has increased over the past decade and is expected to reach $20 billion in 2019. The rise of environmental, social, and governance criteria as a benchmark for investment decisions shows a growing investor preference for companies with strong ethics. For the first time in 2020, the assets under management of sustainable investment funds exceeded $1 trillion (Bialkova & TePaske, 2021).

According to Bikefe et al. (2020), the existence of contemporary Stakeholder Theory, Triple Bottom Line (TBL), and ethical governance practices is due to theoretical models. Businesses should account for the interests of all stakeholders. This approach has made it possible for employees, consumers, communities, and the environment to see a company's responsibilities. The concept encourages businesses to evaluate their performance not only on financial returns but also on social and environmental impact and the essence of sustainable business operations.

The Shared Value concept, elaborated by Porter and Kramer in 2011, says societal needs, not just economic needs, define markets. Businesses that use their resources, innovation, and expertise to tackle societal issues do more than engage in philanthropic activities; they also strategically position themselves for sustainable growth and competitiveness. Integrating social factors into business models has driven corporate innovation (Barrio & Enrique, 2021).

As Carroll (2021) stated, through drives, for example, a maintainable inventory network, the board, moral, and CSR contemplations are placed into action plans. The organization's economic living arrangement intends to decouple its development from its natural impression. Such drives show the development of CSR as an essential resource instead of an expense. Corporate administration rehearses are advancing to upgrade straightforwardness, responsibility, and board variety. In 2015, the level of ladies on the sheets of enormous cap organizations was 15%; however, in 2020, it was 20%.

Indian Perspective and Practices

India significantly represents the reception and change of CSR, corporate administration, and business morals among the perplexing snare of worldwide strategic policies. The Indian business scene is described by its rich social legacy, various cultural standards, and a quickly developing monetary climate, which, on the whole, shape the execution of worldwide business objectives. The segment dives into the fuse practices and difficulties of CSR, corporate administration, and business morals inside the Indian setting, featuring the unique ways that Indian enterprises take on these complex scenes. The commanding of CSR exercises brings up issues about the inspiration of organizations and how lengthy the drives will endure. However, it may only sometimes bring about significant cultural effects because of the chance of check box consistency.

Many Indian corporations have embraced the spirit of CSR to create shared value. It has long been celebrated that ethical practices and governance can coexist with profitable business operations. The Securities and Exchange Board of India (SEBI) tightened its regulations after high-profile governance failures in India. The companies have focused on enhancing transparency, accountability, and board independence. Family loyalty is blended with professional management in the governance of family-owned conglomerates in India. While nepotism and conflicts of interest may be desirable, so can nepotism and nepotism, or worse (Contini et al., 2020).

As per Dathe et al. (2022), India's business ethics are intertwined with sociocultural norms and economic disparities in a highly complex socio-economic Indian society. Aggressive competition and the pressure to meet short-term financial targets can cause ethical issues. Businesses have to follow strict ethical practices to foster a culture of integrity and ethical conduct, progressive Indian companies use global best practices in ethics and compliance.

There is a blend of legislative compulsion and voluntary commitment in the Indian perspective on CSR, corporate governance, and business ethics. Indian corporations slowly incorporate social responsibility, ethical governance, and business ethics into their core operations despite facing numerous challenges. India is a notable player on the global stage of responsible business conduct because of the integration that facilitates compliance with legal mandates (Edinger-Schons et al., 2019). Fallah Shayan et al. (2022) state that the fusion of CSR, corporate governance, and business ethics in tourism management creates a favorable environment for scholarly investigation. More literature is needed regarding the confluence of the themes in the tourism sector. The tourism industry is a vital part of economic development in developing economies, therefore the principles in tourism management with further research.

Firstly, studies need to look at the impact of CSR initiatives on local communities. Concrete data and case studies are required to show the outcomes of CSR initiatives (Sultan, Shaikh, et al., 2024; Sultan, Tunio, et al., 2024). The preservation of cultural heritage and environmentally sustainable tourism practices are included.

Secondly, despite the literature, the challenges that tourism enterprises face in managing tourism enterprises in culturally significant areas still need to be reflected in the literature. The governance structures and practices that balance profit motives with the need to preserve natural and cultural heritage need more investigation (Han et al., 2020). There needs to be more clarity regarding integrating the voices and interests of local communities and other stakeholders directly affected by tourism-based governance mechanisms in tourism.

Thirdly, cultural commodification, exploitation of natural resources, and the impact of tourism on indigenous populations should be explored more in the tourism industry. There is a need for further research that focuses on the ethical aspects of tourism development and presents models and frameworks for ethical decision-making in the tourism sector (Sultan, Shaikh, et al., 2024; Sultan, Tunio, et al., 2024). Technology and ethics in tourism management present an emerging area of interest that needs to be better represented in the literature. There are ethical considerations with the advancement of digital technologies in tourism marketing, operations, and customer engagement (Ibarnia et al., 2020).

As per Jain et al. (2021), policy and regulatory frameworks have a role in tourism. There needs to be more clarity regarding the development of ethical and sustainable tourism through national and international policies. The literature on tourism management gives a foundation but leaves several critical areas that need to be explored. Extensive research is the key to improving academic discourses and providing practical insights and frameworks for businesses, policymakers, and stakeholders in the tourism sector (Nanu et al., 2024). To ensure sustainable and ethical tourism development, it is essential to address the many challenges and opportunities that the tourism industry currently faces and also address the critical gaps in the industry's support for addressing global challenges and opportunities.

Case Studies

Rajasthan's Ethical Gem: Learning Jaipur's Corporate Governance and CSR Magnificence

Jaipur and Its Importance in Tourism

In Rajasthan, 59,039,000 tourists visit Chittaurgarh annually, making it the most famous tourist spot. However, Jaipur is a central hub in the state's tourism network. In Fig. 5.1, Statista's line shows how many people visit many places, but Jaipur's is among the most important. It is even more true when one considers how its cultural and CSR work helps places like the Marble Pavilion at Ana Sagar Lake in Ajmer, which gets 45,692,000 people annually.

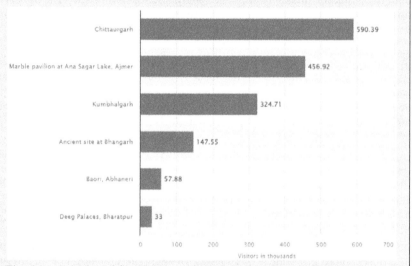

Fig. 5.1. Popular Vising Place and Number of Visitors in Jodhpur and Jaipur in FY2022. *Source*: Statista (2024a, 2024b).

These old buildings in Jaipur, like Amer Fort, City Palace, and Hawa Mahal, tell stories of royal grandeur that draw tourists and show how much the city cares about keeping its past alive. UNESCO has marked the architecture and historical sites in Jaipur. Cities that are well-planned and use eco-friendly tourism methods make cities more appealing to tourists (Khattak et al., 2019). There are now better facilities and services for tourists thanks to the city's CSR efforts in tourism. It could bring in the same number of guests as Kumbhalgarh (32,471,000). Also, these projects show that all of Rajasthan's guest hubs care about people and the economy (Kim et al., 2020). They help Jaipur's tourism business. With this kind of planned CSR integration, Jaipur will continue to amaze tourists with its pink clay skyline. It will also signify a future where tourism grows while communities grow and cultures are kept alive.

Corporate Governance and CSR Activities in Jaipur

Piramal School of Leadership

As per Kim and Park (2020), the Piramal School of Leadership is a paradigm of how corporate social responsibility can impact sectors beyond the immediate focus of tourism management. Spread over 32 acres, this educational edifice is envisioned to become a beacon of learning, offering specialized programs across five schools with the capacity to train over 150,000 middle managers from state and government agencies annually as well as professionals from CSR initiatives and non-profit (TheCSRjournal.in. 2024). India's 30 million public officials are the curriculum's focus, and it addresses crucial development sectors.

Sustainable development and capacity building are the main focus areas for collaborating with the Piramal School of Leadership and Tourism Management in Jaipur. The initiative indirectly contributes to the sustainable development of the tourism sector by giving public officials and professionals involved in CSR and non-profit activities advanced managerial and leadership skills. If officials and CSR professionals are educated, the visitor experience can be improved through better service delivery and infrastructure development (Lee et al., 2021).

As per Lee et al. (2020), the pressing need for responsible tourism management that safeguards Jaipur's cultural and natural heritage while fostering economic growth fits the school's focus on development sectors. Jaipur's tourism industry is thriving thanks to the Piramal School of Leadership, which helps maintain the tourism industry's cultural integrity and the environment without jeopardizing the integrity of the environment.

Lupin Foundation's Mobile Medical Van

The mobile medical van (MMV) project, created by the Lupin Foundation in Jaipur in July 2023, is a prime illustration of a CSR initiative that integrates health considerations with tourism management by contributing to improving the community's well-being. Providing essential diagnostic services and medical support to the underserved areas of Jaipur, this mobile healthcare unit uses a fully equipped MMV mobile unit. The initiative impacts the well-being of local communities by facilitating access to healthcare through screenings, diagnostics, treatment, and disease management capabilities (Lu et al., 2019).

Magno and Cassia (2021) state that the MMV initiative and tourism management in Jaipur are connected by the sustainable tourism framework, which emphasizes the importance of health and well-being in creating resilient communities. Tourists prefer visually and culturally appealing destinations and show a commitment to the health and welfare of their inhabitants. Maintaining a welcoming environment for visitors is one way healthy communities contribute to a robust tourism sector. The tourism sector has a role to play in the promotion of inclusive growth.

Jaipur's reputation as a responsible and sustainable tourist spot is strengthened by the MMV initiative, which focuses on the holistic needs of the community. For tourists, the assurance of being in a region that cares about healthcare accessibility adds to their travel experience (Monfort et al., 2019).

Asian Paints' Project 'Sparsh' for Visually Impaired Children

As per Moehl and Friedman (2021), project 'Sparsh' is an initiative by Asian Paints and Start India that improves Jaipur's community's cultural and social aspects by linking it to tourism management. This project was launched to bring the magic of art to visually impaired children and transform the educational experience at the school. Students can see art through touch with innovative murals that allow them to interact with their cultural heritage. The initiative touches lives personally and integrates the visually impaired more deeply into the societal narrative.

There is more than one contribution to tourism management in Jaipur. Adding a layer of social responsibility is one of the benefits. People interested in socially responsible travel want to travel to inclusive places. Jaipur is appealing to a global audience that values ethical and inclusive tourism experiences because it profoundly respects all its inhabitants (Randle et al., 2019).

According to Rusydiana and Riani (2022), the city is committed to arts and education for all, and such initiatives can become points of interest themselves. Tourists are interested in discovering more about the local people's work to overcome challenges and promote an inclusive society. Jaipur is positioning itself as a leader in integrating social causes with tourism development because of projects like 'Sparsh'.

McDonald's India's 'McDonald's for Youth' Initiative

McDonald's India is committed to empowering the youth of Jaipur by implementing CSR and strategic workforce development through the 'McDonald's for Youth' program. Over 600 workers in Rajasthan have received training and meaningful jobs through partnerships with skill development organizations. The initiative's primary focus is the service industry's crucial service-oriented skills of responsibility, efficiency, teamwork, and responsiveness (Supanti & Butcher, 2019).

According to Tunio et al. (2021), there is a strong link between this CSR activity and tourism management in Jaipur. Local youth, through training and employment, are not only the driving force behind economic growth but also the reason why the tourism and hospitality industries rely on a workforce well-versed in cultural hospitality and service excellence. Jaipur is committed to sustainable tourism practices through community empowerment.

Rajasthan Rural Tourism Scheme

The Rajasthan Rural Tourism Scheme is a big project that will make Jaipur a better place for guests. According to Invest.rajasthan.gov.in (2024), the plan encourages the growth of country tourist areas, not in city zones. These are places like homestays, guest rooms, and camping grounds. It makes Jaipur more attractive as a place to learn about culture and have fun. This project helps tourists stay healthy and gives locals more power, which aligns with CSR ideas.

There are many effects on tourists in Jaipur. Rural areas around Jaipur are becoming popular vacation places because of the scheme's perks, like not having to pay stamp tax or SGST. It gives tourists more to see and explore than just the city's famous forts and buildings. It also helps rural areas grow economically and lets tourists see how people live there (Wong et al., 2022).

CSR benefits everyone, from visitors by supporting new and local artists and businesses. The strategy promotes community growth and culture by prioritizing local artists and business owners (Velte, 2022). Focusing on swift choices and minimal bureaucratic impediments demonstrates a desire to make Jaipur a business-friendly city that complements its rich history and culture, improving its tourism appeal and guaranteeing tourists a more diverse and pleasurable experience.

Analysis and Impact

A paradigm shift toward sustainable organizational performance can be seen in the initiatives undertaken by organizations in Jaipur. The repercussions of these undertakings on the corporate entities involved and the community, with a particular focus on tourism management, are investigated in this examination (Wardhani et al., 2019).

Sustainable Organizational Performance

As stated by Wong and Kim (2020), the integration of CSR into the operational frameworks of organizations has created a relationship between business success and social welfare. Asian paints demonstrated how businesses could leverage their core competencies for societal benefit by being associated with innovative social projects. McDonald's India's focus on empowering young people aligns with its strategic goal of cultivating a talented workforce, leading to improved service quality and a happier customer experience within its Jaipur operations.

The Rajasthan Rural Tourism Scheme improves long-term organizational performance by expanding tourism portfolios. It does this by encouraging businesses to invest in rural experiences that add to cultural offerings, boost local engagement, and boost economic growth. It strengthens their market position and helps the tourism industry in Rajasthan stay strong (Yaseen et al., 2019).

Contributions to the Community

According to Zhong et al. (2022), the societal impact of these initiatives is significant in a culturally rich yet economically diverse setting like Jaipur. Through the Piramal School of Leadership, middle managers and professionals from different sectors will be trained to enhance public service delivery, indirectly benefiting the tourism industry by improving infrastructure and services. The Lupin Foundation's mobile medical van (MMV) addresses critical healthcare needs in underserved areas. It contributes to the community's overall well-being, a fundamental aspect of social sustainability that indirectly supports the tourism industry by fostering a healthy environment for both residents and visitors.

CSR initiatives that take a comprehensive approach promote a more inclusive and equitable development model. Key areas like health, education, and skill development can be addressed to create a more sustainable foundation for the growth of the tourism sector (Zeng, 2021).

Case Study 2: Indore's Ethical Odyssey: Managing Corporate Governance and CSR

Excellence in the Heart of India: Indore and Its Business Landscape

As per Asante Boadi et al. (2020), it is a testament to the dynamic interplay of tradition and modernity that Indore is a focal point for economic, industrial, and tourism activities. Indore's economic growth was based on its past as a trading post between Delhi and the Deccan, which was connected to the rest of India due to its strategic location. Its cultural heritage continues to attract tourists from all over the world as it is considered the state's financial capital.

Indore's economy is multifaceted, with the industrial sector prominently alongside a burgeoning tourism industry. The city's industrial prowess is anchored in areas like textiles, automobiles, and IT, with numerous industrial parks and SEZs, including the Pithampur Industrial Area – dubbed the 'Detroit of India' – attracting both domestic and international investors (theCSRjournal.in, 2023). Supanti and Butcher (2019) highlight the area's role as a hub for major automobile manufacturers.

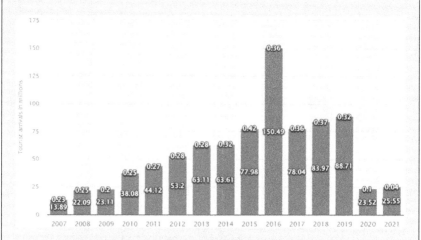

Fig. 5.2.   Tourist Numbers in Madhya Pradesh Over the Years*.
Source: Statista (2024a, 2024b).*Higher numbers (2021, 25.55) are domestic tourists, lower numbers are foreign tourists (2021, 0.04).

Fig. 5.2 showcases in 2021, Madhya Pradesh received 25 million domestic tourists and fewer than 42,000 foreign visitors, demonstrating its appeal as the heart of excellent India and rich cultural and natural resources. Its cultural richness, historical landmarks, and cuisine make Indore appealing. Starting in the city, you may explore Madhya Pradesh's highlights. The Rajwada Palace and Lal Bagh Palace showcase the state's regal history. The bustling Sarafa Bazaar and Chappan Dukan provide distinct eating experiences, enhancing Indore's reputation as a historical city (Lee et al., 2020). Indore's magnificent environment and high-tech city life have made it a model city. Cleaning and urban development prizes have been awarded.

Corporate Governance and CSR Activities in Indore

CSR of HDFC Bank

As stated by Magno and Cassia (2021), the HDFC Bank's CSR initiatives have contributed to the city's sustainable development. The holistic rural development program focuses on comprehensive community upliftment through interventions in natural resource management, education, skill development, financial literacy, and healthcare. The sustainable development model of Indore supports the tourism industry and enhances the quality of life of the rural inhabitants.

As per Wong et al. (2022), a critical aspect of attracting eco-conscious tourists is the bank's efforts in natural resource management, which aims to irrigate 2 lakh acres of land. Rural tourism is an emerging niche in the tourism industry that celebrates traditional lifestyles, agriculture, and nature. In order to prepare the local youth for employment in the burgeoning tourism and hospitality sectors of Indoor, the bank's education and skill development initiatives have been put in place. By promoting financial literacy and healthcare, the bank enhances the resilience and well-being of the community, making it a more attractive destination for tourists seeking authentic, culturally rich experiences in well-developed, sustainable settings.

To elevate Indore's profile as a safe and tourist-friendly city, HDFC Bank's investment in the community's health infrastructure ensures that residents and visitors have access to quality medical services. Though not directly aimed at tourism development, the bank's CSR activities significantly enhance the city's attractiveness as a tourist destination. The bank works with a healthy community to grow tourism. This growth shows Indore as a holistic development model where corporate responsibility and tourism management converge to create a sustainable, inclusive future (Lu et al., 2019).

River Ambulance – CSR of IRCTC in Indore

The Indian Railway Catering and Tourism Corporation (IRCTC) has introduced an innovative healthcare solution for Indore's remote and riverside communities.

The initiative bridges the community's critical healthcare access gap along the waterways by employing a boat with medical facilities and staff. Besides its primary healthcare mission, this mobile medical unit inadvertently contributes to the growth of the tourism industry in the area (Velte, 2022).

According to Wong et al. (2022), Indore's community-centered tourism includes safety and well-being measures for tourists experiencing its riverine settings and rural periphery. This approach builds traveler trust and promotes river-based and country tourism, which helps government and company sustainability initiatives. In 2019, the Madhya Pradesh Tourism Board (MPTB) launched the Bed and Breakfast Establishment (Registration and Regulation) Scheme and the Farm Stay Establishment Scheme, according to Tourism.mp.gov.in (2024). The schemes encouraged homeowners to adapt their houses into tourist hotels. These projects, especially for rural regions, provide affordable lodging and food, making Indore more desirable as an innovative and sustainable city. Local friendliness makes the tourism experience more fascinating and supports the city's long-term, beneficial tourism objective.

Smart Classes in Government Schools

As Wong and Kim (2020) stated, under their CSR initiatives, several corporate entities have funded transforming traditional classrooms into smart classes in government schools in Indore. Smart classrooms aim to create an engaging and interactive learning experience to enhance the education standard for students in disadvantaged sectors.

According to Han et al. (2020), tourism management is positively impacted by this initiative, which promotes socio-economic development in the community through tourism management. Educated and tech-savvy individuals should participate in and benefit from the growing tourism industry in Indore. The local economy is poised to benefit from the employment opportunities that arise from an expanding tourism industry or entrepreneurial ventures catering to tourists, who are the primary beneficiaries of these smart classrooms. Indore has a reputation for being a forward-thinking city due to the presence of innovative educational projects. As a model for integrating CSR into community and economic development, it attracts tourists interested in academic and cultural developments.

Gulf Oil Lubricants' Initiative

Gulf Oil Lubricants' initiative is "Gulf Superfleet Suraksha Bandhan," which is centered on improving the health of truck drivers. Truck drivers are crucial to the logistics and supply chains that facilitate the tourism industry in Indore. Gulf Oil Lubricants wants to ensure that tourists in the tourism industry have access to clean and safe drinking water by installing community water purifiers at strategic transport hubs (Monfort & Villagra, 2019).

As per Jain et al. (2021), the sustainable nature of the tourism sector can be seen in the relationship the initiative has with tourism management in Indore. Ensuring the smooth operation of supply chains for hotels and restaurants to ensure the timely and safe transport of tourists is essential to tourism. Gulf Oil

Lubricants supports the tourism industry by focusing on the health and well-being of the truck drivers. Healthier drivers mean fewer delays, more reliable transport, and a more robust supply chain, all of which contribute to a more robust and resilient tourism sector.

Other Notable CSR Projects

As per Kim (2019), a series of CSR projects have been implemented to enhance the destination's appeal. Swastika Investment promotes the financial independence of persons with disabilities (PwDs) through its "Taare Zameen Par" initiative. Swastika Investment encourages individual empowerment and promotes a more inclusive society by providing PwDs with the necessary skills.

According to Avotra et al. (2021), Medisave's initiative addresses a critical aspect of health and well-being to spread awareness of menstrual hygiene. Medisave improves the quality of life for women and girls by conducting healthcare and menstrual hygiene sessions and distributing sanitary napkins.

Hinduja Global Solutions has a program that transforms traditional learning spaces in government schools into technologically advanced classrooms. Indore's dedication to using technology for social advancement is showcased in this initiative, which improves the educational experience for students. The CSR projects show the relationship between corporate initiatives and the sustainable development of tourism in Indore. Each project contributes to creating a robust, inclusive, and sustainable environment that enhances Indore's attractiveness as a destination that values social progress and community well-being (Bialkova & TePaske, 2021).

Analysis and Impact

Avotra et al. (2021) state that various corporate entities use CSR initiatives to improve corporate governance, social responsibility, and ethical practices. Corporate social responsibility is exemplified by many initiatives, ranging from healthcare reform and education reform to environmental sustainability and inclusivity. All of these initiatives demonstrate a commitment to enhancing the quality of life for the community and the planet.

Sustainable Development

The city's CSR projects have directly contributed to the sustainable development goals. Future generations inherit a better society because of the sustainable development model. The effort of Gulf Oil Lubricants to give truck drivers clean drinking water directly impacts the environment (Wardhani et al., 2019).

Community Empowerment

CSR initiatives have enhanced access to essential services, improved educational outcomes, and fostered economic independence. The smart classes and school adoption program have allowed students from underprivileged backgrounds to access quality education and thus enhance their future employment prospects. Empowerment initiatives boost the local economy and make the community more inclusive (Kim et al., 2020).

Promotion of Ethical Standards

Indore's companies have incorporated CSR into their core business strategies, elevating the bar for ethical business practices. The projects enhance corporate governance and foster a culture of ethics that affects the wider business community outside of the corporate sector. Improving morality is essential in establishing trust between customers, employees, and the community (Awawdeh et al., 2021).

Impact on Community and Environment

The CSR initiatives have positively impacted Indore's community and the city's environment. Besides the immediate benefits, such as improved healthcare access and educational reforms, these projects have also played a role in constructing a solid and sustainable city. Visitors interested in sustainable urban development's cultural and social dynamics are attracted to Indore's appeal as a responsible tourism destination (Khattak et al., 2019). Companies can use sustainable practices through the development and management of tourism assets.

Application in Case Studies

There is a path to achieving sustainable development goals through public-private partnerships, innovative funding mechanisms, and a commitment to sustainable practices. These models show the synergy between preserving cultural and natural heritage.

Jaipur: A Case of Cultural and Heritage Tourism

Jaipur's Amer Fort and City Palace, among other heritage sites in the city, could be managed and protected more effectively with the help of the concession model. The Rajasthan government may grant operational rights to private organizations focused on heritage conservation and tourism management in a partnership based on this model. Advanced preservation techniques and innovative visitor services can be introduced through the private sector's investment capacity. According to the agreement, some of the revenue will be reinvested into the sites' upkeep. Local artisans, guides, and vendors can be included in the tourism value chain if community engagement clauses are included (Edinger-Schons et al., 2019).

Indore: Leveraging Eco-Tourism and Urban Renewal

In Indore, concession models could be significant in developing eco-tourism projects around its natural attractions and revitalizing urban spaces to boost tourism. A public-private partnership can be used to develop the Patalpani waterfall area into an eco-tourism site. Eco-tourism standards would be strictly followed under the concession agreement (Wardhani et al., 2019).

The Rajwada Palace area could be transformed into a cultural and tourism hub with concession agreements. Enhancing the cultural experience for tourists and preserving the historical integrity of the urban landscape are the aims of these projects, funded and managed by private partners. Innovative financing mechanisms like green bonds or impact investments attracted by the project's sustainability goals could be utilized by such initiatives to enhance tourist services and infrastructure (Ibarnia et al., 2020).

Partnerships and Funding Mechanisms

Jaipur and Indore have developed concession models that establish strong partnerships between the government, the private sector, and local communities. Tourism projects can only be developed with the pooling of resources, expertise, and networks. The social responsibility aims of the private sector are compatible with the social responsibility aims of the local communities (Bialkova & TePaske, 2021).

Sustainable Development Goals

The UN goals are directly contributed by concession models in Jaipur and Indore. These models and tourism development that are sustainable, inclusive, and preserve cultural and natural heritage are crucial to achieving these goals.

Conclusion

Sustainable organizational performance is of utmost importance to the Indian tourism sector and has a significant role to play. Various vital conclusions have been drawn from the literature review, case studies in Jaipur and Indore, and the literature review itself.

The literature review shows a shift toward incorporating CSR principles into business strategies to contribute to long-term profitability and societal well-being. Business frameworks, such as the shared value concept, are emerging that demonstrate how businesses can create economic value while addressing societal issues.

The case studies show how to apply principles in India. Private sector entities are working with local communities to address social issues while promoting sustainable tourism in Jaipur. Corporate entities play a significant role in socio-economic development in Indore through initiatives.

Using literature and case studies, the significance of CSR is highlighted in India's tourism sector in promoting sustainable tourism practices. Businesses can contribute to the growth of tourism destinations by embracing these principles. Exploring potential areas for future research to advance sustainable tourism in India is essential. Tourism is experiencing new trends in digitalization, climate change adaptation, and stakeholder engagement in the tourism industry. Taking into account the region's socio-cultural and environmental factors is required to evaluate the effectiveness of various CSR models and governance frameworks.

The significance of responsible tourism practices in achieving the sustainable development goals (SDGs) is being emphasized as the tourism industry evolves and the business climate changes. Future research could use tourism as a catalyst for inclusive growth, environmental protection, and cultural preservation. Government agencies, private enterprises, civil society organizations, and local communities must work together to make sustainable tourism development a reality. Multi-stakeholder platforms, capacity-building programs, and knowledge-sharing networks foster greater synergy and collective action toward achieving sustainable tourism outcomes.

Future Directions

There are several areas for future research and practice that are driven by emerging trends in India and globally. Digital technologies can be utilized by tourism businesses in India to enhance customer experience, sustain operations, and manage tourism destinations. Emerging technologies could affect tourism governance, marketing strategies, and the environment in the future. Climate change threatens the tourism sector with extreme weather events, sea-level rise, and biodiversity loss. Future research is expected to focus on adaptation strategies and resilience-building measures for tourism destinations in India. It includes looking at nature-based solutions, green infrastructure development, and community-based adaptation approaches. And in the case of the *Community Empowerment and Inclusive Tourism Development* which needs to focus on empowering local communities and marginalized groups to ensure equitable distribution of benefits. Future research could look at best practices and innovative models for community engagement, capacity-building, and entrepreneurship development in tourism destinations across India. Inclusion in inclusive growth is examined through community-based tourism enterprises, homestay programs, and cultural heritage preservation initiatives.

Ensuring environmental, social, and moral standards can be achieved by implementing sound policy and governance frameworks through effective policy and governance frameworks. The sustainability of tourism in India through policy instruments, regulatory mechanisms, and institutional arrangements may be investigated in the future. It includes looking at the role of public-private partnerships, destination management organizations, and multi-stakeholder platforms in facilitating governance approaches for sustainable tourism.

References

Asante Boadi, E., He, Z., Bosompem, J., Opata, C. N., & Boadi, E. K. (2020). *Employees' perception of corporate social responsibility (CSR) and its effects on internal outcomes. The Service Industries Journal, 40*(9–10), 611–632. Retrieved March 7, 2024, from https://www.tandfonline.com/doi/abs/10.1080/02642069.2019.1606906

Avotra, A. A. R. N., Chenyun, Y., Yongmin, W., Lijuan, Z., & Nawaz, A. (2021). Conceptualizing the state of the art of corporate social responsibility (CSR) in green construction and its nexus to sustainable development. *Frontiers in Environmental Science, 9*, 541. Retrieved March 27, 2024, from https://www.frontiersin.org/articles/10.3389/fenvs.2021.774822/full

Awawdeh, A. E., Ananzeh, M., El-khateeb, A. I., & Aljumah, A. (2021). Role of green financing and corporate social responsibility (CSR) in technological innovation and corporate environmental performance: a COVID-19 perspective. *China Finance Review International, 12*(2), 297–316.Retrieved March 27, 2024, from https://www. acem.sjtu.edu.cn/ueditor/jsp/upload/file/20230705/1688558879188089569.pdf

Barrio, E., & Enrique, A. M. (2021). *The strategic value of corporate social responsibility CSR: The present and future of its management.* Retrieved March 27, 2024, from https://revista.profesionaldelainformacion.com/index.php/EPI/article/download/83259/62978

Bawai, R., & Kusumadewi, H. (2021). Effect of corporate governance, firm characteristic, disclosure of corporate social responsibility (CSR) on firm value. *Jurnal Economia, 17*(1), 20–33.Retrieved March 27, 2024, from https://pdfs.semanticscholar.org/e14b/88a9ed367ae25e804595098f7f54f0b0cd8b.pdf

Bialkova, S., & TePaske, S. (2021). Campaign participation, spreading electronic word of mouth, purchase: How to optimise corporate social responsibility, CSR, effectiveness via social media?. *European Journal of Management and Business Economics, 30*(1), 108–126. Retrieved March 27, 2024, from https://www.emerald.com/insight/content/doi/10.1108/EJMBE-08-2020-0244/full/html

Bibi, S., Khan, A., Hayat, H., Panniello, U., Alam, M., & Farid, T. (2022). Do hotel employees really care for corporate social responsibility (CSR): A happiness approach to employee innovativeness. *Current Issues in Tourism, 25*(4), 541–558. Retrieved March 27, 2024, from https://www.tandfonline.com/doi/abs/10.1080/13683500.2021.1889482

Bikefe, G., Umaru, Z., Araga, S., Faize, M., Ekanem, E., & Daniel, A. (2020). Corporate social responsibility (CSR) by small and medium Enterprise (SMEs). A systematic review. Retrieved March 27, 2024, from http://repository.futminna.edu.ng:8080/jspui/bitstream/123456789/8406/1/2020%20Bikefe%20et%20al.pdf

Carlini, J., & Grace, D. (2021). The corporate social responsibility (CSR) internal branding model: Aligning employees' CSR awareness, knowledge, and experience to deliver positive employee performance outcomes. *Journal of Marketing Management, 37*(7–8), 732–760.

Carroll, A. B. (2021). Corporate social responsibility: Perspectives on the CSR construct's development and future. *Business & Society, 60*(6), 1258–1278. Retrieved March 27, 2024, from https://www.researchgate.net/profile/Archie-Carroll/publication/352029873_Corporate_Social_Responsibility_Perspectives_on_the_CSR_Construct%27s_Development_and_Future/links/632f533686b22d3db4dbe95b/Corporate-Social-Responsibility-Perspectives-on-the-CSR-Constructs-Development-and-Future.pdf

Contini, M., Annunziata, E., Rizzi, F., & Frey, M. (2020). Exploring the influence of Corporate Social Responsibility (CSR) domains on consumers' loyalty: An experiment in BRICS countries. *Journal of Cleaner Production, 247*, 119158. Retrieved March 27, 2024, from https://www.sciencedirect.com/science/article/pii/S0959652619340284

Dathe, T., Dathe, R., Dathe, I., & Helmold, M. (2022). *Corporate social responsibility (CSR), sustainability and environmental social governance (ESG): Approaches to ethical management.* Springer Nature. Retrieved March 27, 2024, from https://books.google.com/books?hl=en&lr=&id=QdlhEAAAQBAJ&oi=fnd&pg=PR5&dq=Dathe,+T.,+Dathe,+R.,+Dathe,+I.,+%26+Helmold,+M.+(2022).+Corporate+social+responsibility+(CSR),+sustainability+and+environmental+social+governance+(ESG):+Approaches+to+ethical+management.+Springer+Nature.&ots=_0uwrtHNiy&sig=uvlsZdgk1eevqtEgMhoUdQFHN1U

Edinger-Schons, L. M., Lengler-Graiff, L., Scheidler, S., & Wieseke, J. (2019). Frontline employees as corporate social responsibility (CSR) ambassadors: A quasi-field experiment. *Journal of Business Ethics, 157*, 359–373. Retrieved March 27, 2024, from https://link.springer.com/article/10.1007/s10551-018-3790-9

FallahShayan, N., Mohabbati-Kalejahi, N., Alavi, S., & Zahed, M. A. (2022). Sustainable development goals (SDGs) as a framework for corporate social responsibility (CSR). *Sustainability, 14*(3), 1222. Retrieved March 27, 2024, from https://www.mdpi.com/2071-1050/14/3/1222

Han, H., Lee, S., Kim, J. J., & Ryu, H. B. (2020). Coronavirus disease (COVID-19), traveler behaviors, and international tourism businesses: Impact of the corporate social responsibility (CSR), knowledge, psychological distress, attitude, and ascribed responsibility. *Sustainability, 12*(20), 8639. Retrieved March 27, 2024, from https://www.mdpi.com/2071-1050/12/20/8639

Ibarnia, E., Garay, L., & Guevara, A. (2020). Corporate social responsibility (CSR) in the travel supply chain: A literature review. *Sustainability, 12*(23), 10125. Retrieved March, 27, 2024, from https://www.mdpi.com/2071-1050/12/23/10125

Indu, B., & Singh, K. (2021). Does your post-COVID-19 travel dream talk about sustainability? Insights from potential tourists in India. In *Tourism destination management in a post-pandemic context: Global issues and destination management solutions* (pp. 273–288). Emerald Publishing Limited. Retrieved March 28, 2024, from https://www.emerald.com/insight/content/doi/10.1108/978-1-80071-511-020211019/full/html/

Invest.rajasthan.gov.in (2024). *Rajasthan Rural Tourism Scheme 2022.*

Jain, A., Kansal, M., & Joshi, M. (2021). New development: Corporate philanthropy to mandatory corporate social responsibility (CSR)—A new law for India. *Public Money & Management, 41*(3), 276–278. Retrieved March, 27, 2024 from https://www.tandfonline.com/doi/abs/10.1080/09540962.2020.1714280

Khattak, S. I., Jiang, Q., Li, H., & Zhang, X. (2019). Corporate social responsibility (CSR) and leadership: Validation of a multi-factor framework in the United Kingdom (UK). *Journal of Business Economics and Management, 20*(4), 754–776. Retrieved March 27, 2024, from https://jau.vgtu.lt/index.php/JBEM/article/download/9852/8880

Kim, H., Rhou, Y., Topcuoglu, E., & Kim, Y. G. (2020). Why hotel employees care about corporate social responsibility (CSR): Using need satisfaction theory. *International Journal of Hospitality Management, 87*, 102505. Retrieved March 27, 2024, from https://www.sciencedirect.com/science/article/pii/S0278431920300578

Kim, J., & Park, T. (2020). How corporate social responsibility (CSR) saves a company: The role of gratitude in buffering vindictive consumer behavior from product failures. *Journal of Business Research, 117*, 461–472. Retrieved March 27, 2024, from https://www.sciencedirect.com/science/article/am/pii/S0148296320303969

Kim, S. (2019). The process model of corporate social responsibility (CSR) communication: CSR communication and its relationship with consumers' CSR knowledge, trust, and corporate reputation perception. *Journal of Business Ethics, 154*(4), 1143–1159. Retrieved March 27, 2024, from https://link.springer.com/article/10.1007/s10551-017-3433-6

Lee, S., Han, H., Radic, A., & Tariq, B. (2020). Corporate social responsibility (CSR) as a customer satisfaction and retention strategy in the chain restaurant sector. *Journal of Hospitality and Tourism Management, 45*, 348–358. Retrieved March 27, 2024, from https://www.academia.edu/download/83975107/Corporate_social_responsibility_CSR_as_a_customer_satisfaction_and_retention_strategy_in_the_chain_restaurant_sector.pdf

Lee, Y. (2021). Bridging employee advocacy in anonymous social media and internal corporate social responsibility (CSR). *Management Decision, 59*(10), 2473–2495. Retrieved March 27, 2024, from https://www.researchgate.net/profile/Yeunjae-Lee/publication/348937048_Bridging_employee_advocacy_in_anonymous_social_media_and_

internal_corporate_social_responsibility_CSR/links/6018180e45851517ef2f2c4d/
Bridging-employee-advocacy-in-anonymous-social-media-and-internal-corporate-
social-responsibility-CSR.pdf
Lu, J., Ren, L., Lin, W., He, Y., & Streimikis, J. (2019). *Policies to promote corporate social responsibility (CSR) and assessment of CSR impacts.* Retrieved March 27, 2024, from https://otik.uk.zcu.cz/bitstream/11025/33691/1/EM_1_2019_06.pdf
Magno, F., & Cassia, F. (2021). Effects of agritourism businesses' strategies to cope with the COVID-19 crisis: The key role of corporate social responsibility (CSR) behaviours. *Journal of Cleaner Production, 325,* 129292. Retrieved March 27, 2024, from https://www.ncbi.nlm.nih.gov/pmc/articles/PMC9759414/
Moehl, S., & Friedman, B. A. (2021). Consumer perceived authenticity of organizational corporate social responsibility (CSR) statements: A test of attribution theory. *Social Responsibility Journal, 18*(4), 875–893. Retrieved March 27, 2024, from https://www.emerald.com/insight/content/doi/10.1108/SRJ-07-2020-0296/full/html?utm_campaign=Emerald_Strategy_PPV_November22_RoN
Monfort, A., López-Vázquez, B., & Villagra, N. (2019). Exploring stakeholders' dialogue and corporate social responsibility (CSR) on Twitter. *El profesional de la información, 28*(5). Retrieved March 27, 2024, from https://revista.profesionaldelainformacion.com/index.php/EPI/article/download/68763/45382
Nanu, L., Rahman, I., Ali, F., & Martin, D. S. (2024). Enhancing the hospitality experience: A systematic review of 22 years of physical environment research. *International Journal of Hospitality Management, 119,* 103692.
Randle, M., Kemperman, A., & Dolnicar, S. (2019). Making cause-related corporate social responsibility (CSR) count in holiday accommodation choice. *Tourism Management, 75,* 66–77. Retrieved March 27, 2024, from https://ro.uow.edu.au/cgi/viewcontent.cgi?article=2609&context=buspapers
Rusydiana, A. S., & Riani, R. (2022). Does zakat disclosures as corporate social responsibility (CSR) have an impact on Islamic banking performance?. *International Journal of Zakat, 7*(1), 75–90. Retrieved March 27, 2024, from https://ijazbaznas.com/index.php/journal/article/download/376/123
Shaikh, E., Brahmi, M., Thang, P. C., Watto, W. A., Trang, T. T. N., & Loan, N. T. (2022). Should I stay or Should I go? Explaining the turnover intentions with corporate social responsibility (CSR), organizational identification and organizational commitment. *Sustainability, 14*(10), 6030. IF: 3.889
Sieminski, M., Wedrowska, E., & Krukowski, K. (2020). Cultural aspect of social responsibility implementation in SMEs. *European Research Studies Journal, XXIII*(3), 68–84.
Statista.com. (2024a) *India number of domestic visitors to Jaipur and Jodhpur circle monuments* Retrieved April 3, 2024, from https://www.statista.com/statistics/1024566/india-number-of-domestic-visitors-to-jaipur-and-jodhpur-circle-monuments/
Statista.com. (2024b) *India tourist arrivals in Madhya Pradesh by type.* Retrieved April 3, 2024, from https://www.statista.com/statistics/1027303/india-tourist-arrivals-in-madhya-pradesh-by-type/
Sultan, M. F., Shaikh, S. K., & Tunio, M. N. (2024). CSR activities as a neutralizer: Halo effect of CSR for Asian companies. In *Strategies and approaches of corporate social responsibility toward multinational enterprises* (pp. 176–183). IGI Global.
Sultan, M. F., Tunio, M. N., Shaikh, S. K., & Shaikh, E. (2024). Strategic impact of corporate social responsibility: A perspective from the hospitality industry. In *Strategies and approaches of corporate social responsibility toward multinational enterprises* (pp. 23–33). IGI Global.
Supanti, D., & Butcher, K. (2019). *Is corporate social responsibility (CSR) participation the pathway to foster meaningful work and helping behavior for millennials? International Journal of Hospitality Management, 77,* 8–18. Retrieved March 27,

2024, from https://translateyar.ir/wp-content/uploads/2021/12/Is-corporate-social-responsibility-CSR-participation-the-pathway-to-foster-meaningful-work-and-helping-behavior-for-millennials.pdf

Thecsrjournal.in. (2023). *Top CSR projects in Indore.* Retrieved March 28, 2024, from https://thecsrjournal.in/top-csr-projects-indore-corporate-social-responsibility/

Thecsrjournal.in. (2024). *Top CSR projects in Jaipur.* Retrieved March 28, 2024, from https://thecsrjournal.in/top-csr-jaipur-rajasthan-corporate-social-responsibility/

Tourism.mp.gov.in. (2024). *The real India home stay, Madhya Pradesh.* Retrieved April 3, 2024, from https://tourism.mp.gov.in/contents?page=homestay&number=jtgYPf+tmICK2N8tHLothw

Tunio, M. N., Yusrini, L., & Shoukat, G. (2021). Corporate social responsibility (CSR) in Hotels in Austria, Pakistan, and Indonesia: Small and medium Enterprise spillover of COVID-19. In *Handbook of research on entrepreneurship, innovation, sustainability, and ICTs in the post-COVID-19 era* (pp. 263–280). IGI Global. Retrieved from March 27, 2024, https://www.igi-global.com/chapter/corporate-social-responsibility-csr-in-hotels-in-austria-pakistan-and-indonesia/273961

Velte, P. (2022). Meta-analyses on corporate social responsibility (CSR): A literature review. *Management Review Quarterly, 72*(3), 627–675. Retrieved March 27, 2024, from https://link.springer.com/article/10.1007/s11301-021-00211-2

Wardhani, J. V., Widianingsih, L. P., & Karundeng, F. (2019). The effect of company size, profitability, leverage, and management ownership towards the level of corporate social responsibility (CSR) disclosure. *Journal of Accounting, Entrepreneurship and Financial Technology* (Jaef), *1*(1), 39–60. Retrieved March 27, 2024, from https://dspace.uc.ac.id/bitstream/handle/123456789/7229/Plagiarism7229.pdf?sequence=5&isAllowed=y

Wong, A. K. F., & Kim, S. S. (2020). Development and validation of standard hotel corporate social responsibility (CSR) scale from the employee perspective. *International Journal of Hospitality Management, 87*, 102507. Retrieved March 27, 2024, from https://e-tarjome.com/storage/btn_uploaded/2020-11-07/1604731864_11547-etarjome%20English.pdf

Wong, A. K. F., Kim, S., & Hwang, Y. (2022). Effects of perceived corporate social responsibility (CSR) performance on hotel employees' behavior. *International Journal of Hospitality & Tourism Administration, 23*(6), 1145–1173. Retrieved March 27, 2024, from https://www.tandfonline.com/doi/abs/10.1080/15256480.2021.1935390

Yaseen, H., Iskandrani, M., Ajina, A., & Hamad, A. (2019). Investigating the relationship between board diversity & corporate social responsibility (CSR) performance: Evidence from France. *Academy of Accounting and Financial Studies Journal, 23*(4), 1–11. Retrieved March 27, 2024, from https://www.researchgate.net/profile/Majd-Iskandrani/publication/335826872_INVESTIGATING_THE_RELATIONSHIP_BETWEEN_BOARD_DIVERSITY_CORPORATE_SOCIAL_RESPONSIBILITY_CSR_PERFORMANCE_EVIDENCE_FROM_FRANCE/links/5d7dfbf692851c87c389d739/INVESTIGATING-THE-RELATIONSHIP-BETWEEN-BOARD-DIVERSITY-CORPORATE-SOCIAL-RESPONSIBILITY-CSR-PERFORMANCE-EVIDENCE-FROM-FRANCE.pdf

Zeng, T. (2021). Corporate social responsibility (CSR) in Canadian family firms. *Social Responsibility Journal, 17*(5), 703–718. Retrieved March 27, 2024, from https://www.emerald.com/insight/content/doi/10.1108/SRJ-12-2019-0410/full/html

Zhong, M., Lu, F., Zhu, Y., & Chen, J. (2022). What corporate social responsibility (CSR) disclosures do Chinese forestry firms make on social media? evidence from wechat. *Forests, 13*(11), 1842. Retrieved March 27, 2024, from https://www.mdpi.com/1999-4907/13/11/1842

Chapter 6

Brand Building Through CSR Initiatives During Hajj and Umrah: A Study of Tourism Industry

Md Safiullah[a], Anchal[a] and Neha Parveen[b]

[a]*Chanakya National Law University, Patna, India*
[b]*Freelance Researcher, India*

Abstract

Purpose: The primary purpose of this study is to understand how tourism companies are engaged in Corporate Social Responsibility (CSR) initiatives during "Hajj and Umrah" to build the Company's Brand image among Muslim pilgrims.

Design methodology and approach: The present study is exploratory and qualitative and follows a case-based approach. Data were collected mainly from secondary sources like newspapers, articles, news reports, agencies" reports, etc.

Findings: Companies increasingly strive to run their businesses ethically, responsibly, and with a conscience during *Hajj and Umrah*. Companies use their vast network and years of experience processing visas, providing transportation, lodging, and guiding during the journey, aiding people experiencing poverty, providing travel services, medical care, food distribution, and contributing to environmental projects. Building engagement with CSR initiatives wins long-term brand loyalty with internal and external audiences, making the company an agent of positive change. CSR activities during *Hajj and Umrah* also provide companies with global outreach opportunities. India companies engaged in CSR activities gained tax benefits under Section 37 of the Income Tax Act.

Corporate Social Responsibility, Corporate Governance and Business Ethics in Tourism Management: A Business Strategy for Sustainable Organizational Performance, 85–92
Copyright © 2025 by Md Safiullah, Anchal and Neha Parveen
Published under exclusive licence by Emerald Publishing Limited
doi:10.1108/978-1-83608-704-520241006

Original: Present study is interdisciplinary (Law & Management) in nature. The study on CSR has been conducted in many areas, but CSR activities during Hajjj and Umrah, a business strategy of brand building, have yet to be studied. The present study will help academicians in theory building and companies to understand the importance of CSR activities during Hajj and Umrah in strategic decision-making.

Keywords: CSR; brand building; Hajjj and Umrah; CSR strategic decision-making; Islam

Introduction

Over time, corporate social responsibility (CSR) programmers have grown and changed. It began as a humanitarian project and is now a model for running businesses worldwide. CSR is now considered as a business strategy for sustainable organizational performance (Aagaard, 2022). According to CSR, companies must return profits to society and the environment. In the late 19th century, ideas like CSR began to take shape. Companies realized the importance of CSR for communities and sustainable business growth. India was the first place CSR took off because of the country's long history of businesses helping their communities. However, the Companies Act 2013 makes CSR compulsory for companies whose turnover is more than 1000 crore. Under Section 135 of the Act, companies must set up a CSR group, give a certain amount to charity, and work to solve problems like poverty, poor health, and environmental damages (Ministry of Corporate Affairs – Companies Act, 2013).

Evolution of CSR in India

CSR in India has a long and rich tradition of closely involving business in social issues to promote national growth. CSR was first known as social obligation or charity in India. Over time, its definition has changed to encompass a broader range of activities, and it is currently most commonly recognized as CSR. The history of business is deeply ingrained with social and environmental challenges, dating back to its inception and path toward excess prosperity. Corporate philanthropy has a long history in India. In early times, the wealthy constructed temples and donated land for other religious practices. The early 1800s was identified as the industrial welfare period. Businesses considered socially conscious in 1900 included those that supported religious behavior, served the community, improved employee well-being, and made charitable contributions. In the 1950s, the fundamental tenet of CSR was the belief that businesses had a social responsibility. Since then, there has been a growing awareness of the need to contribute to social activities worldwide to enhance the local environment (Shinde, 2005).

Additionally, it has been discovered that businesses that genuinely consider socially conscious behavior are increasingly favored by the general public and are sought after for their products and services. Multinational corporations are currently posing a threat to Indian businesses by providing the same services right in their own neighborhood. An effective strategy for Indian corporations to contend with this competition is to expand their corporate social responsibility endeavors. As a result, India's need for CSR performances has significantly increased (Safiullah et al., 2024). The only way to navigate diverse cultures, languages, and environments is to be adept at and proactive in corporate social responsibilities.

Milestone in Evolution of CSR in India

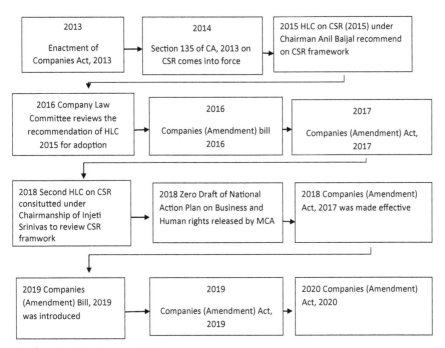

Source: Safiullah et al. (2024).

Literature Review

Nowadays, CSR is more than just something big companies do. It is also reaching out to individuals on a micro level, depending on their means (e.g., *Annadhanams* in nursing homes, homeless shelters, orphanages, houses of worship, and organizations that help those with disabilities and mental illness). People from many walks of life have been touched by this, lending their human and material resources to the cause of CSR in everyday speech. Socially responsible business practices with a charitable focus have deep roots in Indian tradition. *Christianity, Parsi, Jainism*, and *Muslims* are just a few of our nation's religions that have contributed to the growth of CSR in their unique ways. Even if the firm doesn't gain financially from philanthropic CSR, it employs charitable gifts to address external societal concerns and injustices. Lantos (2002) argues that private corporations can practice generous CSR if it comes from their earnings and not from tactics that violate ethical CSR, such as raising customer prices or underpaying staff. The goal of CSR is "business success, and it can accomplished by paying tribute to ethical values and respecting people, societies, and the environment" (Clark, 2006). Although there isn't a universally accepted definition of CSR, most definitions focus on the positive ways in which corporations can influence the community and be excellent corporations to meet public expectations (Redford, 2005). Compared to other countries, India's CSR tradition is among the richest. In recent years, significant efforts have been made to educate Indian business leaders on the importance of social responsibility in their company practices. But so far, India's CSR efforts have gone unnoticed. Philanthropic CSR in India entails establishing charity foundations, non-governmental organizations (NGOs), healthcare and educational institutions, and various trusts that aid community development and environmental preservation.

The present study is exploratory and qualitative and follows a case discussion approach to understand the degree to which companies engage in CSR activities during Hajj and Umrah and consider CSR as a business strategy in band building. The data were collected mainly from secondary sources like newspapers, articles, news reports, agencies reports, etc.

Companies CSR Activities and in Brand Building

A strong brand can support a customer's positive perception and improve their ability to recognize the products (Grewal & Krishnan, 1998). Products are more likely to attract consumers when they positively perceive the brand (Hassan & Sharma, 2011). According to Park et al. (1986), corporate communication efforts impact brand image, a perceptual phenomenon allowing consumers to associate branded items with their thoughts freely. Keller and Lehmann (2006) define brand equity as "the additional value that accrues to a firm because of the presence of the brand name that would not accrue to an equivalent unbranded product." No matter how closely related they are, reputation and brand are different. While the brand focuses on the customer, reputation is mainly on the company (Ettenson & Knowles, 2008). The company's reputation also helps to set the stage for a positive product appeal and increases the brand's value. Customers may recognize a product or service through symbol, name, and design. CSR also helps establish a brand and facilitates the launch of new items (Pride et al., 2006).

CSR Activities During Hajj and Umrah

Hajj and Umrah are sacred pilgrimages that Muslims from around the world visit Macca and Madinah multiple times to fulfill their religious journey. Various institutions are engaged in providing CSR activities during the Hajj and Umrah. Hajj attracts millions of pilgrims, creating a unique opportunity to make a significant difference. CSR activities can address the real needs of a large group of people in a concentrated timeframe. A recent study has shown that the UAE and Saudi Arabian governments emerged as leaders in the

MENA region regarding CSR implementation. India played a crucial role during the activity.

Recognizing different companies for doing Umrah and Hajj shows how important it is to help travelers with these sacred journeys, according to the Indian government. The success of the pilgrimage depends on the efforts of these groups, which range from well-known companies to newer ones (Serrano, 2021).

All India Hajj & Umrah Tours Private Limited is an India-based company. It has a paid-in capital of 100,000 rupees and an authorized capital of Rs.500,000. Travel agency operations, as well as supporting and auxiliary transportation, are encompassed. Accordingly, they look after the tourists who go for Hajj and Umrah (Aihut, 2024).

Akbar Travel Service: A well-known name on the list who has been helping *Muslims* with all aspects of their travel arrangements for Hajj and Umrah for many years. They have a vast network and years of experience in the field to meet the demands of pilgrims with various services, such as processing visas, providing transportation, lodging, and guiding during the journey (Akbar Travels, 2023).

Anam Tours & Travels is another well-known firm committed to offering pilgrims high-quality services. Their dependable companionship for individuals undertaking the spiritual pilgrimages of Hajj and Umrah is due in large part to their dedication to client happiness and meticulousness (Aman Group, 2023)

Gulf Associates is the other prestigious name on the roster, and they all have something unique to offer. Every pilgrim should have a relaxing and rewarding time on their pilgrimage, and these groups work hard to make that happen by coordinating flights, lodging, and group tours.

The individualized attention and unwavering dedication to providing first-rate service set Ahlam Hajj & Umrah Services apart. Each pilgrim is guaranteed an unforgettable and spiritually satisfying tour by their team of seasoned specialists who go out of their way to accommodate their unique needs and preferences.

Indo Gulf Aviation Pvt. Ltd. has received accolades for its commitment to providing exceptional service and happy customers. To ensure that pilgrims are comfortable and well-supported throughout their journey, these groups organize educational seminars and offer 24/7 help.

Iqbalhusen Abdulrahim Shaikh is well-known for offering pilgrimage packages that are both excellent quality and affordable alternatives. Pilgrims can more easily meet their religious commitments without going into debt.

Some companies that focus on helping *Gujarati* pilgrims are *Gujarat Hajj Tours Karnataka Hajj* Group. Pilgrims from the area can rest assured that their journey will be smooth and rewarding thanks to their familiarity with the region and the community's needs.

Al Aksha, Hazrat Khwaja Garib Nawaj, Haj T Molvi, and *Adenwalaare* well known for their dedication to maintaining Islamic traditions and values. For pilgrims looking for a life-changing experience, they are reliable allies thanks to their expert personnel and meticulous attention to detail.

Companies like *Hadi International Imaan International* have stellar reputations for professionalism and dependability. Pilgrims who want a pleasant and trouble-free journey have come to rely on them because of their honest pricing and prompt service (Aihut, 2024). Companies like *Hajj Corporation of India, Al Syed Tours International, and Surat Haj Tours* meet the unique requirements of pilgrims from Surat and other parts of India. Pilgrims looking for a customized and unforgettable pilgrimage experience often choose them because of their local knowledge and personalized service.

Reputable pilgrimage companies that prioritize ethics and responsibility include Rumani Enterprises. Sustainability and community involvement are vital priorities, distinguishing them as market leaders.

Some well-known firms that guarantee safe and pleasurable travel experiences include *Seair Hajj Services, Najath Khidmat Hul Hajja*. Every pilgrim can rest easy on their pilgrimage thanks to their knowledgeable team and rigorous safety standards. *Zam Haj Service, Akbar Travel & Tours, and Al Amal Hajj Umra* Service are well-known for their affordable and extensive offerings. Pilgrims from all over the globe can find something that suits their taste and budget, from affordable packages to five-star accommodations.

Companies like *Madani Haj Group and Rais Enterprises* are well-known for their dedication to providing excellent service and ensuring customer happiness. Every pilgrim is guaranteed a smooth and unforgettable journey by their skilled personnel and meticulous attention to detail.

Among the many reputable pilgrimage companies, *Sayed Ebrahim Badshah Hajj UMF, Good Hope Enterprises, and Barakath Hajj Group* stand out for their commitment to moral and environmentally conscious practices. Sustainability and community involvement are two of their key priorities, which distinguish them as market leaders (Aihut, 2024)

The *Great India Tour Company, Salamath Haj Group, and Air Travel Enterprises India Ltd.* Every pilgrim can rest easy on their pilgrimage thanks to their knowledgeable team and rigorous safety standards. Among the businesses renowned for their commitment to offering safe and comfortable travel experiences are *Al Junaid Hajj Umra Committee and Safar International*.

As reliable allies for pilgrims seeking a life-changing encounter, they stand out due to their emphasis on delivering individualized service. Because of its long history and commitment to its clients' happiness, *Al Madina Haj* Service is one of the top companies in the field. Every pilgrim is guaranteed a smooth and unforgettable journey with their extensive choice of services and meticulous attention to detail. Finally, the Indian government's acknowledgment of these groups highlights their dedication to ensuring pilgrims' well-being and spiritual growth. The sacred pilgrimages of Umrah and Hajj are made possible by these organizations, who are highly regarded for their professionalism, knowledge, and commitment to the complete happiness of their clients.

Discussion and Conclusion

Companies are increasingly compelled to engage in CSR to support communities, the environment, and ethical standards. Today, brand names rely on factors beyond quality, price, and distinctiveness. Companies' image also depends on their interactions with the community, employees, and the organization. CSR is a practice that firms can use to contribute to their long-term growth. The present study attempts to understand the company's corporate social responsibility activities during Hajj & Umrah and its strategy for building a brand image among the Muslim population.

The Muslim pilgrimage during Hajj and Umrah is one of the most significant occasions in the Islamic calendar, where believers thank Allah for their many bounties. Companies attempt to make a big difference by implementing impactful CSR and communications initiatives to ensure everyone has a peaceful Hajj, Umrah, and joyous Eid season. Giving charity is among the most significant tenets of Islam. Companies participating in CSR initiatives create positive impacts on society, build long-term brand loyalty among customers, and position companies in the customer goods list. On the other hand, customers share positive experiences and create a sense of attachment to the company and good feelings. Often, the government uses social media to announce subsidies for Hajj and capitalize on it in their election campaign (Safiullah Pathak, & Singh, 2016a; Safiullah, Pathak, Singh, & Anshul, 2016b, 2017). Political parties also highlight facilities & help provide to Hajj & Umrah pilgrims during their election campaign to make party images better in the eyes of voters (Parveen & Safiullah, 2021; Safiullah, 2019; Safiullah & Parveen 2022; Safiullah et al., 2022). CSR programs communicate and encourage introspection, humanity, gratitude, and kinship. While the pilgrimages concentrate on the individual's spiritual development, adding CSR activities enables pilgrims to expand their good deeds and fulfill the objectives of Umrah and Hajj. Aiding people experiencing poverty, providing travel services, medical care, food distribution, environmental projects, and other services to many companies might take advantage of the big crowds to have a beneficial social impact. Including CSR in the Hajj and Umrah enables pilgrims to perform their spiritual duties and promotes a socially conscious mindset that spreads well beyond the sacred site.

The company engaged with CSR initiatives wins long-term brand loyalty with internal and external audiences, making the company an agent of positive change. CSR activities during Umrah and Hajj also provide companies with global outreach opportunities. India companies engaged in CSR activities gained tax benefits under Section 37 of the Income Tax Act.

References

Aagaard, A. (2022). *Sustainable business: Integrating CSR in business and functions*. River Publishers.

Aihut. (2024). *Atlas Umrah India's National Umrah brand daily Umrah group tours from all over India*. All India Hajj & Umrah Tours Private Limited.

Akbar Travels. (2023, May 18). *Hajj & Umrah pilgrim packages*. https://alakbartravels.com/?page_id=1330

Aman Group (2023, December 4). *India is a key priority market for Haj*. The Anam Group. https://travelbizmonitor.com/india-is-a-key-priority-market-for-the-anam-group-2/

Clark, S. (2006). Corporate social responsibility: A marketing tool for major hotel brands. *HSMAI Marketing Review, 23*(1), 42–45.

Ettenson, R., & Knowles, J. (2008). *Marketing metrics: Managing performance with marketing analytics.* Harvard Business Press.

Grewal, R., & Krishnan, R. (1998). Understanding the role of customer satisfaction in loyalty: An empirical study. *Journal of Marketing, 62*(4), 1–14.

Hassan, S. S., & Sharma, A. (2011). Understanding consumer behavior in emerging markets. *Journal of International Marketing, 19*(3), 45–60.

Keller, K. L., & Lehmann, D. R. (2006). *Brands and branding: Research findings and future priorities.* Marketing Science Institute.

Lantos, G. P. (2002). The ethicality of altruistic corporate social responsibility. *Journal of Consumer Marketing, 19*(5), 205.

Ministry of Corporate Affairs – Companies Act. (2013). https://www.mca.gov.in/mca/html/mcav2_en/home/actsandrules/companies+act++2013/companiesact2013.html#:~:text=The%20Companies%20Act,Gazette%20on%2030th%20August%2C%202013

Park, C. W., Jaworska, B., & Macionin, B. (1986). The effects of advertising on consumer perception. *Journal of Consumer Research, 13*(4), 532–541.

Parveen, N., & Safiullah, M. (2021). Twitter and radio indicators of election outcome – A study of Indian election. *International Journal of Economics and Business Research, 22*(2/3), 278.

Pride, W. M., Ferrell, O. C., Lukas, B. A., Schembri, S., & Niininen, O. (2006). *Marketing: Concepts and strategies.* Cengage Learning.

Redford, K. (2005). Business whizzes get a soul. *Caterer & Hotelkeeper, 195*(4392), 36–39.

Safiullah, A., Parveen, N., & Iqbal, I. (2024). Challenges and opportunities within the evolving CSR landscape in India. In K. Singh, J. Yadav, & R. Abraham (Eds.), *Technology-driven evolution of the corporate social responsibility ecosystem* (pp. 46–60). IGI Global.

Safiullah, M. (2019). Primetime news coverage and electoral harvest – A study of 2014 Indian general election. *International Journal of Business Forecasting and Marketing Intelligence, 5*(4), 424–432.

Safiullah, M., & Parveen, N. (2022). Big data, artificial intelligence and machine learning: A paradigm shift in election campaigns. In S. K. Panda, R. K. Mohapatra, S. Panda, & S. Balamurugan (Eds.), *The new advanced society: Artificial intelligence and industrial internet of things paradigm* (pp. 247–262). Wiley-Scrivener.

Safiullah, M., Pathak, P., & Singh, S. (2016). Emergence of social media and its implications for public policy: A study of Delhi Assembly Election 2013. *Management Insight, 12*(1).

Safiullah, M., Pathak, P., & Singh, S. (2022). The impacts of social media and news media on political marketing: An empirical study of 2014 Indian General Election. *International Journal of Business Excellence, 22*(4), 536–550.

Safiullah, M., Pathak, P., Singh, S., & Anshul, A. (2016). Social media in managing political advertising: A study of India. *Polish Journal of Management Studies, 13*(2), 121–130.

Safiullah, M., Pathak, P., Singh, S., & Anshul, A. (2017). Social media as an upcoming tool for political marketing effectiveness. *Asia Pacific Management Review, 22*(1), 10–15.

Serrano. (2021). *Why corporate social responsibility and giving during Hajj matters, W7Worldwide's Abdulrahman Inayat.* Campaign Middle East. https://campaignme.com/why-corporate-social-responsibility-and-giving-during-hajj-matters-byw7worldwides-abdulrahmaninayat/#:~:text=This%20is%20where%20businesses%20can%20play%20an%20important,for%20the%20spiritual%20reward%20it%20provides%20the%20giver

Shinde, A. (2005). *Consumer behavior in the digital age.* ABC Publishers.

Chapter 7

Conceptualizing of Place Attachment with CSR and Company's Growth: A Conceptual Model for Small-scale Tourism Companies

Muhammad Faisal Sultan[a], Muhammad Nawaz Tunio[b] and Erum Shaikh[c]

[a]KASBIT, Karachi, Pakistan
[b]University of Sufism and Modern Sciences, Bhitshah, Pakistan
[c]Shaheed Benazir Bhutto University, Sindh, Pakistan

Abstract

Purpose: The purpose has multiple purposes. Hence, this study has been conducted not only to shed light on the factors associated with place attachment but also to make people understand the two-way association between firm performance and CSR activities of small-scale tourism companies.

Significance and Scope: This chapter is specifically written in association with the tourism industry to make readers understand the implication of place attachment with CSR activities. This chapter also has a role in theoretical optimization as it highlights possible two-way associations between firm performance and CSR.

Research Gap: The lack of studies associated with this point is the major cause of concern. Therefore, this study has been conducted specifically to understand the importance of place attachment for CSR activities of small-scale tourism companies. Moreover, almost all of the studies conducted in this vein highlighted only the reasons for place attachment and their association with the CSR of the small-scale tourism industry. None of the studies are inclined toward model extension and enhancement.

Corporate Social Responsibility, Corporate Governance and Business Ethics in Tourism Management: A Business Strategy for Sustainable Organizational Performance, 93–101
Copyright © 2025 by Muhammad Faisal Sultan, Muhammad Nawaz Tunio and Erum Shaikh
Published under exclusive licence by Emerald Publishing Limited
doi:10.1108/978-1-83608-704-520241007

Data Collection: Data have been collected through published material to develop postulates and models authentically.

Findings: After the compilation of data, it has been presumed that place attachment is one of the important elements in CSR activities of small-scale tourism businesses. However, the model can be reassessed in two-way association as a decline in the company's performance may also cause a decline in CSR activities and also in place attachment.

Keywords: Tourism; tourism business; CSR; small-scale tourism; businesses & place attachments

Background

Corporate Social Responsibility means that firms are required to consider other purposes than profitability. Hence, firms are required to play their part in the sustainability of society by improving the environment, fair trade practices, and benefiting local communities (Wen et al., 2021). Hence, there is no objection to the importance of corporate social responsibility and its role in the growth of the organization. However, the term became associated with tourism and tourism management very late. Research evident the importance of corporate social responsibility came into the limelight within the passage of 25 years. In 1999, World Tourism Organization recognized the importance of CSR for tourism businesses. Hence, research work on the topic has also increased to understand more about the free movement of capital, people, and ideas, and people have a vivid understanding of thoughts and ideas to behave responsibly (Contreiras et al., 2016). On the other side, CSR is also termed as an important tool and strategy that may have a significant impact on the company's competitiveness and performance. Hence the impact of the controller or head of the company is significantly important for the CSR activities of the firm (Xia et al., 2022).

Introduction

It is difficult to separate an entrepreneur from small-scale companies and their actions. The same is the case for small-scale tourism companies that reflect the traits of their companies. Hence, any action or activity carried out by the small-scale tourism company is based upon the entrepreneur's actions, understanding, and traits. Hence, CSR-related decisions of the firm also hinge mainly on the entrepreneurs managing small-scale tourism companies. Literature associated with CSR in the tourism sector uses the reference to Place Attachment Theory to indicate that the attachment of an individual to a place is a reflection of an individual's perception of responsibility toward the place. Early researchers who explored this concept indicated that the place where we reside is perceived as one of the most important elements of oneself and has the tendency to realize oneself.

However, the place does not provide the same level of attraction and attachment to everyone and this bond has been found mostly in the behavior of entrepreneurs (Hallak et al., 2013). Therefore, the literature highlights the attachment of an individual to the place as an emotional behavior. Moreover, attachment to the place is also based on one's assessment of the place, that is, whether that place is providing some realistic benefits and making entrepreneurs realize themselves and their desired lifestyles. Hence entrepreneurs may find to be involved in civic activities, protective behavior, and incline toward environmental responsibilities (Wen et al., 2021).

Problem Statement

It is unclear what is the importance of CSR to the entrepreneurs running SMEs. Similarly, it is also unclear which element has the most impact on the entrepreneur's assessment of ongoing experiences (Wen et al., 2022). Place attachment is the deep attachment of any person to the physical and social elements of a particular place. Therefore, environmental psychology scholars regularly emphasize the importance of place attachment (Hallak et al., 2013). The importance of place attachment became signified with the CSR activities started to cause a decline in the profit of the function and make entrepreneurs focus more on environmental sustainability. Hence, it is legitimate to declare that the company's purpose to attain maximum profit seems to be shifted toward sustainability and environmental protection of the location (Wen et al., 2022). Hence, further studies must be conducted to understand the place attachment in small tourism business owners (Hallak et al., 2013).

Theoretical Underpinning

Echelon Theory postulated a significant association between managerial background and the activities and strategies of the company (Xia et al., 2022). Therefore, it looks legitimate to use the theory along with the Place identity theory by Proshansky et al. (1983) which terms place association as the complex cognitive structure that also acts as a sub-structure of one's self-identity. Hence, the uses of these theories are legitimate for the research work associated with CSR activities carried out by owners of small-scale tourism companies.

Literature Review

The study by Ayuningtyas et al. (2021) indicated that the framework for place attachment is based on three indicators person, place and processes. The formulated framework for the study is shown in Fig. 7.1.

Person: *The belief* of an individual that he/she belongs to a particular place or community and also perceives that place will provide required resources will become inclined toward the place. The inclination resulted in making one ready to help and provide the community with resources at the time of need (Hallak et al., 2013).

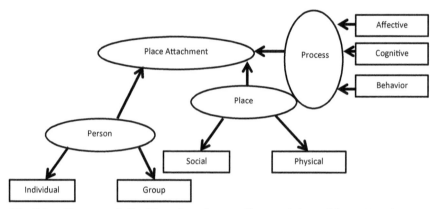

Fig. 7.1.   Framework for Place Attachment. *Source*: Adapted from Ayuningtyas et al. (2021).

Group Association: Hallak et al. (2013) indicated that entrepreneurs from small-scale tourism companies are more inclined toward social interaction. Thus found to be more engaged in community and societal development. Wen et al. (2021) emphasized the personal association and attachment of entrepreneurs with the stakeholders to gain the understanding and experience required for business growth and betterment. Supported by Wen et al. (2022) entrepreneurs of small-scale tourism companies put high importance on conducting business with supportive people and social community.

Individual Association: Place is termed as an important element for influencing individuals either as a part of the group or in an individual capacity. Strong association with place resulted in place-protective behavior and inclination toward civic activities (Ayuningtyas et al., 2021).

Social Association: Hallak et al. (2013) indicated that entrepreneurs handling small-scale businesses are commonly found to be associated with business communities to foster better relationships. Recent studies also indicated that association with the place is based on social relationships as people tend to evaluate the place and its environment either positively or negatively. Moreover, place attachment is also based upon community attachments. Studies reflected that community attachment is based upon attachment to the house, neighbors, and city. Moreover, studies also believe that working in the home environment is positively correlated with production function (Ayuningtyas et al., 2021).

Physical Association: Hallak et al. indicated that small-scale businesses also gain through their CSR activities and functions. Similar points posited by Wen et al. (2022) indicated that physical aspects of the place indicated about availability of resources at the specific place and importance of these resources to carrying out business operations. Hence authors termed the physical aspect of the place as "Place Dependence," on the other side, there is also substantial support for the social aspect of the place that authors termed as "Place identity." Place identity is the degree of emotional attachment of the entrepreneur to the place as place causes group belonging and self-identity. Considering the points of Wen et al. (2021), it is legitimate to believe that CSR activities are the outcome of the strong emotional attachment of entrepreneurs to the place (Wen et al., 2021).

Processes

The entrepreneurial process refers not only to the identification of entrepreneurial opportunity but also includes opportunity evaluation and opportunity exploitation.

These processes are a blend of cognitive and affective components and produce significant over the behavior of entrepreneurs holding small-scale tourism companies (Delgado García et al., 2015). Multiple studies indicated that three types of bonds are potent in the studies related to place association, that is, affective, cognitive, and behavioral bonds (Ayuningtyas et al., 2021).

(a) *Affective Bonds*: These types of bonds might be termed emotional bonds and might have positive as well as negative impacts over the place attachment. Positive impact comes when the place is the one that is fulfilling some of the basic human needs. The negative impact comes with bad memories of the place or when the disruption caused by the place is very high and beyond the control of the person.
(b) *Cognitive Bonds*: Place is associated with social identity and self-image. Therefore, cognitive bonds are based on the mental representation of the place. These bonds also include mental maps and knowledge of how to organize a place.
(c) *Behavioral Bonds*: It is based on the manifestation of place that is the predictor for maintaining good association with the place.

Ayuningtyas et al. (2021) provided a detailed and comprehensive model for place attachment but by combining it with Hallak et al. (2013) we came to understand that an increase in community support by small-scale tourism companies will lead to an improvement of the company's performance. Community support can be rendered through sustainable tourism practices by small tourism companies (Wen et al., 2021, 2022) which may lead to an increase in the performance and goodwill of the firm (Hallak et al., 2013).

Evidences

Initial studies conducted on the community-based tourism enterprises of Kenya highlighted that the place attachment of the owner is a significant predictor of the owner's support to the owner's community that also produces an indirect significant impact on the firm's performance (Manyara & Jones, 2007). These findings are aligned with the self-interest model presented by Wallich and McGowan (1970), which indicated that place attachment also yields monetary benefits to the entrepreneurs. Similar was the indication of previous studies that tourism companies that maintain good connections with the local communities tend to outperform their counterparts.

Studies such as by Liere and Dunlap (1980) and Zelezny et al. (2000) indicated that female entrepreneurs are more inclined toward the place as compared to their counterparts. However, Hernández et al. (2020) indicated that there is no clear evidence that female entrepreneurs have more place inclination or attachment as compared to their counterparts.

However, it is not appropriate to declare gender as the main predictor of place attraction and there are some other variables like language and population group that always have a connection with gender to produce impact over place attachment (Grieve & Van Staden, 1996).

Implications

The model discussed above provided no understanding or research that may indicate the impact of the decrease in performance specifically the financial performance of the small-scale tourism companies over the decrease in CSR concerns and decrease in place attachment. However, an increase in the level of inflation tends to decrease the purchase ability of customers (Anggraini, 2015) and the cost of business may also increase when a company invests in CSR activities (Saeed, 2021). Hence by considering Ayuningtyas et al. (2021), Hallak et al. (2013), and Wen et al. (2021, 2022), a conceptual framework has been developed to provide a detailed illustration of the two-sided progression of place attachment with the CSR activities and firm's performance (Fig. 7.2).

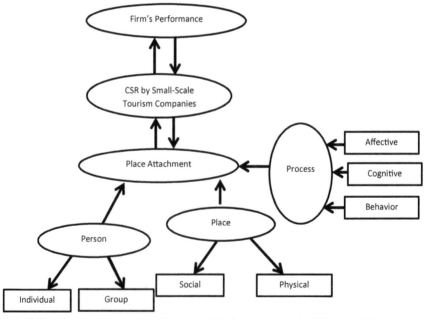

Fig. 7.2.   The Interaction of Company Performance and CSR Activities.
Source: Own illustration through combining Ayuningtyas et al. (2021), Hallak et al. (2013), and Wen et al. (2021, 2022).

Contribution

Fig. 7.2 provides a detailed overview of the conceptual framework associated with the CSR activities of small-scale companies in the tourism industry. However, the study adds one additional postulate that has been added to Fig. 7.2 which is two-way arrows which means previous studies explored and indicated that an increase in place attachment of entrepreneurs heading small-scale tourism companies may lead to an increase in CSR activities that ultimately result in improved company's performance.

Philanthropic CSR activities can be harmful to companies that are operating in economies with lower GDPs, higher inflation, and low exports like Pakistan (Sehar, 2017). Moreover, it is also important to consider the impact of political competitiveness on the performance of the firm (Jaffery & Kalim, 2014). These are the points that may negatively influence the performance of the firm and hence the reverse relationship between firm performance and CSR activities is also possible. The postulate is valid as most of the studies associated with place attachment and CSR activities of small-scale tourism companies are based in the developed and Western world. However, the scenario of Pakistan and the developing world is indicating a different scenario. Therefore, it is required to be evaluated whether the decrease in the financial performance of small-scale tourism companies may result in the decrease of CSR activities and may also cause a decline in place attachment of entrepreneurs. Therefore, effective to believe the points and indications made by Anggraini (2015) and Saeed (2021) that companies operating in declining economies or under hyperinflation, etc., may not prefer to conduct CSR activities.

Research Methodology

The purpose of this research is two-fold. The initial purpose of this study is to understand the importance of place association in CSR activities of small-scale tourism businesses Therefore; the data are collected from published material to develop material and models effectively and efficiently. Hence the purpose of this study is descriptive as it defines all the elements that increase place associations. The researcher's interference is minimal as work has been done through analyzing literature published in research papers and the time horizon is cross-sectional as the study has been developed within a time frame of a few months. All these points coincide effectively with the parameters indicated by Sekaran and Bougie (2016). However, to develop a rigorous and thorough methodology, this chapter also utilizes the parameters highlighted by Saunders et al. (2007). Hence, the philosophy of this study is Epistemology, the research strategy is archival and the method of the study is mono-method.

Conclusion and Significance

This is one of the premier studies that indicated the two-sided effect of CSR activities on the performance of small-scale tourism companies. This study provides a fundamental postulate that is particularly important and seems to be valid for developing economies. Therefore, this study will not only be treated as a work that fosters further research but will also result in a theoretical contribution to the literature on the construct of place attachment. Moreover, this study may also have some practical implications as considering this study entrepreneurs and tourism companies may also formulate effective strategies for organizing CSR activities that may be different in under-developed, developing, and developed sides of the world.

References

Anggraini, D. (2015). Proven again: Corporate social responsibility as one of influential factors towards stock return. *European Journal of Business and Management, 7*(3), 151–160.

Ayuningtyas, G., Santosa, H. R., & Septanti, D. (2021). Place attachment of entrepreneurs: A proposed analytical framework. *IPTEK Journal of Proceedings Series*, (6), 261–267.

Contreiras, J. P., Machado, V., & Duarte, A. P. (2016). Corporate social responsibility in tourism: The case of Zoomarine Algarve. *Tourism & Management Studies, 12*(1), 127–135.

Delgado García, J. B., De Quevedo Puente, E., & Blanco Mazagatos, V. (2015). How affect relates to entrepreneurship: A systematic review of the literature and research agenda. *International Journal of Management Reviews, 17*(2), 191–211.

Grieve, K. W., & Van Staden, F. J. (1985). Environmental concern in South Africa: An attitudinal study. *South African Journal of Psychology, 15*(4), 135–136.

Hallak, R., Brown, G., & Lindsay, N. J. (2013). Examining tourism SME owners' place attachment, support for community and business performance: The role of the enlightened self-interest model. *Journal of Sustainable Tourism, 21*(5), 658–678.

Hernández, B., Hidalgo, M. C., & Ruiz, C. (2020). Theoretical and methodological aspects of research on place attachment. In *Place attachment* (2nd ed., 94–110). Routledge. e-ISBN 9780429274442

Jaffery, A., & Kalim, R. (2014). Political competition, rising prices and economic augmentation: Evidence from Pakistan. In *4th international conference on business management* (pp. 1408–1422). Sukkur Institute of Business Administration. ISBN: 978-969-9978-01-2

Liere, K. D. V., & Dunlap, R. E. (1980). The social bases of environmental concern: A review of hypotheses, explanations and empirical evidence. *Public Opinion Quarterly, 44*(2), 181–197.

Manyara, G., & Jones, E. (2007). Community-based tourism enterprises development in Kenya: An exploration of their potential as avenues of poverty reduction. *Journal of Sustainable Tourism, 15*(6), 628–644.

Proshansky, H. M. (1983). Place identity: Physical world socialisation of the self. *Journal Environmental Psychology, 3*, 299–313.

Saeed, K. (2021). *Impact of corporate social responsibility disclosure reports on sale performance: Evidence from Pakistani non financial firms* [Doctoral dissertation]. https://thesis.cust.edu.pk/UploadedFiles/KiranSaeed-MMS193026.Pdf

Saunders, M., Lewis, P., & Thornhill, A. (2007). *Research methods for business students* (4th ed.). Pearson Education Limited.

Sehar, Z. (2017). How economic recession effect the corporate philanthropy? Evidence from Pakistani corporate sector. *APSTRACT: Applied Studies in Agribusiness and Commerce, 11*, 89–96.

Sekaran, U., & Bougie, R. (2016). *Research methods for business: A skill building approach.* John Wiley & Sons.

Wallich, H. C., & McGowan, J. J. (1970). Stockholder interest and the corporation's role in social policy. In *A new rationale for corporate social policy* (pp. 39–59). Committee for Economic Development.

Wen, T., Zhang, Q., & Li, Y. (2021). Why small tourism enterprises behave responsibly: Using job embeddedness and place attachment to predict corporate social responsibility activities. *Current Issues in Tourism, 24*(10), 1435–1450.

Wen, T., Zhang, Q., Song, L., & Li, Y. (2022). Corporate social responsibility, social bonding and place attachment among entrepreneurs of small and medium-sized tourism enterprises. *International Journal of Tourism Research, 24*(2), 189–201.

Xia, J., Wu, Z., Dang, Z., & Zhang, R. (2022). Hometown attachment and corporate social responsibility: Evidence from overseas Chinese entrepreneurs. *Frontiers in Psychology, 13*, 943701.

Zelezny, L. C., Chua, P. P., & Aldrich, C. (2000). New ways of thinking about environmentalism: Elaborating on gender differences in environmentalism. *Journal of Social Issues, 56*(3), 443–457.

Chapter 8

Confluence of Corporate Social Responsibility, Sustainability and Financial Performance in Tourism and Hospitality

Sheikh Najam-mu-Sahar[a] *and Hafizullah Dar*[b]

[a]*Department of Management, Mittal School of Business, Lovely Professional University, Phagwara, Punjab, India*
[b]*Department of Tourism and Airlines, School of Hotel Management and Tourism, Lovely Professional University, Phagwara, Punjab, India*

Abstract

Purpose: Recent years have seen a tremendous surge in research into corporate social responsibility (CSR). One noticeable aspect is the increasing relevance of CSR in the tourist and hospitality industry, which reflects the industry's fast growth and emphasis on solving societal issues. The current study aimed to assess CSR in tourism and hospitality offering a thorough understanding of CSR in a wider context of sustainability, financial performance and ethical considerations.

Methodology: A qualitative desk research approach was undertaken to conduct this study. Thorough review of contemporary research literature, including content analysis, was done for data gathering.

Findings: Findings show that CSR is rising as a key trend in the worldwide tourism and hospitality business, with a significant impact on the industry's performance and development. Tourism and hospitality industry shows both positive and negative economic impacts on the environment and society. To offset negative impacts, this industry is progressively embracing CSR initiatives. An integration between CSR and sustainable tourism, highlights the stability of socioeconomic, environmental, and cultural growth while considering interests of all stakeholders. The effect of CSR on the financial

Corporate Social Responsibility, Corporate Governance and Business Ethics in Tourism
Management: A Business Strategy for Sustainable Organizational Performance, 103–118
Copyright © 2025 by Sheikh Najam-Mu-Sahar and Hafizullah Dar
Published under exclusive licence by Emerald Publishing Limited
doi:10.1108/978-1-83608-704-520241008

performance of the tourist and hospitality industry reveals that CSR has a favorable influence on financial performance of hotels, but mixed outcomes are shown in restaurants, cruises, and airlines. Highlighting insights on tourism corporations incorporating strategic and ethical CSR ideals into their activities, this study concludes with practical implications.

Originality: This study creates a unified integrated framework based on intersection of strategic CSR, financial performance, sustainability, and ethical aspects in tourism and hospitality.

Keywords: Corporate social responsibility; sustainability; financial performance; ethics; tourism and hospitality

1. Introduction

Recent years have seen a substantial surge in research on CSR. Cheng et al. (2014) and Tang (2011) have focused on why corporations should practice CSR. Increased public awareness of CSR has prompted firms to share information about their environmental and social initiatives with their customers (Hamrouni et al., 2019). By incorporating environmental and social concerns into firm operations (Bocquet et al., 2017), CSR has become an essential component of corporate strategy. CSR helps firms to achieve "triple bottom line," including financial, social, and environmental outcomes (Coles et al., 2013).

The advancement of CSR in the tourism and hospitality sector has become one of the most recent developments in the global tourism business. CSR is especially important for tourism businesses and organizations because of the sector's dynamic growth within the national economy, as well as its social orientation toward meeting people's needs (Kumar & Kumar, 2018). Tourism relies on local people, communities, and natural resources, concerns related to environment, human rights, and fair trade. This has upsurged the relevance of CSR practices in tourism (Hadj, 2020). CSR confluences with sustainable tourism, prioritizing balance between social, economic, environmental, and cultural development, taking into account, the concerns of all stakeholders (Blinova et al., 2018). Tourism and hospitality firms are engaging in strategic CSR to improve their bottom line and create value to society (Camilleri, 2017). These strategic CSR activities impact the financial performance of tourism and hospitality firms as well. Further, tourism and hospitality sector is incorporating ethical ideals into their activities, frequently under the pretense of CSR. This study aims to understand the CSR in hospitality and tourism in the context of sustainability, organizational performance and ethical aspects and enlists the responsible corporate activities of different stakeholders in hospitality and tourism.

This research work is qualitative in nature and aimed to ascertain the importance of CSR in tourism and hospitality. Hence, it employed the desk research approach and was done using different secondary research sources including research papers, articles, reports, thesis, book chapters and other published and unpublished sources. An extensive literature review of recent research from reputable sources like journals, magazines, and websites was done for data gathering. This literature review proceeded with content analysis in order to identify key concepts related to CSR in tourism and hospitality. The literature focused on the impact of CSR on financial performance in different sectors of the said industry. Further, the integration of CSR and sustainability was also studied. The study contributes to the literature by substantially widening the perspective of CSR in hospitality and tourism, thus opening new avenues of research. This study is structured as follows. It begins by introducing the concepts related to CSR. In addition, this study reviews the previous research of CSR in the field of hospitality and tourism. Then, it describes the CSR and financial performance in different elements of tourism. Finally, with the discussion about integration of ethical aspects and CSR, the conclusion, and further implications are provided.

2. Corporate Social Responsibility

CSR as per Coles et al. (2013), since many decades, has been a topic of discussion in the scientific community, serving as a focal point for debates on the link between business and society. According to Nyahunzvi (2013), conventionally CSR is defined as firm investment activities that provide environmental or social advantages outside the corporation, with activities mostly chosen by head office and shareholder interests. Currently, CSR refers to an organization's obligation to all stakeholders involved in business and society as a whole as highlighted by Kotler et al. (2010). Singh et al. (2021) viewed CSR as an amalgam of both institutionalization of company practices and competitive constraints. This shows that CSR is fundamentally a multi-theoretical and multi-stakeholder construct. According to Abaeian et al. (2019), CSR adheres to company objectives, personal ethical values, and cultural conventions while deciding on different environmental and social projects. Hence it necessitates a delicate balance between company aims, individual beliefs, and social expectations, requiring intelligent decision making and strategic alignment with varied stakeholder interests. Coles et al. (2013) described CSR as a firm's commitment to achieve the "triple bottom line," which includes financial, social, and environmental outcomes, encompassing a variety of activities like as employee well-being schemes, stakeholder engagement, charitable giving, community involvement, responsible supply chain management, environmental conservation, and ethical leadership.

Past literature has shown difference between internal and external CSR and the framework has been rightly explained by Font and Lynes (2018) (Fig. 8.1). Further, Servaes and Tamayo (2013) demonstrated that CSR and business value are positively associated for firms.

The internal corporate social policy as per Romanova et al. (2017) focuses on the company's employees and is restricted within its framework. External corporate social policy refers to the social policy implemented by the corporation or certain of its subsidiaries for the benefit of the local community. Hence, businesses utilize corporate responsibility strategies accordingly to establish programs

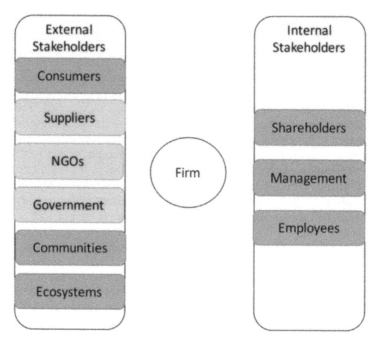

Fig. 8.1.   Overview of External and Internal Stakeholders Related to a Firm's CSR Practices. *Source*: Font and Lynes (2018).

that promote human resource development, community support, and natural resource protection as highlighted by Ivanova and Bikeeva (2016). Ultimately, effective business performance is crucial for a country's social and economic stability, welfare, and quality of life.

3. CSR in Tourism Industry

International hotel firms were the first to apply CSR in the tourist industry in the late 1990s. According to European Cities Marketing (2011), CSR actions in the tourism sector include the responsible use of cultural and resources, minimizing pollution and waste, conserving landscapes, cultural heritage and biodiversity, fair treatment of employees, suppliers, guests, using local products and services fairly, and local community participation. CSR has emerged as a key trend in the worldwide tourist business and has become a pertinent factor in the success and growth of the tourism industry as per Madanaguli et al. (2022). CSR in the tourist sector has garnered more attention during the last decade as described by Putra et al. (2019). Tourism companies are increasingly addressing destination development concerns through CSR activities, as indicated by numerous company CSR reports, websites and social media profiling, economic, social and environmental initiatives. Donations to schools and hospitals, water and energy conservation, environmental preservation, local produce procurement, and equal opportunity recruiting and training are some examples of these programs.

Recently, the notion of CSR as per Kang et al. (2016) has been widely adopted by enterprises in the hospitality and tourist industry; large publicly listed hotel corporations and casino firms produce CSR reports, outlining the aims, strategies, and CSR activities, Kumar and Kumar (2018) highlights that tourism firms and organizations prioritize the social responsibility system due to the sector's rapid growth and focus on serving people's needs and increasing their quality of life. Hadj (2020) stated that the importance of CSR practices in tourism has grown since the business relies on local communities, people and natural resources, and the environment, as well as concerns addressing the environment, human rights, and fair trade. According to Sharpley and Telfer (2023), CSR in tourism is a critical component of achieving sustainable development in general. Hence, CSR has become a pertinent factor in the success and growth of the tourism industry.

As per Blinova et al. (2018), CSR in tourism should embody a wide range of activities, including the following:

1. Fostering local attractions via financial assistance for cultural and historical assets, educational and sporting facilities, and charitable causes.
2. Promoting environmental conservation and sustainability via responsible use of natural resources, pollution prevention, and effective environmental management in tourism.

Madanaguli et al. (2022) examined that tourist industry's CSR activities address two dimensions: community and environment. This sector prioritizes environmental measures including carbon offsetting, anti-poaching, and ecological rehabilitation. As per Chilufya et al. (2019), tourism may both benefit the economy and pose a harm to the environment and society. Hence to prevent negative repercussions, the tourist sector is increasingly implementing CSR activities as stated by Han et al. (2020).

By implementing CSR initiatives, tourism companies can promote economic growth and improve the quality of life for employees, families, and the community. According to Muafi (2017), tourism organizations can be considered socially responsible if they consider both good and negative impacts of their activities on the environment, economy, and society. As per Nyahunzvi (2013), CSR programs are a vital method for the tourist industry, especially in the lodging sector, to contribute to community development. CSR is traditionally viewed as firm investment activities that offer environmental or social advantages outside the corporation, with activities often governed, in large part, by head office and shareholder interests.

Font and Lynes (2018) used a stakeholder lens to examine the evolution of CSR in tourism and hospitality. It goes on to clarify that the research focused on both internal stakeholders such as shareholders, staff, and management, as well as outward stakeholders such as customers. Other external stakeholders, such as communities and ecosystems, are now increasingly being discussed in the literature. Melubo and Carr (2021) investigated the relevance of CSR implementation in Tanzanian tourist firms. They found several motivations driving enterprises to embrace CSR including adhering to community standards and environmental concerns. For companies seeking long-term existence, outward stakeholders or tourists (consumers) are central to their CSR initiatives as per Curras-Pérez et al. (2018) and Jones et al. (2017). Chilufya et al. (2019) considered that in the tourism industry, consumers play an important role in shaping CSR practices, thus representing a critical aspect of the community's local development.

As noted by Lin et al. (2018), CSR literature in tourism has mainly focused on hotels and environmental features rather than intermediaries, regardless of the fact that these enterprises are significant stakeholders in the tourism sector. The majority of the research focuses on how tourism intermediaries have only just begun to adopt CSR policies in their firms, and those that are devoted to implementing them tend to focus on environmental measures, owing to their simplicity and visibility. In this regard, a study by Ibarnia et al. (2020) emphasizes the innovative nature of CSR as a critical factor in the survival of such intermediaries, not only in terms of potential internal control and process management measures, but also in a clear commitment to co-creating value throughout the supply chain.

4. CSR as a Tool for Sustainable Development in Tourism

Conceptual confluence between CSR and sustainability is that they mutually emphasize on creating a balance between economic affluence, environmental responsibility, social and ethical integrity as per Bansal and Song (2015). Blinova et al. (2018) state that CSR aligns with sustainable tourism development, which prioritizes balancing economic, environmental, social, and cultural development objectives while considering the interests of all stakeholders (tourists, sending and receiving destinations, and local population) which is achieved through rational use of tourism resources and collaborative efforts. Tourist engagement in CSR is typically considered in terms of tourist demand for ethical practices (de Grosbois, 2012) or satisfying tourist expectations to enjoy pristine ecosystems and local culture.

In a study by Ertuna et al. (2019), it was examined that, in developing country contexts, how sustainability and CSR discourses and procedures emerge in multinational companies (MNC) and local hotels through the lens of institutional logics that are derived from certain institutional orders, like market, corporation, state and community. The findings show that there are disparities in how sustainability and CSR are interpreted and resulting logics are established. While CSR logic serves the aim of PR and is matched well with the local hotel's marketing and branding function, sustainability looks to be more ingrained and layered inside the organizations flowing via multiple functions (beginning with the core business of service production).

Despite its potential to contribute to sustainable development, the usefulness of CSR in tourism is debatable. Longitudinal research by Hatipoglu et al. (2019) extended beyond providing the immediate results of a CSR programs in sustainable tourism and highlighted intermediate effects such as capital, well-being of community, and at large society's shared value. According to the findings of this study, in tourism, CSR programs have immense potential to significantly contribute to economic development by creating entrepreneurial ability for small tourism enterprises across a large geographical region. This strengthens rural communities, empowers women and other disadvantaged groups, and revitalizes rural and cultural places.

CSR activities as per Chubchuwong (2019) can be used as tools for influencing revisit intention of convention participants. and corporate meetings. CSR activities during a business trip is a new concept and destination management firms as well as national tourism organizations can use it for developing satisfying and sustainable tourism products.

5. Impact of CSR on Financial Performance in Tourism Sector

Financial performance is one of the most important outcomes for firm shareholders; without strong financial backing, businesses would not exist. So, to examine the financial effects of CSR, a lot of studies have researched about the association between CSR and financial performance (Benavides-Velasco et al., 2014; García & Armas, 2007; Singal, 2014). The majority of these research produces consistent findings regarding the direct and positive association between CSR and corporate financial success. Other academics, however, stated that CSR activities are not directly connected to corporate financial success; rather, CSR plays an important moderating role in firm's financial performance. Tamajón and Font (2013) investigated the correlation between CSR and financial performance in small and medium-sized tourist firms in Europe and Latin America. Results implied that companies that apply sustainability initiatives outshine their competitors in terms of financial performance.

According to Inoue and Lee (2011), all CSR aspects have a positive financial impact, with varying implications on short-term and long-term profitability across tourism-related companies. According to them, CSR activity causes a significant decrease in the airline industry's short-term profitability while there is an increase in the restaurant and hotel industry's long and short-term profitability. Some researches were done on the relationship between airline firms' CEP and CFP. Lee et al. (2013) and Inoue and Lee (2011) found out that CEP does not affect airlines' CFP. Goffi et al. (2022) suggested that tour operators with a high level of CSR participation had much greater short-term profit and sales growth. The results from this study also suggested that adopting CSR principles, promoting CSR ideals, and building local economic links have a good and significant impact on tour operators' performances.

5.1. CSR in Financial Performance of Hotel Sector

Study by Rhou et al. (2016) implies that stakeholders' CSR knowledge influences the manner in which CSR actions might result in financial improvements in corporate performance. Number of research works have investigated the effect of CSR activity on firm performance in tourism-related industries. Kang et al. (2010) found out that in the tourism industry, CSR activity has both positive and negative impact on company's financial performance. This suggests that, in the hotel industry, there is a positive correlation between CSR and financial performance of the firm. Further, CSR has an impact on both financial and non-financial performance in hotels. Such assessments have both practical and intellectual importance, contributing to CSR decision making, particularly in settings outside of Western industrialized nations. Ghaderi et al. (2019) investigated the relationship between CSR and performance, with a focus on four and five-star hotels in Tehran, Iran. Results showed that CSR directly and positively affects hotel performance. These results applied to social, economic, legal, ethical and environmental dimensions of CSR.

5.2. CSR in Financial Performance of Restaurant Business

Restaurants, have received a relatively small amount of attention from CSR researchers, although being a significant part of hospitality and tourism industry. Although, research works are being done in this area, while much is unknown, a large number of findings are also conflicting. Several studies (Kang et al., 2010; Kim & Kim, 2014; Lee et al., 2013c; Rhou et al., 2016) have shown conflicting results on the correlation between CSR and financial success. Kang et al. (2010) found a positive correlation between CSR and financial success. However, Kim and Kim (2014) and Rhou et al. (2016) found a positive correlation only under certain conditions, such as a recession and increased CSR efforts. Lee et al. (2013c) study found no significant correlation between operation-related and non-operational CSR and a firm's financial success during a non-recessionary time. Mixed results also appeared in this industry. While Lee and Heo (2009) found that restaurants' CEP (Corporate environmental performance) has a neutral impact on CFP (Corporate financial performance (CFP)). And according to Inoue and Lee (2011), there was a non-significant impact of CEP on CFP on restaurants.

5.3. CSR in Financial Performance of Aviation Sector

The airline sector is another essential component of the tourist system that has gained significant attention in CSR research (Inoue & Lee, 2011). Along with the remarkable rise of the global economy, the number of airline passengers is fast expanding, and airlines are emerging as one of the most significant transportation service industries (Low & Lee, 2014). Most significantly, CSR programs are the most effective approach for airlines to acquire a competitive edge and increase customer loyalty.

The literature on CSR in the airline sector continues to focus solely on financial success and customer happiness. Researchers (Kang et al., 2010; Lee et al., 2013b; Lee & Park, 2010) have studied the impact of CSR activities on financial profitability and long-term corporate value. These researches yielded slightly different conclusions. According to Kang et al. (2010), positive CSR activities have a negative impact on profitability, whereas bad CSR activities have a negative impact on company value, implying that CSR activities only generate additional money for investment. Lee and Park (2010) research partially corroborated this viewpoint; their findings demonstrated a positive and substantial association between CSR activities and value performance but no relationship between CSR activities and financial success.

5.4. CSR in Financial Performance of Cruises

Casino corporations are implementing CSR initiatives to address societal issues associated with their business model. The casino sector has implemented CSR activities to offset its growing gaming business. MGM, a global casino industry leader, has created the "MGM Cares" program to promote labor diversity, environmental sustainability, philanthropy, and community participation (MGM Report, 2017). Unlike in other sectors, CSR researchers have not extensively studied the impact of CSR activities and the link between CSR efforts and financial success in casinos. Few studies (Inoue & Lee, 2011; Lee & Park, 2009; Theodoulidis et al., 2017) investigated the impact of CSR and the relationship between CSR and financial performance in the casino industry, and none found a significant relationship between casino profitability and long-term value. Instead, Kang et al. (2010) discovered that in the casino business, there is a positive relationship between CSR and return on equity. As a result, there is a paucity of research outlining the fundamental reasons why CSR measures do not improve a company's financial success in the casino business.

6. Strategic Use of CSR in Tourism and Hospitality

CSR at the firm level, involves a strategic approach influencing the operations and decision making of firms to meet the demands of its stakeholders. Tourism firms tend to engage in strategic CSR when they have responsible conduct in their operations (Camilleri, 2019). Strategic CSR activities may usually improve their bottom line, while taking into account their legitimate stakeholders' interests (Garay & Font, 2012). Their motivation behind their engagement in strategic CSR practices is to increase their profits and to create value to society (Camilleri, 2017). The hospitality and tourism industry has indicated a growing attention to CSR issues similar to other industries. For example, Starbucks (2017) has committed to CSR activities, focusing on four goals (i.e., sustainable coffee, greener retail, creating opportunities, and strengthening communities). Such CSR strategies appear to be more important in the hotel and tourist industries due to unique industry-specific traits that distinguish them from other businesses. In the hospitality and tourism industry, effective CSR strategies enable firms to adapt to local business environments and gain a competitive advantage across multiple regions, both domestically and internationally. One of the significant factors to be comprehended when implementing CSR strategies across various locations is national culture. Hence, Song and Kang (2019) proposed a four-step culture-based framework as explained in Fig. 8.2, for implementing CSR strategies to provide a practical tool and a guideline for better implementations of CSR strategies:

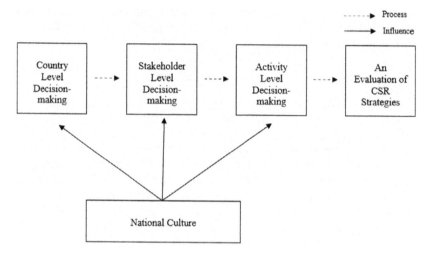

Fig. 8.2.   A Culture-based Model for Implementing CSR Strategies.
Source: Song and Kang (2019).

1. Identify important nations for CSR emphasis based on a variety of criteria, including market presence, societal effect, and regulatory climate.
2. Allocation of CSR resources to each stakeholder group and challenges in each country.
3. Decide whether to prioritize expanding good CSR activities or decreasing each stakeholder group's negative CSR activities.
4. Post-implementation, evaluate CSR efforts by analyzing their influence on corporate performance, taking into account both good and negative CSR actions.

National culture influences total CSR operations in a given country, hence multinational hospitality and tourist companies should investigate the link between national culture characteristics and CSR activities in order to optimize their worldwide CSR portfolios. Hospitality and tourist companies, which deal actively and extensively with communities, customers, workers, and even franchisees as key assets, should design CSR plans for each stakeholder group by considering a unique set of concerns in each.

As noted by Lin et al. (2018), CSR literature in tourism has mainly focused on hotels and environmental features rather than intermediaries, regardless of the fact that these enterprises are significant stakeholders in the tourism sector. The majority of the research focuses on how tourism intermediaries have only just began to adopt CSR policies and strategies in their firms, and those that are devoted to implementing them tend to focus on environmental measures, owing to their simplicity and visibility. In this regard, study by Ibarnia et al. (2020) emphasizes the innovative nature of CSR as a critical factor in the survival of such intermediaries, not only in terms of potential internal control and process management measures, but also in a clear commitment to co-creating value throughout the supply chain.

7. CSR and Ethical Aspects in Tourism and Hospitality

The ethical framework outlines the core philosophy and organizational aims in specific terms, as well as rules for the organization's legal and efficient governance. An ethical approach is becoming increasingly important for corporate success and a strong corporate image, and it applies to all elements of company activity and interaction among individuals and businesses as a whole. Though many hotels and firms in the tourism industry are encompassing ethical values into their activities, usually under the guise of CSR, but their CSR activities are limited to PR exercises, cost-saving (e.g., energy efficiency) or sideline activities that primarily benefit the company. Hence, In tourism, CSR typically correlates with Burns' (1999) notion of Tourism First planning, in which economic growth and benefits take preference, with development viewed as a natural result. Other development concerns, such as developing capacity, empowering the poor and protecting human rights, that have the potential to significantly impact local community developments are often disregarded. Hughes and Scheyvens (2020) thus proposed a Development First framework as a means of assessing tourism company efforts to support local destination development. This framework encompasses a more holistic, sustainable, people-centered approach to CSR than the norm.

Horng et al. (2017) combined the content of ethics and CSR of the tourism industry in Taiwan through the *Confucianism* (Romar, 2004), which is a strong foundation for Chinese people and it demands every individual to play a proper role appropriate for a community, an organization, or an institution and that establishes a good connection with others in order to create a business environment full of harmony. Horng et al. (2017) presented an integrated model of CSR and ethics for tourism business with several indicators (Fig. 8.3) of its dimensions – intra, inter, and external organization ethics, individual ethics precursors to adopting CSR, inside and outside forces; strategies for implementing CSR, including environment, economy, society, and culture; the outcome, including consequence; and several sub-dimensions. Following this conceptual framework, ethics serves as the cornerstone of the CSR method, with each stage having a tie to ethics. This framework adhered to Carrol's model (Nalband & Kelabi, 2014), the triple bottom line (Coles et al., 2013) and Epstein (1989) assertion of four separate degrees of corporate ethics. Thus, it incorporates the full process of ethics and CSR implementation.

8. Conclusion

In conclusion, the findings of this chapter showed that CSR in tourism and hospitality is emerging as an important trend at global level with successful expansion of the sector. The chapter findings revealed that to offset the negative socio-environmental impacts of tourism, this sector is increasingly implementing sustainable CSR initiatives, and tourism businesses promote economic growth while improving the quality of life for employees, families, and the community as a whole. Findings further showed the confluence sustainable CSR practices in tourism emphasizes a congenial stability of socio-economic, environmental, and

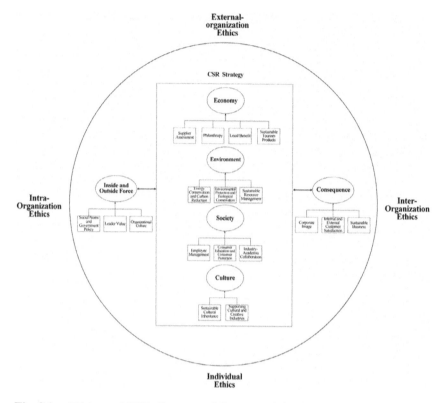

Fig. 8.3.   Ethics and CSR Conceptual Framework in the Tourism Industry.
Source: Horng et al. (2017).

cultural progression, while having a concern for the interests of all stakeholders. On the other hand, the impact of CSR on financial performance of businesses is significant in hotel sector and partially significant in other sub-domains in the industry. This study theoretically, contributes to the CSR literature in tourism and hospitality domain by widening its perspectives in the context of strategic sustainability, financial performance and ethical aspects.

9. Implications

Tourism and hospitality organizations must focus on incorporating CSR efforts into their entire business plan. This requires connecting CSR initiatives with the company's mission, vision, and extended goals for making the businesses sustainable. Acknowledging the value of stakeholders such as local communities, employees and tourists, businesses firms should actively engage and partner with them on CSR initiatives. This engagement not only will improve the success of CSR activities, but also will develop positive connections and trust in the community. Tourism and hospital firms must undertake frequent reviews to determine the impact of CSR activities on financial performance. Monitoring the relationship between CSR activities and financial outcomes may help with strategic decision making and resource allocation by emphasizing areas where CSR expenditures produce the best returns.

References

Abaeian, V., Khong, K. W., Kyid Yeoh, K., & McCabe, S. (2019). Motivations of undertaking CSR initiatives by independent hotels: A holistic approach. *International Journal of Contemporary Hospitality Management, 31*(6), 2468–2487.

Bansal, P., & Song, H. (2015). Similar but not the same: Differentiating corporate sustainability from corporate responsibility. *Academy of Management Annals, 11*(1), 105–149.

Benavides-Velasco, C. A., Quintana-García, C., & Marchante-Lara, M. (2014). Total quality management, corporate social responsibility and performance in the hotel industry. *International Journal of Hospitality Management, 41*, 77–87.

Blinova, E., Gregoric, M., Dedusenko, E., & Romanova, M. (2018). Corporate social responsibility in tourism: International practices. *European Research Studies Journal, 21*(3), 636–647.

Bocquet, R., Le Bas, C., Mothe, C., & Poussing, N. (2017). CSR, innovation, and firm performance in sluggish growth contexts: A firm-level empirical analysis. *Journal of Business Ethics, 146*(1), 241–254.

Burns, P. (1999). Paradoxes in planning tourism elitism or brutalism? *Annals of Tourism Research, 26*(2), 329–348.

Camilleri, M. A. (2017). Corporate sustainability and responsibility: Creating value for business, society and the environment. *Asian Journal of Sustainability and Social Responsibility, 2*(1), 59–74.

Camilleri, M. A. (2019). The circular economy's closed loop and product service systems for sustainable development: A review and appraisal. *Sustainable Development, 27*(3), 530–536.

Cheng, B., Ioannou, I., & Serafeim, G. (2014). Corporate social responsibility and access to finance. *Strategic Management Journal, 35*(1),1–23.

Chilufya, A., Hughes, E., & Scheyvens, R. (2019). Tourists and community development: Corporate social responsibility or tourist social responsibility? *Journal of Sustainable Tourism, 27*(10), 1513–1529.

Chubchuwong, M. (2019). The impact of CSR satisfaction on destination loyalty: A study of MICE travelers in Thailand. *Asia Pacific Journal of Tourism Research, 24*(2), 168–179.

Coles, T., Fenclova, E., & Dinan, C. (2013). Tourism and corporate social responsibility: A critical review and research agenda. *Tourism Management Perspectives, 6*, 122–141.

Curras-Pérez, R., Dolz-Dolz, C., Miquel-Romero, M. J. & Sanchez-García, I. (2018). How social, environmental, and economic CSR affects consumer-perceived value: Does perceived consumer effectiveness make a difference? *Corporate Social Responsibility and Environmental Management, 25*(5), 733–747.

Epstein, E. M. (1989). Business ethics, corporate good citizenship and the corporate social policy process: A view from the United States. *Journal of Business Ethics, 8*(8), 583–595.

Ertuna, B., Karatas-Ozkan, M., & Yamak, S. (2019). Diffusion of sustainability and CSR discourse in hospitality industry: Dynamics of local context. *International Journal of Contemporary Hospitality Management, 31*(6), 2564–2581.

European Cities Marketing. (2011). *Corporate social responsibility and tourism.* http://www. europeancitiesmarketing.com/corporate-social-responsibility-and-tourism.

Font, X., & Lynes, J. (2018). Corporate social responsibility in tourism and hospitality. *Journal of Sustainable Tourism, 26*(7), 1027–1042.

Garay, L., & Font, X. (2012). Doing good to do well? Corporate social responsibility reasons, practices and impacts in small and medium accommodation enterprises. *International Journal of Hospitality Management, 31*(2), 329–337.

García, R., & Armas, C. (2007). Relation between social-environmental responsibility and performance in hotel firms. *International Journal of Hospitality Management, 26*(4), 824–839. https://doi.org/10.1016/j.ijhm.2006.08.003

Ghaderi, Z., Mirzapour, M., Henderson, J. C., & Richardson, S. (2019). Corporate social responsibility and hotel performance: A view from Tehran, Iran. *Tourism Management Perspectives, 29*, 41–47.

Goffi, G., Masiero, L., & Pencarelli, T. (2022). Corporate social responsibility and performances of firms operating in the tourism and hospitality industry. *The TQM Journal, 34*(6), 1626–1647.

de Grosbois, D. (2012). Corporate social responsibility reporting by the global hotel industry: Commitment, initiatives and performance. *International Journal of Hospitality Management, 31*(3), 896–905.

Hadj, T. B. (2020). Effects of corporate social responsibility towards stakeholders and environmental management on responsible innovation and competitiveness. *Journal of Cleaner Production, 250,* 119490.

Han, S., Li, G., Lubrano, M., & Xun, Z. (2020). Lie of the weak: Inconsistent corporate social responsibility activities of Chinese zombie firms. *Journal of Cleaner Production, 253,* 119858.

Hamrouni, A., Uyar, A., & Boussaada, R. (2019). Are corporate social responsibility disclosures relevant for lenders? Empirical evidence from France. *Management Decision, 58*(2), 267–279.

Hatipoglu, B., Ertuna, B., & Salman, D. (2019). Corporate social responsibility in tourism as a tool for sustainable development: An evaluation from a community perspective. *International Journal of Contemporary Hospitality Management, 31*(6), 2358–2375.

Horng, J. S., Hsu, H., & Tsai, C. Y. (2017). The conceptual framework for ethics and corporate social responsibility in Taiwanese tourism industry. *Asia Pacific Journal of Tourism Research, 22*(12), 1274–1294.

Hughes, E., & Scheyvens, R. (2020). Corporate social responsibility in tourism post-2015: A development first approach. In *Tourism and sustainable development goals* (pp. 74–87). Routledge.

Ibarnia, E., Garay, L., & Guevara, A. (2020). Corporate social responsibility (CSR) in the travel supply chain: A literature review. *Sustainability, 12*(23), 10125.

Inoue, Y., & Lee, S. (2011). Effects of different dimensions of corporate social responsibility on corporate financial performance in tourism related industries. *Tourism Management, 32*(4), 790–804. https://doi.org/10.1016/j.tourman.2010.06.019

Ivanova, A. I., & Bikeeva, V. M. (2016). Corporate social responsibility: Specificity, formation mechanism, estimation of management efficiency. *European Research Studies Journal, 19*(3) Part A, 167–184.

Jones, R. J., Reilly, T. M., Cox, M. Z., & Cole, B. M. (2017). Gender makes a difference: Investigating consumer purchasing behaviour and attitudes toward corporate social responsibility policies. *Corporate Social Responsibility and Environmental Management, 24*(2), 133–144.

Kang, K. H., Lee, S., & Huh, C. (2010). Impacts of positive and negative corporate social responsibility activities on company performance in the hospitality industry. *International Journal of Hospitality Management, 29*(1), 72–82. https://doi.org/ 10.1016/j.ijhm.2009.05.006

Kang, K. H., Lee, S., & Yoo, C. (2016). The effect of national culture on corporate social responsibility in the hospitality and tourism industry. *International Journal of Contemporary Hospitality Management, 28*(8), 1728–1758.

Kim, M., & Kim, Y. (2014). Corporate social responsibility and shareholder value of restaurant firms. *International Journal of Hospitality Management, 40*, 120–129.

Kotler, P., Berger, R., & Bickhoff, N. (2010). *The quintessence of strategic management: what you really need to know to survive in business.* Springer Berlin Heidelberg.

Kumar, R. B., & Kumar, M. (2018). Corporate social responsibility in Indian tour operation industry. *International Journal of Hospitality and Tourism Systems, 11*(2), 82–88.

Lee, S., & Heo, C. Y. (2009). Corporate social responsibility and customer satisfaction among US publicly traded hotels and restaurants. *International Journal of Hospitality Management, 28*(4), 635–637. https://doi.org/10.1016/j.ijhm.2009.02.007

Lee, S., & Park, S. Y. (2009). Do socially responsible activities help hotels and casinos achieve their financial goals? *International Journal of Hospitality Management, 28*(1), 105–112.

Lee, S., & Park, S. Y. (2010). Financial impacts of socially responsible activities on airline companies. *Journal of Hospitality & Tourism Research, 34*(2), 185–203.

Lee, S., Seo, K., & Sharma, A. (2013). Corporate social responsibility and firm performance in the airline industry: The moderating role of oil prices. *Tourism Management, 38*, 20–30. https://doi.org/10.1016/j.tourman.2013.02.002

Lin, L. P. L., Yu, C. Y., & Chang, F. C. (2018). Determinants of CSER practices for reducing greenhouse gas emissions: From the perspectives of administrative managers in tour operators. *Tourism Management, 64*, 1–12.

Low, J. M., & Lee, B. K. (2014). Effects of internal resources on airline competitiveness. *Journal of Air Transport Management, 36*, 23–32. https://doi.org/10.1016/j.jairtraman.2013.12.001

Madanaguli, A., Srivastava, S., Ferraris, A., & Dhir, A. (2022). Corporate social responsibility and sustainability in the tourism sector: A systematic literature review and future outlook. *Sustainable Development, 30*(3), 447–461.

Melubo, K., & Carr, A. (2021). Developing indigenous tourism in the bomas: Critiquing issues from within the Maasai community in Tanzania. In *Indigenous heritage* (pp. 41–54). Routledge.

MGM Report (2017). *Corporate social responsibility report.* MGM Resorts.

Muafi, M. (2017). From company reputation to environmental performance. The context of corporate social responsibility port manager in Indonesia. *Journal of Environmental Management and Tourism, 8*(7), 1386–1398.

Nalband, N. A., & Kelabi, S. A. (2014). Redesigning Carroll's CSR pyramid model. *Journal of Advanced Management Science, 2*(3), 236–239.

Nyahunzvi, K. D. (2013). CSR reporting among Zimbabwe's hotel groups: A content analysis. *International Journal of Contemporary Hospitality Management, 25*(4), 595–613.

Putra, N., Rawi, S., Amin, M., Kusrini, E., Kosasih, E. A., & Mahlia, T. M. I. (2019). Preparation of beeswax/multi-walled carbon nanotubes as novel shape-stable nanocomposite phase-change material for thermal energy storage. *Journal of Energy Storage, 21*, 32–39.

Rhou, Y., Singal, M., & Koh, Y. (2016). CSR and financial performance: The role of CSR awareness in the restaurant industry. *International Journal of Hospitality Management, 57*, 30–39. https://doi.org/10.1016/j.ijhm.2016.05.007.

Romanova, O. G. A., Berg, D. B., & Matveeva, Y. A. (2017). Creating competitive strategies of industrial enterprises from the standpoint of corporate social responsibility. *Ekonomicheskie i Sotsialnye Peremeny* (54), 138–152.

Romar, E. J. (2004). Managerial harmony: The Confucian ethics of Peter F. Drucker. *Journal of Business Ethics, 51*(2), 199–210.

Servaes, H., & Tamayo, A. (2013). The impact of corporate social responsibility on firm value: The role of customer awareness. *Management Science, 59*(5),1045–1061.

Sharpley, R., & Telfer, D. J. (2023). Tourism supply in a growth-based economy. In *Rethinking tourism and development* (pp. 102–129). Edward Elgar Publishing.

Singal, M. (2014). Corporate social responsibility in the hospitality and tourism industry: Do family control and financial condition matter? *International Journal of Hospitality Management, 36*, 81–89. https://doi.org/10.1016/j.ijhm.2013.08.002.

Singh, S., Khare, A., Pandey, S. K., & Sharma, D. P. (2021). Industry and community peers as drivers of corporate social responsibility in India: The contingent role of institutional investors. *Journal of Cleaner Production, 295*, 126316.

Song, H. J., & Kang, K. H. (2019). Implementing corporate social responsibility strategies in the hospitality and tourism firms: A culture-based approach. *Tourism Economics, 25*(4), 520–538.

Starbucks. (2017). *Global social impact 2017 performance report.* Retrieved August 10, 2018, from https://news.starbucks.com/uploads/documents/Starbucks_Social_Impact_Report_2017.pdf

Tamajón, L. G., & Font, X. (2013). Corporate social responsibility in tourism small and medium enterprises evidence from Europe and Latin America. *Tourism Management Perspectives, 7*, 38–46.

Tang, Y. (2011). Literature review for the stakeholders CSR motivations research. *Management World, 8*, 184–185.

Theodoulidis, B., Diaz, D., Crotto, F., & Rancati, E. (2017). Exploring corporate social responsibility and financial performance through stakeholder theory in the tourism industries. *Tourism Management, 62*, 173–188. https://doi.org/10.1016/j.tourman.2017.03.018

Chapter 9

Empirical Investigation of Relationship Between CSR and Financial Performance: Study of Tata Companies

Premendra Kumar Singh[a], Dikshit Gupta[b], Rajinder Kumar[c], Raju Ganesh Sunder[a] and Bidhu Kanti Das[d]

[a]*Sharda University, India*
[b]*Lovely Professional University, India*
[c]*University of Ladakh, India*
[d]*Mizoram University, India*

Abstract

Purpose: This study examines how corporate social responsibility (CSR) affects Tata enterprises' financial performance. Numerous studies have examined how CSR affects company FP, with mixed results. The large variety of outcomes may have been due to erroneous analysis or insignificantly controlled variables, but the most likely explanation is that different research utilised different approaches. This study examines the relationship between CSR and financial performance in India using Tata Group companies listed on the BSE100.

Methodology: The BSE100-listed Tata companies were chosen for investigation because Tata's are pioneer in philanthropy and CSR. The present investigation relies on data obtained from annual reports and sustainability reports of the respective companies for a period of 10 years (2013–2022). Regression analysis was performed using Stata version 14 to evaluate the relationship between CSR spending and financial performance.

Research limitation: The study is confined to 7 Tata companies indexed in the BSE100 for 10 years (FY2013–FY2022).

Corporate Social Responsibility, Corporate Governance and Business Ethics in Tourism
Management: A Business Strategy for Sustainable Organizational Performance, 119–135
doi:10.1108/978-1-83608-704-520241009

Social implication: Tata companies' ethics and philanthropy activities are landmarks in Indian society that can be used to motivate the business stakeholders to contribute more to CSR. The tourism companies can use Tata's CSR model to grow their financial performance.

Findings: The findings of the study depict that financial performance is positively impacted by the amount spent on CSR by the companies. Companies that invest more in CSR have higher profitability, ROA, ROE, EPS, MB Ratio and MR_Daily.

Originality: This chapter will add comprehensive knowledge about the relationship of CSR and financial performance.

Keywords: Corporate social responsibility; financial performance; Tata; TCS; tourism

Introduction

The term CSR refers to an organisational practice known as considering the interests of society by addressing the impact their activities have on Stakeholders as well as the environment. Also, according to Carroll (1999, p. 268),

> The concept of corporate social responsibility (CSR) has a long and varied history. It is possible to trace evidence of the business world's centuries-old concern for society. However, the formal literature on social responsibility is largely a product of the 20th century, especially the last 50 years.

This commitment is perceived as surpassing the minimum legal obligation and making additional endeavours to improve the well-being of employed individuals and their dependents, as well as for the community at large and society (Ahmad et al., 2023). The responsibility for the economy and the environment is included in social responsibility. The fundamental idea behind CSR is that companies have a responsibility to meet the standards that are set forth by society in their practices (Pfajfar et al., 2022). The CSR have multidimensional performance, that is, corporate social performance (Esteban-Sanchez et al., 2017; Griffin & Mahon, 1997; McWilliams & Siegel, 2001); corporate financial performance (Callan & Thomas, 2009; Esteban-Sanchez et al., 2017); value creation (Freudenreich et al., 2020; Pera et al., 2016); social impact (Barnett et al., 2020; Pfajfar et al., 2022). It is commonly understood that the companies make use of society for its various inputs in the form of raw materials, resources, skilled, and unskilled labours which are nothing, but part of society and the finished products create wealth for them (Ceil, 2012). This signifies that the two are interrelated and they need each other for their existence. Therefore, this interdependency should be understood by the enterprises and accept the fact that they should bear some cost for the growth of the society at large (Sharma & Sathish, 2022). At the same time, these initiatives should not compromise the profitability of the organisations. The term refers to the idea that private businesses have a moral obligation to fulfil their role as guardians of the community. Institutional theory can provide an explanation for yet another reason why businesses are engaging in CSR activities. The investigation of institutional theory in connection with CSR is a more recent trend (Brammer et al., 2012).

According to the older theory, businesses participate in CSR activities because of pressures from the outside world, and not necessarily because they are concerned with being good and accountable (Avars & Lee, 2011). Many recent studies, such as the one conducted by Brammer et al. (2012), assert that businesses in developed nations that engage in international trade or that are partially owned by individuals from other countries tend to be more engaged in the sustainability approach. This chapter explored the spending on CSR of various Tata companies and its impact on financial performance.

Literature Review

CSR, Business, and Prosperity

In today's parlance, CSR would also involve financial, environmental, and governance considerations. CSR can be defined as the actions taken by organisations towards their internal and external stakeholders, including financial, environmental, and governance practices (Aguinis, 2011; Rupp, 2011). The pursuit of the greatest possible profit should not be the sole objective of for-profit businesses. Businesses as such are obligated to comprehend and carry out their business plans in a way that is morally commensurate and socially responsible (Buchholz, 1991) to the various stakeholders both internal and external to the organisation. It is of utmost significance to understand the connection between the monetary success of a business and its commitment to CSR. The obligation that a company must maintain and preserve well-being both now and time to come by creating long-term prosperity for its stakeholders is what is meant by the term CSR (Hay et al., 1976). In post-Covid-19 era CSR and business had a strong commitment towards philanthropy and resulted in prosperity (Carroll, 2021; Schwartz & Kay, 2023).

CSR and Financial Performance

According to the findings of some scholars, an investment in CSR by the company's results in a better financial return, which, in turn, leads to an improvement in the firm's reputation (Griffin & Mahon, 1997; Preston & O'Bannon, 1997; Solomon & Hanson, 1985). Comparable research on CSR's effects on financial results for 1,222 Korean companies was conducted empirically by Choi et al. (2010). According to their findings, CSR had a very favourable impact on the company's financial performance. The findings are in line with those of a study that was conducted in 2012 by the Nigerian firms Uadiale and Fagbemi (2012). Bragdon and Marlin (1972) and Vance (1975) found that there is a negative correlation between CSR and CFP (Abbott & Monsen, 1979; Alexander & Buchholz, 1978) found no definite relationship between the two properties. Coelho et al. (2023) conducted a detailed study on the relationship of CSR and FP and advocated that the relationship between these two variables is not clear or questionable.

CSR, Financial Performance, and Stakeholders Theory

The stakeholder theory was developed by Freeman in 1984. It postulates that higher levels of CSR practices will eventually lead to improved business performance. According to this theory, a company's level of success is directly related to how well it can keep good ties with all of its stakeholders. Garcia-Castro et al. (2010) conducted research from 1991 to 2005 that examined the impact that social production had on the financial results of 658 companies located in the United States. With the help of the pooled data and the ordinary least square (OLS) model, the researchers were able to reach the conclusion that the correlation was both positive and significant. Studies in various countries have also shown results where positive relationship between CSR and financial performance has been seen (Bragdon & Marlin, 1972; Davis & Blomstrom, 1975; Godfrey, 2005; Heinz, 1976; Jain et al., 2016; McWilliams & Siegel, 2001; Moskowitz, 1972; Parket & Eilbirt, 1975; Solomon & Hanson, 1985; Sturdivant & Ginter, 1977).

It can be inferred from the above literature that across the globe research is conducted to explore the relationship between CSR and financial performance of a company (Coelho et al., 2023; Kaur & Singh, 2021; Lund-Durlacher, 2015; Sameer, 2021). Also, there is a dearth of studies in connection with India and specifically a group of Tata companies in post-Covid-19 era (Ntasis et al., 2021). Hence the following hypothesis was assumed:

H1. The financial performance of organisations is significantly impacted by their CSR investment.

Research Methodology

The companies selected for study are Tata companies which are listed in the BSE100 and it was purposive as the Tatas' are considered as the pioneers in the area of philanthropy and CSR. Seven of the Tata companies are found to be listed in the BSE100 list, hence the study was carried out on these companies. The current analysis relies on secondary data acquired from the annual and sustainability reports of the individual companies for a period of 10 years (2013–2022). For the analysis of the collected data, Stata version 14 was used, and regression analysis was done to evaluate the relationship between CSR spending and financial performance of the selected companies. The variables used in the study for analysis are explained below.

Measurement of CSR

There are different ways of measuring CSR, some researchers suggest measuring CSR through disclosures, content analysis making use of Global Reporting Initiative (GRI) framework (Beck et al., 2018; Laskar & Maji, 2016; Waworuntu et al., 2014). For the study, CSR expenses as measurement of CSR (Menezes, 2019; Singh & Das, 2020) was used.

Measurement of Financial Performance

There are studies that suggest different ways to measure financial performance of firms. (Griffin & Mahon, 1997) identified 80 measurements of financial performance which were used in over 50 studies, and could be classified into accounting-based measures, market-based measures, measures of risk and other firms specific characteristics. For this study, Accounting-based measures which include Return on Equity (ROE), Earning Per Share (EPS), Return on Assets (ROA), Net Profit (NP) (Maqbool & Zameer, 2018; Pava & Krausz, 1996) and Market-based measurements consisting of Market to Book (MB) Value, PE Ratio and Market Return (MR) (Freedman & Jaggi, 1986; Maqbool & Zameer, 2018; Pava & Krausz, 1996; Vance, 1975) were considered. Accounting-based performance measures as observed from literature reviews relate to preceding or interim financial performance of firms, whereas market-based measures capture forthcoming or long-haul financial performance of firms (Gentry & Shen, 2010).

Dependent Variable

In this analysis, the firms' financial performance serves as the dependent variable; it is the variable upon which other factors can have an influence. For the purpose of carrying out the research, accounting measurements comprising of ROE, EPS, ROA, NP and MB value, PE Ratio and MR as an indicator for Market-based measurements (Freedman & Jaggi, 1986; Pava & Krausz, 1996; Vance, 1975) were considered.

Independent Variable

Factors whose influence must be analysed in relation to the variables that are being studied are referred to as the Independent Variables. The money spent by businesses on CSR projects, that is, CSR spending is the independent variable for this study.

Control Variable

Those factors might influence the CSR expenditure of firms as well as their overall financial performance. Following an analysis of the relevant prior research, it was chosen to make use of specific control variables, such as size and DE ratio, which may influence the findings of the study. For measuring the size of the companies, Natural Logarithm of Total Assets is used (Claessens et al., 2002; Gorton & Schmid, 2000; Kapoor & Sandhu, 2010; Siueia et al., 2019). The study incorporates the DE ratio as a secondary control variable.

Results

The impact of CSR spending on the companies' financial performance was assessed using a variety of variables, including profitability, ROA, ROE, EPS, PE Average, MR Daily, and MB Ratio. The ratio of a company's net profit to its total assets was used to determine how profitable the firms were. A company's ability to make money from its assets is shown by both the ROE and ROA, which are both expressed as percentages. The annual reports of the corresponding companies provided the ROA and ROE values. A company's earnings from each of its individual shares is expressed as earnings per share (EPS) for short. The EPS data were obtained from the annual reports of each of the firms. 'PE Average' is an acronym for 'Average Price Earning Ratio', a performance metric that varies according to the market. The ratio of the average stock price to the EPS was the metric that was used to determine it. Taking the daily market price average allowed for accurate calculation of the MR Daily indicator, also known as the Daily MR, which is a market-based performance measurement. MB Ratio is another essential indication of market-based measures. This ratio assists in determining how current market valuations of firms compare to their book value. The MB Ratio was determined by taking the total shareholder money and dividing that figure by the entire number of equity shares held by the company. CSR Spend is the amount of money spent by firms, which can be determined by calculating the Natural Log of the actual amount spent by companies on CSR endeavours. This gives the total amount of money spent by companies. The Natural Logarithm of the Total Assets was utilised as the basis for the calculation of the firms' sizes. The Debt Equity Ratio, often known as the DE Ratio, is the second control variable that is utilised in this study. The study additionally makes use of a time-specific dummy variable to control the time-specific influence that is having on the study.

Descriptive Statistics

The descriptive statistics are provided for better understanding of the correct background information. The variables are segmented into means, medians, and standard deviations in Table 9.1. It is expected that there would not be a significant gap between the variables' mean and median values, and the data in Table 9.1 demonstrates that this expectation has been met, that is, mean and median values do not have a significant. The degree to which the variables deviate from each other is indicated by the value of the standard deviation (SD).

Correlation Matrix

The association between the factors that were examined in the study is represented in Table 9.2. It indicates a statistically significant positive correlation between profitability and financial performance indicators at a significance level of 1%. This correlation holds true. There exists a negative correlation between Profitability and DE Ratio at 1% significance level which justifies the argument of Pecking order theory of Capital Structure (Myers, 1984; Myers &

Table 9.1. Descriptive Statistics.

Variables	Mean	Median	SD	Min	Max
Profitability	0.110	0.078	0.114	−0.116	0.347
ROA	10.829	7.780	11.161	−11.640	32.070
ROE	0.160	0.125	0.180	−0.400	0.490
EPS	32.301	9.745	44.687	−21.060	270.330
PE	28.711	26.775	128.736	−739.500	580.530
MR	−0.159	−0.140	0.158	−0.570	0.160
M/B Ratio	6.804	5.850	6.241	0.410	34.390
CSR_Spend	3.146	3.011	1.823	−0.163	6.589
Size	9.873	10.520	1.714	5.869	12.310
DE Ratio	0.386	0.305	0.461	0.000	2.270

Source: Calculated from annual reports of Tata companies (2012–2013 to 2021–2022).

Majluf, 1984) while there does not exist any correlation between profitability and size, CSR_Spend, and PE_Average Ratio. At 1% significance level, a positive connection is discovered between ROA and ROE, EPS, MR Daily, and MB Ratio, however, there is a negative association between ROA and DE Ratio and Size. On the other hand, there is no link identified between ROA and PE Average and CSR Spend. It is evident from Table 9.2 that at 1% significance level, ROE has a positive association with EPS, MR Daily, and MB Ratio. It is possible to deduce from the table that there is an inverse link between ROE and DE Ratio and Size. It has been determined that there is no connection between ROE, PE Average, and CSR Spend. A negative correlation has been observed between EPS and DE Ratio, whereas no significant relationship has been established between EPS and PE Average or MB Ratio. A statistically significant positive association has been observed between EPS and MR Daily, CSR Spend at a significance level of 1%, and Size at a significance level of 5%. At a significance level of 1%, a statistically significant positive relationship is shown between the PE Average and MR Daily. However, no significant association is observed between the PE Average and the MB Ratio, CSR Spend, Size, or DE Ratio. A positive correlation is depicted between MR Daily and MB Ratio at a significance level of 1%. Conversely, at a level of 5% significance, a negative correlation is observed between MR Daily and DE Ratio. There is a statistically significant negative relationship between MB Ratio and DE Ratio. Similarly, at 5% significance level, there exists a significant negative connection between MB Ratio and Size.

Multicollinearity

Severe multicollinearity is anticipated when the Variance Inflation Factor (VIF) exceeds 10 (Gujarati et al., 2012). Table 9.3, which assesses multicollinearity by

126   *Premendra Kumar Singh et al.*

Table 9.2.   Correlation Matrix.

Variables	Profitability	ROA	ROE	EPS	PE	MR	M/B Ratio	CSR_Spend	Size	DE Ratio
Profitability	1									
ROA	0.99*	1								
ROE	0.93*	0.93*	1							
EPS	0.59*	0.59*	0.56*	1						
PE	0.05	0.04	0.07	−0.02	1					
MR	0.35*	0.36*	0.36*	0.29*	0.30*	1				
M/B Ratio	0.47*	0.46*	0.46*	0.13	0.15	0.37*	1			
CSR_Spend	0.22	0.21	0.15	0.58*	0.05	0.21	−0.03	1		
Size	−0.22	−0.24**	−0.24**	0.27**	−0.03	0.03	−0.27**	0.81*	1	
DE Ratio	−0.69*	−0.70*	−0.64*	−0.39*	−0.19	−0.24**	−0.29*	−0.076	0.39*	1

Source: Calculated from annual reports of Tata companies (2012–2013 to 2021–2022).

* and ** denote coefficients are statistically significant at 1% and 5%, respectively.

Table 9.3.   Variance Inflation Factor (VIF).

Variables	Profitability	ROA	ROE	EPS	MR_Daily	PE_Average	MB
CSR_Spend	7.14	7.14	7.14	7.14	7.14	7.14	7.14
Size	8.13	8.13	8.13	8.13	8.13	8.13	8.13
DE Ratio	2.76	2.76	2.76	2.76	2.76	2.76	2.76
Year_2014	1.8	1.8	1.80	1.8	1.8	1.8	1.8
Year_2015	1.87	1.87	1.87	1.87	1.87	1.87	1.87
Year_2016	1.85	1.85	1.85	1.85	1.85	1.85	1.85
Year_2017	1.91	1.91	1.91	1.91	1.91	1.91	1.91
Year_2018	1.89	1.89	1.89	1.89	1.89	1.89	1.89
Year_2019	1.92	1.92	1.92	1.92	1.92	1.92	1.92
Year_2020	1.83	1.83	1.83	1.83	1.83	1.83	1.83
Year_2021	1.86	1.86	1.86	1.86	1.86	1.86	1.86
Year_2022	1.92	1.92	1.92	1.92	1.92	1.92	1.92

Source: Calculated from annual reports of Tata companies' (2012–2013 to 2021–2022).

comparing the VIF values of each independent variable with the values of the dependent variables, indicates that the maximum value observed is 8.13. This finding suggests that there is no evidence of multicollinearity, thereby allowing us to proceed with the regression analysis without any concerns.

Discussion

It can be observed from Table 9.4, even without considering expenses on CSR by the Tata companies it is evident that the companies reflect higher profitability, ROA, ROE and MB Ratio which may not be said about the other measures of financial performance viz. EPS, MR_Daily and PE_ Average as these are not significant. Companies that invest more in CSR undoubtedly have higher profitability, ROA, ROE, EPS, MB Ratio and MR_Daily as the values are significant at 1%, 5%, and 10%, respectively. There is a significant negative correlation between profitability and size, Debt Ratio of the companies which aligns with the findings of (Chechet & Olayiwola, 2014; Hasan et al., 2014; Lee & Liu, 2015; Nguyen & Nguyen, 2015). There is a significant negative correlation between ROA and size, Debt Ratio of the companies which is aligned with the study by Chechet and Olayiwola (2014), Goyal (2013), Hasan et al. (2014), Qayyum and Noreen (2019), Rouf (2015), and Zeitun (2012). There is a significant negative correlation between ROE and size, Debt Ratio of the companies which is justified by the findings of Patel (2018). At a significance threshold of 10%, a notable inverse relationship exists between the EPS and debt ratio of the corporations. A notable inverse relationship exists between the MB Ratio and the size of companies. The time dummy variables were used in order to control the time-specific impact and

Table 9.4.   Regression Analysis.

Variables	Profitability	ROA	ROE	EPS	MR_Daily	PE_Average	MB Ratio
Constant	0.463 (3.98)*	46.524 (4.13)*	0.702 (3.56)*	59.8 (1.28)	0.052 (0.25)	5.052 (0.03)	27.954 (3.61)*
CSR_Spend	0.048 (3.42)*	4.778 (3.51)*	0.065 (2.71)*	19.612 (3.47)*	0.042 (1.68)***	-3.994 (-0.17)	1.968 (2.11)**
Size	-0.047 (-2.97)*	-4.81 (-3.11)*	-0.067 (-2.48)*	-8.069 (-1.26)	-0.03 (-1.07)	9.238 (0.36)	-2.928 (-2.76)*
DE Ratio	-0.091 (-2.63)*	-8.783 (-2.62)*	-0.137 (-2.33)**	-24.54 (-1.76)***	-0.029 (-0.47)	-58.226 (-1.03)	0.127 (0.06)
Year_2014	0.019 (0.44)	2.115 (0.51)	0.017 (0.24)	4.397 (0.26)	0.079 (1.04)	-0.981 (-0.01)	0.309 (0.11)
Year_2015	-0.008 (-0.17)	-0.952 (-0.23)	-0.049 (-0.67)	-3.147 (-0.18)	-0.069 (-0.89)	-42.907 (-0.61)	1.626 (0.56)
Year_2016	-0.007 (-0.15)	-0.484 (-0.12)	-0.036 (-0.49)	-12.48 (-0.72)	-0.129 (-1.67)***	37.773 (0.54)	-0.07 (-0.02)
Year_2017	-0.033 (-0.75)	-2.866 (-0.67)	-0.094 (-1.27)	-14.71 (-0.83)	-0.012 (-0.15)	-38.378 (-0.54)	-0.72 (-0.25)
Year_2018	-0.023 (-0.54)	-1.357 (-0.32)	-0.093 (-1.26)	-15.333 (-0.87)	-0.015 (-0.2)	-58.208 (-0.82)	0.539 (0.19)
Year_2019	0.006 (0.13)	0.758 (0.18)	-0.014 (-0.19)	-2.841 (-0.16)	-0.105 (-1.34)	-31.09 (-0.43)	-0.049 (-0.02)

Year_2020	0.001 (0.01)	0.474 (0.11)	−0.059 (−0.81)	0.934 (0.05)	−0.154 (−2.02)**	−142.171 (−2.03)**	0.078 (0.03)
Year_2021	−0.006 (−0.13)	0.213 (0.05)	−0.042 (−0.57)	4.84 (0.28)	0.07 (0.91)	−20.969 (−0.3)	3.968 (1.38)
Year_2022	0.037 (0.84)	3.588 (0.84)	0.062 (0.83)	37.691 (2.13)**	0.014 (0.18)	−28.434 (−0.4)	9.473 (3.24)*
F-Statistics	7.05*	7.28*	5.44*	6.44*	2.42*	0.9	3.23*
BP Test	0.79	1.42	19.26*	51.33*	0.7	26.59*	25.11*
SK Test	6.97	6.52**	6.99**	38.19*	3.94	26.46*	4.47
Adjusted R^2	0.51	0.52	0.53	0.49	0.19	−0.018	0.28

Source: Author's original work.

*, ** and *** denotes coefficients are statistically significant at 1%, 5% and 10%, respectively.

Table 9.4 reflects that as the coefficients are insignificant except for EPS in 2022, MR_Daily in 2016 and 2020, PE_Average in 2020, and MB Ratio in 2022, it cannot be concluded that there is difference in the profitability, ROA, ROE, EPS, MR_Daily, PE_Average and MB_Ratio of the companies during the base year, that is, 2013 and the other years in which the study was conducted.

The insignificance of the BP test result indicates the absence of heteroscedasticity in the profitability data, and the F-statistics were determined to be significant at the 1% level of significance. The skewness and kurtosis test, often known as the SK test, is performed to check for normalcy. SK test is performed and insignificant result for this test indicates that residuals are normally distributed. Based on the adjusted R^2 value, it appears that the independent variables utilised in the model explain approximately 51% of the variations in the dependent variable. For MR_Daily variable, the BP and SK tests are insignificant which depicts the absence of heteroscedasticity and even the residuals are normally distributed. The model incorporates an independent variable that accounts for approximately 19% of the observed fluctuations in the dependent variable.

The ROA model used in the study was insignificant because SK test reflected such that the residuals deviated from a normal distribution hence it was not used for further consideration. Whereas in the other models, as there was heteroscedasticity, Robust Estimation method was utilised to control the heteroscedasticity and further check was conducted so that to understand if those models could be considered for the study.

As it can be seen from Table 9.5, Even after adjusting for heteroscedasticity, it was discovered that there was no normal distribution for residuals, except for the MB Ratio. As a result of the fact that the results of the Skewness Kurtosis test indicated that it was significant, it may be deduced that there was no normal distribution for residuals, which goes against one of the most important postulations of OLS regression. Because of the potential for these models' outputs to provide inaccurate conclusions, additional research does not take them into account once Robust Estimation has been applied and the model of MB Ratio is considered as the heteroscedasticity is controlled and the residuals are normally distributed.

Conclusion and Implications

Our study aided the earlier studies conducted in Indian context which depicts that the money spent by the companies in India helps improve their financial performances. The reason for the positive impact of CSR expenses on financial performance may be linked to the ideology of the Tata group, as they are not involved in any business, which may directly harm the society. This study considered the actual spending on CSR as the measure of CSR which is the first known study in Indian context. Therefore, tourism companies can use Tata's CSR model to grow their financial performance.

Limitations and Future Directions

There are some limitations about this work which may point the way to promising avenues for further research. Companies that fall under one umbrella, that is, TATA

Table 9.5. Regression Analysis After Robust Estimation.

Variables	Robust ROE	Robust PE	Robust MB
Constant	0.70	5.05	27.95
	(3.68)*	(0.03)	(3.28)*
CSR_Spend	0.06	−3.99	1.97
	(2.84)*	(−0.17)	(2.28)**
Size	−0.07	9.24	−2.93
	(−2.47)*	(0.37)	(−2.68)
DE Ratio	−0.14	−58.23	0.13
	(−1.32)	(−1.38)	(0.06)
Year_2014	0.02	−0.98	0.31
	(0.27)	(−0.02)	(0.12)
Year_2015	−0.05	−42.91	1.63
	(−0.64)	(−0.96)	(0.58)
Year_2016	−0.04	37.77	−0.07
	(−0.58)	(0.38)	(−0.03)
Year_2017	−0.09	−38.38	−0.72
	(−1.51)	(−0.79)	(−0.29)
Year_2018	−0.09	−58.21	0.54
	(−1.41)	(−1.15)	(0.2)
Year_2019	−0.01	−31.09	−0.05
	(−0.21)	(−0.66)	(−0.02)
Year_2020	−0.06	−142.17	0.08
	(−0.71)	(−1.24)	(0.03)
Year_2021	−0.04	−20.97	3.97
	(−0.58)	(−0.43)	(1.49)
Year_2022	0.06	−28.43	9.47
	(0.66)	(−0.57)	(2.12)**
F-Statistics	5.89*	0.78	3.04*
SK Test	6.99**	26.46*	4.47
Adjusted R^2	0.53	0.16	0.41

Source: Author's original work.
*, ** and *** denotes coefficients are statistically significant at 1%, 5% and 10%,

Group are included as a sample in this study. Thus, by comparing it to samples from various industries and larger number of companies from similar industries, future research could either validate or disprove the model presented in the present study. This study can be extended to National Stok Exchange listed tourism service suppliers' company to explore the relationship between CSR and FP.

References

Abbott, W. F., & Monsen, R. J. (1979). On the measurement of corporate social responsibility: Self-reported disclosures as a method of measuring corporate social involvement. *The Academy of Management Journal, 22*(3), 501–515.

Aguinis, H. (2011). Organizational responsibility: Doing good and doing well. In S. Zedeck (Ed.), *APA handbook of industrial and organizational psychology, Vol 3: Maintaining, expanding, and contracting the organization* (3rd ed., pp. 855–879). American Psychological Association.

Ahmad, N., Ullah, Z., Ryu, H. B., Ariza-Montes, A., & Han, H. (2023). From corporate social responsibility to employee well-being: Navigating the pathway to sustainable healthcare. *Psychology Research and Behavior Management, 16*, 1079–1095.

Alexander, G. J., & Buchholz, R. A. (1978). Corporate social responsibility and stock market performance. *The Academy of Management Journal, 21*(3), 479–486.

Avars, A., & Lee, M. (2014). *Why your company should produce a sustainability report.* http://www.sustainability.com/library/why-your-company-should-produce-a-sustainability-report#.T4W7cfW6WSo

Barnett, M. L., Henriques, I., & Husted, B. W. (2020). Beyond good intentions: Designing CSR initiatives for greater social impact. *Journal of Management, 46*(6), 937–964.

Beck, C., Frost, G., & Jones, S. (2018). CSR disclosure and financial performance revisited: A cross-country analysis. *Australian Journal of Management, 43*(4), 517–537.

Bragdon, J. H., & Marlin, J. (1972). Is pollution profitable. *Risk Management, 19*(4), 9–18.

Brammer, S., Jackson, G., & Matten, D. (2012). Corporate social responsibility and institutional theory: New perspectives on private governance. *Socio-economic Review, 10*(1), 3–28.

Buchholz, R. A. (1991). Corporate responsibility and the good society: From economics to ecology. *Business Horizons, 34*(4), 19–31. https://doi.org/10.1016/0007-6813(91)90003-E

Choi, J.-S., Kwak, Y.-M., & Choe, C. (2010). Corporate social responsibility and corporate financial performance: Evidence from Korea. *Australian Journal of Management, 35*(3), 291–311. https://doi.org/10.1177/0312896210384681

Callan, S. J., & Thomas, J. M. (2009). Corporate financial performance and corporate social performance: An update and reinvestigation. *Corporate Social Responsibility and Environmental Management, 16*(2), 61–78.

Carroll, A. B. (1999). Corporate social responsibility: Evolution of a definitional construct. *Business & Society, 38*(3), 268–295.

Carroll, A. B. (2021). Corporate social responsibility (CSR) and the COVID-19 pandemic: Organizational and managerial implications. *Journal of Strategy and Management, 14*(3), 315–330.

Ceil, C. (2012). *Corporate Social Responsibility and Wealth Maximization.* Available at SSRN 2051857.

Chechet, I. L., & Olayiwola, A. B. (2014). Capital structure and profitability of Nigerian quoted firms: The Agency Cost Theory Perspective. *American International Journal of Social Science, 3*(1), 139–158.

Claessens, S., Djankov, S., Fan, J. P. H., & Lang, L. H. P. (2002). Disentangling the incentive and entrenchment effects of large shareholdings. *Journal of Finance, 57*(6), 2741–2771.

Coelho, R., Jayantilal, S., & Ferreira, J. J. (2023). The impact of social responsibility on corporate financial performance: A systematic literature review. *Corporate Social Responsibility and Environmental Management, 30*(4), 1535–1560.

Davis, K., & Blomstrom, R. L. (1975). *Business and society: Environment and responsibility* (3rd ed., Issue v. 1). McGraw-Hill.

Esteban-Sanchez, P., de la Cuesta-Gonzalez, M., & Paredes-Gazquez, J. D. (2017). Corporate social performance and its relation with corporate financial performance:

International evidence in the banking industry. *Journal of Cleaner Production, 162,* 1102–1110.

Freedman, M., & Jaggi, B. (1986). An analysis of the impact of corporate pollution disclosures included in annual financial statements on investment decisions. *Advances in Public Interest Accounting, 1*(2), 193–212.

Freudenreich, B., Lüdeke-Freund, F., & Schaltegger, S. (2020). A stakeholder theory perspective on business models: Value creation for sustainability. *Journal of Business Ethics, 166*(1), 3–18.

Garcia-Castro, R., Ariño, M. A., & Canela, M. A. (2010). Does social performance really lead to financial performance? Accounting for endogeneity. *Journal of Business Ethics, 92*(1), 107–126. https://doi.org/10.1007/s10551-009-0143-8

Gentry, R. J., & Shen, W. (2010). The relationship between accounting and market measures of firm financial performance: How strong is it? *Journal of Managerial Issues, 22*(4), 514–530.

Godfrey, P. C. (2005). The Relationship Between Corporate Philanthropy and Shareholder Wealth: A Risk Management Perspective. *Academy of Management Review, 30*(4), 777–798.

Gorton, G., & Schmid, F. A. (2000). Universal banking and the performance of German firms. *Journal of Financial Economics, 58*(1–2), 29–80.

Goyal, A. M. (2013). Impact of capital structure on performance of listed public sector banks in India. *International Journal of Business and Management Invention, 2*(10), 35–43.

Griffin, J. J., & Mahon, J. F. (1997). The corporate social performance and corporate financial performance debate: Twenty-five years of incomparable research. *Business & Society, 36*(1), 5–31.

Gujarati, D. N., Porter, D. C., & Gunasekar, S. (2012). *Basic econometrics.* McGraw-Hill Education (India) Private Limited.

Hasan, Md. B., Ahsan, A. F. M. M., Rahaman, Md. A., & Alam, Md. N. (2014). Influence of Capital Structure on Firm Performance: Evidence from Bangladesh. *International Journal of Business and Management, 9*(5), 184–194.

Heinz, D. C. (1976). Financial correlates of a social measure. *Akron Business and Economic Review, 7*(1), 48–51.

Jain, P., Vyas, V., & Chalasani, D. P. S. (2016). Corporate social responsibility and financial performance in SMEs: A structural equation modelling approach. *Global Business Review, 17*(3), 630–653.

Kapoor, S., & Sandhu, H. S. (2010). Does it pay to be socially responsible? An empirical examination of impact of corporate social responsibility on financial performance. *Global Business Review, 11*(2), 185–208.

Kaur, N., & Singh, V. (2021). Empirically examining the impact of corporate social responsibility on financial performance: evidence from Indian steel industry. *Asian Journal of Accounting Research, 6*(2), 134-151.

Laskar, N., & Maji, S. G. (2016). Disclosure of corporate social responsibility and firm performance: evidence from India. *Asia-Pacific Journal of Management Research and Innovation, 12*(2), 145–154.

Lee, J.-H., & Liu, W.-S. (2015). Pecking order prediction of debt changes and its implication for the retail firm. *Journal of Distribution Science, 13*(10), 73–82.

Lund-Durlacher, D. (2015). Corporate social responsibility and tourism. In P. Moscardo & G. Benckendorff (Eds.). *Education for sustainability in tourism: A handbook of processes, resources, and strategies* (pp. 59–73). Springer.

Maqbool, S., & Zameer, M. N. (2018). Corporate social responsibility and financial performance: An empirical analysis of Indian banks. *Future Business Journal, 4*(1), 84–93.

McWilliams, A., & Siegel, D. (2001). Corporate social responsibility: A theory of the firm perspective. *The Academy of Management Review, 26*(1), 117–127.

Menezes, G. (2019). Impact of CSR Spending on firm's financial performance. *International Journal of Advance Research, Ideas and Innovations in Technology, 5*(2), 613–617.

Moskowitz, M. (1972). Choosing socially responsible stocks. *Business & Society Review, 1*, 71–75.

Myers, S. C. (1984). The capital structure puzzle. *The Journal of Finance, 39*(3), 574–592. https://doi.org/10.1111/j.1540-6261.1984.tb03646.x

Myers, S. C., & Majluf, N. S. (1984). Corporate financing and investment decisions when firms have information that investors do not have. *Journal of Financial Economics, 13*, 187–221.

Nguyen, T., & Nguyen, H.-C. (2015). Capital structure and firms' performance: Evidence from Vietnam's stock exchange. *International Journal of Economics and Finance, 7*(12), 1–10.

Ntasis, L., Koronios, K., & Pappas, T. (2021). The impact of COVID-19 on the technology sector: The case of TATA Consultancy Services. *Strategic Change, 30*(2), 137–144.

Parket, I. R., & Eilbirt, H. (1975). The practice of business social responsibility: The underlying factors. *Business Horizons, 18*(4), 5–10.

Patel, A. M. (2018). Relationship between financial leverage and profitability of textile companies of India. *Research Review International Journal of Multidisciplinary, 3*(6), 24–27.

Pava, M. L., & Krausz, J. (1996). The association between corporate social-responsibility and financial performance: The paradox of social cost. *Journal of Business Ethics, 15*(3), 321–357.

Pera, R., Occhiocupo, N., & Clarke, J. (2016). Motives and resources for value co-creation in a multi-stakeholder ecosystem: A managerial perspective. *Journal of Business Research, 69*(10), 4033–4041.

Pfajfar, G., Shoham, A., Małecka, A., & Zalaznik, M. (2022). Value of corporate social responsibility for multiple stakeholders and social impact – Relationship marketing perspective. *Journal of Business Research, 143*, 46–61.

Preston, L. E., & O'Bannon, D. P. (1997). The corporate social-financial performance relationship: A typology and analysis. *Business & Society, 36*(4), 419–429.

Qayyum, N., & Noreen, U. (2019). Impact of capital structure on profitability: A comparative study of Islamic and conventional banks of Pakistan. *Journal of Asian Finance, Economics and Business, 6*(4), 65–74.

Rouf, M. A. (2015). Capital structure and firm performance of listed non-financial companies in Bangladesh. *The International Journal of Applied Economics and Finance, 9*(1), 25–32.

Rupp, E. D. (2011). An employee-centered model of organizational justice and social responsibility. *Organizational Psychology Review, 1*(1), 72–94.

Sameer, I. (2021). Impact of corporate social responsibility on organization's financial performance: evidence from Maldives public limited companies. *Future Business Journal, 7*(1), 29.

Schwartz, M. S., & Kay, A. (2023). The COVID-19 global crisis and corporate social responsibility. *Asian Journal of Business Ethics, 12*(1), 101–124.

Sharma, E., & Sathish, M. (2022). "CSR leads to economic growth or not": An evidence-based study to link corporate social responsibility (CSR) activities of the Indian banking sector with economic growth of India. *Asian Journal of Business Ethics, 11*(1), 67–103.

Singh, P. K., & Das, B. K. (2020). Relationship between CSR and firms' Financial Performance: Empirical Evidence from Indian Banks. *Studies in Indian Place Names, 40*(60), 3483–3490.

Siueia, T. T., Wang, J., & Deladem, T. G. (2019). Corporate Social Responsibility and financial performance: A comparative study in the Sub-Saharan Africa banking sector. *Journal of Cleaner Production, 226*, 658–668.

Solomon, R. C., & Hanson, K. R. (1985). *It's Good Business*. Atheneum.

Sturdivant, F. D., & Ginter, J. L. (1977). Corporate Social Responsiveness: Management attitudes and economic performance. *California Management Review*, *19*(3), 30–39.

Vance, S. G. (1975). Are socially responsible corporations good investment risks? *Management Review*, *64*(8), 18–24.

Waworuntu, S. R., Wantah, M. D., & Rusmanto, T. (2014). CSR and Financial Performance Analysis: Evidence from Top ASEAN Listed Companies. *Procedia – Social and Behavioral Sciences*, *164*, 493–500.

Zeitun, R. (2012). Determinants of Islamic and conventional banks performance in GCC countries using panel data analysis. *Global Economy and Finance Journal*, *5*(1), 53–72.

Chapter 10

Digital Disruption: 'Transforming Tourism Education for the 21st Century'

Shiv Raj[a], Suman Sharma[a] and Dev Dutt[b]

[a]*Department of Tourism and Travel, Central University of Himachal, Dharamshala, India*
[b]*Jawahar Navodaya Vidyalaya, Himachal Pradesh, India*

Abstract

This study investigates the impact of digital disruption on tourism education in the 21st century.

Research problem: Digital disruption is causing a major upheaval in the tourism education sector, which is affecting how teachers instruct and how students learn. The purpose of this study is to investigate ways in which educators can adjust to these changes and to comprehend the impact of digital disruption on tourism education.

Research significance: This study is important because it clarifies the opportunities and problems associated with the digital disruption of tourism education. It offers guidance to educators, decision-makers, and industry participants on how to successfully incorporate digital technologies into curricula for tourism education.

Methods: A mixed-methods strategy integrating quantitative and qualitative methods was employed. An online survey and in-depth interviews with 100 participants – students, professionals in the industry, and educators – were used to gather data. For qualitative data, thematic analysis was employed, whereas descriptive statistics were used for quantitative data.

Frameworks: The study is set up in relation to the theory of digital disruption and how it affects education. The literature on digital technologies in

Corporate Social Responsibility, Corporate Governance and Business Ethics in Tourism
Management: A Business Strategy for Sustainable Organizational Performance, 137–145
Copyright © 2025 by Shiv Raj, Suman Sharma and Dev Dutt
Published under exclusive licence by Emerald Publishing Limited
doi:10.1108/978-1-83608-704-520241010

education, transformative learning theory, and the necessity of developing 21st-century skills are also consulted.

Results: Participants generally perceived a moderate to high level of disruption, suggesting that there is a significant level of digital disruption in tourism education. The study emphasizes how critical it is to incorporate new technologies into curricula, stress the value of sustainable development, enhance intercultural competency, and promote cooperation between academic institutions and the travel and tourism sector.

Originality/value: Overall similarity 2%.

Keywords: Digital disruption; tourism education; intercultural competencies; 21st century skills; transformative learning; sustainable development; teamwork

Introduction

Today's industries are being shaped by digital disruption on a broad scale, and the tourism education sector is no different. With the advent of digital technologies, the educational landscape is undergoing a significant transformation as we approach the 21st century. This shift involves a fundamental rethinking of how we teach, learn, and interact with the subject of tourism, not just adding digital tools to the curriculum.

The introduction of digital technologies has completely changed how we communicate, obtain information, and carry out business. Digital disruption has created new opportunities for global collaboration, immersive learning experiences, and real-time industry insights in the context of tourism education.

Additionally, it has brought in a new era of personalized learning, in which students can modify their course of study to fit their unique interests and learning preferences.

But these opportunities also bring with them difficulties. Because technology is changing so quickly, educators must constantly update their knowledge and skills to stay up to date with new developments. Furthermore, many students still face obstacles as a result of the digital divide, especially those from underprivileged backgrounds, which emphasizes the need of inclusive strategies in digital education.

In light of this, it is critical that educators and decision-makers working in the tourism education sector see digital disruption as a chance for development and creativity. We can give students a more dynamic, interesting, and pertinent education by utilizing digital technologies, enabling them to succeed in the quickly changing tourism industry.

The tourism industry (Raj et al., 2023) is undergoing major changes due to digital transformation. Digital technology has revolutionized the way businesses operate and the way consumers consume travel and hospitality services. In this rapidly evolving landscape, the role of education in training (Amoah et al., 1997) future professionals is becoming increasingly important. This research chapter examines the impact of digital transformation on tourism education and the strategies educators can use to provide students with the skills and knowledge they need to succeed in the 21st century tourism industry.

In the 21st century, the digital revolution has reshaped numerous aspects of our lives, including the way we learn and acquire knowledge. The field of tourism education (Raj & Sharma, 2023) is no exception, as digital disruption has brought about transformative changes in how tourism-related subjects are taught and understood. According to recent studies (Smith, 2022), the integration of digital technologies in tourism education has not only enhanced the learning experience but has also revolutionized the industry's practices and approaches. This chapter explores the profound impact of digital disruption on tourism education, highlighting its implications for both educators and learners in the 21st century.

Literature Review

The rapid development and integration of new technologies are changing perceptions in all aspects of education, including tourism education (Kallou et al., 2021). The COVID-19 pandemic has further accelerated the need for digital transformation in education, leading to changes in learning environments, teaching methods, and curricula. This led to the proposal of a pedagogical framework using transformative learning theory and digital technologies that enables modern learning design and flexible use of digital tools in tourism education (Kallou et al., 2021). Although YouTube is increasingly being used in blended learning and online education, its use in tourism research has lagged behind. The Travel Professors YouTube channel aims to disseminate tourism research and provide useful reference materials for face-to-face and online learning by highlighting the opportunities and challenges of using YouTube in tourism education (Tolkach et al., 2021). The use of digital devices and tools in the classroom and home is being explored to create a 21st century digital learning experience (Hover et al., 2020). As digital technologies continue to permeate our lives, schools are expected to make room for them and teachers should be prepared to incorporate digital tools into their teaching practices (Karsenti, 2019). Advances in information and communication technology (ICT) have facilitated growth in various fields, including education, creating new opportunities for individuals in the 21st century. This has increased the importance of digital literacy and its impact on various aspects of people's daily lives, including the education sector (Reddy et al., 2020). In summary, integrating digital technologies into tourism education is crucial to prepare students for the new challenges of the 21st century.

The use of platforms such as YouTube and the implementation of digital competency models can contribute to the transformation of tourism education (Gangotia et al., 2022) and the development of students according to the needs of modern society.

In the 21st century, the use of digital technology in education has become increasingly important. Prensky (2012) discusses the impact of digital natives on education and the need to rethink traditional teaching methods to better meet the needs of these learners. Lai (2011) also highlights the importance of digital technologies in higher education and points out that digital technologies can support changes in cultural practices in teaching and learning. Wang et al. (2011) further discussed the need to bring schools into the 21st century, highlighting the importance of integrating 21st century skills into the curriculum and preparing teachers for the changing educational environment. Higgins (2014) argues that 21st century education curricula require critical thinking and 21st century skills, but are not sufficient. The author emphasizes the importance of knowing and understanding different cultural perspectives and values, as well as the specific technical and historical requirements of his 21st century related to digital skills. Morrell (2012) also highlights the importance of her 21st century literacy and critical media pedagogy in language teaching, and the need for educators to integrate new tools and communication methods into traditional literacy approaches. I'm emphasizing.

Overall, the literature suggests that digital transformation is transforming education and that teaching and learning practices need to adapt to better meet the needs of her 21st century learners. This includes integrating digital technologies into the curriculum, preparing teachers for the changing educational environment, and incorporating new skills and critical media pedagogy into traditional educational approaches (Higgins, 2014; Lai, 2011; Morrell, 2012; Prensky, 2012; Wan et al., 2011). See Fig. 10.1.

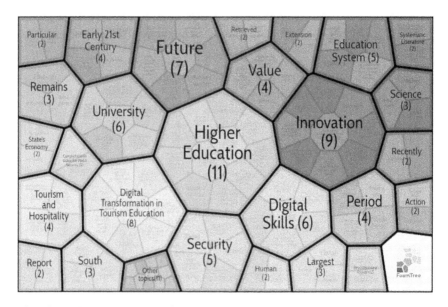

Fig. 10.1   Tree Map (Researcher Data).

Research Methodology

This study investigated the effects of digital disruption on tourism education using a mixed-methods approach that combined qualitative and quantitative techniques. To ensure representation from a variety of stakeholder groups, the sample size was 100 participants, chosen through purposive sampling, which included students, professionals in the tourism industry, and educators. While quantitative data were obtained via an online survey, qualitative data were obtained through in-depth interviews. To analyze the qualitative data and find themes and patterns, thematic analysis was used. Descriptive statistics were utilized for the quantitative data analysis in order to look at the distribution and frequency of responses. Confidentiality and informed consent were guaranteed by adherence to ethical standards. The validity and reliability of the results were improved by using member verification and triangulation of data sources.

Data Analysis

Descriptive statistics show that the average perception score of 100 respondents on digital disruption in tourism education is 4.3653, which indicates a relatively high level of perceived disruption. A standard deviation of 0.12444 suggests that responses varied moderately around this mean. A skewness of 0.108 indicates a slightly right-skewed distribution, suggesting that while most respondents experience moderate levels of disturbance, some respondents experience higher levels. A kurtosis value of -0.467 indicates that the distribution is slightly smoother than a normal distribution, with fewer outliers than a completely normal distribution. Overall, these statistics suggest that respondents generally see significant digital disruption in tourism education, with respondents' perceptions somewhat varied (Table 10.1).

The mean score of 4.3653 suggests that respondents see an average moderate to high digital disconnect in tourism education on average. This is also supported

Table 10.1. Perception of Respondent.

Descriptive Statistics						
N	**Mean**	**Std. Deviation**	**Skewness**		**Kurtosis**	
Statistic	**Statistic**	**Statistic**	**Statistic**	**Std. Error**	**Statistic**	**Std. Error**
Digital Disruption	100	4.3653	0.12444	0.108	0.241	−0.467	0.478
Valid N (listwise)	100						

Source: Survey respondent data.

by the average score of 4.3333, which is close to the mean and shows a relatively symmetrical distribution of responses around the central value. The mode of 4.33 indicates that respondents chose this particular score most often, reinforcing the perception of concentrated perception around that value (Table 10.2).

The standard deviation of 0.12444 indicates that there is some variability in respondents' perceptions and that the scores are scattered about average. A skewness value of 0.108 indicates a slightly right-skewed distribution, indicating that while most respondents perceive a moderate level of harassment, some perceive it as higher.

A kurtosis value of −0.467 indicates that the distribution is slightly smoother than normal with fewer extremes. Overall, these statistics suggest that although there is general agreement among respondents on the level of digital disruption in tourism education, there are also some differences in understanding, with some respondents perceiving the disruption as stronger.

Table 10.3 shows the respondents' understanding of digital disruption in tourism education. The majority of respondents, 41%, gave a digital disruption level of 4.33, indicating a significant impact. Additionally, 13% of respondents rated it 4.20, 14% as 4.40, and 12% as 4.53, indicating significant agreement on the idea of ?major digital disruption in the industry. A smaller but significant percentage of respondents rated the disturbance slightly lower or higher, with 6% at 4.13 and 4.60, and 7% at 4.47. These findings suggest that respondents generally agree on the existence and importance of digital disruption in tourism education, and most see it as an important factor shaping the field.

Table 10.2.   Statistics.

Statistics		
Digital Disruption		
N	Valid	100
	Missing	0
Mean		4.3653
Median		4.3333
Mode		4.33
Std. Deviation		0.12444
Variance		0.015
Skewness		0.108
Std. Error of Skewness		0.241
Kurtosis		−0.467
Std. Error of Kurtosis		0.478

Source: Survey respondent data.

Table 10.3.   Understanding of Digital Disruption in Tourism Education.

Digital Disruption

		Frequency	Percent	Valid Percent	Cumulative Percent
understanding of digital disruption in tourism education	4.13	6	6.0	6.0	6.0
	4.20	13	13.0	13.0	19.0
	4.33	41	41.0	41.0	60.0
	4.40	14	14.0	14.0	74.0
	4.47	7	7.0	7.0	81.0
	4.53	12	12.0	12.0	93.0
	4.60	7	7.0	7.0	100.0
	Total	100	100.0	100.0	

Source: Survey respondent data.

Discussion

Based on the comes about of the information examination, it is obvious that advanced disturbance includes a noteworthy effect on tourism instruction, as seen by both understudies and teachers. The larger part of members appraised the level of disturbance as direct to tall, showing a far-reaching affirmation of the transformative impacts of computerized innovations in this field. These discoveries emphasize the significance of coordination advanced innovations in tourism instruction educational program to guarantee that understudies are enough arranged for the challenges and openings of the 21st-century tourism industry. Teachers ought to proceed to investigate inventive ways to use advanced instruments and stages to enhance learning encounters and create the abilities and competencies required for victory within the advanced age. Generally, this consideration contributes to the developing body of writing on advanced disturbance in instruction and highlights the requirements for continuous inquiry about and advancement in this region. By grasping computerized change, tourism education can advance to meet the demands of a progressively computerized world and engage understudies to flourish within the tourism industry in long-term.

Recommendations

The data clearly show that digital disruption is a major factor shaping the future of tourism education. To effectively address this disruption, educational institutions and policy makers should consider the following recommendations.

Educational institutions should integrate new technologies such as virtual reality and artificial intelligence into their curricula to provide students with practical skills and knowledge in digital technology age.

Due to the importance of sustainable development in the field of tourism, educational programs should emphasize the principles of sustainable development and responsible tourism so that students are prepared for the changing demands of the field.

Improvement of multiculturalism. competencies: As tourism becomes increasingly globalized, students must have the necessary intercultural competencies to communicate effectively with different travelers and communities.

Collaboration between educational institutions and the tourism industry is essential to ensure the delivery of education. programs remain relevant and responsive to industry needs.

Due to the dynamic nature of the tourism industry, educational programs must continually adapt to new trends and technologies to prepare students for careers in the industry.

Conflict of Interest Statement

The authors declare that they have no conflicts of interest regarding the publication of this research chapter. All authors have full control of all primary data and agree to allow the journal to review the data if requested.

References

Amoah, V. A., & Baum, T. (1997). Tourism education: policy versus practice. *International Journal of Contemporary Hospitality Management, 9*(1), 5–12.

Buhalis, D., & Amaranggana, A. (2014). Smart tourism destinations enhancing tourism experience through personalization of services. In *Information and communication technologies in tourism 2014* (pp. 377–389). Springer.

Dredge, D., & Jamal, T. (2015). Progress in tourism management: A review of website evaluation in tourism research. *Tourism Management, 50*, 51–61.

European Commission. (2017). *Digital skills in the tourism sector*. https://ec.europa.eu/growth/sectors/tourism/education_en

Gangotia, A., Bhatt, K., & Kumar, S. (2022). Vocational education in tourism at schools and colleges of Himachal Pradesh, India: A qualitative inquiry on challenges encountered by trainers. *Journal of Teaching in Travel & Tourism, 22*(4), 378–399.

Gretzel, U., & Fesenmaier, D. R. (2009). eTourism: Towards a new paradigm for tourism management. In *Information and communication technologies in tourism 2009* (pp. 37–48). Springer.

Gretzel, U., & Yoo, K. H. (2008). Use and impact of online travel reviews. *In Information and communication technologies in tourism 2008* (pp. 35–46). Springer.

Gursoy, D., & Saayman, M. (2016). Disruptive technologies: Advances that will transform life, business, and the global economy. *Tourism Management, 59*, 59–60.

Hall, C. M. (2009). Tourism education and its relevance in a rapidly changing world. *Journal of Hospitality & Tourism Education, 21*(4), 18–27.

Hall, C. M., & Page, S. J. (2009). *The geography of tourism and recreation: Environment, place, and space*. Routledge.

Han, H., & Ryu, K. (2012). The role of social media in knowledge sharing. In *Information and communication technologies in tourism* 2012 (pp. 153–164). Springer.

Hjalager, A. M. (2010). A review of innovation research in tourism. *Tourism Management, 31*(1), 1–12.

Neuhofer, B., Buhalis, D., & Ladkin, A. (2015). Technology as a catalyst of change: Enablers and barriers of the tourist experience and their consequences. In *Information and communication technologies in tourism 2015* (pp. 789–802). Springer.

Pappas, N. (2020). The transformative power of blockchain technology in the travel industry. *Journal of Tourism, Heritage & Services Marketing*, *6*(1), 46–49.

Raj, S., & Sharma, S. (2023). Tourism education and career readiness: A case study of Himachal Pradesh Government Schools. *Journal of Tourism Education*, *3*(2), 85–92.

Raj, S., Sharma, S., Kaushal, N., & Choudhary, V. (2023). Assessing the impacts of tourism education on employment opportunities: A study of the schooling population of Himachal Pradesh. *Journal of Survey in Fisheries Sciences*, *10*(2), 777–779.

Sigala, M. (2017). The digital platform: A research agenda. *Journal of Hospitality and Tourism Technology*, *8*(1), 10–29.

UNWTO. (2020). *Tourism education in the digital age: Opportunities and challenges.* https://www.unwto.org/tedigitalage2020

UNWTO. (2021). *Tourism recovery tracker.* https://www.unwto.org/covid-19-dashboard

Chapter 11

Analyzing Tourist Satisfaction and Revisit Intention Using the 7 As of Tourism: A Case Study of Kachchh Rann Utsav

Bhumi Vyas[a] and Vijay H. Vyas[b]

[a]*Marwadi University, India*
[b]*Kachchh University, India*

Abstract

Purpose: Understanding consumer wants is crucial for improving service quality and gaining a competitive edge. This study's primary goal is to examine how satisfied tourists are with Kachchh Rann Utsav and whether they plan to revisit.

Methodology: The researcher used tourists who have visited Kachchh Rann Utsav previously as a sample based on the cluster sampling method. The sample size for this research was 478. The present study has considered the 7As of tourism: attraction, accessibility, amenities, accommodation, activities, awareness, and ancillary service to measure the underlying satisfaction. The researcher used multinomial logistic regression to predict the travelers' intention to revisit.

Findings: Surprisingly, the researcher observed that the other six A's of tourism have been found not to affect tourists' revisit intention, although accommodation does. Thus, the researcher thinks that a shift in the quality of lodging services offered to visitors during Kachchh Rann Utsav will have a big influence on the extent and direction of their desire to return to Kachchh Rann Utsav.

Originality: As to Kachchh Rann Utsav is an unexplored area. So to bridge the gap the researcher's study on this topic. As it will enhance the knowledge of Kachchh Tourism.

Corporate Social Responsibility, Corporate Governance and Business Ethics in Tourism
Management: A Business Strategy for Sustainable Organizational Performance, 147–157
Copyright © 2025 by Bhumi Vyas and Vijay H. Vyas
Published under exclusive licence by Emerald Publishing Limited
doi:10.1108/978-1-83608-704-520241011

Implication: This study will be helpful for all Gujarat's and Kachchh's tourism industry stakeholders in framing the policy regarding Kachchh Rann Utsav.

Keywords: 7As of tourism; tourist satisfaction; revisit intention; Kachchh Rann Utsav; event tourism

1. Introduction

Prior studies have established the significance of recurrent travel in ensuring the long-term viability of the tourism sector (Chen & Gursoy, n.d.; Hung et al., 2016; Kozak, 2001; Stylos et al., 2017; Quintal & Polczynski, 2010). According to Um et al. (2006), relying on repeat tourists is more cost-effective in the long term compared to relying on first-time visitors. Therefore, the growth of a destination's tourism business depends largely on attracting repeat visitors. Extensive research has been conducted to comprehend the factors that influence tourists' intention to return, considering the importance of return travel. Consumer behavior study has demonstrated that visitor happiness is a crucial motivation.

Korstanje (2024) conducted research on post-COVID-19 behavior in the new normal. COVID-19 significantly halted several service industries, such as the tourism industry, to an unprecedented extent. Consequently, the travel and tourism industry served as both the primary transmitter and recipient of this virus. In order to manage the spread of the virus, governments enforced rigorous measures such as implementing border closures, airspace restrictions, and the shutdown of bus terminals and airports. Additionally, they imposed lockdowns to restrict individuals from leaving their homes. Academics fervently debated whether this founding event signified a fresh opportunity for degrowth tourism and a more sustainable form of consumption, or a new hindrance for the field of tourism studies (Chin et al., 2018). The findings of this research demonstrate that prospective tourists' perceptions of a tourist destination during COVID-19 act as a bridge between the impact of a destination's image and their interest in visiting there. This demonstrates that one factor to take into account is how prospective visitors perceive the risk of COVID-19.

West Kachchh tourist place developed after Rann Utsav and Its Impact on the livelihood of Bhachau Taluka only. The Kachchh is rich in nature, ancient architecture, culture, heritage, and tradition, making this place a tourist destination (Kalaiya & Kumar, 2015).

The proposed study has given the profile of the sightseers and featured their temperament of travel, understanding of tourist place products, and amenities they devour or like. It has been supportive in anticipating the travel industry demand pattern; with the help of this target market can be recognized, and focus can be given to it. This study will also assist in lowering the cost of promotion and improving the effectiveness of marketing methods. Through planned research, the local people's perception has assisted with drawing specific outcomes with respect to Kachchh Rann Utsav. It will likewise help policymakers, organizers, and developers better understand the prominent region of Kachchh and create awareness, leading to the framing of plans and policies that are helpful for the development of Kachchh Tourism through a live research study.

2. Literature Review

Alegre and Cladera (2006) examine the impact that rates of return visits have on travelers' satisfaction levels and their intentions to return to the location. According to Kim et al. (2013), the research aims to (a) analyze the characteristics of food regarding tourists and (b) determine whether their satisfaction and intention to return varied significantly depending on how much they spent. The current study is an attempt to gauge visitor satisfaction in Kashmir Valley due to the growing significance of visitor satisfaction for tourism promotion (Bhat & Qadir, 2013). Three ideas that are the antecedents of passengers' behavioral intentions – traveler-perceived freedom of choice, destination image, and satisfaction – are examined to evaluate a theory-based pattern (Liu et al., 2016).

Seetanah et al. (2020) examine the correlation between the satisfaction levels of tourists with the quality of airport services at a destination and their desire to revisit. Focused on the ideas of geographic proximity and personal affiliation. The purpose of the study by Foroudi et al. (2018) is to close a gap in place identification research about the impact of a place website on consumers', visitors', and tourists' perceptions of their location. The goal of Abbasi et al. (2023) is to identify the variables that affect travelers' intentions to return. Liao et al. (2021) offer a valuable resource for destination marketers to formulate marketing strategies, as the challenges surrounding destination consumption have to be further validated. A few other noteworthy works are Petrick (2002).

The study conducted by Chi and Qu (2008) investigates the interconnections between destination image, tourist satisfaction, and destination loyalty through the utilization of an integrated methodology. The study model offered consisted of seven well-established hypotheses. The study conducted by Meng et al. (2008) examined the connections among travel motivation, satisfaction, the significance of destination attributes, and performance. The present study aims to create and evaluate a comprehensive theoretical framework for destination branding that takes into account the notions of brand credibility, client brand attachment, and brand attachment to the brand. Based on the principles discussed earlier, it is hypothesized that the relationships between the four constructs of destination source credibility, destination image, and destination attachment are factors that come before destination satisfaction (Veasna et al., 2013). In Bandung, West Java, Indonesia (Putri, 2017) carried out a case study on Saung Angklung Udjo, with a focus on visitors' pleasure at cultural sites. Currently, destination managers must work in extremely competitive markets, which compels them to search for cutting-edge strategies and durable competitive advantages, such as cultivating visitor loyalty. Adinegara (2019) set out to investigate the aspects of service quality that guests considered important as well as the perceived level of performance they encountered.

The goals of Ungasan. (2020) were to (1) examine the association between tourism destination attributes and tourists' intentions to return to Melasti Beach; (2) examine the association between service quality and visitors' intent to return to Melasti Beach; and (3) examine the association between guest satisfaction and visitor intents to return. Examining how foreign guests' dining experiences impact their contentment and loyalty when consuming regional cuisine in Bali is the aim of Hendriyani et al. (2020). This study, which uses Thailand as its starting point, assesses the relevance and efficacy of Islamic characteristics used to analyze the travel destinations chosen by Muslims and to measure overall visitor satisfaction.

3. Research Methodology

The researcher used primary and secondary data for this investigation. To collect primary data, structured questionnaires have been utilized. The researcher surveyed 470 tourists of Kachchh Rann Utsav as the respondents by cluster sampling method in this study. Gujarat is divided into four zones: North Gujarat, South Gujarat, West Gujarat, and Central Gujarat. The researcher analyzed the data by multinomial logistic regression through the SPSS 22 version.

3.1. Problem Statement

The idea is to study Kachchh tourism as Rann Utsav as a product to examine its tourist offerings. Destination branding as a sphere of study is evolving rapidly. Therefore, a more holistic tactic must be applied to study any destination brand in contemporary times. So one has to explore the various areas and examine them. This study highlights the satisfaction level of travelers based on the 7 A's of tourism (Attractions, Accessibility, Amenities, Accommodation, Activities, Awareness, and Ancillary Services).

3.2. Objective

To analyze the underlying satisfaction of tourists with destination attributes based on the 7 A's of Tourism regarding Kachchh Rann Utsav.

3.3. Hypothesis

H0. Tourist satisfaction from a visit to Kachchh Rann Utsav does not influence their revisit intention.

H1. Tourist satisfaction from a visit to Kachchh Rann Utsav does influence their revisit intention.

3.4. Research Design

The framework of research methodologies and procedures that a researcher selects to carry out an investigation is referred to as the research design. Because of the design, researchers can hone down on research methodologies that are

Table 11.1.   Sample Design.

Population	Tourist of Kachchh
Sampling Method	Cluster Sampling Method
Sampling Elements	Tourists of Kachchh Rann Utsav
Sample Size	478
Survey Area	Kachchh District

Source: Author's own compilation.

Table 11.2.   Sources of Scale.

Sr. No.	Variable	Source of Variable
1.	Satisfaction Level "Experience at Kachchh Rann Utsav"	Asmelash and Kumar (2019), Warbung et al. (2021), Madhani (2018), Mistry (2018), Katoch (2016), Kozak and Rimmington (2016), Rami (2015), Manaktola and Jauhari (2007), Thaker (2004), and Chaudhary (2000)

Source: Author's own compilation.

appropriate for the topic matter and properly organize their investigations to ensure their success. Table 11.1 shows the sample design of this research.

3.5. Sources of Scale

Tourists' satisfaction level is based on the 7 A's of Tourism: attraction, accessibility, amenities, accommodation, activities, awareness, ancillary services, and other aspects mentioned in Table 11.2.

4. Analysis and Results

Multinomial logistic regression is used to describe the overall association test, which assesses the link between the independent and dependent variables. Table 11.3 displays the model fitting information, namely the statistical significance of the final model chi-square. This table is used to analyze the relationship between the dependent variable and a group of independent variables. Since the p-value is less than 0.05, the model is considered statistically significant.

The researcher rejected the null hypothesis that the independent variable model and the model without independent variables were identical. The validated alternative (*H1*) hypothesis was corroborated by the association between the independent and dependent variables, as evidenced in Table 11.4.

Table 11.5 indicates if the model fits the data effectively. Again, the p-values (sig) should be greater than 0.05 (Tabachnick & Fidell, 2018). Therefore, we may infer that this model fits the data well.

Table 11.3.   Model Fitting Information for Tourist Satisfaction and Their Revisit Intention.

Model	Model Fitting Criteria	Likelihood Ratio Tests		
	−2 Log Likelihood	Chi-Square	df	Sig.
Intercept Only	1,134.967			
Final	533.083	601.884	400	<0.001

Source: Author's original work.

Table 11.4.   Goodness-of-Fit for Tourist Satisfaction and Their Revisit Intention.

	Chi-Square	df	Sig.
Pearson	849.789	760	0.013
Deviance	528.411	760	1.000

Source: Author's original work.

Table 11.5.   Pseudo R-Square for Tourist Satisfaction and Their Revisit Intention.

Cox and Snell	0.722
Nagelkerke	0.790
McFadden	0.523

Source: Author's original work.

In this example, the level of variation in the dependent variable is determined by using the Cox and Snell R^2 and the Nagelkerke R^2 value. It is described as a pseudo R^2. Table 11.5 shows that the values are 0.722 and 0.790, respectively, implying that this collection of variables in the model explains between 72.2% and 79% of the variability.

The accuracy rate was computed using the methodology described by Bayaga (2010). The proportionate by chance accuracy rate was calculated by multiplying the number of instances in each group by the proportion of cases in each group, then squaring and summing the proportions of cases in each group [$(0.4851)^2$ + $(0.2234)^2$ + $(0.29145)^2$]. However, 46.27% of the proportionate by chance accuracy standards were met (0.3016∗1.25). This necessitates a comparison of accuracy rates. The classification accuracy rate was 73.5% (see Table 11.6), higher than the 46.27% proportionate by chance accuracy threshold, indicating that the model was helpful.

Understanding the concept of the preceding argument and referring to Table 11.7, the independent variable out of 7 'A of Tourism accommodation and the dependent variable – revisit intention have a statistically significant association. Table 11.8 shows the summary of hypothesis in which null hypothesis has been rejected.

Table 11.6. Classification of Cases.

Observed	Predicted			
	Yes	**No**	**May Be**	**Percent Correct**
Yes	183	19	26	80.3
No	31	66	8	62.9
May Be	28	13	96	70.1
Overall Percentage	51.5	20.9	27.7	73.4

Source: Author's original work.

Table 11.7. Likelihood Ratio Tests for Tourist Satisfaction and Their Revisit Intention.

Effect	Model Fitting Criteria	Likelihood Ratio Tests		
	−2 Log Likelihood of Reduced Model	**Chi-Square**	**df**	**Sig.**
Intercept	533.083[a]	0.000	0	.
Attraction	610.608[a]	77.525	64	0.119
Accessibility	578.913[a]	45.830	40	0.243
Amenities	606.994[a]	73.911	64	0.186
Accommodation	997.166[a]	464.083	52	<0.001
Activities	595.400[a]	62.317	56	0.262
Awareness	577.212[a]	44.129	56	0.875
Ancillary Services	585.871[a]	52.788	40	0.085

Source: Author's original work.

The chi-square statistic is the difference in −2 log-likelihoods between the final model and a reduced model. The reduced model is formed by omitting an effect from the final model. The null hypothesis is that all parameters of that effect are 0.

[a]This reduced model is equivalent to the final model because omitting the effect does not increase the degrees of freedom.

Table 11.8. Summary of Hypothesis.

Sr. No.	Hypothesis	Test	P-Value	Result
1	Tourist satisfaction from a visit to Kachchh Rann Utsav does not influence their revisit intention	Multinomial Logistic Regression	0.00	Reject H_0

Source: Author's original Work.

5. Discussion and Conclusion

The current study has considered the 7A's of tourism: attraction, accessibility, amenities, accommodation, activities, awareness, and ancillary service to measure the underlying satisfaction. The relationships between the 7A's of tourism and their revisit intention of tourists to Kachchh Rann Utsav were shown using multinomial logistic regression. Surprisingly, the other six A's of tourism have been found not to affect tourists' revisit intention, although accommodation does.

Additionally, prior research indicates a robust and affirmative correlation between revisit intention and happiness concerning destination (Kuo, 2011). The past study describes that a higher satisfaction level of tourists leads to a stronger revisit intention. According to previous research on visitors who visit natural regions, visitor satisfaction with destination locations can accurately predict future visiting behavior. The current findings support that Mensah (2013), Chin et al. (2018), and Bala Banki et al. (2014) found that the affective destination image plays a moderating role in the association between visitor pleasure and behavior. More precisely, individuals who had a strong positive emotional perception of the destination had more favorable actions toward the resort compared to those who had a weak positive emotional perception of the destination. Hence, the researcher posits that any alteration in the quality of lodging services offered to tourists during Kachchh Rann Utsav will have a substantial effect on the extent and inclination of their intention to revisit Kachchh Rann Utsav. Although all the 7A's are essential to measuring the satisfaction level of tourists, as for the current study, revisit purpose is found dependent on the underlying satisfaction of tourists concerning accommodation provided during Kachchh Rann Utsav. As Kachchh represents culture, Hense offers various accommodation facilities, from basic guest houses or hotels to a wide range of tents available in Tent City and Bhunga at various resorts or villages. Tentcity and Bhunga offer a cultural experience to attract tourists to Kachchh Rann Utsav. Traditional homes known as bhungas are only found in the Gujarati Kutch area. The houses have thatched roofs and circular walls. They are renowned for being climate-sensitive and having structural resilience during earthquakes. Additionally, it defends against cyclonic winds and sandstorms.

Numerous recreational activities should be developed to build visitor loyalty and encourage return visits to the Kachchh. Due to its extensive coastline, numerous beaches and sea sports should be created in Kachchh. Scuba diving, underwater aquariums, boats, jet skiing, and parasailing have a lot of development potential, as most tourists like to visit Kachchh Rann Utsav due to the satisfaction of accommodation facilities. So it can be suggested that more work be done on the other six A's of tourism to attract more tourists.

The study suggested appropriate measures for the sustainable development of Kachchh Rann Utsav to overcome the challenges and problems tourists face in the Kachchh district. The present study has supported outlining the critical facets of Kachchh Rann Utsav in the Kachchh district.

References

Abbasi, A., Ghanooni, F., & Celardo, L. (2023). Tourist destination loyalty: A case study of Rome. *Rivista Italiana di Economia Demografia e Statistica*, *77*(4), 37–48.

Adinegara, G. N. J. (2019). Perception of tourism satisfaction: A study at Blimbingsari tourism village in Bali. *Sriwijaya International Journal of Dynamic Economics and Business*, *3*(2), 157–170.

Alegre, J., & Cladera, M. (2006). Repeat visitation in mature sun and sand holiday destinations. *Journal of Travel Research*, *44*(3), 288–297.

Asmelash, A. G., & Kumar, S. (2019). The structural relationship between tourist satisfaction and sustainable heritage tourism development in Tigrai, Ethiopia. *Heliyon*, *5*(3). https://doi.org/10.1016/j.heliyon.2019.e01335

Bala Banki, M., Nizam Ismail, H., Dalil, M., & Kawu, A. (2014). Moderating role of affective destination image on the relationship between tourists satisfaction and behavioural intention: Evidence from Obudu Mountain Resort. *Journal of Environment and Earth Science*, *4*(4). www.iiste.org

Bayaga, A. (2010). Multinomial logistic regression: Usage and application in risk analysis. *Journal of Applied Quantitative Methods*, *5*(2), 288–297.

Bhat, M. A., & Qadir, N. (2013). Tourist satisfaction in Kashmir: An empirical assessment. *Journal of Business Theory and Practice*, *1*(1), 152–166.

Chaudhary, M. (2000). India's image as a tourist destination – A perspective of foreign tourists. *Tourism Management*, *21*(3), 293–297. https://doi.org/10.1016/S0261-5177(99)00053-9

Chen, J. S., & Gursoy, D. (n.d.). *An investigation of tourists' destination loyalty and preferences*. http://www.emerald-library.com/ft

Chi, C. G. Q., & Qu, H. (2008). Examining the structural relationships of destination image, tourist satisfaction and destination loyalty: An integrated approach. *Tourism Management*, *29*(4), 624–636.

Chin, C. H., Law, F. Y., Lo, M. C., & Ramayah, T. (2018). The impact of accessibility quality and accommodation quality on tourists' satisfaction and revisit intention to rural tourism destination in Sarawak: The moderating role of local communities' attitude. *Global Business and Management Research: An International Journal*, *10*(2), 115–127. https://www.researchgate.net/publication/328899252

Foroudi, P., Akarsu, T. N., Ageeva, E., Foroudi, M. M., Dennis, C., & Melewar, T. C. (2018). Promising the dream: Changing destination image of London through the effect of website place. *Journal of Business Research*, *83*, 97–110.

Hendriyani, I. G. A. D., Budiarsa, M., Antara, M., & Sudiarta, N. (2020). The loyalty model of foreign tourists consuming traditional Balinese food. *Global Business & Finance Review (GBFR)*, *25*(3), 34–48.

Hung, W. L., Lee, Y. J., & Huang, P. H. (2016). Creative experiences, memorability and revisit intention in creative tourism. *Current Issues in Tourism*, *19*(8), 763–770. https://doi.org/10.1080/13683500.2013.877422

Kalaiya, A. B., & Kumar, A. (2015). Tourism as a development tool: A study on role of tourism in economic development, employment generation and poverty reduction: Special focus on Kachchh. *International Journal of Advance Research in Computer Science and Management Studies*, *3*(7), 189–197.

Katoch, A. (2016). *The impacts of rural tourism on local community development: A study of Himachal Pradesh, India*. Central University of Himachal Pradesh.

Kim, K., Uysal, M., & Sirgy, M. J. (2013). How does tourism in a community impact the quality of life of community residents? *Tourism Management*, *36*, 527–540. https://doi.org/10.1016/j.tourman.2012.09.005

Korstanje, M. E. (2024). How has travel behavior changed after the new normal. In S. W. Maingi, V. G. Gowreesunkar, & M. E. Korstanje (Eds.), *Tourist behaviour and the new normal* (Vol. I). Palgrave Macmillan. https://doi.org/10.1007/978-3-031-45848-4_2

Kozak, M. (2001). Repeaters' behavior at two distinct destinations. *Annals of Tourism Research, 28*(3). www.elsevier.com/locate/atoures

Kozak, M., & Rimmington, M. (2016). Tourist satisfaction with Mallorca, Spain, as an off-season holiday destination. *Journal of Travel Research, 38*(3), 260–269. https://doi.org/10.1177/004728750003800308

Kuo, C. T. (2011). Tourist satisfaction and intention to revisit Sun moon lake. *Journal of International Management Studies, 6*(1), 32–37.

Liao, Y. K., Wu, W. Y., Truong, G. N. T., Binh, P. N. M., & Van Vu, V. (2021). A model of destination consumption, attitude, religious involvement, satisfaction, and revisit intention. *Journal of Vacation Marketing, 27*(3), 330–345.

Liu, X. R., Li, J. J., & Fu, Y. D. (2016). Antecedents of tourists' behavioral intentions: The role and influence of tourists' perceived freedom of choice, destination image, and satisfaction. *Tourism Analysis, 21*(6), 577–588.

Madhani, A. (2018). *Changing scenario of tourism in Saurashtra Region: A economic analysis.* Saurastra University.

Manaktola, K., & Jauhari, V. (2007). Exploring consumer attitude and behaviour towards green practices in the lodging industry in India. *International Journal of Contemporary Hospitality Management, 19*(5), 364–377. https://doi.org/10.1108/09596110710757534

Meng, F., Tepanon, Y., & Uysal, M. (2008). Measuring tourist satisfaction by attribute and motivation: The case of a nature-based resort. *Journal of vacation marketing, 14*(1), 41–56.

Mensah, C. (2013). Residents' satisfaction and behavioural intention with Asogli Yam Festival in Ghana. *International Journal of Asian Social Science, 3*(3). http://www.aessweb.com/journal-detail.php?id=5007

Mistry, R. B. (2018). Influence of destination attributes importance to tourists' satisfaction – Gujarat tourism. *Amity Journal of Management Research, 3*(1), 14–26.

Petrick, J. F. (2002). An examination of golf vacationers' novelty. *Annals of Tourism Research, 29*(2), 384–400.

Putri, M. (2017). Tourist satisfaction at cultural destination. *International Journal of Tourism & Hospitality Reviews, 4*(1), 35–43.

Quintal, V. A., & Polczynski, A. (2010). Factors influencing tourists' revisit intentions. *Asia Pacific Journal of Marketing and Logistics, 22*(4), 554–578. https://doi.org/10.1108/13555851011090565

Rami, A. (2015). A study of tourist satisfaction in Ahmedabad city within SERVQUAL dimension. *Kaav International Journal of Economics, Commerce and Business Management, 2*(2), 94–104.

Seetanah, B., Teeroovengadum, V., & Nunkoo, R. (2020). Destination satisfaction and revisit intention of tourists: Does the quality of airport services matter? *Journal of Hospitality & Tourism Research, 44*(1), 134–148.

Stylos, N., Bellou, V., Andronikidis, A., & Vassiliadis, C. A. (2017). Linking the dots among destination images, place attachment, and revisit intentions: A study among British and Russian tourists. *Tourism Management, 60*, 15–19. https://doi.org/10.1016/j.tourman.2016.11.006

Tabachnick, B. G., & Fidell, L. S. (2018). *Using multivariate statistics* (7th ed.). Pearson.

Thaker, M. (2004). *Problems and prospects of tourism industry in Gujarat.* Saurashtra University.

Um, S., Chon, K., & Ro, Y. H. (2006). Antecedents of revisit intention. *Annals of Tourism Research, 33*(4), 1141–1158. https://doi.org/10.1016/j.annals.2006.06.003

Ungasan, D. (2020). Atribut destinasi pariwisata dan kualitas pelayanan mempengaruhi niat wisatawan berkunjung kembali di pantai melasti. *Jumpa: Jurnal Master Pariwisata, 6*(2), 425–451.

Veasna, S., Wu, W. Y., & Huang, C. H. (2013). The impact of destination source credibility on destination satisfaction: The mediating effects of destination attachment and destination image. *Tourism Management, 36*, 511–526.

Warbung, C. J. E., Tulung, J. E., & Saerang, R. T. (2021). Analysis of tourist satisfaction based on 5A's of tourism elements towards tourist revisit intention to Tomohon city [analisa kepuasan turis berdasarkan element pariwisata 5A terhadap minat kunjungan kembali di kota tomohon]. *Jurnal EMBA, 9*(2). https://doi.org/10.35794/emba.v9i2.33336

Chapter 12

Community-based Tourism in Bangladesh: A Strategic Approach

Mohammad Badruddoza Talukder[a], Kamarun Muhsina[b], Tanjila Afroz Mou[b] and Sanjeev Kumar[c]

[a]*College of Tourism and Hospitality Management, International University of Business Agriculture and Technology, Dhaka, Bangladesh*
[b]*Department of Tourism and Hospitality Management, Daffodil Institute of IT, Dhaka, Bangladesh*
[c]*School of Hotel Management and Tourism, Lovely Professional University, Phagwara, India*

Abstract

Purpose: This chapter provides a thorough explanation of the growth of community-based tourism in Bangladesh, encompassing its historical background, challenges faced, and potential strategies for future advancement.

Methodology: We employed a descriptive analysis based on the literature review of the development and expansion of community-based tourism in Bangladesh. This study looks at the development of community-based tourism (CBT) throughout history, as well as the innovative contributions made by Non-Governmental Organizations (NGOs) and local groups in CBT initiatives, government policies, international recognition, challenges encountered (such as environmental and economic concerns), and potential strategies for future expansion.

Findings: The chapter suggests various methods for future growth, including developing policies, involvement of the private sector, execution of marketing strategies, and empowerment of the community through training and enhancing their abilities.

Corporate Social Responsibility, Corporate Governance and Business Ethics in Tourism Management: A Business Strategy for Sustainable Organizational Performance, 159–175
Copyright © 2025 by Mohammad Badruddoza Talukder, Kamarun Muhsina, Tanjila Afroz Mou and Sanjeev Kumar
Published under exclusive licence by Emerald Publishing Limited
doi:10.1108/978-1-83608-704-520241012

Value: The study provides insightful information regarding the distinctive characteristics of community-based tourism in Bangladesh, drawing attention to the country's long-standing tradition of extended hospitality and cultural heritage. Moreover, the study analyzes the difficulties and opportunities that CBT efforts encounter in the region and the proposition of individualized solutions for sustainable growth.

Implications: This study not only improves the quality of experiences that tourists have, but it also gives a voice to underrepresented groups by prioritizing local communities. In addition, it instills a sense of ownership and pride in the community's residents, motivating them to make a long-term commitment to preserving the legacy of developing CBT in Bangladesh.

Keywords: Community-based tourism; potential strategies; economic challenges; marketing strategies; Bangladesh

Introduction

Bangladesh's community-based tourism (CBT) has emerged as a powerful mechanism for sustainable development. It capitalizes on the country's abundant cultural and natural heritage while empowering its communities. The desire of communities to utilize tourism as a means of economic upliftment while simultaneously preserving their cultural identity and environment has been the driving force behind the flourishing of CBT projects (Kwangseh, 2014). These projects have their origins in grassroots initiatives and traditional hospitality practices. CBT was established by early pioneers, who were frequently supported by non-governmental organizations (NGOs) and local organizations. This demonstrates that CBT has the potential to have a positive impact on both communities and visitors. The growth of cognitive behavioral therapy has been facilitated over time by policies and support mechanisms implemented by the government, which has led to its expansion and recognition on both the domestic and international levels. Currently, CBT in Bangladesh is undergoing continuous development, with the primary objectives being the enhancement of community participation, the adoption of technological innovations, the diversification of tourism experiences, and the promotion of collaboration with educational institutions to promote economic growth and cultural exchange (Talukder, Kumar, & Das, 2024a, 2024b Talukder, Kabir, Kaiser, et al., 2024.

Literature Review

Historical Development of Community-based Tourism in Bangladesh

The origins of CBT in Bangladesh can be traced back to indigenous communities' traditional hospitality practices and grassroots initiatives (Hoque, 2020). Initially, according to Ahmed (2007), CBT was shaped by the profound hospitality deeply rooted in Bangladeshi culture, where extending warm and welcoming receptions to visitors is customary. Local communities frequently initiated initial CBT projects in search of sustainable tourism opportunities to capitalize on their natural and cultural resources (Shahmirzadi, 2012). These initiatives aimed to sustain the local populace economically while safeguarding their cultural legacy and natural surroundings. NGOs and local organizations that assisted communities interested in participating in CBT initiatives with training, capacity building, and support were indispensable during this time (Talukder, 2021). The concept of CBT began to gain significant traction and international and domestic recognition as these initiatives accumulated momentum. It exhibited favorable results concerning tourism sustainability and community development (Jørgensen & Thoning, 2017). Governmental policies and support mechanisms, such as funding initiatives, regulatory frameworks, and training programs, were progressively implemented to facilitate the expansion of CBT. International acclaim and awards were bestowed upon the innovative strategies Bangladeshi communities involved in CBT employed to advance sustainable tourism development (Talukder, Kabir, Kaiser, et al., 2024; Talukder, Kumar, & Das, 2024a, 2024b). This recognition enhanced the standing of CBT programs in Bangladesh and inspired additional communities to engage actively.

As time has passed, cognitive-behavioral therapy has increasingly shifted its focus toward fostering community empowerment and participation (Ahsani et al., 2022). This has increased residents' prominence in decision-making processes and benefit-sharing arrangements (Kumar, Talukder, Kabir, et al., 2024; Kumar, Talukder, & Pego, 2024). Recent developments in CBT encompass incorporating technological innovations to enrich visitors' experiences, expanding tourism offerings to accommodate diverse interests and preferences, and partnerships with academic institutions to foster learning and exchanging knowledge (Jung, 2022).

The historical progression of CBT in Bangladesh embodies a line characterized by indigenous ingenuity, conventional notions of hospitality, NGO assistance, an official endorsement from the government, global acclaim, and continuous endeavors to augment community engagement and empowerment in sustainable tourism advancement.

Challenges and Opportunities

The origins of CBT in Bangladesh can be traced back to indigenous communities' traditional hospitality practices and grassroots initiatives. Initially, CBT was shaped by the profound hospitality deeply rooted in Bangladeshi culture, where extending warm and welcoming receptions to visitors is customary (Das et al., 2024). Local communities frequently initiated initial CBT projects in search of sustainable tourism opportunities to capitalize on their natural and cultural resources (Shahmirzadi, 2012). These initiatives aimed to sustain the local populace economically while safeguarding their cultural legacy and natural surroundings. NGOs and local organizations that assisted communities interested in participating in CBT initiatives with training, capacity building, and support were indispensable during this time (Talukder et al., 2022). The concept of CBT began to gain significant traction and international and domestic recognition as these initiatives accumulated momentum. It exhibited favorable results concerning tourism sustainability and community development. According to AlAbabneh (2019), to facilitate the expansion of CBT, governmental policies and support mechanisms, such as funding initiatives, regulatory frameworks, and training programs, were progressively implemented (Dodds et al., 2018).

International acclaim and awards were bestowed upon the innovative strategies employed by Bangladeshi communities involved in CBT to advance sustainable tourism development. This recognition enhanced the standing of cognitive-behavioral therapy (CBT) programs in Bangladesh and inspired additional communities to engage actively.

As time has passed, cognitive-behavioral therapy (CBT) has increasingly shifted its focus toward fostering community empowerment and participation (Ahsani et al., 2022). This has increased residents' prominence in decision-making processes and benefit-sharing arrangements. The study done by Burbano and Meredith (2021) highlighted recent developments in CBT encompass incorporating technological innovations to enrich visitors' experiences, expanding tourism offerings to accommodate diverse interests and preferences, and partnerships with academic institutions to foster learning and knowledge exchange within communities (Talukder et al., 2022).

The historical progression of CBT in Bangladesh embodies a path characterized by indigenous ingenuity, conventional notions of hospitality, NGO assistance, an official endorsement from the government, global acclaim, and continuous endeavors to augment community engagement and empowerment in sustainable tourism advancement. The challenges are shown in Fig. 12.1.

Environmental Concerns

Bangladesh's CBT is susceptible to environmental issues from infrastructure development in ecologically sensitive areas and heightened visitor traffic. Destruction of habitats, pollution, waste management issues, and disturbance of wildlife populations are among these concerns. These challenges are compounded by the exponential growth of urbanization and industry, which strains natural resources and ecosystems. Incorporating sustainable practices into tourism operations, educating visitors and local communities about conservation issues, and

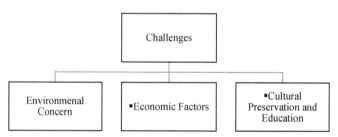

Fig. 12.1.   Challenges of Developing Community-based Tourism. *Source*: Authors compiled based on Cernat and Gourdon (2012).

implementing efficient management strategies to mitigate adverse environmental effects are all essential components of a comprehensive approach to addressing environmental concerns (Sonter et al., 2018).

Bangladesh's many ecosystems, like its mangrove forests, wetlands, and wildlife reserves, protect biodiversity and provide ecosystem services (Islam et al., 2023). Promoting ecotourism while protecting these ecosystems is essential to ensure they will be around long (Sonter et al., 2018). To do this, steps need to be taken to control the activities of tourists. For example, tourist sites need to be given carrying capacities, protected areas need to be named, and rules must be enforced to stop habitat destruction and wildlife disturbance. Ecotourism practices that help conservation goals and give communities economic benefits are made possible by projects that bring together government agencies, local communities, NGOs, and tourism operators (Salkin & Lavine, 2008).

Bangladeshi communities that depend on natural resources and farming for a living are facing big problems because of climate change. Coastal communities and farming methods are in danger because the sea level is rising, extreme weather events are happening more often, and the way rain falls is changing (Sumarmi & Aliman, 2020). These effects can make it harder for people to go on vacation, make resources less available, and worsen socioeconomic problems (Craig & Douglas, 2006). Adaptation strategies, like finding other ways to make money, encouraging farming methods resistant to climate change, and spending money on infrastructure to stop coastal flooding and erosion, are essential for making communities that depend on tourism more resilient (Sumarmi & Aliman, 2020).

Sustainable resource management is essential to protect the environment and help community-based tourism projects in Bangladesh last for a long time (Jaafar et al., 2015). Conservation, sustainable development, and community involvement must be a part of tourism planning and operations for sustainable resource management strategies (Hoque, 2020). This includes encouraging responsible tourism practices like recycling and reducing waste, using as little energy as possible, and helping with conservation efforts in the area (Mohammad et al., 2023, 2024b). Using programs that build people's skills, training for ecotourism, and ways to share profits can help local communities take care of their natural resources, making them feel like they own them and encouraging conservation efforts (Talukder, 2024). For adaptive management and making intelligent decisions, it is also essential to regularly monitor and evaluate how tourism affects natural ecosystems (Khalid et al., 2019).

Economic Factors

The long-term success and sustainability of community tourism development depend on economic factors, including many things that affect the industry's ability to make money and grow and positively affect the economy (Muhsina, 2021, 2023). Some of these factors are tourism-related activities that bring in money, like lodging and guided tours, which help reduce poverty and give communities more economic power (Tubey et al., 2019). Tourism spending also affects local industries like transport and retail, which helps the economy grow and opens up new business

Fig. 12.2.   Economic Factors of CBT. *Source*: Authors compiled based on Jørgensen and Thoning (2017).

opportunities. Effective revenue distribution mechanisms ensure that everyone in the community gets an equal share of the money made from tourism. This helps bring people together and lowers income inequality. Capacity building and skills development programs give people the skills they need to work in tourism-related businesses, which makes them more employable and increases their ability to make money (Sarker, 2014). To get the most favorable economic effects from community tourism while minimizing any adverse effects, it is also essential to consider market diversification, outside economic influences, and sustainability measures (Jørgensen & Thoning, 2017). See Fig. 12.2.

Financial Models for CBT Stability

For Bangladesh's CBT projects to be stable and last long, they must develop long-term financial models. Traditional funding sources, like grants and donations, might not always work or be enough to keep CBT projects going in the long term (Talukder et al., 2023a, 2023b). So, looking into new financial models that can generate steady money streams is essential. Several strategies could be used to achieve this, such as community-based enterprises and businesses related to tourism that are run and benefited by the local community (Block, 2018). Examples of these are homestays, tour guides, and handicraft sales. Additionally, communities can get money from tourism through revenue-sharing agreements with tour operators or government agencies. Adding user fees or entrance fees for people to visit cultural or natural attractions can also help pay for CBT programs while limiting the number of visitors to protect the environment (Walker & McCarthy, 2010).

Employment Opportunities and Local Economic Growth

Bangladesh could use community-based tourism to create jobs and boost the local economy. This is especially true in rural and underprivileged areas where job opportunities may be limited. Local people can help with CBT programs by working as guides, cooks, artisans, and service providers. This can create direct and indirect jobs, raising household incomes and lowering poverty rates. Also, tourist spending can help other businesses grow, such as transportation services, food vendors, and souvenir shops, called the "multiplier effect." This makes the local economy even more substantial. For the social and economic benefits of tourism development to be fully realized, programs that train and build people's skills and abilities to make them more employable are necessary (Talukder, 2020a, 2020b). Connecting CBT businesses and nearby supply chains can help small companies grow and strengthen communities' economies.

Exploring Alternate Revenue Streams

Along with traditional tourism-related activities, looking for other ways to make money can help community-based tourism projects in Bangladesh stay financially stable (Dodds et al., 2018). To do this, tourism products might need to be expanded to include unique experiences like agrotourism, culinary tours, and cultural immersion programs that are designed to meet the needs of specific groups of people. To make more money, communities can partner with local farmers, crafters, and business owners to promote agricultural products, traditional arts and crafts, and cooperatives (Talukder et al., 2021). Using digital platforms for marketing and e-commerce can also help CBT products and services reach more people in the United States and other countries, leading to more sales. Working with educational institutions to offer study tours, research opportunities, and hands-on learning programs can also help people learn about each other's cultures and make extra money. CBT projects can make them more financially stable by using a variety of income streams (Lusby & Eow, 2015). This will also help the long-term growth of tourism in Bangladesh.

A Conceptual Model for CBT Development

The model shown below in Fig. 12.3 was developed to show how community factors ensure the development of CBT.

Policy Development and Governmental Role

A big part of how CBT works is how policies are made and what the government does. Governments are significant for making an environment that is good for business by making and enforcing policies and rules that help (Talukder & Kumar, 2023; Zielinski et al., 2021). For example, this could mean making rules for eco-friendly tourism, giving money or grants to CBT projects, and ensuring that natural and cultural resources are safe. Governments can also help different groups form partnerships, like local communities, NGOs, and the private sector.

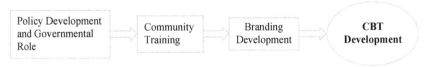

Fig. 12.3.   Community-based Tourism Development. *Source*: Authors developed based on Lusby and Eow (2015).

This will encourage everyone to work together and coordinate efforts to develop tourism. As governments get more involved in making policies, they can help CBT grow and be successful while protecting the environment and the interests of local communities (Minhus & Huie, 2021).

Designing Inclusive Tourism Policies

To ensure that everyone in society, including vulnerable and marginalized groups, gets an equal share of the benefits of tourism, we need inclusive policies. Governments can make policies that encourage social inclusion by giving underrepresented groups chances to participate in tourism activities and benefit from job and business opportunities related to tourism. This could mean implementing affirmative action programs, helping marginalized groups get training and skills-building opportunities, and encouraging the growth of community-owned tourism businesses. Governments can help reduce social gaps, boost community unity, and support long-term growth by making inclusive tourism policies a top priority (Diekmann et al., 2018).

Incentives for Private Sector Involvement

To encourage investment, new ideas, and business in the tourism sector, it is important to offer incentives for the private sector to get involved. There are many ways for governments to get the private sector engaged in CBT projects. These include tax breaks, grants, subsidies, and better ways to get money (Rahaman et al., 2020). Providing regulatory support and streamlining bureaucratic processes can also make it easier for people in the private sector who want to invest in CBT. By incentivizing the private sector to get involved, governments can use the private sector's resources and knowledge to improve the quality of tourism goods and services, create jobs, and help the economy grow.

Community Empowerment and Training

Giving people in the community the tools and training they need is essential for getting them involved and feeling like they own tourism development projects. Governments can help empower communities by giving people the training and resources they need for tourism-related activities through programs that build people's skills and knowledge. This could mean setting up workshops on customer service, hospitality, business, and environmentally friendly tourism and giving people access to financial and technical help. Making it easier for communities to make decisions and setting up ways for people to share profits and benefits can also give communities the power to manage tourism development well and benefit from it (Ibrahim & Falola, 2021). By giving communities the necessary tools, training, and support, governments can ensure that tourism projects are inclusive, long-lasting, and aligned with local needs and goals.

Capacity-building workshops for locals are essential for giving people in the community the information, skills, and tools they need to do well in tourism-related activities. Governments can hold workshops to build people's skills in various areas of community-based tourism, such as customer service, hospitality, preserving culture, environmentally friendly tourism practices, and running a business. These workshops can be put on with the help of local groups, NGOs, schools, or experts in the field. They can be customized to fit the needs and interests of the people attending (Hoque, 2020). By giving locals workshops on building their skills, governments can provide communities with the tools they need to play an active role in tourism development, improve the quality of tourist experiences, and create jobs for locals.

Leadership development in communities is essential for ensuring local leaders can run and manage tourism projects well. Governments can help develop leaders by giving community leaders involved in tourism development training, mentoring, and chances to meet other leaders in the field (Jung, 2022). This could mean setting up leadership workshops, seminars, and conferences covering community involvement, handling conflicts, making decisions, and managing projects (Loulanski & Loulanski, 2011). Creating partnerships between community leaders, government agencies, and other interested parties can also help people share information and support the best methods for managing community-based tourism (Sotiriadis & Shen, 2017).

Marketing and Branding Strategies

For community-based tourism destinations to get more visitors, they must have strong marketing and branding plans. The governments of CBT destinations can create branding and marketing campaigns that highlight those places' unique cultural, natural, and heritage attractions (Rahaman et al., 2020). This could mean promoting real experiences, cultural festivals, and traditional food through several marketing channels, such as websites, social media, travel blogs, and tourism fairs (Cuomo et al., 2021). Working with tour operators, travel influencers, and media outlets can also help CBT destinations get more attention and reach more people (Kerdpitak, 2022). Governments can make CBT destinations stand out as appealing and competitive tourist spots by putting money into marketing and branding plans (Lenzerini, 2011). This will increase demand for visitors and help local economies.

Digital marketing and a social media presence are becoming increasingly crucial for connecting with and reaching modern travelers (Crespi & Taibi, 2020). Governments can use digital marketing tools and social media sites to promote community-based tourist spots, share real experiences, and talk to people who might want to visit (Lenzerini, 2011). This could mean making interesting content like blogs, videos, and photos showing the unique attractions and cultural heritage of CBT destinations (Simpson, 2008). Keeping up with social media and joining online communities can also help you connect with travelers and influential people, create buzz, and get more people to visit CBT websites and booking platforms. Governments can use digital marketing and social media to make CBT destinations more visible and competitive in the global tourism market (Kar et al., 2022).

To make Bangladesh stand out as a special place for CBT, it is essential to show off its rich cultural history, beautiful natural scenery, and authentic experiences (Hall, 2023). Governments can develop branding plans that make Bangladesh stand out as a unique CBT destination, giving tourists immersive and meaningful experiences (Shaikh et al., 2020). This could mean promoting less well-known places to visit, showing off local crafts and traditions, and stressing how friendly and welcoming Bangladeshi communities are (Khandaka & Muzahid, 2015). Another way to help Bangladesh's CBT sector build a strong brand identity is to work with tourism stakeholders like local communities, tour operators, and cultural groups (Plzáková, 2015). By marketing Bangladesh as a one-of-a-kind CBT destination, governments can bring in discerning tourists looking for authentic cultural experiences and help the country's tourism industry grow in a way that lasts (Fu & Luo, 2023).

Case Studies and Comparative Analysis

Success Stories in Bangladesh

Many examples of CBT businesses have done well in Bangladesh. These businesses use the country's natural and cultural resources to make money (Akagawa, 2014). For instance, the tea garden communities in the Sylhet region have set up homestay programs that let tourists fully experience traditional ways of growing tea, cultural performances, and local food (Xue & Kerstetter, 2018). The communities that live in the Sundarbans mangrove forests have also started ecotourism programs (Bala et al., 2023). These include guided tours, boat cruises, and nature walks that show off the area's biodiversity and bring in money for those who live there. These success stories show how CBT can help communities in Bangladesh get ahead financially, protect their cultural heritage, and promote environmental protection (Aas et al., 2005).

Analysis of Thriving CBT Projects

Community-led tourism projects doing well in Bangladesh show that they can help reach sustainable development goals (Cardona et al., 2017). Looking at these projects more closely, they were successful because they involved and engaged the community well, worked well with other parties, used sustainable resource management methods, and devised new ways to market themselves (Hlengwa & Maruta, 2020). Also, capacity building is often a big part of successful CBT projects (Artal-Tur et al., 2020). These give locals the skills and knowledge they need to run tourism businesses responsibly. By providing people in the community a sense of ownership and pride, these projects help tourism initiatives last longer while also helping local economies and ecosystems the most.

International Benchmarks

International standards for CBT are used to judge the success, usefulness, and long-term viability of CBT projects worldwide (Lavarack & Ryan, 2015). These standards cover many areas, such as community involvement and empowerment, practices for protecting the environment, sharing economic benefits, efforts to keep cultures alive, and overall visitor satisfaction (Kwangseh, 2014). By comparing CBT projects in Bangladesh to international standards, stakeholders can find areas where the projects are doing well and could be better. This will improve the country's quality and effectiveness of CBT programs (Lak et al., 2020).

CBT Models from Other Countries

Several countries have created successful community-based tourism models that Bangladesh can use as examples and learn from. Ecotourism models in places like Costa Rica emphasize protecting the environment and involving people in the community (Kichurchak, 2020). On the other hand, Nepal has set up homestay programs that give tourists real cultural experiences. In the same way, Thailand and Vietnam have built community tourism into their national tourism strategies (Dodds et al., 2018). These countries use their natural and cultural attractions to promote long-term tourism growth. Bangladesh can improve its own CBT sector and get the most out of its social, economic, and environmental benefits by looking at and adopting successful CBT models from other countries (Hull & Sassenberg, 2012).

Adaptability of International Practices in Bangladesh

Many things affect how well international practices work in Bangladesh. These include cultural, social, economic, and environmental factors. Some parts of international CBT models might immediately work in Bangladesh (Cuomo et al., 2021). However, other parts might need to be changed or tailored to fit the country's needs and priorities (Agrawal & Gibson, 1999). When applying international best practices to Bangladesh, we need to consider things like the community's readiness and ability, the government's support and policies, the availability of infrastructure, the market's demand, and the long-term health of the environment (King, 2003). Bangladesh can make its CBT programs more effective and successful by carefully examining whether international practices are appropriate and doable and then adapting them to meet Bangladesh's needs and circumstances (Richards, 2007).

Collaborative Initiatives with International Communities

In community-based tourism, working together on projects with communities from other countries is a great way to share knowledge, build skills, and learn from each other (Kirshenblatt-Gimblett, 2004). Bangladesh can strengthen its CBT sector by working with international organizations, NGOs, universities, and other groups (Horaira & Devi, 2021). This way, it can get advice, resources, and the best ways to do things worldwide. Joint research projects, training programs, technical help, and cross-cultural exchange programs can all be part of collaborative initiatives (Mohammad et al., 2024a). The goal is to improve local communities and tourism professionals' skills and abilities (Chatkaewnapanon & Lee, 2022). Partnering with other countries can also help connect markets, encourage cross-border tourism routes, and raise awareness of Bangladesh as a global CBT destination. Working with people from other countries can improve

Bangladesh's CBT sector and help the country reach its long-term development goals (Annisa & Tabassum, 2023).

Upcoming CBT Projects and Expectations

Communities can use their cultural and natural assets for tourism development through upcoming CBT projects. These projects will also help communities deal with current and future problems. Homestay programs, ecotourism programs, cultural festivals, and heritage trails may be set up as part of these projects. People usually look forward to upcoming CBT projects because they think they will benefit the economy, cultural heritage, the environment, and community health (Mtapuri et al., 2022). Local communities, governments, NGOs, and private sector partners are all involved in these projects. They all want to make meaningful tourism experiences, have an impact, and help the region's economic growth while honoring and celebrating its natural and cultural heritage (Artal-Tur et al., 2020).

Fostering Next-Generation CBT Leaders

Training the next generation of CBT leaders is essential to ensure that community-based tourism projects last long. This means putting money into the growth of young professionals, business owners, and community members who will lead the CBT sector in innovation, management, and leadership (Witchayakawin & Tengkuan, 2018). To help the next generation of CBT leaders grow, there may be mentorship programs, training workshops, internships, and learning opportunities focusing on eco-friendly tourism, community involvement, and starting your own business. Communities can ensure their tourism programs are ongoing, creative, and flexible by giving the next generation of CBT leaders the necessary tools (de Beer & Elliffe, 1997). This will also help people feel like they own and are proud of their heritage and culture.

Conclusion

In conclusion, CBT in Bangladesh has a bright future ahead of it as long as people involved keep coming up with new ideas, working together, and investing in projects that promote sustainable development. By working on projects that look to the future, new CBT programs can use creative methods and technology, giving people more power to make meaningful tourism experiences that are meaningful and have an impact. Many people hope these projects will help the economy, protect cultural heritage, protect the environment, and improve the community's health. Bangladesh can also ensure its CBT sector stays solid and alive by mentoring, training, and providing educational opportunities for the next generation of CBT leaders. As Bangladesh moves forward, it will be essential to use international standards, teamwork, and new methods to help community-based tourism reach its full potential and make the tourism industry more sustainable and open to everyone.

Along with these efforts, the future of community-based tourism in Bangladesh depends on how well it can adapt to international standards and build partnerships with communities worldwide. Working with international groups and studying successful CBT models from other countries can help Bangladesh improve its own CBT sector by giving it access to helpful information, resources, and the best ways to do things. Bangladesh can also enhance visitor experiences, become more competitive in the market, and attract a wide range of tourists by using new technologies and approaches in its tourism offerings. Bangladesh can become a top spot for sustainable and authentic community-based tourism by adopting these forward-thinking strategies and investing in training the next generation of CBT leaders. This will help the country's efforts to improve its economy and keep its culture alive.

References

Aas, C., Ladkin, A., & Fletcher, J. (2005). Stakeholder collaboration and heritage management. *Annals of Tourism Research, 32*(1), 28–48. https://doi.org/10.1016/j.annals.2004.04.005

Agrawal, A., & Gibson, C. C. (1999). Enchantment and disenchantment: The role of community in natural resource conservation. *World Development, 27*(4), 629–649. https://doi.org/10.1016/S0305-750X(98)00161-2

Ahmed, I. (2007). *The heritage of Shankharibazar: Peoples participation in the conservation process to promote cultural tourism. BRAC University Journal IV*(2), 7–16. https://doi.org/10.4157/geogrevjapanb.94.65

Ahsani, R. D. P., Wulandari, C., Dinata, C., Azmi, N. A., & Fathani, A. T. (2022). The challenges and opportunities for developing community-based tourism in Indonesia. *Journal of Governance: Jurnal Ilmu Pemerintahan Universitas Sultan Ageng Tirtayasa, 7*(4), 864–876. https://doi.org/10.31506/jog.v7i4.16232

Akagawa, N. (2014). *Heritage conservation and Japan's cultural diplomacy: Heritage.* National Identity and National Interest. Routledge. https://doi.org/10.4324/9781315886664

Al-Ababneh, M. M. (2019). Creative cultural tourism as a new model for cultural tourism. *Journal of Tourism Management Research, 6*(2), 109–118. https://doi.org/10.18488/journal.31.2019.62.109.118

Annisa, N. N., & Tabassum, N. (2023). Challenges of multiculturalism: Integration of religion in state policy. *Religion and Policy Journal, 1*(1), https://doi.org/10.15575/rpj.v1i1.433

Artal-Tur, A., Villena-Navarro, M., & Alamá-Sabater, L. (2020). The relationship between cultural tourist behaviour and destination sustainability. In A. Artal-Tur, M. Villena-Navarro, & L. Alamá-Sabater (Eds.), *Culture and cultures in tourism* (pp. 71–85). Routledge. https://doi.org/10.4324/9780429054891-8

Bala, B., Ibragimov, A., Shamsuddoha, M., & Abdursaupov, R. (2023). Modeling of mangrove forests and ecotourism of the Sundarbans in Bangladesh. *Journal of Coastal Conservation, 27*(6), 68. https://doi.org/10.1007/s11852-023-00993-5

Burbano, D. V., & Meredith, T. C. (2021). Effects of tourism growth in a UNESCO World Heritage Site: Resource-based livelihood diversification in the Galapagos Islands, Ecuador. *Journal of Sustainable Tourism, 29*(8), 1270–1289. https://doi.org/10.1080/09669582.2020.1832101

Cardona, A. R., Sun, Q., Li, F., & White, D. (2017). Assessing the effect of personal cultural orientation on brand equity and revisit intention: Exploring destination branding in Latin America. *Journal of Global Marketing, 30*(5), 282–296. https://doi.org/10.1080/08911762.2017.1336827

Cernat, L., & Gourdon, J. (2012). Paths to success: Benchmarking cross-country sustainable tourism. *Tourism Management, Elsevier, 33*(5), 1044–1056.

Chatkaewnapanon, Y., & Lee, T. J. (2022). Planning sustainable community-based tourism in the context of Thailand: Community, development, and the foresight tools. *Sustainability, 14*(12), 7413. https://doi.org/10.3390/su14127413

Craig, C. S., & Douglas, S. P. (2006). Beyond national culture: Implications of cultural dynamics for consumer research. *International Marketing Review.* https://psycnet.apa.org/record/2006-12521-004

Crespi, I., & Taibi, M. (2020). Cultural differences and social amplification of risk of a tourism destination: Foreign media coverage after 2016/2017 earthquakes in central Italy. *Italian Sociological Review, 10*(2), 201A–237. https://doi.org/10.1016/S0160-7383(01)00008-1

Cuomo, M. T., Tortora, D., Foroudi, P., Giordano, A., Festa, G., & Metallo, G. (2021). Digital transformation and tourist experience co-design: Big social data for planning cultural tourism. *Technological Forecasting and Social Change, 162*, 120345. https://doi.org/10.1016/j.techfore.2020.120345

de Beer, G., & Elliffe, S. (1997). *Tourism development and the empowerment of local communities. DPRU industrial strategy project: Phase two* (Working Paper No. 11). https://idl-bnc-idrc.dspacedirect.org/items/8f179042-7bc7-4ec0-8a95-b1ab6f2c40ef

Das, I. R., Talukder, M. B., & Kumar, S. (2024). Implication of artificial intelligence in hospitality marketing. *Utilizing smart technology and ai in hybrid tourism and hospitality.* IGI Global. https://doi.org/10.4018/979-8-3693-1978-9.ch014

Diekmann, A., McCabe, S., & Ferreira, C. C. (2018). Social tourism: Research advances, but stasis in policy. Bridging the divide. *Journal of Policy Research in Tourism, Leisure and Events, 10*(3), 181–188. https://doi.org/10.1080/19407963.2018.1490859

Dodds, R., Ali, A., & Galaski, K. (2018). Mobilizing knowledge: Determining key elements for success and pitfalls in developing community-based tourism. *Current Issues in Tourism, 21*(13), 1547–1568. https://doi.org/10.7176/EJBM/15-17-01

Fu, Y., & Luo, J. M. (2023). An empirical study on cultural identity measurement and its influence mechanism among heritage tourists. *Frontiers in Psychology, 13*, 8718. https://doi.org/10.3389/fpsyg.2022.1032672

Hall, S. (2023). Whose heritage? Un-settling 'the heritage', re-imagining the post-nation. In S. Hall (Ed.), *Whose heritage?* (pp. 13–25). Routledge. https://doi.org/10.4324/9781003092735-3

Hlengwa, D. C., & Maruta, A. T. (2020). A framework for facilitation of community participation in and beneficiation from CBT around the Save Valley Conservancy. *African Journal of Hospitality, Tourism and Leisure, 9*(2), 1–11. https://doi.org/10.1002/inc3.31

Hoque, M. A. (2020). *Community-based indigenous tourism, NGOs and indigenous poverty in Bangladesh.* University of Otago. https://doi.org/10.5367/te.2014.0456

Horaira, M. A., & Devi, A. (2021). Cultural tourism in Bangladesh, a potential and profound tourism destination: Developing a model for cultural tourism development in Bangladesh. *International Tourism and Hospitality Journal, 4*(10), 1–22. https://doi.org/10.37227/ITHJ-2021-08-1187

Hull, J. S., & Sassenberg, U. (2012). Creating new cultural visitor experiences on islands: Challenges and opportunities. *Journal of Tourism Consumption and Practice, 4*(2), 91–110. https://doi.org/10.3390/su122410313

Ibrahim, A. H., & Falola, J. (2021). Assessing the factors that can enhance or hinder community support for ethno-cultural tourism development in some selected local government areas of kaduna state. *Fudma Journal of Sciences, 5*(1), 85–93. https://doi.org/ https://doi.org/10.33003/fjs-2021-0501-540

Islam, M. K., Farjana, F., Nasrin, N., & Ahmed, M. S. (2023). The economic, social and environmental implications of heritage tourism: Evidence from Bangladesh. *SN Business & Economics, 3*(2), 42. https://doi.org/10.1007/s43546-022-00411-2

Jaafar, M., Noor, S. M., & Rasoolimanesh, S. M. (2015). Perception of young local residents toward sustainable conservation programmes: A case study of the Lenggong World Cultural Heritage Site. *Tourism Management, 48*, 154–163. https://doi.org/10.1016/j.tourman.2014.10.018

Jørgensen, S. V., & Thoning, S. D. (2017). *Participation, empowerment and the role of external actors in community-centered tourism.*

Jung, M. (2022). *The role of social capital and trust in community-based tourism stakeholder.* Collaboration University of Surrey. https://doi.org/10.21776/ub.jitode.2019.007.02.02

Kar, N. S., Basu, A., Kundu, M., & Giri, A. (2022). Urban heritage tourism in Chandernagore, India: Revival of shared Indo-French Legacy. *GeoJournal, 87*(3), 1575–1591. https://doi.org/10.1007/s10708-020-10328-8

Kerdpitak, C. (2022). The effects of innovative management, digital marketing, service quality and supply chain management on performance in cultural tourism business. *Uncertain Supply Chain Management, 10*(3), 771–778. https://doi.org/10.5267/j.uscm.2022.4.005

Khalid, S., Ahmad, M. S., Ramayah, T., Hwang, J., & Kim, I. (2019). Community empowerment and sustainable tourism development: The mediating role of community support for tourism. *Sustainability, 11*(22), 6248. https://doi.org/10.3390/su11226248

Khandaka, S., & Muzahid, M. A. U. (2015). *Community based tourism: A potential tool for alleviating poverty in Bangladesh. IIUC Business Review, 4*, 137–154. https://doi.org/10.1080/02508281.2012.11081686

Kichurchak, M. (2020). Evaluation of cultural sphere development in the European Union countries as a factor of forming social capital and creative industries: Experience for Ukraine. *Економічний часопис-XXI, 184*(7–8), 68–78. https://doi.org/10.21003/ea.V184-07

King, T. F. (2003). *Places that count: Traditional cultural properties in cultural resource management* (Vol. 5). Rowman Altamira. https://doi.org/10.1177/1942778614007002

Kirshenblatt-Gimblett, B. (2004). Intangible heritage as metacultural production. *Museum International, 56*(1–2), 52–65. https://doi.org/10.1111/j.1350-0775.2004.00458.x

Kumar, S., Talukder, M. B., Kabir, F., & Kaiser, F. (2024). Challenges and sustainability of green finance in the tourism industry: Evidence from Bangladesh. In S. Taneja, P. Kumar, S. Grima, E. Ozen, & K. Sood (Eds.), *Advances in finance, accounting, and economics* (pp. 97–111). IGI Global. https://doi.org/10.4018/979-8-3693-1388-6.ch006

Kumar, S., Talukder, M. B., & Pego, A. (Eds.). (2024). *Utilizing smart technology and AI in hybrid tourism and hospitality.* IGI Global. https://doi.org/10.4018/979-8-3693-1978-9

Kwangseh, B. E. (2014). *Community based tourism (CBT) planning – An analysis of opportunities and barriers: A case study of Cameroon.* Unpublished Master Thesis, Eastern Mediterranean University, Gazimağusa, North Cyprus. https://doi.org/10.22080/JTPD.2021.21341.3528

Lak, A., Gheitasi, M., & Timothy, D. J. (2020). Urban regeneration through heritage tourism: Cultural policies and strategic management. *Journal of Tourism and Cultural Change, 18*(4), 386–403. https://doi.org/10.1080/14766825.2019.1668002

Lavarack, J., & Ryan, R. (2015). Cultural development and local government: Analytical frames, insights and observations. *Asia Pacific Journal of Public Administration, 37*(1), 44–55. https://doi.org/10.1080/23276665.2015.1018373

Lenzerini, F. (2011). Intangible cultural heritage: The living culture of peoples. *European Journal of International Law, 22*(1), 101–120. https://doi.org/10.1093/ejil/chr006

Loulanski, T., & Loulanski, V. (2011). The sustainable integration of cultural heritage and tourism: A meta-study. *Journal of Sustainable Tourism, 19*(7), 837–862. https://doi.org/10.1080/09669582.2011.553286

Lusby, C., & Eow, K. (2015). Tourism development in a new democracy: Residents' perceptions of community-based tourism in Mawlamyine, Myanmar. *Journal of Tourism and Recreation, 2*(1), 23–40. https://doi.org/10.12735/jotr.v2i1p23

Minhus, S., & Huie, L. (2021). The tendency of traditional costume at heritage festival for cultural revival. *SAGE Open, 11*(2), 21582440211016905. https://doi.org/10.1016/j.tmp.2019.100555

Mohammad, B. T., Firoj, K. M., & Das, I. R. (2023). Emerging concepts of artificial intelligence in the hotel industry: A conceptual paper. *International Journal of Research Publication and Reviews, 4*, 1765–1769. https://doi.org/10.55248/gengpi.4.923.92451

Mohammad, B. T., Sanjeev, K., & Das, I. R. (2024a). Implications of blockchain technology-based cryptocurrency in the cloud for the hospitality industry. In D. Darwish (Ed.), *Emerging trends in cloud computing analytics, scalability, and service models* (p. 19). https://doi.org/10.4018/979-8-3693-0900-1.ch018

Mohammad, B. T., Sanjeev, K., & Das, I. R. (2024b). Perspectives of digital marketing for the restaurant industry. In G. Erol & M. Kuyucu (Eds.), *Advancements in social-ized and digital media communications* (p. 17). https://doi.org/10.4018/979-8-3693-0855-4.ch009

Mtapuri, O., Camilleri, M. A., & Dłużewska, A. (2022). Advancing community-based tourism approaches for the sustainable development of destinations. *Sustainable Development, 30*(3), 423–432. https://doi.org/10.1002/sd.2257

Muhsina, K. (2021). Prospects of parasailing activities in Bangladesh: A study on the opportunities and challenges. *International Journal of Management and Accounting, 3*, 43–51. https://doi.org/10.34104/ijma.021.043051

Muhsina, K. (2023). Evolution of tourism through travel agencies: A case study on Bangladesh. *International Journal of Research and Innovation in Social Science, 7*(12), 541–549. https://doi.org/10.47772/IJRISS.2023.7012044

Plzáková, L. (2015). Economic and social impacts of cultural tourism. *International Multidisciplinary Scientific Conference on Social Sciences and Arts SGEM 2015.* https://doi.org/10.5593/SGEMSOCIAL2015/B23/S7.026

Rahaman, A., Uddin, A. J., & Hossain, M. S. (2020). Origin and socio-cultural forma-tion of Bihari identity: A study on Bihari community in Bangladesh. *International Journal of Social, Political and Economic Research, 7*(4), 879–903. https://doi.org/ https://doi.org/10.1080/13602000902943682

Richards, G. (2007). *Cultural tourism: Global and local perspectives.* Psychology Press. https://doi.org/10.1007/s10824-008-9069-8

Salkin, P. E., & Lavine, A. (2008). Understanding community benefits agreements: Equitable development, social justice and other considerations for developers, municipalities and community organizations. *UCLA Journal of Environmental Law and Policy, 26*, 291. https://doi.org/10.5070/L5262019560

Sarker, S. (2014). Competitive marketing strategies for tourism industry in the light of "Vision 2021" of Bangladesh. *European Journal of Business and Management, 6*(4), 210–220. https://doi.org/10.13140/RG.2.2.16786.96968

Shahmirzadi, E. K. (2012). *Community based tourism (CBT) planning and possibilities: The case of Shahmirzad.* Iran Eastern Mediterranean University (EMU). https:// doi.org/10.32598/JSRD.02.02.30

Shaikh, S., Sultan, M. F., & Akbar, W. (2020). *Identifying the opportunities and challenges in potential cultural heritage tourism destination – A case of Sindh, Pakistan.* Editorial board. https://doi.org/10.52700/assap.v4i2.307

Simpson, M. C. (2008). Community benefit tourism initiatives – A conceptual oxymoron? *Tourism Management, 29*(1), 1–18. https://doi.org/10.1016/j.tourman.2007.06.005

Sonter, L. J., Ali, S. H., & Watson, J. E. (2018). Mining and biodiversity: Key issues and research needs in conservation science. *Proceedings of the Royal Society B, 285*(1892), 20181926. https://doi.org/10.1098/rspb.2018.1926

Sotiriadis, M., & Shen, S. (2017). The contribution of partnership and branding to des-tination management in a globalized context: The case of the UNWTO Silk Road Programme. *Journal of Tourism, Heritage & Services Marketing, 3*(2), 8–16. https:// doi.org/10.3390/su13041920

Sumarmi, K. E., & Aliman, M. (2020). Community based tourism (CBT) to establish blue economy and improve public welfare for fishing tourism development in Klatak Beach, Tulungagung, Indonesia. *GeoJournal of Tourism and Geosites, 31*(3), 979–986. https://doi.org/10.30892/gtg.31307-530

Talukder, M. B. (2020a). An appraisal of the economic outlook for the tourism industry, specially Cox's Bazar in Bangladesh. *i-manager's Journal on Economics & Commerce, 2*(1), 23–35. https://doi.org/10.26634/jecom.2.1.17285

Talukder, M. B. (2020b). The future of culinary tourism: An emerging dimension for the tourism industry of Bangladesh. *I-Manager's Journal on Management*, *15*(1), 27. https://doi.org/10.26634/jmgt.15.1.17181

Talukder, M. B. (2021). An assessment of the roles of the social network in the development of the tourism Industry in Bangladesh. *International Journal of Business, Law, and Education*, *2*(3), 85–93. https://doi.org/10.56442/ijble.v2i3.21

Talukder, M. B. (2024). Implementing artificial intelligence and virtual experiences in hospitality. In *Innovative technologies for increasing service productivity* (pp. 145–160). IGI Global. https://doi.org/10.4018/979-8-3693-2019-8.ch009

Talukder, M. B., & Hossain, M. M. (2021). Prospects of future tourism in Bangladesh: An evaluative study. *I-Manager's Journal on Management*, *15*(4), 1–8. https://doi.org/10.26634/jmgt.15.4.17495

Talukder, M. B., Kabir, F., Kaiser, F., & Lina, F. Y. (2024). Digital detox movement in the tourism industry: Traveler perspective. In *Business drivers in promoting digital detoxification* (pp. 91–110). IGI Global. https://doi.org/10.4018/979-8-3693-1107-3.ch007

Talukder, M. B., & Kumar, S. (2023a). Revisit intention in hotel industry of Bangladesh: A critical review of present literatures' limitations and suggestions for further study. ResearchGate. Retrieved April 2023 from https://www.researchgate.net/publication/371503587_Revisit_Intention_in_Hotel_Industry_of_Bangladesh_A_Critical_Review_of_Present_Literatures'_Limitations_and_Suggestions_for_Further_Study

Talukder, M. B., & Kumar, S. (2023b). *The effect of food service quality on customer satisfaction in the hotel industry: A conceptual paper*. ResearchGate, Jun.10, 2023. https://www.researchgate.net/publication/371503829_The_Effect_of_Food_Service_Quality_on_Customer_Satisfaction_in_the_Hotel_Industry_A_Conceptual_Paper

Talukder, M. B., Kumar, S., & Das, I. R. (2024a). Mindfulness of digital detoxification: Healthy lifestyle in tourism. In *Contemporary management and global leadership for sustainability* (pp. 56–71). IGI Global. https://doi.org/10.4018/979-8-3693-1273-5.ch004

Talukder, M. B., Kumar, S., & Das, I. R. (2024b). Food wastage on the economic outcome: Evidence from the hotel industry. In *Sustainable disposal methods of food wastes in hospitality operations* (pp. 68–80). IGI Global. https://doi.org/10.4018/979-8-3693-2181-2.ch005

Talukder, M. B., Kumar, S., Sood, K., & Grima, S. (2023). Information technology, food service quality and restaurant revisit intention. *International Journal of Sustainable Development and Planning*, *18*(1), 295–303. https://doi.org/10.18280/ijsdp.180131

Talukder, M., Shakhawat Hossain, M., & Kumar, S. (2022). Blue ocean strategies in hotel industry in Bangladesh: A review of present literatures' gap and suggestions for further study. *SSRN Electronic Journal*. https://doi.org/10.2139/ssrn.4160709

Tubey, W. C., Kyalo, D. N., & Mulwa, A. (2019). Socio-cultural conservation strategies and sustainability of community based tourism projects in Kenya: A case of Maasai Mara conservancies. *Journal of Sustainable Development*, *12*(6), 90–102. https://doi.org/10.5539/jsd.v12n6p90

Walker, E. T., & McCarthy, J. D. (2010). Legitimacy, strategy, and resources in the survival of community-based organizations. *Social problems*, *57*(3), 315–340. https://doi.org/10.1525/sp.2010.57.3.315

Witchayakawin, P., & Tengkuan, W. (2018). Community based tourism development and participation of ageing villagers in Ban Na Ton Chan, Thailand. *International Journal of Mechanical and Production Engineering Research and Development*, *8*(3), 969–976. https://doi.org/10.24247/ijmperdjun2018102

Xue, L., & Kerstetter, D. (2018). Discourse and power relations in community tourism. *Journal of Travel Research*, *57*(6), 757–768. https://doi.org/10.1177/0047287517714908

Zielinski, S., Jeong, Y., & Milanés, C. B. (2021). Factors that influence community-based tourism (CBT) in developing and developed countries. *Tourism Geographies*, *23*(5–6), 1040–1072. https://doi.org/10.1080/14616688.2020.1786156

Chapter 13

Strategies for Sustainable Tourist Destination Benchmarking: Insights and Frameworks

Shikha Dhakad

Jiwaji University, Gwalior, India

Abstract

Purpose: The purpose of this study is to give comprehensive strategies for developing sustainable tourism destinations by incorporating case studies, conceptual frameworks, and existing research. By addressing the lack of holistic approaches in sustainable tourism practices, this study seeks to provide insightful information that can guide stakeholders, policymakers, and destination managers in effective decision-making and planning.

Methodology/study design/approach: A comprehensive literature review has been conducted for analyzing peer-reviewed journal papers, case studies, and conceptual frameworks relevant to sustainable tourism benchmarking. Peer-reviewed journal papers, case studies, and conceptual frameworks pertaining to sustainable tourism benchmarking have all been examined through a thorough assessment of the literature. In this study, numerous information on sustainable tourism and benchmarking strategies allows for a meticulous understanding of benchmarking and its relevancy to sustainable tourist destination development.

Findings: The study distinguishes essential strategies for benchmarking sustainable tourist destinations, which include stakeholder engagement, integration of the triple bottom line framework, choosing appropriate indicators, promotion of certification and standards, and encouraging collaborations among destinations. The case studies highlight, the significance of

Corporate Social Responsibility, Corporate Governance and Business Ethics in Tourism
Management: A Business Strategy for Sustainable Organizational Performance, 177–194
Published under exclusive licence by Emerald Publishing Limited
doi:10.1108/978-1-83608-704-520241013

having a long-term commitment, governance, and stakeholder involvement while implementing sustainable tourism policies.

Value: This study presents a combination of existing literature and frameworks to evolve comprehensive strategies for benchmarking sustainable tourist destinations. By incorporating perceptions from various sources, this study gives valuable direction for practitioners and researchers seeking to advance sustainable tourism practices.

Keywords: Sustainable tourism; benchmarking; destination management; triple bottom line; stakeholder engagement; case studies; conceptual frameworks

Introduction

Globally, tourism has become an integral part of development and economic growth for many countries. With increasing tourist flow, it is necessary to adopt strategies to promote sustainability while maintaining the competitiveness of tourist destinations. To give basic sustainable tourism benchmarking criteria for applying to all major destinations to sustain their environment and culture, and ensure the long-term success of tourist destinations through implementing the "Triple Bottom Line" (Weaver, 2010).

Triple Bottom Line (TBL) incorporates three sustainability dimensions that are environment, economy, and social (Blancas et al., 2018; Janusz & Bajdor, 2013; Nguyen et al., 2023; Weaver, 2010). Sustainable tourism manages to handle the negative impacts on economic, environmental, and social elements of tourist destinations (Nguyen et al., 2023). Triple bottom line aspects of tourist destinations attract and satisfy tourists and also contribute to the well-being of local communities and preserve natural resources. These dimensions highlight the memorable experiences of tourists arising from interacting with destinations surrounding and give a "small self" feeling in big nature also shows the positive emotions of tourists toward nature-based experiences (Breiby et al., 2020) because it gives

> An experience that raises deep, meaningful emotions and memories that can encourage tourists' contribution toward destination sustainability. (Breiby et al., 2020)

Furthermore, they contribute to the preservation of natural and cultural heritage, support local economies, and enhance community well-being. Hence benchmarking destinations as sustainable destinations plays a crucial role in fostering experiences and encouraging tourists' commitment toward sustainability.

Benchmarking is a process of identifying best practices, setting benchmarks and targets, and monitoring progress (Blancas et al., 2018). Benchmarking destinations as sustainable tourism includes the evaluation and comparison of different destinations which are practicing and performing sustainability and giving positive results. Using it as a strategic tool to implement best practices focusing on issues like garbage, water pollution, climate change, and preservation of old buildings (Breiby et al., 2020) to address these concerns and ensure the continuous improvement, long term-viability of destination, and inflate competitiveness in the market through develop strategies that align with the principles of sustainability.

This study aims to assess and improve sustainable tourism practices and performances by formulating strategies to benchmark all destinations with universal indicators, engaging the triple bottom line approach, indicators, and certification and standards of GSTC, GreenGlobe and EarthCheck By utilizing literature review using Scopus, Google Scholar, and Academia, the study highlights the importance of benchmarking destinations as sustainable tourism destinations by incorporating sustainable tourism benchmarking frameworks, dimensions, indicators, stakeholders, and certification and standards, and case studies. The case studies highlight the significance of having a long-term commitment, governance, and stakeholder involvement while implementing of sustainable tourism policies. The study emphasizes five strategies for benchmarking sustainable tourist destinations that are incorporation of a triple bottom line approach, enhancing collaboration among stakeholders and participants, identification of indicators relevant to all tourist destinations, adoption of sustainability certification and standards of achieving sustainability, and establishing collaboration and partnership between destinations to encourage innovation and technology adoption and continuous learning, improvement, monitoring, and evaluation. Lastly, this study demonstrates the significance of sustainable tourism benchmarking destination for transforming tourism practices for a more sustainable future.

Conceptual Frameworks on Sustainable Tourism Benchmarking

Acknowledging the complexities of globalization, mapping relationships between tourism phenomena and developing appropriate indicators and policies can enhance the association between tourism academia, political geographers, and scientists for interdisciplinary synergy (Weaver, 2010). It is crucial to have a conceptual framework that incorporates the economic, social, and environmental dimensions of sustainable tourism destinations. To serve as a guide for benchmarking and evaluating the performance of tourist destinations in terms of sustainability. Furthermore, the framework should take into account key factors such as waste management, resource conservation, community engagement, cultural preservation, and the use of renewable energy. Erroneously planned tourist destinations can destroy the economic, environmental, and social resources of tourism destinations meanwhile developing tourism with planning works sustainably because developing sustainable tourism aims to uphold and preserve all three dimensions of the tourist area (Byrd, 2007; Nguyen et al., 2023). The development of a conceptual framework for benchmarking sustainable tourist destinations is crucial to effectively assess and improve sustainability performances. The process of developing a conceptual framework for sustainable tourism destination benchmarking involves various steps starting from defining essential dimensions and appropriate indicators and then delving into cross-country comparisons to form a conceptual chart (Cernat & Gourdon, 2007). Sustainable development has to ensure and support the social, cultural, and economic development of locals, nature, and cultural environment to be a sustained tourist destination by offering quality products and ensuring appropriate management and monitoring (Tardivo et al., 2014). Overall the sustainable tourism destination benchmarking framework aims to balance economic growth, environmental preservation, and social inclusivity. Some authors gave benchmarking models, as mentioned in Fig. 13.1.

Cernat and Gourdon (2012) gave a sustainable tourism benchmarking tool framework in their study as shown in Fig. 13.1, based on seven dimensions that are assets, activity, linkages, leakages, sustainability and infrastructure, and complex integration between each dimension. Their framework allows to identification of specific issues related to tourism in developing countries through analyzing linkages between specific areas.

Travel & Tourism Development Index 2021 provides a strategic tool for benchmarking businesses (Fig. 13.2), governments, organizations, and other sectors. Consists of five subindexes, 17 pillars, and 112 individual indicators, distributed among the different pillars. This index gives a platform to formulate strategies, policies, and actions to be taken at local, national, and international levels.

Punzo et al. (2022) gave a SusTour-Index in their study formed of 75 elementary indicators under environmental, economic, and social dimensions with further divisions into pillars. Whereas the environmental dimension contains 21 elementary indicators, structured into four pillars, the economic dimension contains 34 elementary indicators, structured into five pillars, and the social dimension consists of 20 elementary indicators, structured into four pillars. This framework

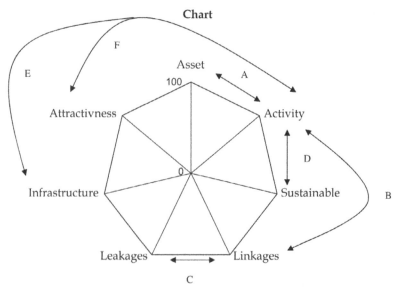

Fig. 13.1.   Benchmarking Tool Framework (Cernat & Gourdon, 2012).

Fig. 13.2.   Travel & Tourism Development Index 2021 (The T&T Competitiveness Index 2019 Framework).

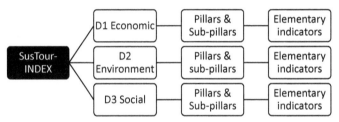

Fig. 13.3.   The Hierarchical Structure of the SusTour-Index (adapted from Punzo et al., 2022).

provides a comprehensive summary of the dimensions with a broad set of elementary indicators, structured in pillars and sub-pillars of sustainability in tourism (Fig. 13.3).

Sustainability Dimensions

Sustainability Dimensions include the various aspects that contribute to the altogether sustainability of a tourist destination. Sustainable experiences are connected to positive emotions like joy, novelty and awe which result from the interaction of sustainable dimensions (Breiby et al., 2020). Several different dimensions are discussed in various research articles including:

Sustainable development incorporates three dimensions that are environmental, economic, and social (Nugraheni et al., 2020; Purvis et al., 2019) known as the TBL and considered as three pillars of sustainability (Purvis et al., 2019; Weaver, 2010), these dimensions are very much compatible and mutually supportive. Sustainable tourism includes environmental protection, and improving local living conditions with the social and economic dimension of tourist areas. Government and local authorities around the globe started implementing strategies for reducing hotel energy, water use, mass tourists, and involvement of locals to boost their income (Janusz & Bajdor, 2013) (Fig. 13.4).

Place, permanence, and person are the new three Ps of sustainability. This three P's triangle represents five sustainability dimensions, place represents physical, geographical, and cultural dimensions whereas permanence represents the temporal dimension, and lastly, personal represents a symbol of individual human beings and not as undifferentiated members of society (Seghezzo, 2009).

Breiby et al. (2020) fostered four sustainable dimensions to create a sustainable experience among tourists that are interaction with the natural environment, cultural environment, insights and views, and contextual activities. These dimensions are further divided into subcategories, memorable experiences, and future concerns.

Cernat and Gourdon (2011) singled out seven dimensions in their study for sustainable tourism which are tourism assets, international tourism activity, tourism-related linkages, tourism-related leakages, environmental, and social sustainability, overall infrastructure and other attractive aspects like cheap prices, human resources, risk factors, etc.

Tardivo et al. (2014) identified five dimensions in their study that are environmental management, ecotourism/natural assets, supporting assets, and cleaner production.

To create a sustainable tourism destination, this study focused on environmental, economic, and social dimensions of sustainable tourism development. It is also essential to consider all the given dimensions under the triple bottom line as all given dimensions cover all the essential aspects mentioned in numerous studies including to create a sustainable tourism destination. All these aspects include all the essential dimensions for creating a sustainable destination including place, permanence, person, interaction with natural and cultural environment, insights and views, tourism assets, international tourism activity, tourism-related linkages, tourism-related leakages, complete infrastructure, and supporting assets.

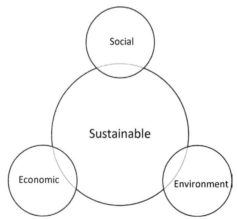

Fig. 13.4.   Three Pillars of Sustainability (adapted from Purvis et al., 2019).

Similarly, environmental dimensions include aspects like environmental management, ecotourism/natural assets, and cleaner production. Similarly, the economic dimension includes aspects like employment income, stability of commodity prices, and equality of working opportunities, and social dimensions encompass aspects like the stability of cultural identity, social order, and social structure in the destination. Lastly, the integration of place, permanence, and person dimensions creates a comprehensive and holistic approach within the broader environmental, economic, and social dimensions.

Environmental Sustainability

It is a key dimension to achieving sustainability. It includes practices and strategies aiming to minimize negative impacts on nature and to conserve ecosystems for coming generations. It includes implementing measures like waste management, conservation of biodiversity, and reducing carbon emissions to maintain the ecological balance.

Social Sustainability

Social sustainability is a dynamic concept of SD that will keep changing in the future. In developing sustainable tourist destinations, social sustainability plays a major role but it is the least developed dimension among all the three dimensions of sustainable development (Nugraheni et al., 2020). Social sustainability aspects include the efforts that have been made by standard setters, planners, and practitioners in various fields, including forest certification, organic and conventional agriculture, urban and regional planning, corporate social and environmental management, reporting, responsibility and fair-trade certification (Nugraheni et al., 2020). Nugraheni et al. (2020) gave 25 aspects of the social sustainability dimension in their study which are related to basic needs, quality of life, good governance, and community participation. However, it is important to understand the specific conditions of the destination, type of tourism, culture of the host community, and political and regulatory environment to develop a complete insight into the social dimension.

It includes community engagement and empowerment, cultural preservation and heritage conservation, and socio-economic benefits for local communities. It also includes aspects like safety, inclusivity, and respect for local customs and traditions.

Economic Sustainability

In tourism, Economic development is a motivation for sustainability. (Nguyen et al., 2023)

Economic sustainability includes the generation of economic benefits to support the long-term viability of the destination, involving activities like supporting small and medium-sized enterprises (SMEs) and local businesses (Nguyen et al., 2023), promoting local economic development and employment opportunities, and ensuring a fair distribution of tourism-related income within the community.

It involves promoting economic growth and development that benefits the local community and stakeholders to make any destination a sustainable tourist destination. Cernat and Gourdon (2011) divided economic sustainability into four subcategories that are Tourism Assets, International Tourism Activities: tourists frequenting and spending, Linkages: tourism revenue for the all economy, and Leakages: missed opportunities. In selecting a destination, Tourism Assets play a major role in influencing tourists whether the tourist destination is offering required natural resources and cultural assets which could lead to assessing long-term potential. Afterwards, international tourism activity measures tourism activities including the number of tourists visited and created revenue generated from tourism. Another subcategory, Linkages enhances the national economy by linking long value supply chains including agriculture, construction, fisheries, manufacturing, communication, and so on to create more value-added benefits by creating and producing tourism products results in benefiting the whole economy and society (Cernat & Gourdon, 2007; Nguyen et al., 2023), and the last subcategory is Leakages, which account the loss of foreign change and different hidden prices deriving from tourism-associated activities. It included two main components that are internal leakages and external leakages (Cernat & Gourdon, 2007).

Economic sustainability in turn builds on the strategies of enhancing local economic development and job creation, ensuring equitable distribution of tourism revenue across stakeholders, supporting SMEs & local business enterprises, assessing the long-term potential of tourism assets, measuring tourism activities and revenue generated from tourism, and reducing leakages from touristic income. Local economic development, job creation, fair distribution of tourism revenues to all stakeholders, support for SMEs and local businesses, assessment of tourism assets, measurement of tourist activities and revenue generated by the sector as well as stakeholder involvement and reduction in leakages are other dimensions discussed alongside environmental and sociocultural consideration to ensure a more holistic approach for developing tourism. That is to say that economic sustainability in sustainable destinations signifies not just boosting economic growth but also impacts the locals while preserving naturalness and cultural heritage.

Benchmarking Methods

In tourism, benchmarking is an important tool for quality improvement and performance evaluation. In a highly competitive and diverse tourism industry, benchmarking is very important because it can be tailored to meet the demands of a diverse tourism industry (Jovičić & Ivanović, 2006; Cano et al., 2001; Weicker, 1998). The process involves a comparison of a tourist destination's performance to enhance the destination's image and achieve market leadership (Thomas, 2013). In the international tourism field, benchmarking models are used to compare and enhance performances, with a focus on data accessibility, kinds, and regions of benchmarking (Frenţ et al. 2017).

Benchmarking is a method of comparing the performance and practices at tourist destinations with those of other destinations that are considered to be leaders or best practices in certain areas. It is a process of identifying and analyzing successful practices to improve performance and achieve desired outcomes. It has become a widely used tool for sustainable destination management. Benchmarking methods in sustainable tourism destination management can include performance indicators, qualitative indicators, stakeholder interviews and surveys, site visits and assessments, and comparative analysis of destination management plans and strategies (Sulistyadi et al., 2019). These methods help identify areas for improvement and provide insights on how to achieve sustainable outcomes (Saraswati et al., 2018).

Cernat and Gourdon (2011), broke the dimensions into variables and then variables into indicators, gave five indicators: tourism assets indicator (natural & cultural), tourism activity (frequenting and spending by characteristics of tourists), linkages with other economic sectors (constrained access to input-output matrix), tourism-related leakages (constrained input-output matrix and data on origin of tourism operators), and indicators for tourism-related infrastructure.

Rasoolimanesh et al. (2023) discussed indicators in their study which are performance indicators, quantitative indicators, objective indicators, and subjective indicators. Whereas performance indicators are aligned with SDGs, the importance of governance, stakeholder involvement, and subjective versus objective measures are all the four criteria of sustainable tourism indicators. Qualitative indicators measure the sustainability performance in each dimension. Objective indicators measure revenue, employment rates, energy efficiency, availability, and usage of clean potable water, biodiversity conservation, and crime rate by employing instruments or evaluation tools. Lastly, subjective indicators, highly contextual based, measure personal feelings and attitudes of people as it is associated with attitudes, experiences, perceptions, and satisfaction levels.

According to Czarnecki (1996), benchmarking involves the analysis of performance within or between businesses with the purpose of improvement. Two forms of benchmarking can be achieved that are outcome-based and process-based. Outcome-based analyses performance against an average and process-based compares critical processes to those of a more successful organization. Zairi et al. (1996) further examine the further depth of benchmarking which entailed in-depth competitor products and processes. Meanwhile, Rebeka et al. (2015) highlight the usefulness of benchmarking in achieving quality improvement, and Lucertini et al. (1995) emphasize the significance of incorporating benchmarking into the company's evaluation and improvement processes.

Certification and Standards

Green Globe

Green Globe is an international certification program that awards companies with green solutions and a sustainable future and provides sustainability certification and standards to tourist destinations. It works on 3S, Safety, Security, and Sustainability. It gives certification of ensuring the highest standards of sustainability by ensuring the safety and security of any tourism destination based on an internationally recognized set of criteria developed over 17 years. The Green

Globe also provides education, training, and marketing services in a total of 83 countries around the globe (Ásványi, 2021). Green Globe certification standards involve 4 dimensions (environmental, cultural heritage, social economic, and sustainable management), 44 criteria and 380 compliance indicators based on the different geographical features and local factors of countries across the globe (www.greenglobe.com/criteria-indicators). All four dimensions include the criteria listed as follows:

A. **Sustainable Management Dimension**:
   1. Implement a Sustainability Management System
   2. Legal Compliance
   3. Employee Training
   4. Customer Satisfaction
   5. Accuracy of Promotional Materials
   6. Local Zoning, Design, and Construction
      6.1 Design and Construction – Compliance with Legal Requirements
      6.2 Sustainable Design and Construction of Buildings and Infrastructure – New Buildings (Constructed Within the Last 5 years) and Existing Buildings
   7. Experiential or Interpretative Tourism
   8. Communications Strategy
   9. Health and Safety
   10. Disaster Management & Emergency Response
B. **Social/Economic Dimension**:
   1. Community Development
   2. Local Employment
   3. Fair Trade
   4. Support Local Entrepreneurs
   5. Respect Local Communities
   6. Exploitation
   7. Equitable Hiring
   8. Employee Protection
   9. Access to Basic Services
   10. Local livelihood
   11. Bribery and Corruption
C. **Cultural Heritage Dimension**:
   1. Code of behavior
   2. Historical Artefacts
   3. Protection of Sites
   4. Incorporation of Culture
D. **Environmental Dimension**:
   1. Conserving Resources
      1.1 Purchasing Policy
      1.2 Consumable Goods
      1.3 Energy Consumption
      1.4 Water Consumption

      1.5 Food and Beverage
      1.6 Green Meetings
2. Reducing Pollution
      2.1 Greenhouse Gas Emissions
      2.2 Wastewater
      2.3 Waste Management Plan (Plan, Reduce, Reuse, Recycle)
      2.4 Harmful Substances
      2.5 Other Pollutants
3. Conserving Biodiversity, Ecosystems, and Landscapes
      3.1 Wildlife Species
      3.2 Wildlife in Captivity
      3.3 Landscaping
      3.4 Biodiversity Conservation
      3.5 Interactions with Wildlife

Global Sustainable Tourism Council (GSTC)

It establishes and manages worldwide requirements for sustainable journeys and tourism, referred to as the GSTC criteria. It contains three sets of criteria that are destination criteria, industry criteria, and MICE criteria, structured in four pillars that are sustainable management, socioeconomic impacts, cultural impacts, and environmental impacts. Based on environmental, cultural, customs, and laws GSTC created criteria, the organization issues accreditation services for certification bodies that certify hotels/accommodations, tour operators, and destinations as sustainable, GSTC destination criteria, and global standards for sustainability in travel and tourism and ensures best practices are adopted and implemented by the industry and the tourist for sustainable tourism (www.gstcouncil.org).

Earth Check

Earth Check provides sustainability certification and programs for tourism businesses, hotels, destinations, governments, developers and building designers, terrestrial and marine parks, and events. It is the world's leading scientific benchmarking certification and advisory group for sustainable travel and tourism (https://earthcheck.org). Earth Check follows five steps before providing a sustainable destination certificate. The five steps are as follows:

1. Create your destination's sustainability authority
2. Establish your environmental, cultural, social, and economic sustainability policy
3. Benchmark your destination or precinct
    a) Energy efficiency, conservation, and management
    b) Greenhouse gas emissions
    c) Air quality protection, noise control, and light pollution
    d) Management of freshwater resources
    e) Wastewater management, drainage, and streams

    f)   Ecosystem conservation and management
    g)   Land use planning and development
    h)   Transport
    i)   Solid waste management
    j)   Management of environmentally harmful substances
    k)   Cultural and social management
    l)   Economic management
4.   Certify your destination or precinct
5.   Audit and promote your certification level annually

Stakeholder Engagement

For successful sustainable tourism development, it is crucial to involve stakeholders in destination development plans for benchmarking destinations (Byrd, 2007), as development requires approvals from all stakeholders including ecological maintenance, local community, and tourist satisfaction (Tardivo et al., 2014). For managing all stakeholders, managers seek to establish strategies and operational procedures that lead to achieving sustainable practices at destination (Tardivo et al., 2014).

There are several indicators and sub-indicators to measure and identify the participation of stakeholders in the community by engaging tourism organizations and local communities for better tourism development by adopting sustainable practices and communicating effectively with both visitors and locals to create a more positive and mutually beneficial relationship (Byrd, 2007).

Limited research articles have included tourists as stakeholders but they should be regarded as very important stakeholders as their experiences and feedback give valuable input which could help in improving visitors' behaviour and further help in deciding to enhance sustainable tourist destinations (Rasoolimanesh et al., 2023).

Strategies for Benchmarking Sustainable Destination

Several strategies for benchmarking sustainable tourist destinations have been proposed in the literature. Tardivo et al. (2014) recommended best practices from sustainable tourism locations, while Nguyen et al. (2023) emphasized the significance of resolving sustainable inefficiencies and technological gaps. Fuchs et al. (2002) proposed a benchmarking destination efficiency indicator system emphasizing resource stewardship and tourist satisfaction. Salazar and Cardoso (2019) also gave a comprehensive set of sustainable strategic planning indicators, including economic, sociocultural, psychological, political/administrative, tourism/commercial, and environmental/physical. Dolnicar (2002) highlights the understanding of focused segments that focus on environmental protection. Riva and Pilotti (2021) point out the need for cooperative, international benchmarking for exchanging best practices and improving strategies. This study highlights the importance of a holistic approach to sustainable tourism and the necessity of a multifaceted approach for benchmarking, considering both internal and external aspects. It also signifies a continuous improvement in sustainable tourism management taking into account tourist happiness, market segmentation, visitor satisfaction, and collaboration.

Insights from Existing Research: Strategies for Sustainable Tourism Destination

The formulation of successful sustainable tourism initiatives demands a comprehensive strategy that incorporates various analytical techniques and considers regional objectives into account. Kisi (2019) used a variety of approaches, such as the A'WOT technique, the TOWS matrix, and SWOT analysis to present a strategic blueprint for the development of sustainable tourist destinations with a focus on Zonguldak province in Turkey. The establishment of the region's vision statement and main sustainable tourism, which are drawn from national and tourism strategies and sustainable tourism literature.

The pivotal strategy proposed in the study is to support product diversity and event management, emphasizing the significance of the importance of leveraging policies for diversification, and collaborating with public–private organizations to curate high-quality visitor experiences. Enhancing the destination image is considered as a crucial objective, necessitating investments in infrastructure modernization and cultural heritage site preservation. These strategies support the overall objective of sustainable tourism by stimulating economic growth within host communities while also aligning to provide visitors with better experiences.

The Kisi (2019) study emphasizes the importance of establishing sustainable visitor management systems to mitigate environmental impacts and promote year-round tourism activities. This involves distributing tourism policies in place to protect the environment and cultural identity. To make a place more visible and competitive in the global tourism market, effective branding and promotion methods are necessary. Additionally, the study builds alliances and cooperative efforts among stakeholders is essential for sustainable tourism development, emphasizing the collective accountability of corporations, governments, communities, and academic institutions.

Kisi (2019) outlined framework strategies that provide a systematic approach to decision-making in the development of sustainable tourism, with potential applicability beyond Zonguldak province through the integration of analytical approaches and goals particular to complex challenges and capitalize on opportunities for sustainable growth. Kisi's (2019) study gives a holistic strategy for tourist development that prioritizes environmental conservation socioeconomic advantages, and cultural preservation, paving the way for a more resilient inclusive tourism industry.

While criticizing the strategies and policies for the development of Smart Tourist Destination, Verduzco Villaseñor et al. (2023) observe the significant impact of governance dynamics. Achieving sustainability development goals needs effective collaboration among a diverse stakeholder including local communities, businesses, and government agencies. The innovative actions that Spain undertakes in conceiving and executing smart tourist destinations highlight the critical role of cooperative networks in destination management. Similarly, Tequila, Mexico, highlights the transformative potential of public-private partnerships in converting a conventional tourist destination into an astute one.

Tequila's and Spain's success, foster an insight showing effective governance, coupled with strategies for a common vision of revolutionizing tourist destinations into intelligent and sustainable entities that involve the active involvement of corporate stakeholders, government agencies, and the local population in advancing sustainable development initiatives to drive innovation, enhance visitor experiences, and foster long-term socio-economic growth within tourist destinations (Verduzco Villaseñor et al., 2023).

Case Studies in Sustainable Tourism Policy Implementation:

Andalusia's Coastal Municipalities: A Model for Sustainable Tourism

Blancas et al. (2018) examined the sustainability in Andalusia's coastal communities thriving coastal communities. The coastal region of Andalusia generates substantial tourism income. Blancas et al. (2018) spotlighted 53 coastal municipalities and analyzed what sustainability means in these dynamic places. A comprehensive set of 65 indicators including social, economic, and environmental aspects is essential to achieve sustainability. Balncas et al. (2018) further added that these indicators function as compasses guiding policymakers toward well-informed choices. They bridge the gap between theory and practice by encapsulating the essence of sustainability. Blancas et al. (2018) used a differential dynamic index to guide the way toward sustainable tourist practices. Through meticulous analysis, the study presents a sustainability dynamic and developed as powerful visual tools, rendering complex data accessible to policymakers to understand complicated data and map out revolutionary paths. Moreover, Blancas et al. (2018) study gave a clear call for demand for action to invite policymakers, stakeholders, and communities to entrail on a common path of sustainability. Andalusia's coastal municipality turns up as the leader of sustainable tourism, fostering economic growth and protecting the natural heritage while safeguarding the ecological heritage. This study highlights detailed information for implementing strategies beyond academic corridors. Andalusia coastal settlement is equipped with a resilient spirit and data-driven insights, the municipalities are ready to steer clear of the turbulent seas of tourism charting a course toward a sustainable tomorrow.

Thailand's 7 Greens Tourism Policy: Challenges and Opportunities

Muangasame and McKercher (2015) explored Thailand's 7 Greens Tourism policy in their study which has received great attention and recognition since its launch in 2008 for the development of sustainable policy by including stakeholders' perspectives to glean lessons for sustainable policy formulation. The tourism authority of Thailand launched a pilot project in Koh Saumui, which is a microcosm of the broader issues that the 7 Green Strategies were facing. Muangasame and McKercher's thorough evaluation of stakeholders clearly revealed a severe concern that raised doubts about the policy's efficacy. The analysis indicates a patchwork of challenges impacting the 7 Green policy of Thailand as initially stakeholders applaud the conceptual framework, but when faced with the reality of execution, their enthusiasm wanes, hence the policy faces significant obstacles due to its limited legislative power and lack of long-term commitment. The Muangasame and McKercher study reveals that the conflict between idealism and pragmatism emphasizes the policy's inherent challenges. While laudable in its intent, the 7 Green policy faces conflicts with stakeholder interests and the limits of bureaucratic machinery. The study points to potential paths for future policy refinement that encourage stakeholder engagement and emphasize long-term commitment as critical components of sustainable policy implementation. It is also very crucial to move beyond rhetoric and infuse policy frameworks with substantive substance that resonates as a clarion call to action. At last, Muangasame and McKercher exemplified the embodies the broader drive for sustainability in the tourist environment. Policymakers can plan a road toward a more inclusive, resilient, and sustainable tourism paradigm and in crucible problems, calling stakeholders to forge a collective path toward a greener and equitable future for tourism.

Concepts and Strategy Formulation for Benchmarking Sustainable Tourist Destinations

Sustainable tourism has become a crucial aspect of development, combining economic growth of environment conservation and social inclusivity. The benchmarking concept highlights the necessity to effectively balance sustainability dimensions. Highlighting from scholarly literature to formulate key concepts and strategies for benchmarking sustainable tourist destinations.

This study suggests integrating the triple bottom line framework, other sustainability indicators, and certification criteria to make a common sustainable tourism benchmarking model that can apply to every destination and is not affected by any aspects like geographical features, rural or urban destinations, etc.

To make a common sustainable tourism benchmarking model, integrating a triple bottom line framework, sustainability indicators, and certification and standards is important. This study has used a triple bottom-up line for strategy formulation as it includes all the narrowed dimensions like place, permanence, person, interaction with natural and cultural environment, insights and views, tourism assets, international tourism activity, tourism-related linkages, tourism-related leakages, complete infrastructure, and supporting assets under environmental, economic, and social dimensions of triple bottom line. The formulated strategies for the common benchmarking of sustainable tourism destinations are:

1. Integrate the triple bottom line framework, which considers economic, environmental, and social aspects of sustainability as these are comprehensive dimensions considered as three pillars of all types of tourism destinations.

2. Encourage stakeholder engagement and participation to actively incorporate tourism organizations, local communities, and tourists themselves in governing, implementing, and promoting sustainable practices.
3. Identification of appropriate indicators that are present on every destination level which are measurable, reliable, and relevant to tailored strategies and initiatives applicable to all tourism destinations and to get a more accurate reflection of the sustainable performance of the destination.
4. Promote certification and standards for continuous learning, encouragement, and recognition to understand the need for consistency and credibility, to know standardized criteria and guidelines, and to improve sustainability practices.
5. Establish partnerships and collaboration among destinations for continuous sharing of best practices followed at their destinations, exchanging experiences, knowledge, and expertise for continuous improvement and innovation. Lastly, learn from each other, build a healthy sustainable relationship, and create a network of sustainable destinations.

Discussion and Conclusion

The key concepts and strategies for benchmarking sustainable tourism destinations include incorporating the triple bottom line, engagement of stakeholders, using appropriate indicators, promoting certification and standards, and fostering partnerships and collaboration among destinations to ensure that sustainability is applicable at all levels and dimensions of destination. This approach ensures positive impacts on the environment, economy, and society and allows for continuous improvement, learning, and exchange of knowledge, following standardized criteria, indicators and guidelines, stakeholder involvement, partnership among destinations and continuous evaluation and improvement.

Moreover, case studies on the coastal municipality of Andalusia and Thailand's 7 Green Tourism policy highlight the need for well-informed policy decisions, giving insightful information about the significance of the extensive indicators to achieve sustainability, also shared sustainable path for calls to action from stakeholders, communities, and governments. Evaluating tourism policies of Thailand 7 Green policies reveals significant difficulties arise from limited legislative power and lack of consistent commitment. It also emphasizes the need to involve stakeholders in implementing sustainable policies and stresses the need to move beyond just words and go beyond rhetoric to develop policy frameworks to emphasize the growing need for sustainability in tourism environments.

Enforcing these strategies can contribute to overall sustainability and the equitable distribution of benefits and improvements to the community and the destination. The study gave five key strategies for formulating a benchmark to apply to every destination that is active participation and involvement of stakeholders, incorporation of the triple bottom line, identification of appropriate indicators, promotion of certification and standards, and establishment of partnerships and collaboration.

References

Ásványi, K. (2021). Green globe certification. In London Metropolitan University, Guildhall Faculty of Business and Law (Ed.), *Encyclopedia of sustainable management* (pp. 1–3). Springer.

Blancas, F. J., Lozano-Oyola, M., González, M., & Caballero, R. (2018). A dynamic sustainable tourism evaluation using multiple benchmarks. *Journal of Cleaner Production, 174*, 1190–1203.

Breiby, M. A., Duedahl, E., Øian, H., & Ericsson, B. (2020). Exploring sustainable experiences in tourism. *Scandinavian Journal of Hospitality and Tourism, 20*(4), 335–351.

Byrd, E. T. (2007). Stakeholders in sustainable tourism development and their roles: Applying stakeholder theory to sustainable tourism development. *Tourism Review, 62*(2), 6–13.

Cano, M., Drummond, S., Miller, C., & Barclay, S. (2001). Learning from others: Benchmarking in diverse tourism enterprises. *Total Quality Management, 12*, 974–980.

Cernat, L., & Gourdon, J. (2007). *Is the concept of sustainable tourism sustainable?* (pp. 89–95). United Nations.

Cernat, L., & Gourdon, J. (2012). Paths to success: Benchmarking cross-country sustainable tourism. *Tourism Management, 33*(5), 1044–1056.

Dolnicar, S. (2002). *Profiling vacation segments with an environment protection attitude—A strategic marketing approach towards sustainability*.

Frenţ, C., Niculescu, A. C., & Creinicean, N. (2017). Comparative aspects on some benchmarking models applied in the tourism field at international level. *Romanian Economic and Business Review, 12*, 52–64.

Fuchs, M., Peters, M., & Weiermair, K. (2002). Tourism sustainability through destination benchmarking indicator systems: The case of alpine tourism. *Tourism Recreation Research, 27*(3), 21–33.

Green Globe. www.greenglobe.com/criteria-indicators

Jovičić, D., & Ivanović, V. (2006). Benchmarking and quality managing of tourist destinations. *Tourism and Hospitality Management, 12*(2), 123–134.

Janusz, G. K., & Bajdor, P. (2013). Towards sustainable tourism–framework, activities and dimensions. *Procedia Economics and Finance, 6*, 523–529.

Kişi, N. (2019). A strategic approach to sustainable tourism development using the A'WOT hybrid method: A case study of Zonguldak, Turkey. *Sustainability, 11*(4), 964.

Lucertini, M., Nicolò, F., & Telmon, D. (1995). Integration of benchmarking and benchmarking of integration. *International Journal of Production Economics, 38*(1), 59–71.

Muangasame, K., & McKercher, B. (2015). The challenge of implementing sustainable tourism policy: A 360-degree assessment of Thailand's "7 Greens sustainable tourism policy". *Journal of Sustainable Tourism, 23*(4), 497–516.

Nanu, L., Rahman, I., Ali, F., & Martin, D. S. (2024). Enhancing the hospitality experience: A systematic review of 22 years of physical environment research. *International Journal of Hospitality Management, 119*, 103692.

Nguyen, D. T., Kuo, K. C., Lu, W. M., & Nhan, D. T. (2023). How sustainable are tourist destinations worldwide? An environmental, economic, and social analysis. *Journal of Hospitality & Tourism Research, 48*(4), 698–711.

Nugraheni, A. I. P., Priyambodo, T. K., Sutikno, B., & Kusworo, H. A. (2020). The social dimensions' aspects of sustainable tourism development analysis: A systematic literature review. *Digital Press Social Sciences and Humanities, 4*, 00001.

Punzo, G., Trunfio, M., Castellano, R., & Buonocore, M. (2022). A multi-modelling approach for assessing sustainable tourism. *Social Indicators Research, 163*(3), 1399–1443.

Purvis, B., Mao, Y., & Robinson, D. (2019). Three pillars of sustainability: In search of conceptual origins. *Sustainability Science, 14*, 681–695.

Rasoolimanesh, S. M., Ramakrishna, S., Hall, C. M., Esfandiar, K., & Seyfi, S. (2023). A systematic scoping review of sustainable tourism indicators about the sustainable development goals. *Journal of Sustainable Tourism, 31*(7), 1497–1517.

Rebeka, E., Veronica, E.V., & Indradevi, R. (2015). Perspective of benchmarking. *EXCEL International Journal of Multidisciplinary Management Studies, 5*, 43–48.

Riva, A., & Pilotti, L. (2021). Benchmarking for sustainable touristic development: The Case of Pavia (Lombardy, Italy). *Economia Aziendale Online, 12*(2), 241–261.

Salazar, A., & Cardoso, C. (2019). Tourism planning: Impacts as benchmarks for sustainable development plans. *Worldwide Hospitality and Tourism Themes, 11*(6), 652–659.

Saraswati, E., & Athia, I. (2018). Building strategy to promote tourism destination attractiveness and competitiveness in developing area: A Case of Bojonegoro regency, East Java, Indonesia. *International Journal of Academic Research in Business and Social Sciences, 8*(4), 77–88.

Seghezzo, L. (2009). The five dimensions of sustainability. *Environmental Politics, 18*(4), 539–556.

Sulistyadi, Y., Eddyono, F., & Entas, D. (2019). Implementation of sustainable tourism model in Taman Wisata Alam Pantai Carita Pandeglang Banten, Indonesia. In *3rd international seminar on tourism (ISOT 2018)* (pp. 390–396). Atlantis Press.

Tardivo, G., Scilla, A., & Viassone, M. (2014). How to become a benchmark sustainable tourist destination? A descriptive model. *Business Systems Review, 3*(2), 207–230.

Thomas, T. K. (2013). Conceptualizing destination performance evaluation for internal destination benchmarking: A review. *ATNA Journal of Tourism Studies, 8*(1), 57–75. https://doi.org/10.12727/ajts.9.5

Verduzco Villaseñor, M. D. C., Cornejo Ortega, J. L., & Espinoza Sánchez, R. (2023). Governmental strategies and policies in the projection of smart tourist destination: An approach to the conceptual and theoretical qualitative analysis. *Sustainability, 15*(9), 7166.

Weaver, D. B. (2010). Geopolitical dimensions of sustainable tourism. *Tourism Recreation Research, 35*(1), 47–53.

Weicker, R. (1998). Benchmarking. *Home Health Care Management & Practice, 10*, 81–83.

www.weforum.org (2021), Benchmarking the enablers of Travel and Tourism development. Travel & Tourism Development Index 2021: Rebuilding for a Sustainable and Resilient Future.

www.weforum.org (2021), The T&T Competitiveness Index 2019 framework.

Zairi, M., & Leonard, P. (1996). *Practical benchmarking: The complete guide* (pp. 47–50). Springer.

Chapter 14

Achieving Net-zero in the Global Economy: Identifying Key Drivers and Their Connection to Corporate Social Responsibility

Bandna and Mushtaq Ahmad Shah

Mittal School of Business, Lovely Professional University, Punjab, India

Abstract

Purpose: The integration of corporate social responsibility (CSR) with the worldwide push toward a net-zero carbon economy is becoming more and more apparent, as both place a high priority on sustainability and environmental stewardship. This book chapter examines the elements and main influences that drive the shift to a net-zero economy, with a particular focus on the relationship between net-zero, CSR, and the creation of sustainable value.

Methodology: This research employs a secondary data analysis methodology of systematic review of scholarly research articles, reports, and online resources. Sources such as SAGE and EBSCO are scrutinized, alongside focused inquiries for qualitative data in academic databases like Emerald and Scopus.

Findings: The findings reveal that a variety of factors, including climate change awareness, governmental policy and regulation, corporate sustainability initiatives, technological advancements, investor pressure, economic possibilities, and environmental and social movements, all contribute to the shift to a net-zero economy in an interconnected way.

Originality: This chapter examines the factors that contribute to the shift to a net-zero economy, the critical factors for successful adoption, and the

Corporate Social Responsibility, Corporate Governance and Business Ethics in Tourism
Management: A Business Strategy for Sustainable Organizational Performance, 195–209
Copyright © 2025 by Bandna and Mushtaq Ahmad Shah
Published under exclusive licence by Emerald Publishing Limited
doi:10.1108/978-1-83608-704-520241014

relationship between CSR and the net-zero economy, all of which provide valuable insights for businesses, policymakers, and stakeholders as they navigate the complexities of achieving a sustainable future.

Keywords: Corporate social responsibility; critical factors; environment; net-zero economy; sustainability

1. Introduction

The idea of achieving net-zero carbon emissions originates from the principles of physical climate science, but its practical implementation involves navigating complex social, political, and economic systems (Fankhauser et al., 2022). A "net-zero economy" refers to an economic system where the amount of greenhouse gases emitted into the atmosphere is balanced by an equivalent amount of greenhouse gases removed or offset, resulting in a net emission of zero.

> Net-zero economy: Amount of greenhouse gases emitted into the atmosphere = Amount of greenhouse gases removed or offset.

Amidst a backdrop of slowed growth and amplified inequalities compounded by the climate crisis and the global economic effects of COVID-19, there's a pressing call for a fresh, inclusive approach to growth that's environmentally sustainable. Central to this is directing investments toward "clean" innovations and their widespread adoption, alongside investments in sustainable infrastructure, and the nurturing of human, natural, and social resources. This approach not only contributes to achieving net-zero greenhouse gas emissions but also enhances productivity, living standards, and individual prospects (Stern & Valero, 2021). This idea is intricately linked to endeavors aimed at tackling climate change and lessening its consequences. The three most critical success factors of net-zero adoption with respect to the automobile industry are identified as emphasizing research and development efforts, fostering international partnerships, and engaging in strategic planning with a well-structured roadmap (Virmani et al., 2022).

2. Key Elements of a Net-zero Economy

Investing in and adopting innovative technologies, such as Carbon Capture and Storage (CCS), sustainable agriculture practices, and electric vehicles, can contribute to achieving a net-zero economy. Governments play a critical role in setting regulations and policies that encourage businesses and individuals to transition to low-carbon practices. This may include carbon pricing, renewable energy targets, and other regulatory measures. Educating the public about the importance of reducing emissions and promoting sustainable practices is essential for fostering widespread support and behavioral changes. Encouraging a circular economy, where products are designed for reuse, recycling, and minimal waste generation, can contribute to reducing the environmental impact of consumption and production.

The net-zero concept gained prominence in the context of international climate agreements, such as the Paris Agreement, where countries commit to limiting global temperature increases to well below 2°C above pre-industrial levels, with efforts to limit it to 1.5°C. Achieving a net-zero economy is seen as a critical step in meeting these climate goals and avoiding the worst impacts of climate change. Businesses are leading the charge in attempts to lessen the effects of climate change as the globe struggles with this serious issue. This study explores the drivers that are propelling the shift to a net-zero economy by dissecting the social, economic, and regulatory aspects influencing business choices. Examining the complex relationship between this shift and CSR, the study clarifies how companies incorporate sustainability into their primary business plans. In the end, the study advances knowledge of the dynamic field of sustainable business by highlighting the critical role that companies play in guiding society as a whole toward a future that is more socially and ecologically responsible.

3. Review of Literature

Tangible assets, human expertise, and intangible assets all have a positive impact on the adoption of a sustainable net-zero economy. Nonetheless, it is worth noting that intangible resources exert a more pronounced influence on the actual implementation of a sustainable net-zero economy (Bag, 2024). This underscores the importance of embracing a set of common practices that encompass fostering a culture of sustainability, providing employee training and knowledge management, and necessitates managers to develop action plans accordingly (Sippel, 2020). Furthermore, the embrace of a sustainable net-zero economy has a beneficial effect on financial, environmental, and social performance (Bag, 2024). However, it is noteworthy that its impact on social performance is more substantial. Consequently, transitioning to a net-zero economy is likely to bring greater advantages to society and local communities (Bonsu, 2020; Gençsü et al., 2020). The recognition of the critical impact of an unstable climate on sustainability and human existence requires human insight. This awareness should serve as a catalyst for a commitment to achieving net-zero emissions, whether through the restoration of ecosystems, the substitution of renewable resources, or their judicious limitation. The imperative to enhance life on earth necessitates a heightened focus on the effective implementation and refinement of net-zero technologies (Sindhwani et al., 2022)

The world must steer toward a more carbon-neutral direction, supported by mounting evidence that emphasizes the existential risk brought about by uncontrolled greenhouse gas emissions (O'Flynn et al., 2021). A four-part action plan has been developed in-house to realize the University's net-zero 2030 goals. This action plan comprises (1) on-site renewable energy generation, (2) demand reduction, (3) off-site renewable energy generation, and (4) offsetting (Sippel, 2020).

Our climate is undergoing rapid changes, intensifying the need for both organizations and individuals to wholeheartedly dedicate themselves to taking action toward a carbon-neutral future (Robbins, 2016). The imperative for the global community to adopt a more carbon-neutral trajectory is evident, as underscored by the dire consequences of unchecked greenhouse gas emissions, as emphasized during the COP21 conference (Sovacool et al., 2023). Typical obstacles encompass susceptibility to the impacts of extreme climatic events, such as natural disasters like landslides and floods, as well as ecosystem deterioration, including ocean acidification, coastal erosion, and deforestation. The accelerated climate change can be attributed to the increase in human-caused greenhouse gases since the pre-industrial period. Climate science has clearly communicated the imperative for a significant overhaul to prevent the most severe outcomes of climate change. This shift should initiate early and result in substantial emissions reductions, well in advance of the year 2030 according to United Nations Climate Change. Businesses are leading the charge in attempts to lessen the effects of climate change as the globe struggles with this serious issue. Conducting a thorough investigation of the key drivers and variables that will lead to a net-zero economy is crucial as it will help navigate the intricate junction of environmental sustainability, business practices, and societal responsibility.

4. Material and Methods

In order to clear understanding of the complex relationship between the adoption of a net-zero economy and CSR, this chapter comprehensively investigates the drivers and critical factors toward the adoption of a net-zero economy and the interconnection between net-zero economy, CSR, and sustainable value creation. This research employs secondary data obtained from various sources like published papers, websites, and reports, aligning with the systematic literature review approach commonly adopted by scholars in diverse academic fields. This study uses secondary data analysis from sources like SAGE and EBSCO, as well as focused searches for qualitative information inside scholarly databases like Emerald and Scopus. This method rigorously gathers, analyzes, and synthesizes existing research to provide a comprehensive understanding of a specific subject or area (Nanu et al., 2024).

5. Analyses and Discussion

5.1. Drivers for the Adoption of a Net-zero Economy

The factors behind the development of a net-zero economy are critical because they are driving a paradigm-shifting worldwide movement toward environmental responsibility and sustainability. Businesses, governments, and people are compelled to reassess and adjust their practices due to the growing worries over climate change, which are further reinforced by stricter legislation and regulations (Deangelo & Harvey, 1998). The forces behind a net-zero economy represent a comprehensive response to the interrelated problems of climate change, encouraging creativity, resilience, and a common commitment to a healthier, more sustainable future for the earth. These forces (Fig. 14.1) are growing as global cooperation strengthens and consumer awareness grows. The drivers of the net-zero economy are covered in detail in this section.

1. *Climate Change Awareness*: Climate change represents a persistent altera-tion in weather patterns from the tropics to the poles (Reichler, 2009). This phenomenon poses a worldwide peril, exerting pressure on multiple sectors (Abbass et al., 2022). Earth's temperature has risen by an average of 0.14°F (0.08°C) per decade since 1880, or about 2°F in total. The rate of warming since 1981 is more than twice as fast 0.32°F (0.18°C) per decade. 2022 was the sixth warmest year on record based on NOAA's temperature data. The 2022 surface temperature was 1.55°F (0.86°C) warmer than the 20th-century average of 57.0°F (13.9°C) and 1.90°F (1.06°C) warmer than the pre-industrial period (1880–1900). The extent of future warming on Earth hinges on the quantity of carbon dioxide and other greenhouse gases released in the com-ing decades. Presently, our actions, such as the combustion of fossil fuels and deforestation, contribute approximately 11 billion metric tons of carbon (equivalent to slightly over 40 billion metric tons of carbon dioxide) into the atmosphere annually. This exceeds what natural processes can remove, lead-ing to a yearly rise in atmospheric carbon dioxide levels. Growing awareness of the urgent need to combat climate change and its severe consequences has led to increased support for net-zero goals. Extreme weather events, rising global temperatures and scientific evidence have made people more concerned about the environment. Climate change is a matter of worldwide

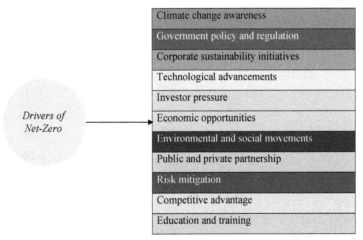

Fig. 14.1.   Drivers for the Adoption of a Net-zero Economy. *Source*: Authors compilation.

apprehension due to its impact on environmentally friendly expansion and the promotion of sustainable development. It jeopardizes ecosystems and the variety of life, impacts the availability of water resources, human communities, and the occurrence and magnitude of extreme weather occurrences, leading to noteworthy repercussions for food production, human welfare, socio-economic operations, and economic productivity (OECD).

In Table 14.1, the top 10 countries with the highest CO_2 emissions globally are listed, which are measured in million metric tons (Mt), as per the EU JRC 2020 data.

2. *Government Policy and Regulation*: Governments around the world are implementing policies and regulations to reduce greenhouse gas emissions (Deangelo & Harvey, 1998). These include carbon pricing mechanisms, renewable energy incentives, and stringent emissions targets, which incentivize businesses to adopt sustainable practices. Table 14.2 Specific policy instruments according to the report of the Organization for Economic Co-operation and Development (OECD).

There are several international environmental conventions and agreements aimed at addressing various environmental issues. Here, Table 14.3 is a list of some of the major ones.

These are just a few examples of international environmental agreements that address a range of environmental issues, from climate change and biodiversity conservation to ozone layer protection and the management of hazardous waste.

Table 14.1.   Top 10 CO_2-Emitting Countries in the World (Total CO_2 in Mt) – EU JRC 2020.

S. No.	Countries	CO_2 Emission
1	China	11,680.42
2	United States	4,535.30
3	India	2,411.73
4	Russia	1,674.23
5	Japan	1,061.77
6	Iran	690.24
7	Germany	636.88
8	South Korea	621.47
9	Saudi Arabia	588.81
10	Indonesia	568.27

Source: https://edgar.jrc.ec.europa.eu/report_2023.

Table 14.2.   Specific Policy Instruments (OECD).

Taxes	Taxes are part of the policy mix used by some Annex I countries (Australia, Austria, Belarus, Belgium, Bulgaria, Canada, etc.) to reduce GHG emissions. These include carbon taxes, carbon/energy taxes as well as taxes on process emissions such as N_2O.
Carbon/energy taxes	Carbon taxes were first introduced in the early 1990s in a handful of northern European countries. Carbon or carbon/energy taxes are becoming increasingly used by countries to reduce CO_2 emissions, despite significant concerns raised by industry.
Taxes on other gases	Emissions of non-CO_2 gases from industry are more commonly limited by non-tax policies such as regulations or voluntary approaches. However, France has put in place a tax on emissions of non-CO_2 gases.
Voluntary approaches	The use of voluntary approaches (VAs) as a tool to reduce emissions from industry is widespread and has been used as a tool to reduce GHG emissions since the early 1990s in some countries.

Source: https://www.oecd.org/.

Table 14.3.   List of International Environmental Conventions.

Name	Year
Ramsar Convention	1971
CITES	1973
Bonn Convention	1979
Vienna Convention	1985
Montreal Protocol	1987
Basel Convention	1989
Convention on Biological Diversity	1992
United Nations Framework Convention on Climate Change (UNFCCC)	1992
Rio Summit	1992
UNCCD	1994
Kyoto Protocol	1997
Rotterdam Convention	1998

(*Continued*)

Table 14.3.   (*Continued*)

Name	Year
Cartagena Protocol on Biosafety	2000
Stockholm Convention	2001
UN-REDD	2008
Nagoya Protocol	2010
Minamata Convention	2013
COP21	2016
Kigali Amendment	2016
COP24	2018
COP25	2019

Source: World Meteorological Organization and Escobar-Pemberthy and Ivanova (2020).

3. *Corporate Sustainability Initiatives*: Sustainable Development Goal 13 (SDG 13) is one of the 17 goals established by the United Nations General Assembly in 2015 as part of the 2030 Agenda for Sustainable Development (Carlsen & Bruggemann, 2022). The goal aims to take urgent action to combat climate change and its impacts. In recent years, the Indian government has taken several steps toward achieving SDG 13, including the development of renewable energy and energy efficiency policies, as well as efforts to promote sustainable transportation and reduce greenhouse gas emissions. However, achieving SDG 13 requires a collective effort from all stakeholders, including businesses, governments, and civil society. Many companies are recognizing the long-term benefits of sustainability and are making commitments to achieve net-zero emissions.

4. *Technological Advancements*: Advances in renewable energy technologies, energy efficiency, and carbon capture and storage have made it more feasible and cost-effective for organizations to reduce their carbon footprints (Abolhosseini et al., 2014). Consumers are increasingly looking for sustainable products and services, and they are willing to support companies that align with their values. This creates a market incentive for businesses to adopt more eco-friendly practices.

5. *Investor Pressure*: The main objective of corporations, is to optimize the prosperity of their stakeholders (Xiang et al., 2022). Investors, including institutional investors, are pressuring companies to disclose their environmental impact and transition to net-zero (Gözlügöl & Ringe, 2022). ESG (Environmental, Social, and Governance) criteria are now a significant consideration for investment decisions. The shift toward a net-zero economy can lead to economic opportunities, such as the creation of green jobs and growth in sustainable industries (Nyangchak, 2022). This economic potential encourages businesses and governments to invest in sustainable solutions.

6. *International Agreements*: Global agreements like the Paris Agreement provide a framework for countries to work together toward net-zero emissions, fostering international cooperation and commitments (Levin et al., 2020). Grassroots movements and NGOs play a crucial role in advocating for climate action. Protests, awareness campaigns, and public pressure can influence policies and corporate practices (Jeudy-Hugo et al., 2021). Collaborative efforts between governments, businesses, and non-governmental organizations can drive innovation, research, and the development of sustainable technologies and practices (Harangozó & Zilahy, 2015). Businesses are increasingly recognizing that a failure to address climate change risks can harm their operations and supply chains. They are adopting sustainability measures to mitigate potential risks (Giannakis & Papadopoulos, 2016). Companies that embrace sustainability and achieve net-zero goals can gain a competitive edge in the marketplace by attracting environmentally-conscious customers and partners (Naidoo & Gasparatos, 2018).

These drivers, in combination, are pushing society toward adopting a net-zero economy, and the transition is expected to continue as climate change concerns grow and the benefits of sustainability become more apparent. While there is a growing global push toward a net-zero economy, several barriers and critical factors can influence the speed and success of this transition. Understanding these challenges is essential for addressing them effectively.

5.2. Critical Factors for the Adoption of a Net-zero Economy

The characteristics that have been determined to be crucial for the implementation of a net-zero economy are extremely important since they serve as the cornerstones required to successfully negotiate the challenging shift toward environmental sustainability. A roadmap is provided by explicit and enforced policy frameworks, which provide individuals and companies the direction they need to match their operations with net-zero goals. The identification of critical factors for the adoption of a net-zero economy is explained (Fig. 14.2) in depth in the section that follows:

1. *Ambitious and Effective Climate Policies*: It is crucial for governments, around the world to establish climate policies that are enforceable and set clear targets for reducing emissions in all sectors (Fekete et al., 2021). These policies should include mechanisms like carbon pricing, investments in energy sources, promotion of energy efficiency and encouragement of practices. Carbon pricing can take forms, such as carbon taxes or emissions trading systems. It assigns a cost to carbon emissions, which makes polluting activities more expensive and encourages both businesses and individuals to opt for alternatives. Governments can impose regulations on energy efficiency and offer financial rewards for adopting energy-saving measures. Governments may promote the adoption of sustainable practices in a number of ways, such as by offering tax breaks for green buildings, subsidizing electric vehicles, and launching public awareness campaigns that support sustainable lifestyles.

Fig. 14.2.   Critical Factors for the Adoption of a Net-zero Economy.
Source: Authors compilation.

2. *Technological Innovation and Deployment*: Innovation plays a pivotal role in developing and deploying low-carbon technologies that enable emissions reductions across various sectors (Malhotra & Schmidt, 2020). This includes advancements in renewable energy, energy storage, electric vehicles, sustainable materials, and carbon capture and storage technologies. Continuous innovation is necessary to improve the efficiency, cost-effectiveness, and scalability of renewable energy technologies, making them more competitive with fossil fuels. Advancements in battery technology and charging infrastructure are essential for making electric vehicles more affordable, reliable, and accessible, reducing emissions from the transportation sector. Carbon Capture and Storage (CCS) technologies have the potential to capture carbon dioxide emissions from industrial processes and power plants, preventing their release into the atmosphere. While CCS still faces challenges in terms of cost and efficiency, it could play a role in achieving net-zero emissions.

3. *International Cooperation and Collaboration*: Achieving a zero economy requires a united effort, where countries come together to cooperate and collaborate (Stern & Valero, 2021). This involves sharing approaches facilitating the transfer of technology and supporting developing nations in their decarbonization efforts. By learning from each other's experiences and achievements, in implementing climate policies developing low-carbon technologies and promoting practices countries can make progress. Developed nations can play a role by assisting developing countries in accessing and adopting low-carbon technologies empowering them to embrace a development path. Moreover, developed nations can extend technical support to aid developing countries in transitioning toward a low-carbon economy while building resilience, against the impacts of climate change.

4. *Financing and Investment*: Transitioning to a net-zero economy requires significant upfront investments in clean technologies, infrastructure, and research and development. Governments, financial institutions, and private investors must work together to mobilize the necessary capital and create a supportive environment for green investments (Clark et al., 2018). Governments can play a key role in mobilizing financial resources by issuing green

bonds, providing subsidies or tax breaks for green investments, and establishing public-private partnerships. Financial institutions can reduce the perceived risks of green investments by improving the availability of data and information, developing innovative financing mechanisms, and investing in green investment funds. Encouraging the incorporation of Environmental, Social and Governance (ESG) criteria into investment decisions can steer capital toward sustainable businesses and projects.

5. *Public Awareness and Behavioral Change*: Public awareness and engagement are essential for driving behavioral changes that contribute to emissions reduction (Whitmarsh et al., 2011). This includes promoting sustainable consumption patterns, encouraging energy efficiency practices, and supporting the adoption of cleaner transportation options. Governments and organizations can raise public awareness about climate change and the need for a net-zero transition through educational campaigns, public service announcements, and community outreach programs. During crises, CSR initiatives strategically influence customer perceptions by mitigating negative rumors or information spread via local media, customer interactions, or online platforms, cultivating a favorable and socially responsible corporate image (Sultan et al., 2024).

6. *Circular Economy Principles*: Embracing circular economy principles, which aim to eliminate waste and extend the lifecycle of resources, can significantly reduce emissions associated with production, consumption, and disposal (Velenturf & Purnell, 2021). Promoting a circular economy mindset encourages consumers to reduce their consumption, reuse items whenever possible, and recycle materials efficiently, minimizing waste generation and resource depletion.

5.3. CSR and a Net-zero Economy Are Interconnected

Growing environmental consciousness and the advancement of environmental laws worldwide are associated with the rise of CSR as a major global movement (Sultan et al., 2024). CSR and the transition to a net-zero economy are closely related, as they both reflect a company's commitment to sustainability, environmental responsibility, and social impact. Here's how CSR and a net-zero economy are interconnected.

CSR and the Net-zero Economy: In the face of pressing environmental challenges, particularly climate change, businesses are increasingly recognizing the importance of integrating sustainability principles into their operations. CSR has emerged as a strategic approach for businesses to manage their environmental, social, and governance (ESG) impacts, while also contributing to a more sustainable future. The net-zero economy, an ambitious goal of achieving a balance between greenhouse gas emissions and removals, offers a framework for businesses to align their CSR efforts with a global effort to mitigate climate change.

CSR as a Catalyst for Net-zero: CSR, when implemented effectively, can play a crucial role in driving the transition to a net-zero economy. By integrating sustainability into their core business strategies, companies can reduce their environmental footprint, enhance their social impact, and improve their long-term financial performance. Businesses can significantly contribute by adopting renewable energy sources. Transitioning to clean energy sources, such as solar, wind, and geothermal power, can significantly reduce a company's carbon footprint (Kabeyi & Olanrewaju, 2022). Implementing energy-efficient practices and technologies can lower energy consumption and associated emissions (Al-Ghandoor et al., 2008). Implementing waste reduction strategies, such as recycling, composting, and resource recovery, can minimize a company's environmental impact (Ahluwalia & Patel, 2018). Strong corporate governance practices can enhance CSR efforts and contribute to a net-zero economy (Helfaya & Aboud, 2023).

6. Conclusion

The adoption of a net-zero economy is being pushed by a number of factors working together to push society in that direction. As awareness of climate change and the advantages of sustainability grows, this shift is anticipated to continue. The adoption of a net-zero economy and the accomplishment of global climate targets depend on overcoming obstacles and utilizing crucial elements. Reaching net-zero emissions has benefited underprivileged populations, resulting in a more equitable distribution of climate-related benefits, reduction of negative health effects, and lessening of social inequalities, particularly in areas with low economic status (Sovacool et al., 2023). It necessitates a multifaceted strategy including many local, national, and international players. Because both CSR and the shift to a net-zero economy emphasize sustainability, environmental responsibility, and social effect, they are related. The adoption of a sustainable net-zero economy has a positive impact on financial, environmental, and social performance. Notably, it exerts a stronger influence on social performance. Consequently, transitioning to a net-zero economy will bring greater benefits to both society and local communities (Bag, 2024). The interconnectedness of CSR and the net-zero economy highlights the critical role that businesses can play in achieving a sustainable future. By integrating sustainability principles into their operations, companies can simultaneously reduce their environmental footprint, enhance their social impact, and improve their long-term financial performance. Embracing CSR as a strategic approach can position businesses as leaders in the transition to a net-zero economy, contributing to a more sustainable and resilient world.

References

Abbass, K., Qasim, M. Z., Song, H., Murshed, M., Mahmood, H., & Younis, I. (2022). A review of the global climate change impacts, adaptation, and sustainable mitigation measures. *Environmental Science and Pollution Research, 29*(28), 42539–42559. https://doi.org/10.1007/s11356-022-19718-6

Abolhosseini, S., Heshmati, A., & Altmann, J. (2014). *A review of renewable energy supply and energy efficiency technologies* [SSRN Scholarly Paper 2432429]. IZA Institute of Labor Economics. https://doi.org/10.2139/ssrn.2432429

Ahluwalia, I. J., & Patel, U. (2018). *Solid waste management in India: An assessment of resource recovery and environmental impact* [Working Paper 356]. Indian Council for Research on International Economic Relations. https://www.econstor.eu/handle/10419/203690

Al-Ghandoor, A., Al-Hinti, I., Jaber, J. O., & Sawalha, S. A. (2008). Electricity consumption and associated GHG emissions of the Jordanian industrial sector: Empirical analysis and future projection. *Energy Policy, 36*(1), 258–267. https://doi.org/10.1016/j.enpol.2007.09.020

Bag, S. (2024). From resources to sustainability: A practice-based view of net zero economy implementation in small and medium business-to-business firms. *Benchmarking: An International Journal, 31*(6), 1876–1894. https://doi.org/10.1108/BIJ-01-2023-0056

Bonsu, N. O. (2020). Towards a circular and low-carbon economy: Insights from the transitioning to electric vehicles and net zero economy. *Journal of Cleaner Production, 256*, 120659. https://doi.org/10.1016/j.jclepro.2020.120659

Carlsen, L., & Bruggemann, R. (2022). The 17 United Nations' sustainable development goals: A status by 2020. *International Journal of Sustainable Development & World Ecology, 29*(3), 219–229. https://doi.org/10.1080/13504509.2021.1948456

Clark, R., Reed, J., & Sunderland, T. (2018). Bridging funding gaps for climate and sustainable development: Pitfalls, progress and potential of private finance. *Land Use Policy, 71*, 335–346. https://doi.org/10.1016/j.landusepol.2017.12.013

Deangelo, B. J., & Harvey, L. D. D. (1998). The jurisdictional framework for municipal action to reduce greenhouse gas emissions: Case studies from Canada, the USA and Germany. *Local Environment, 3*(2), 111–136. https://doi.org/10.1080/13549839808725553

Escobar-Pemberthy, N., & Ivanova, M. (2020). Implementation of multilateral environmental agreements: Rationale and design of the environmental conventions index. *Sustainability, 12*(17), Article 177098. https://doi.org/10.3390/su12177098

Fankhauser, S., Smith, S. M., Allen, M., Axelsson, K., Hale, T., Hepburn, C., Kendall, J. M., Khosla, R., Lezaun, J., Mitchell-Larson, E., Obersteiner, M., Rajamani, L., Rickaby, R., Seddon, N., & Wetzer, T. (2022). The meaning of net zero and how to get it right. *Nature Climate Change, 12*(1), 15–21. https://doi.org/10.1038/s41558-021-01245-w

Fekete, H., Kuramochi, T., Roelfsema, M., Elzen, M. den, Forsell, N., Höhne, N., Luna, L., Hans, F., Sterl, S., Olivier, J., van Soest, H., Frank, S., & Gusti, M. (2021). A review of successful climate change mitigation policies in major emitting economies and the potential of global replication. *Renewable and Sustainable Energy Reviews, 137*, 110602. https://doi.org/10.1016/j.rser.2020.110602

Gençsü, I., Grayson, A., Mason, N., & Foresti, M. (2020). *Migration and skills for the low-carbon transition* [Working Paper]. Overseas Development Institute. https://apo.org.au/node/307391

Giannakis, M., & Papadopoulos, T. (2016). Supply chain sustainability: A risk management approach. *International Journal of Production Economics, 171*, 455–470. https://doi.org/10.1016/j.ijpe.2015.06.032

Gözlügöl, A. A., & Ringe, W.-G. (2022). Private companies: The missing link on the path to net zero. *Journal of Corporate Law Studies, 22*(2), 887–929. https://doi.org/10.1080/14735970.2023.2191779

Harangozó, G., & Zilahy, G. (2015). Cooperation between business and non-governmental organizations to promote sustainable development. *Journal of Cleaner Production, 89*, 18–31. https://doi.org/10.1016/j.jclepro.2014.10.092

Helfaya, A., & Aboud, A. (2023). Editorial for the special issue "corporate governance, social responsibility, innovation, and sustainable business development goals". *Sustainability, 15*(12), Article 129471. https://doi.org/10.3390/su15129471

Jeudy-Hugo, S., Re, L. L., & Falduto, C. (2021). *Understanding countries' net-zero emissions targets.* OECD. https://doi.org/10.1787/8d25a20c-en

Kabeyi, M. J. B., & Olanrewaju, O. A. (2022). Sustainable energy transition for renewable and low carbon grid electricity generation and supply. *Frontiers in Energy Research, 9.* https://www.frontiersin.org/articles/10.3389/fenrg.2021.743114

Levin, K., Rich, D., Ross, K., Fransen, T., & Elliott, C. (2020). *Designing and communicating net-zero targets* [Working Paper]. World Resources Institute. https://apo.org.au/node/307656

Malhotra, A., & Schmidt, T. S. (2020). Accelerating low-carbon innovation. *Joule, 4*(11), 2259–2267. https://doi.org/10.1016/j.joule.2020.09.004

Naidoo, M., & Gasparatos, A. (2018). Corporate environmental sustainability in the retail sector: Drivers, strategies and performance measurement. *Journal of Cleaner Production, 203,* 125–142. https://doi.org/10.1016/j.jclepro.2018.08.253

Nanu, L., Rahman, I., Ali, F., & Martin, D. S. (2024). Enhancing the hospitality experience: A systematic review of 22 years of physical environment research. *International Journal of Hospitality Management, 119,* 103692. https://doi.org/10.1016/j.ijhm.2024.103692

Nyangchak, N. (2022). Emerging green industry toward net-zero economy: A systematic review. *Journal of Cleaner Production, 378,* 134622. https://doi.org/10.1016/j.jclepro.2022.134622

O'Flynn, C., Seymour, V., Crawshaw, J., Parrott, T., Reeby, C., & Silva, S. R. P. (2021). The road to net zero: A case study of innovative technologies and policy changes used at a medium-sized university to achieve C_{zero} by 2030. *Sustainability, 13*(17), Article 179954. https://doi.org/10.3390/su13179954

Reichler, T. (2009). Changes in the atmospheric circulation as indicator of climate change. In T. M. Letcher (Ed.), *Climate change* (Chap. 7, pp. 145–164). Elsevier. https://doi.org/10.1016/B978-0-444-53301-2.00007-5

Robbins, A. (2016). How to understand the results of the climate change summit: Conference of Parties21 (COP21) Paris 2015. *Journal of Public Health Policy, 37*(2), 129–132. https://doi.org/10.1057/jphp.2015.47

Sindhwani, R., Singh, P. L., Behl, A., Afridi, Mohd. S., Sammanit, D., & Tiwari, A. K. (2022). Modeling the critical success factors of implementing net zero emission (NZE) and promoting resilience and social value creation. *Technological Forecasting and Social Change, 181,* 121759. https://doi.org/10.1016/j.techfore.2022.121759

Sippel, S. (2020). Climate change now detectable from any single day of weather at global scale. *Nature Climate Change, 10,* 35–41.

Sovacool, B. K., Del Rio, D. F., & Zhang, W. (2023). The political economy of net-zero transitions: Policy drivers, barriers, and justice benefits to decarbonization in eight carbon-neutral countries. *Journal of Environmental Management, 347,* 119154. https://doi.org/10.1016/j.jenvman.2023.119154

Stern, N., & Valero, A. (2021). Innovation, growth and the transition to net-zero emissions. *Research Policy, 50*(9), 104293. https://doi.org/10.1016/j.respol.2021.104293

Sultan, M. F., Shaikh, S. K., & Tunio, M. N. (2024). CSR activities as a neutralizer: Halo effect of CSR for Asian companies. In *Strategies and approaches of corporate social responsibility toward multinational enterprises* (pp. 176–183). IGI Global. https://doi.org/10.4018/979-8-3693-0363-4.ch010

Sultan, M. F., Tunio, M. N., Shaikh, S. K., & Shaikh, E. (2024). Strategic impact of corporate social responsibility: A perspective from the hospitality industry. In *Strategies and approaches of corporate social responsibility toward multinational enterprises* (pp. 23–33). IGI Global. https://doi.org/10.4018/979-8-3693-0363-4.ch002

Velenturf, A. P. M., & Purnell, P. (2021). Principles for a sustainable circular economy. *Sustainable Production and Consumption, 27,* 1437–1457. https://doi.org/10.1016/j.spc.2021.02.018

Virmani, N., Agarwal, S., Raut, R. D., Paul, S. K., & Mahmood, H. (2022). Adopting net-zero in emerging economies. *Journal of Environmental Management, 321*, 115978. https://doi.org/10.1016/j.jenvman.2022.115978

Whitmarsh, L., Seyfang, G., & O'Neill, S. (2011). Public engagement with carbon and climate change: To what extent is the public 'carbon capable'? *Global Environmental Change, 21*(1), 56–65. https://doi.org/10.1016/j.gloenvcha.2010.07.011

Xiang, H., Shaikh, E., Tunio, M. N., Watto, W. A., & Lyu, Y. (2022). Impact of corporate governance and CEO remuneration on bank capitalization strategies and payout decision in income shocks period. *Frontiers in Psychology, 13*. https://doi.org/10.3389/fpsyg.2022.901868

Chapter 15

Corporate Social Responsibility: A Strategic Move to Achieve Sustainability for Better Organizational Performance in the Tourism Sector

Aaliya Ashraf and Nancy Sahni

Mittal School of Business, Lovely Professional University, Punjab, India

Abstract

Purpose: This chapter will look closely at CSR in its first section. The necessity of striking a balance between company aims and CSR goals will be covered next. The significance of CSR in the travel and tourism industry will also be discussed. Lastly, a thorough discussion of how CSR may be used as a tactical move to guarantee sustainability and market competitiveness will round off the chapter.

Methodology/study design/approach: This chapter benefits from the wide range of secondary data sources that are cited as well as the inclusion of important industry reports and assessments.

Findings: Incorporating CSR into the tourism industry is not just a moral duty but also a critical strategic move toward attaining sustainability and maximizing corporate effectiveness. In light of the ever-changing global landscape that is marked by social inequality, environmental concerns, and issues related to cultural preservation, the future course that tourism-related businesses will follow is increasingly being determined by CSR.

Corporate Social Responsibility, Corporate Governance and Business Ethics in Tourism
Management: A Business Strategy for Sustainable Organizational Performance, 211–229
Copyright © 2025 by Aaliya Ashraf and Nancy Sahni
Published under exclusive licence by Emerald Publishing Limited
doi:10.1108/978-1-83608-704-520241015

Originality/value: The paradigm presented in this chapter offers a fresh and systematic perspective on CSR as a strategic instrument for attaining sustainability in the travel and tourist industry.

Keywords: Corporate Social Responsibility; sustainability; organizational performance; strategic move; multi-stakeholder

Introduction

Although the idea of CSR is not new, interest in it among academics and practitioners is expanding. Many see CSR as an ideology and collection of actions that help the environment, society, and economy. This viewpoint is based on the understanding that businesses have more responsibilities than just making money. CSR is becoming more frequently acknowledged as a holistic approach that acknowledges enterprises' involvement in fostering beneficial effects beyond their current financial interests. Its goal is to create benefits for shareholders and the larger community. It might be challenging to acknowledge and carry out these obligations since it's not always clear what constitutes the best way to show dedication. However, the tourism sector appears to have distinct and definite responsibilities that go beyond its business dealings because of its intimate ties to target environments and communities which are crucial parts of its services.

The negative effects of commercial operations have given rise to several historical instances of social agitation, such as the British West Indian slave farms case. Early social entrepreneurs' main objective was to enhance the well-being of their workers; these initiatives are seen as the precursors of corporate social responsibility initiatives (Werther & Chandler, 2011). Contemporary Corporate Social Responsibility (CSR) originated with the publication of Howard Bowen's groundbreaking book "Responsibilities of a Businessman" in the 1950s. Bowen (1953) defined CSR as the obligations placed on businesses to make sure that their operations are consistent with societal norms and values. In his discussion on CSR, Bowen stressed the need of having a positive effect on society at large. During this time, businesses began to gain greater public acclaim for their ability to solve environmental and social issues in addition to their business goals.

Although CSR is broadly accepted, there has been strong opposition to it. Friedman (1970) presented a contrasting viewpoint in his paper "The Social Responsibility of Enterprise is to Increase Profits," arguing in favor of a shareholder-centric strategy that puts the owners of the company's profits first. That being said, opinions about the place of businesses in society have changed over time. More and more people see corporations as essential components of society, with duties to uphold moral corporate conduct, solve social and environmental issues, and meet economic commitments. This method of approaching CSR using sociology draws attention to the ways in which firm's impact society at large and promotes a more thorough comprehension of CSR that extends beyond making financial gains.

The notion of CSR was further refined after it was first conceived, with different scholars coming up with different definitions and frameworks. By providing unique viewpoints on the obligations of corporations to society, Frederick (1960), McGuire (1963), Davis (1967), Walton (1967), and Carroll (1979, 1991) contributed to the creation of CSR. Stakeholder Theory (Freeman 1984) was introduced by R. Edward Freeman in 1984. It asserts that firms have connections to various societal groups, referred to as stakeholders. This argument contends that ethical companies ought to take into account the interests of all stakeholders, not just shareholders when making decisions. Corporate responsibility is increasingly more widely defined to encompass the welfare of various stakeholders, including suppliers, workers, communities, and the environment, in addition to financial benefits, thanks to the adoption of this stakeholder approach.

Review of Literature

According to Peters (2018), CSR in the tourism industry refers to travel businesses' social obligations, which include abiding by the moral, legal, and ethical norms of the community. According to the World Travel & Tourism Council (2019) and the United Nations World Tourism Organization (2021), the tourism industry is currently one of the most significant sectors of the global economy. It is highly dependent on open, healthy natural resources, a positive social environment, and other factors, but it also has a significant impact on the environment, society, economy, and a thriving economic climate. As a result, the travel and tourism industry needs to arrange travel in a way that benefits both businesses and society as a whole. The attainment of a competitive advantage through social responsibility and anticipating social obligations are prerequisites for the success of this strategy, as noted by Fifka (2016). As a result, CSR plays a major role in the travel and tourism sector. Over the past half-century, there has been a discernible increase in CSR awareness and adoption in numerous industries, including multinational enterprises. Developed and developing nations' small and medium-sized businesses (SMEs) are also covered. Corporate spending on CSR strategy and implementation has been connected to this growth (Palacios-Marqués & Devece-Carañana, 2013).

Nonetheless, because corporate social responsibility is a controversial topic, there is not a universally accepted definition of it. According to the Sustainable Development Council of World Business (1999), CSR refers to an organization's continuous efforts to maintain ethical standards in its business practices, foster economic expansion, and simultaneously enhance the standard of living for its workers, their families, the local community, and the general public. Fernandez-Kranz and Santalo (2010) assert that this demonstrates that CSR is not a commercial event or activity, but rather the primary goal of a corporation that goes above and beyond what is needed by law and business in order to serve society (Torelli et al., 2010). It seems that CSR is essentially a strategic decision. CSR is defined by Kucukusta et al. (2016) as an organization's commitment to recognize and carry out its social and environmental duties in addition to its business obligations. As a result, when we talk about duty in relation to tourism, we are talking about the social duties that travel agencies have to preserve the moral, ethical, and legal norms of a community (Peters, 2018). CSR is the term for this.

In the 1950s, there was an exponential rise in international travel, and this corresponded with businesses paying more attention to CSR. Merely 25 million foreign visitors arrived compared to the estimated 1.5 billion foreign visitors at the end of 2019 (United Nations World Tourism Organization 2021). The company's internal corporate social policy is restricted to the company's structure and serves as the social policy for its employees. The social policy that the corporation, or certain of its subsidiaries, pursues for the local community is known as social policy. In light of this, businesses employ the corporate responsibility approach to carry out corporate initiatives targeted at the advancement of human resources, community assistance, conservation of natural resources, etc. (Ivanova & Bikeeva, 2016). In the end, successful corporate performance determines social and economic stability, social welfare, and the standard of living for the nation's population.

Dedusenko (2017) discovered common tendencies and patterns in the contributions provided by international and Russian tourism firms in Russia through an exploration of corporate responsibility concerns, as demonstrated by the experiences of tourism organizations (Blinova, 2018). In the meantime, one of the most recent developments in the global tourist business is the growth of CSR in the travel and tourism sector. The social responsibility system is especially important for tourism-related enterprises and organizations because of the sector's rapid growth within the national economy, social focus on satisfying the requirements of individuals, and raising the standard of living (Kumar & Kumar, 2018).

Activities that a business engages in beyond its immediate profit-making goals and legal requirements are commonly referred to as CSR (McWilliams & Siegal, 2001, p. 117). It considers business ethics and recognizes the significance of parties other than owners, investors, and shareholders, according to Schmidheiny et al. (1997). CSR is based on the principle that businesses have obligations to society that extend above their personal financial goals and that they should prioritize societal requirements, including environmental preservation (Hopkins, 1999). The case for CSR and sustainable development have been intertwined (UN, 2004). The United Nations has more recently promoted a "global compact" encouraging responsible business companies to collaborate with other stakeholders, in an attempt to fulfill a vision of a more environmentally friendly and inclusive global economy (UN Global Compact, 2005). Sustainable development puts the welfare of the person and the advancement of society above the protection of the environment. The triple bottom line paradigm, which takes into account not only financial advantages but also social and environmental repercussions, is frequently used in conjunction with this holistic approach (Zadek, 2002).

While making money and turning a profit continue to be the main objectives, CSR is recognized to have practical financial and cost-saving benefits in a number of areas, such as employee attraction and retention, brand perception enhancement, advertising, distinctiveness, as opposed to competitive positioning

(Pearce & Doh, 2005). Though its commonly believed that CSR efforts will result in both non-monetary and monetary benefits, the direct impact of CSR on financial and other outcomes is a subject of debate (Griffin & Mahon, 1997; Knox & Maklan, 2004). Furthermore, the execution of corporate social responsibility programs could necessitate extra costs, such as higher labor and material costs. This may result in inherent tensions between business goals and environmental and social interests. Hence, in order to avoid having their dedication to CSR initiatives interfere with the pursuit of crucial business objectives, organizations need to carefully manage these conflicts by finding the right balance.

CSR although not without its ambiguities and difficulties in practice, has been increasingly popular in the last few decades. It has grown in importance on business agendas and practically developed into a separate industry (BBC, 2004; PR Week. 2005). The increased interest in CSR is a reflection of broader societal trends as well as internal company incentives. The breadth and complexity of corporate obligations have grown as a result of globalization, especially for businesses operating in less developed areas. Nowadays, a lot of people think that corporations can help Third World nations develop (Twigg, 2001). These days, there are social norms about the conduct of private companies, and individuals and groups are speaking up and stepping up to effect change. In addition, environmental rules are becoming increasingly harsh in some countries, and breaching them has legal repercussions.

The majority of case studies and academic research on CSR come from North America and Europe, and the majority of the coverage of CSR occurs in Western environments. In contrast, although some local and foreign businesses support it, In Asia, the concept of CSR is still somewhat new. A few branded product companies have initiated talks and implemented inspections and standards of behavior with the local factories they operate with. However, considering the constant reports of corporate misuse and wrongdoing that appear in a new magazine dedicated to the subject, it would be inaccurate to imply that CSR methods are widely applied throughout Southeast Asia (CSR Asia Weekly, 2006).

Corporate Social Responsibility and Tourism

The tourism industry can benefit from discussions about CSR in the broader business world, but there are certain unique challenges that make it unique. Tourism entails the provision of services by individuals, providing participants with experiences that include lodging, entertainment, and transportation; this introduces possibly disruptive elements into the picture. Several scholarly investigations have explored the significant influence of tourism on the economics, society, cultures, and environments of the places visited; the industry has faced significant criticism due to its adverse effects (Tourism Concern, 2005). It is crucial to recognize, nevertheless, that tourism can also offer the essential jobs, revenue, and infrastructure that support the growth of destination economies and raise living standards. Furthermore, tourism has the potential to strengthen the case for protecting endangered resources and help fund conservation initiatives.

It's clear that travel agencies have unique and significant responsibilities with regard to a variety of conditions at the destinations they promote, which may eventually lead them to embrace CSR. The government is calling for improved tourism management and planning. The environmental movement and changing consumer preferences have all contributed to this trend. Companies exhibit a range of comprehension regarding corporate social responsibility, even as their reactions to these impacts differ. Nonetheless, there seems to be a discernible trend toward acknowledging these obligations and attempting to meet them.

With an emphasis on protecting the environment and cultural heritage, an increasing number of tourism businesses are pledging to use more sustainable practices (Diamantis, 1999; Stabler, 1997). These businesses claim to actively participate in industry efforts, work with governmental authorities, and base their operations on sustainability. The ambitiously sets 12 targets of a sustainable tourism agenda and offers suggestions for their implementation in a UNEP book (UNEP, 2005, pp. 18–19). Goals pertaining to local prosperity, social equity, employment quality, economic viability, visitor happiness, autonomy locally, community health, preservation of culture, integrity of the environment, nature, resource effectiveness, and environmental cleanliness have all been moved closer to, according to the World Travel and Tourism Council (WTTC, 2002). The tourism industry has made significant developments in a number of areas, including airlines (ICAO, 2001), hotels (UNEP, 2003), and tour operators (Kalisch, 2002).

However, similar to general skepticism, there are doubts over the level of commitment and accuracy of declarations of purpose and accomplishment, which typically have a propensity to be vague and difficult to verify. A lot of marketing makes strong claims about sustainability and ecotourism, implying that the products support and benefit both the natural and human surroundings (Wight, 1993). But the evidence for these assertions is sometimes ambiguous and sometimes inconsistent, suggesting that there may have been "green washing." Furthermore, individual organizations may find it difficult to implement significant change due to industry complexity, cost and control limitations, and other factors (Miller, 2001). Improvements across the board are still desperately needed, and outside pressure could be needed to hasten the process (Forsyth, 1995).

The terms sustainable development and CSR have a lot in common, and they are occasionally used synonymously. Sustainable tourism businesses are socially sensitive by nature, and CSR incorporates some basic sustainability principles. However, sustainable development aims to involve all pertinent stakeholders and give their opinions equal weight. Contrarily, CSR mainly emphasizes the company's perspective, keeping social and environmental agendas secondary and financial concerns at the forefront. A deeper and wider commitment is required for sustainable development, which is a component of a larger conversation that is pertinent to many facets of human activity and influences decisions made in both the public and commercial sectors. CSR, on the other hand, is exclusive to industry participants and focuses on a special voluntary aspect. CSR should therefore be analyzed in the context of the larger sustainability discourse, as it falls closer to the softer end of the sustainability continuum.

Research Questions:

RQ1. What is corporate social responsibility all about?
RQ2. Why is it important to strike a balance between CSR initiatives and business goals?
RQ3. What is the role of CSR in the tourism sector?
RQ4. How can CSR act as a strategic tool for attaining sustainability in the market?

Research Methodology

This chapter benefits from the wide range of secondary data sources that are cited as well as the inclusion of important industry reports and assessments. These studies provide a useful lens through which to study theoretical topics by offering insightful perspectives on current trends, issues, and opportunities within the tourist sector. Additionally, speaking with professionals and specialists in the field can provide firsthand knowledge and complex viewpoints that enhance the chapter's discussion. Through the utilization of the expertise and experiences of people who are actively engaged in the tourist sector, the chapter can offer a more thorough comprehension of developing concerns and real-world dynamics.

Moreover, case studies that provide noteworthy problems or effectively illustrate successful tourist projects can function as instructive examples to contextualize theoretical frameworks and empirical data. By providing readers with tangible examples to anchor abstract ideas in, the chapter has become more relevant and approachable. To present a comprehensive picture of the complex nature of tourism, the chapter also incorporates multidisciplinary research from disciplines including economics, sociology, psychology, and environmental studies. By fusing ideas from several academic fields, the chapter offers a more sophisticated understanding of the complex interactions that exist between vacationing, culture, society as a whole, and the environment.

Corporate Social Responsibility

CSR protects workers' health since it fosters a positive working relationship between the company and its sales force through supportive leadership. Employees are less likely to intend to leave an employer where there is greater alignment between their beliefs and the organization's (Fritz et al., 2017). Contented workers are more likely to be dedicated and fulfilled, which makes them desire to stick with the company (George et al., 2011). According to Aguinis and Glavas (2012), CSR initiatives have a noteworthy impact on the efficacy of firms, captivating and retaining their workforce. Nevertheless, prior research failed to identify a connection between employees' intentions to leave the company and the ethical atmosphere within it (Gong et al., 2021). Instead, studies highlighted the indirect impact that employees' intentions to leave the company have on CSR when they feel satisfied and show a commitment to the company (Govindarajo et al., 2020).

CSR programs foster a sense of pride among participants, which aids organizations in defining themselves (Tiep et al., 2022). Because of this, workers are more likely to be content with their current working connections and wwould not waste their time looking for new jobs elsewhere. The impact of insightful CSR on employee resigning intentions has not been extensively studied. According to the Islam et al. (2020), there is a negative correlation between employee involvement in CSR and employees' inclinations to quit their jobs. According to the Jaramillo et al., (2006), there is a direct and positive association between CSR and loyalty intention, and this relationship is mediated by perceived organizational trust. In an empirical study conducted by Jin et al. (2021) on the Dutch ABN-AMRO bank, staff members freely participated in a range of corporate social responsibility initiatives. The program participants, community volunteers, and non-volunteers had similar attitudes toward the value of their personal careers, their level of Organizational Citizenship Behavior (OCB), and their intention to leave their jobs. The authors discovered no differences in these groups' attitudes.

According to a study by Jones Christensen et al. (2014), CSR initiatives help people to identify with the company, which has a favorable impact on workers' intentions to stick around. There was no evidence for mediation over the claimed supervisor's behavior, despite the fact that there was favorable support in the mediation between the employees' want to stay and OCB loyalty. In light of the dearth of empirical evidence and inconsistent results, more research is needed to determine whether employees' opinions of CSR influence their inclination to quit their jobs. Prior research indicates a favorable and strong correlation between corporate social responsibility and organizational commitment. In a similar spirit, Jurkowska-Gomulka et al. (2021) contended that an organization's CSR initiatives raise organizational commitment.

An organization's efforts to advance sustainable development are referred to as CSR. While CSR has several meanings and terminologies, its fundamental components are the effects that a company's actions have on the economy, society, and environment; also, CSR is voluntary and takes stakeholder relationships into account. Stakeholder involvement, social effect, economic performance, volunteer efforts, and environmental responsibility are the five main elements of CSR that were highlighted in a recent study using frequency counts obtained through Google searches (Dahlsrud, 2008, as referenced in Carroll & Shabana, 2010).

A number of definitions of CSR can be found in academic literature; however, in more recent times, definitions have been introduced by institutions like the European Communities Commission. CSR, according to the European Commission (2011), is a strategic approach in which companies voluntarily incorporate social and environmental considerations into their operations, stakeholder connections, business strategy, and tactics. Archie B. Carroll is recognized for creating one of the most popular definitions of CSR in scholarly literature. Carroll presented a pyramid model that depicts four aspects of CSR. Within this framework, the legal, ethical, and charitable components are built upon the economic component. Reaching great performance at the basic levels is considered to be crucial for reaching the goals mentioned in the upper categories, even though firms should continually aim to succeed across all categories (Carroll, 1991).

Companies interact with and are a part of many societal groups. Society provides vital resources including markets, trained labor, and infrastructure, which are crucial for commercial operations. Changes in social structures that include historical, sociological, anthropological, and economic elements are what constantly sculpt the field of CSR. The development and perception of CSR activities are significantly influenced by the many ways that cultures define the interaction between business and society. According to Werther and Chandler (2011), CSR argues that maintaining societal legitimacy requires meeting stakeholder demands, which in turn guarantees a company's long-term financial sustainability. According to the moral case for CSR, a company's ability to succeed is influenced by external as well as internal variables, including acts that are consistent with society's ideals. The logical justification for CSR stems from companies' desire to maximize profits by minimizing operational limitations by doing voluntary and legally mandated measures.

CSR is a means for firms to minimize operational and financial restrictions by anticipating and resolving public worries, as social repercussions like activism and boycotts are becoming more and more influential in shaping corporate prosperity. The business case for CSR is predicated on the idea that including stakeholders and attending to their needs will increase the company's market value and contribute value (Werther & Chandler, 2011). A critical analysis of the ethical framework surrounding CSR marketing is provided by Van de Ven (2008). CSR should be differentiated from marketing geared toward a cause, which lacks strategic intent, and from green washing, in which businesses misrepresent themselves as environmentally conscious without actually integrating ecological principles into their operations, potentially misleading consumers.

Importance of Striking a Balance Between CSR Initiatives and Business Goals

Contemporary companies that aspire to thrive in a competitive and socially aware market need to reconcile their CSR initiatives with their financial goals. CSR is a company's commitment to operating in a way that sustainably affects the economy, society, and environment while balancing the interests of stakeholders. Conversely, firm goals encompass long-term viability, expansion, profitability, and market share. Engaging in corporate social responsibility initiatives can enhance a company's standing and perception. A growing number of stakeholders, including investors and customers, want to work with socially conscious companies. Companies can employ CSR initiatives to bolster their brand, set themselves apart from rivals, and draw in and hold on to ethically minded investors and customers by coordinating these efforts with their business objectives.

Integrating CSR initiatives with business goals can lower risks in a variety of ways. Addressing environmental issues or encouraging moral work standards, for instance, can reduce the possibility of bad press, legal repercussions, or consumer reactions. Companies may protect their reputation and financial line and develop resilience against future disasters by proactively tackling social and environmental challenges. CSR programs have the potential to improve staff retention, engagement, and satisfaction. Workers are drawn to businesses that show a dedication to responsibility for society and the environment because they are looking for meaning and purpose in their employment. Organizations can cultivate a sense of accomplishment and meaning among staff members, resulting in increased morale, productivity, and loyalty, by integrating CSR into business goals.

In an organization, pursuing CSR efforts can stimulate innovation and cultivate a continuous improvement culture. Innovative solutions to societal problems provide businesses with a competitive advantage in the marketplace. Including CSR in corporate objectives promotes innovation, teamwork, and the search for sustainable practices that may lead to financial savings, increased productivity, and new business prospects. Maintaining the organization's long-term viability and profitability requires striking a balance between CSR programs and business objectives. Companies that take Environmental, Social, and Governance (ESG) factors into account when making decisions are better able to predict and adjust to changing market trends, stakeholder expectations, and legal requirements. In a world that is changing quickly, this proactive strategy aids firms in being resilient, competitive, and relevant.

Successful CSR programs can improve communication and foster trust across a range of stakeholders, including communities, suppliers, investors, employees, and customers. By exhibiting a sincere dedication to social responsibility and moral corporate conduct, corporations can cultivate benevolence and faithfulness among interested parties, resulting in enduring collaborations and joint advantages. By incorporating CSR into corporate objectives, companies may guarantee adherence to all applicable laws, rules, and industry standards. Companies are required by law in many jurisdictions to report on their social and environmental impacts; not doing so may have negative legal and financial repercussions. Organizations may proactively manage compliance risks and fulfill their ethical and legal obligations by incorporating CSR issues into strategic planning and day-to-day operations.

Striking a Balance Between CSR Initiatives and Business Goals in the Tourism Industry

The tourist industry has a unique set of issues that make it crucial to strike a balance between corporate objectives and CSR efforts. By its very nature, tourism entails interaction with a wide range of stakeholders, including the environment, local populations, cultural heritage sites, and the economy. The preservation of animals, natural settings, and cultural heritage places is vital to the tourism sector. Participating in CSR projects that support cultural preservation, responsible tourism, and environmental protection helps to protect these priceless resources for coming generations. Tourism operators may ensure the long-term sustainability of their business while reducing the adverse effects of tourism operations on fragile ecosystems and cultural heritage sites by coordinating their CSR efforts with their commercial objectives.

Tourism places may become more attractive and competitive by implementing CSR programs. More and more tourists are looking for real, sustainable experiences that benefit the environment and nearby people. Tourism operators may stand out in the market, draw ethical tourists, and obtain an advantage over places that overlook sustainability and social responsibility by incorporating CSR principles into their business plans. For nearby towns, tourism has the potential to have a large positive socioeconomic impact, including the creation of jobs, revenue, and infrastructure. But these advantages are not always shared fairly, and travel can occasionally make socioeconomic gaps and racial tensions worse. Tourism businesses can cultivate positive relationships with local communities, empower underrepresented groups, and ensure equitable sharing of tourism benefits by giving priority to CSR projects that emphasize involvement in the community, capacity building, and inclusive economic development.

Negative social and environmental effects of tourism may include congestion, pollution, cultural eroding, and resource exploitation. Tourist organizations need to incorporate CSR programs into their operations in order to reduce these consequences and encourage sustainable tourist practices. This could entail putting into effect ethical waste management procedures, encouraging environmentally friendly modes of transportation, aiding regional environmental initiatives, and upholding the rights and customs of indigenous people. Tourism operators can reduce their environmental impact and improve the well-being of target communities by coordinating their CSR initiatives with their business objectives. Tourism businesses can improve their brand and reduce risks by taking part in CSR programs. Adverse effects on the environment or society may result in harm to one's reputation, regulatory examination, and a decline in the contentment of tourists. Tourism operators can enhance their brand reputation, establish trust with stakeholders, and reduce potential risks by taking proactive measures to solve these concerns through CSR efforts. Furthermore, showcasing a dedication to responsible tourism practices might draw in investors and passengers who respect moral business methods and social responsibility.

Numerous laws and guidelines pertaining to community involvement, cultural preservation, and environmental protection apply to the tourism sector. Tourism operators can ensure compliance with applicable laws and regulations and cultivate beneficial interactions with lawmakers, local authorities, and other stakeholders by incorporating CSR programs into their business goals. By fostering cooperation and collaboration with key stakeholders, this proactive strategy not only lowers regulatory risks but also facilitates easier operations and sustained growth. Maintaining the long-term viability and robustness of the tourism industry requires balancing corporate objectives with CSR initiatives. In the face of global concerns like climate change, financial turmoil, and public health crises, destinations must continue to be appealing and competitive. Sustainable tourism practices that stress the preservation of the environment, social inclusion, and economic prosperity are essential. Tourism operators can enhance their business strategies, adjust to evolving market conditions, and guarantee the sustained prosperity of their establishments and locations by incorporating CSR concepts.

Role of CSR in the Tourism Sector

Howard Bowen first proposed the idea of CSR in his groundbreaking 1953 book "Social Responsibilities of the Businessman." According to Carroll and Shabana

(2010), CSR started to emphasize performance, responsiveness, and responsibility by the 1970s. Frederick (1994) defined CSR as a business's dedication to the well-being of society. This generates concerns about how businesses react and the consequences that follow. As a result, corporate social responsiveness became the benchmark for measuring CSR. As a result, scholars began dissecting the many facets of business operations in this context.

Numerous tourism-related studies have examined different facets of CSR. For example, Cvelbar and Dwyer (2013) identified seven sustainable variables applicable to hotels using the Triple Bottom Line (TBL) approach. These included overall financial performance, hotel-specific performance, resource-usage practices that are environmentally conscious, interactions with the local community, customer and employee relations, and relationships with each other. Each of these factors had multiple indicators. A similar paradigm was used by Font et al. (2016) to investigate CSR in the cruise sector. Factors that they identified included economic ones (like economic outcomes and effects on the destination), social ones (like labor and employment rights and human rights), cultural factors, product accountability, environmental ones (such as waste, emissions, water, biodiversity, and effluents), as well as the standard of products and services. Some researchers have employed elements of the Triple Bottom Line (TBL) paradigm, albeit in varying degrees. Levy and Park (2011) identified four CSR components in the hotel industry, for instance, relationships with the community, employee relations, environmental difficulties, and product quality.

Hughes and Scheyvens (2016) have noted in recent years that culture is a crucial component of CSR. The specifics of every measurement found in the following are reviewed in earlier research. Numerous research works in the tourist domain have examined different facets of CSR. Cvelbar and Dwyer (2013) identified seven sustainability factors relevant to hotels using the Triple Bottom Line (TBL) approach. These include overall financial performance, hotel-specific accomplishments, resource-use practices, environmental awareness, involvement in the community, customer relations, and employee relationships. Each of these factors has multiple associated metrics.

A similar methodology was applied by Font et al. (2016) in their cruise industry study. Their model included social factors (human rights, labor rights, and employment rights), considerations related to the environment (water management, preservation of biodiversity, emissions control, and waste management), societal impacts, product responsibility, and economic aspects (economic outcomes and the economic influence on destinations). It also included product and service quality.

Several studies have employed the Triple Bottom Line (TBL) idea, albeit to differing degrees. In the hotel industry, for instance, Levy and Park (2011) emphasized four components of CSR operations: employee relations, community relations, environmental issues, and product quality. They noted that there was regular discussion of the three main facets of CSR practices: societal, environmental, and economic. Other factors that have been used to analyze CSR include the CSR triangle (economic, legal, ethical, and philanthropic), location social responsibility, CSR focused on society and stakeholders, self-referential CSR, other-centric CSR, and concerns of present situations and innovation.

Prior studies frequently described the characteristics of CSR without assessing how successful they are. Furthermore, as stressed by the European Communities (2001), being socially responsible entails going above and beyond the call of duty in addition to making additional investments in stakeholder engagement, environmental preservation, and human capital. As a result, the CSR pyramid's legal and moral obligations are essential to business operations and form a crucial part of the Triple Bottom Line (TBL). However, the tourism industry's CSR components go beyond the TBL framework to encompass the economy, environment, society, and most significantly, the cultural dimension which is not specifically mentioned in the CSR pyramid but is crucial to the sector.

CSR Acts as a Strategic Tool for Attaining Sustainability in the Market

CSR is a strategic instrument that helps companies traverse the intricate web of contemporary markets while also improving society. Fundamentally, CSR is incorporating ethical, social, and environmental factors into a business's operations and decision-making procedures. This strategic approach involves proactive devotion to ethical conduct, sustainability, and stakeholder engagement; it goes beyond simple altruism or regulatory compliance. First of all, CSR helps businesses stand out in cutthroat markets and improve the reputation of their brands. Businesses may win over customers who value sustainability and ethical behavior more and more by exhibiting a sincere dedication to social and environmental principles. Customers who share the company's values and mission can be drawn in by a robust CSR plan, which can also function as an effective marketing tool.

Second, by reducing risks and improving operational effectiveness, CSR supports long-term financial sustainability. By implementing strategies like supply chain transparency, ethical procurement, and environmental stewardship, businesses can lessen the probability of negative consequences to their reputation, fines from regulators, and interruptions to operations. Furthermore, through resource optimization, waste reduction, and energy efficiency improvements, CSR programs frequently result in cost savings. Additionally, CSR improves linkages with local communities, suppliers, investors, employees, and other stakeholders. Organizations can cultivate a healthy corporate culture and draw in top talent by allocating resources toward employee development, diversity and inclusion initiatives, and workplace health and safety. Furthermore, by interacting with local communities via volunteer work, charity endeavors, and sustainable development initiatives, businesses can foster a sense of trust and goodwill that will facilitate smoother operations and lessen opposition to their operations.

Furthermore, CSR is becoming more widely acknowledged as a catalyst for innovation and corporate expansion. Businesses that place a high priority on corporate social responsibility are frequently better able to predict and seize market opportunities because they are more aware of new trends, consumer preferences, and regulatory developments. In addition, interacting with stakeholders via CSR programs can yield insightful comments and insights that help shape marketing plans, new business models, and product development. In today's linked and socially conscious world, corporate social responsibility is a strategic instrument that helps organizations achieve sustainable growth and a competitive edge. Companies can improve their brand image, reduce risks, cultivate connections with stakeholders, spur innovation, and ultimately provide long-term value for shareholders and society at large by coordinating commercial objectives with societal and environmental goals.

Tourism enterprises are encouraged by CSR to implement sustainable practices that reduce adverse environmental effects, protect natural resources, and maintain cultural heritage. This covers programs like encouraging environmentally friendly modes of transportation, putting energy-saving technology into practice, funding regional conservation efforts, and honoring the customs and cultures of indigenous people. In order to guarantee local communities' participation in and benefits from tourist-related activities, CSR initiatives in the tourism sector frequently entail working with them. Programs for increasing capacity, developing skills, creating jobs, and fostering regional business and cultural endeavors are a few examples of this. Tourism firms have the potential to cultivate positive relationships, boost destination authenticity, and alleviate social disparities by means of meaningful and inclusive community engagement.

Businesses in the tourism industry have an obligation to make sure that their supply chains follow morally and environmentally sound standards. This entails obtaining goods and services from regional vendors and craftspeople, encouraging fair trade principles, and guaranteeing decent pay and working conditions for workers and subcontractors all the way down the supply chain. Through their assistance to small enterprises and support of local economies, tourist companies help to reduce poverty and foster community development. Tourism has a significant environmental impact, hence CSR efforts frequently aim to reduce adverse effects on ecosystems, biodiversity, and natural habitats. This can entail putting in place initiatives for recycling and trash reduction, preserving water supplies, safeguarding wildlife habitats, and advocating for environmentally friendly travel strategies including eco-friendly tours and low-impact travel. The attractiveness and long-term profitability of destinations are enhanced by tourism firms through their preservation of natural resources and mitigation of environmental damage.

For CSR in the tourist sector to be successful, local communities, governmental bodies, non-governmental organizations (NGOs), and other stakeholders need to be actively involved. Establishing trust, resolving issues, and coordinating CSR projects with stakeholder expectations, all depend on open communication, stakeholder consultation, and teamwork. Through promoting communication and collaboration, tourism enterprises may pinpoint common goals, make the most of available resources, and work together to effect positive change. By encouraging sustainable tourism development, community involvement, ethical supply chain management, environmental preservation, and stakeholder engagement, CSR is very important to the travel and tourism sector. Businesses in the tourism sector can help to maintain the industry's resilience and long-term existence by implementing CSR principles into their daily operations and decision-making procedures. This will improve their competitiveness, build brand recognition, and contribute to the well-being of destinations and communities.

Findings

Incorporating CSR into the tourism industry is not just a moral duty but also a critical strategic move toward attaining sustainability and maximizing corporate effectiveness. In light of the ever-changing global landscape that is marked by social inequality, environmental concerns, and issues related to cultural preservation, CSR is playing an increasingly important role in determining the direction that tourism enterprises will take in the future. Tourism firms may seize a multitude of chances for expansion, creativity, and resilience by considering CSR as more than just a collection of charitable deeds but rather as an essential part of strategic decision-making. Businesses can achieve a careful balance between social inclusion, environmental preservation, and economic prosperity by implementing sustainable tourism development techniques. In the long run, adopting programs like the creation of environmentally friendly infrastructure, the management of trash, and the promotion of real cultural experiences not only reduces adverse effects but also raises the competitiveness and appeal of the destination.

Moreover, the core of implementing CSR in the tourism industry effectively is community participation. Tourism businesses may cultivate authentic collaborations that beyond transactional relationships by providing equitable economic opportunities, skill development initiatives, and capacity-building programs to local communities. This cooperative strategy guards against future disputes and backlash by ensuring that tourism operations benefit the host communities and by encouraging a sense of pride and ownership among locals. Furthermore, since the procurement of goods and services frequently involves crossing many regional and cultural boundaries, responsible supply chain management becomes an essential component of CSR in the tourism industry. Tourism businesses can aid in the reduction of poverty, the preservation of local culture, and the economic diversification of destination areas by placing a high priority on fair labor standards, ethical sourcing methods, and the assistance of local artists and business owners.

Conclusion

For tourism companies navigating the tricky junction of social fairness, environmental stewardship, and economic prosperity, corporate social responsibility acts as a strategic compass. Tourism organizations may create value for all stakeholders and help to preserve our planet's natural and cultural legacy for future generations by adopting CSR as a comprehensive and integrated approach to business management. The time has come for tourism businesses to embrace CSR as an essential component of their managerial DNA, driving beneficial and sustainable growth in the pursuit of a better, more inclusive future for all. We are at the cusp of a new era marked by previously unheard-of challenges and opportunities.

Furthermore, the core of ethical tourism activities is environmental sustainability. In order to mitigate the environmental effects of travel and tourism-related activities while maintaining the natural resources that are vital to their long-term viability, tourism businesses can play a critical role in implementing energy-efficient technologies, reducing waste, and supporting biodiversity conservation and ecosystem restoration initiatives. In the end, CSR is a strategic necessity as well as a moral imperative for tourism firms that want to thrive in a world that is changing swiftly. When tourism organizations truly commit to sustainable and ethical practices and align their financial aims with broader societal objectives, they may ensure long-term prosperity, enhance their reputation, and advance the welfare of people and the environment.

References

Aguinis, H., & Glavas, A. (2012). What we know and don't know about corporate social responsibility: A review and research agenda. *Journal of management, 38*(4), 932–968.

Asia Society. (2005). *Corporate social responsibility in action: Private sector summit on post-tsunami rehabilitation and reconstruction.* Retrieved August 27, 2005, from http://www.asiasociety.org

BBC. (2004). *Green reports shun supply chain.* BBC News. Retrieved August 22, 2005, from http://www.bbc.co.uk

Blinova, E., Gregorić, M., & Jelačića, B. J. (2018). Corporate social responsibility of international and local hotels operating in Russian and Croatian markets. In *Mediterranean Islands Conference MIC-Vis* (pp. 115–124).

Bowen, H. R. (2013). *Social responsibilities of the businessman.* University of Iowa Press.

Canavan, B. (2016). Tourism culture: Nexus, characteristics, context and sustainability. *Tourism Management, 53,* 229–243.

Carroll, A. B. (1979). A three-dimensional conceptual model of corporate social performance. *Academy of Management Review, 4,* 497–505.

Carroll, A. B. (1991). The pyramid of corporate social responsibility: Toward the moral management of organizational stakeholders. *Business Horizons,* (July–August), 39–48.

Carroll, A. B., & Shabana, K. M. (2010). The business case for corporate social responsibility: A review of concepts, research and practice. *International Journal of Management Reviews, 12*(1), 85–105. 10.1111/j.1468-2370.2009.00275.x

Corporateeurope.org. (2024). Corporate Europe Observer 3-june 1999. Retrieved September 26, 2024, from https://archive.corporateeurope.org/observer0/wbcsd.html

Cvelbar, L. K., & Dwyer, L. (2013). An importance–performance analysis of sustainability factors for long-term strategy planning in Slovenian hotels. *Journal of Sustainable Tourism, 21*(3), 487–504.

Dahlsrud, A. (2008), How corporate social responsibility is defined: An analysis of 37 definitions. *Corp. Soc. Responsib. Environ. Mgmt, 15,* 1–13. https://doi.org/10.1002/csr.132

Davis, K. (1960). Can business afford to ignore social responsibilities? *California Management Review, 2,* 70–76.

Dedusenko, E. A. (2017). Impact investing trends in Russia and tourism. *Journal of Environmental Management and Tourism (JEMT), 8*(08(24)), 1474–1481. doi:https://doi.org/10.35808/ersj/555.

Diamantis, D. (1999). Green strategies for tourism worldwide. *Tourism and Tourism Analyst, 4,* 89–112.

Esparon, M., Gyuris, E., & Stoeckl, N. (2014). Does ECO certification deliver benefits? An empirical investigation of visitors' perceptions of the importance of ECO certification's attributes and of operators' performance. *Journal of Sustainable Tourism, 22*(1), 148–169.

European Commission. (2011). *A renewed EU strategy 2011–14 for corporate social responsibility.* Retrieved September 4, 2013, from http://eur-lex.europa.eu/LexUriServ/LexUriS-erv.do?uri=COM:2011:0681:FIN:EN:PDF

European Communities. (2001). *Green paper: Promoting a European framework for corporate social responsibility.* Commission of the European Communities.

Fernández-Kranz, D., & Santaló, J. (2010). When necessity becomes a virtue: The effect of product market competition on corporate social responsibility. *Journal of Economics & Management Strategy, 19*(2), 453–487.

Fifka, M. S. (2016). The impact of socioeconomic and political factors on stakeholder dialogs. In *A stakeholder approach to corporate social responsibility* (pp. 5–24). Routledge.

Font, X., Guix, M., & Bonilla-Priego, M. J. (2016). Corporate social responsibility in cruising: Using materiality analysis to create shared value. *Tourism Management, 53,* 175–186.

Forsyth, T. (1995). Business attitudes to sustainable tourism: Self-regulation in the UK outgoing tourism industry. *Journal of Sustainable Tourism, 3*(4), 210–231.

Frederick, W. C., Davis, K., & Post, J. E. (1992). *Business and society: Corporate strategy, public policy, ethics.* McGraw-Hill.

Friedman, M. (2007). *The social responsiblity of business is to increase its profits* (pp. 173–178). Springer.

Fritz, K., Schoenmueller, V., & Bruhn, M. (2017). Authenticity in branding–exploring antecedents and consequences of brand authenticity. *European journal of marketing, 51*(2), 324–348.

George, E., & Ng, C. K. (2011). Nonstandard workers: Work arrangements and outcomes. In S. Zedeck (Ed.), *APA handbook of industrial and organizational psychology, Vol. 1. Building and developing the organization* (pp. 573–596). American Psychological Association. https://doi.org/10.1037/12169-018

Gong, Y., & Ho, K. C. (2021). Corporate social responsibility and managerial short-termism. *Asia-Pacific Journal of Accounting & Economics, 28*(5), 604–630.

Govindarajo, N. S., & Khen, M. H. S. (2020). Effect of service quality on visitor satisfaction, destination image and destination loyalty–practical, theoretical and policy implications to avitourism. *International Journal of Culture, Tourism and Hospitality Research, 14*(1), 83-101.

Griffin, J. J., & Mahon, J. F. (1997). The corporate social performance and corporate financial performance debate: Twenty-five years of incomparable research. *Business & Society, 36*(1), 5–31.

Hopkins, M. (2016). *The planetary bargain: Corporate social responsibility comes of age.* Springer.

Hughes, E., & Scheyvens, R. (2016). Corporate social responsibility in tourism post-2015: A development first approach. *Tourism Geographies, 18*(5), 469–482.

ICAO (2001). *Aviation and sustainable development. Department of Economic and Social Affairs.* International Civil Aviation Organisation.

Islam, T., Islam, R., Pitafi, H., Xiaobei, P., Rehmani, M., Irfan, M., & Mubarik, M. (2020). The impact of corporate social responsibility on customer loyalty: The mediating role of corporate reputation, customer satisfaction, and trust. *Sustainable Production and Consumption, 25.* 10.1016/j.spc.2020.07.019.

Ivanova, I. A., & Bikeeva, M. V. (2016). Corporate social responsibility: Specificity, formation mechanism, estimation of management efficiency. *European Research Studies Journal, XIX*(Issue 3A), 167–184.

Jaramillo, F., Mulki, J. P., & Solomon, P. (2006). The role of ethical climate on salesperson's role stress, job attitudes, turnover intention, and job performance. *Journal of Personal Selling & Sales Management, 26*(3), 271-282.

Jones Christensen, L. I. S. A., Mackey, A., & Whetten, D. (2014). Taking responsibility for corporate social responsibility: The role of leaders in creating, implementing, sustaining, or avoiding socially responsible firm behaviors. *Academy of Management Perspectives, 28*(2), 164–178.

Jurkowska-Gomulka, A., Kurczewska, K., & Bilan, Y. (2021). Corporate social responsibility in public administration. Case of Polish central administrative institutions. *Administratie si Management Public, 36,*116–133.

Kalisch, A. (2002). *Corporate futures: Social responsibility in the tourism industry: Consultation on good practice.* Tourism Concern.

Knox, S., & Maklan, S. (2004). Corporate social responsibility: Moving beyond investment towards measuring outcomes. *European Management Journal, 22*(5), 508–516.

Kucukusta, D., Denizci Guillet, B., & Chan, H. L. (2016). The effect of CSR practices on employee affective commitment in the airline industry. *Journal of China Tourism Research, 12*(3–4), 451–469.

Kumar, P., & Kumar, A. (2018). Corporate social responsibility disclosure and financial performance: Further evidence from NIFTY 50 firms. *International Journal of Business Insights & Transformation, 11*(2).

Levy, S. E., & Park, S. -Y. (2011). An analysis of CSR activities in the lodging industry. *Journal of Hospitality and Tourism Management, 18*(1), 147–154.

McGuire, J. (1963). *Business and society.* McGraw-Hill.

McWilliams, A., & Siegel, D. (2001). Corporate social responsibility: A theory of the firm perspective. *Academy of Management Review, 26*(1), 117–127.

Mehnaz, Jin, J., Hussain, A., Warraich, M. A., & Waheed, A. (2021). Impact of perceived CSR practices on customers loyalty. The mediating role of reputation and customer satisfaction. *Corporate Social Responsibility and Environmental Management.*

Miller, G. (2001). Corporate responsibility in the UK tourism industry. *Tourism Management, 22*(6), 589–598.

Palacios-Marqués, D., & Devece-Carañana, C. A. (2013). Policies to support corporate social responsibility: The case of Telefónica. *Human Resource Management, 52*(1), 145–152.

Pearce, J. A., II, & Doh, J. P. (2005). The high impact of collaborative social initiatives. *MIT Sloan Management Review, 46*(3).

Peters, T. D. (2018). Corporations, sovereignty and the religion of neoliberalism. *Law and Critique, 29*(3), 271–292.

PR Week. (2005). CSR: Who's responsible? *PR Wee.* Retrieved August 12, 2005, from https://www.prweek.com/article/490873/csr-whos-responsible

Schmidheiny, S., & Gentry, B. (1997). Privately financed sustainable development. *Thinking ecologically: The new generation of environmental policy,* 118–135.

Stabler, M. J. (1997). *Tourism and sustainability: Principles to practice.* CAB International.

Tiep Le, T., & Nguyen, V. K. (2022). The impact of corporate governance on firms' value in an emerging country: The mediating role of corporate social responsibility and organisational identification. *Cogent Business & Management, 9*(1), 2018907.

Torelli, C., & Shavitt, S. (2010). Culture and concepts of power. *Journal of Personality and Social Psychology, 99,* 703–723.

Tourism Concern. (2005). *Tourism concern.* Retrieved August 7, 2005, from http://www.tourismconcern.org.uk

Twigg, J. (2001). *Corporate social responsibility and disaster reduction: A global overview.* Benfield Greig Hazard Research Centre.

UN Global Compact. (2005). What is the global compact? *UN Global Compact.* Retrieved August 19, 2005, from http://www.unglobalcompact.org

UN. (2004). Agenda 21: UN department for economic and social affairs. *Division for Sustainable Development.* Retrieved August 19, 2005, from http://www.un.org

UNEP. (2003). *A practical guide to good practice: Managing environmental and social issues in the accommodation sector.* United Nations Environment Programme.

UNEP. (2005). *Making tourism more sustainable: A guide for policy makers.* United Nations Environment Programme.

UNWTO. (2021). International Tourism Highlights, 2020 Edition. *International Tourism Highlights.* [online] doi:https://doi.org/10.18111/9789284422456.

Van de Ven, B. (2008). An ethical framework for the marketing of corporate social responsibility. *Journal of Business Ethics, 82*(2), 339–352. 10.1007/s10551-008-9890-1.

Walton, C.C. (1967). *Corporate social responsibilities.* Wadsworth.

Wells, V. K., Manika, D., Gregory-Smith, D., Taheri, B., & McCowlen, C. (2015). Heritage tourism, CSR and the role of employee environmental behaviour. *Tourism Management, 48,* 399–413. 10.1016/j.tourman.2014.12.015

Werther, W. B., Jr, & Chandler, D. (2010). *Strategic corporate social responsibility: Stakeholders in a global environment.* Sage.

Wight, P. (1993). Ecotourism: Ethics or eco-sell? *Journal of travel research, 31*(3), 3–9.

WTTC. (2002). *Corporate social leadership in travel and tourism.* World Travel and Tourism Council.

Zadek, S. (2002). *Third generation corporate citizenship.* AccountAbility. Retrieved August 2, 2005, from www.accountability.org.uk

Chapter 16

Strategic Corporate Social Responsibility: A Foundation for Successful Tourism Management

Muhammad Haseeb Shakil[a,b], Junaid Khalil[a], Ali Sajjad[c], Muhammad Mukarram[c] and Qasim Ali Nisar[d,e]

[a]*Department of Management Sciences, Faculty of Business Administration, COMSATS University Islamabad, Lahore, Pakistan*
[b]*Faculty of Engineering & Technology, The Superior University, Lahore, Pakistan*
[c]*Chaudhary Abdul Rehman Business School, Faculty of Business & Management Sciences, The Superior University, Lahore, Pakistan*
[d]*School of Media and Communication Studies, Faculty of Social Sciences & Leisure Management, Taylor's University, Subang Jaya, Malaysia*
[e]*School of Business and Law, RMIT University, Melbourne, Australia*

Abstract

Purpose: This chapter aims to review and brief the role of Strategic Corporate Social Responsibility (SCSR) in the tourism industry, targeting its impact on the performance and sustainability of the tourism industry. This chapter seeks to provide insights into how SCSR can lead to a positive transformation and competitive advantage.

Methodology: The chapter incorporates a brief literature review to examine current trends, hurdles, and benchmarking in the implementation of SCSR in the tourism industry. Comparative analysis and recent literature are used to extract valuable results and implications for effective tourism management.

Research limitations: The current chapter has limited potential biases in the selection of literature and the evolving nature of CSR in the tourism sector. Future research is required to check the developments in tourism and CSR.

Corporate Social Responsibility, Corporate Governance and Business Ethics in Tourism Management: A Business Strategy for Sustainable Organizational Performance, 231–249
Copyright © 2025 by Muhammad Haseeb Shakil, Junaid Khalil, Ali Sajjad, Muhammad Mukarram and Qasim Ali Nisar
Published under exclusive licence by Emerald Publishing Limited
doi:10.1108/978-1-83608-704-520241016

Results: This chapter shed light on the complex association between the performance of CSR and business in the tourism industry, highlighting the importance of governance qualities and new initiatives for achieving financial sustainability.

Originality/value: This chapter adds valuable insights to the existing literature by shedding light on the most recent literature on SCSR in the tourism industry and provides inputs for setups looking for sustainability.

Keywords: Strategic corporate social responsibility; sustainability; CSR performance; tourism management; ethical considerations

1. Introduction

Recent studies have described recent developments in the literature on Strategic Corporate Social Responsibility (SCSR) in the tourism industry and suggested future explorations (Ahmad et al., 2023; Coles et al., 2013). According to Hatipoglu et al. (2019), SCSR involves ethical, social, environmental, and financial practices to achieve the requirements of stakeholders. This fact gained attention to the exploration of SCSR in the early stages of the tourism industry. Barriers in the tourism industry come under the interest of academicians and researchers (Shahzalal & Elgammal, 2023). A crucial response along with SCSR guidelines is supposed to recommend research and achieve these objectives. The tourism industry and various firms are forced to incorporate SCSR guidelines to meet social and financial performance (Alatawi et al., 2023). Organizations ought to consolidate ecologically, socially, and monetarily mindful practices into their tasks to further develop sustainability in the tourism industry. Tourism professionals must adopt SCSR as a long-term strategy for increasing competitiveness and ensuring corporate sustainability (Camilleri, 2021).

1.1. Significance of SCSR in Tourism Management

In the tourism industry, SCSR is a business strategy that incorporates social and environmental factors into a company's fundamental operations and decision-making processes (Madanaguli et al., 2022). Beyond simple philanthropy, this strategy emphasizes ongoing involvement with stakeholders and positive influence on the locations where a company operates. Fair labor standards, employee well-being, environmental conservation, and cultural preservation are just a few of the many facets of this (Goffi et al., 2022; Sánchez et al., 2022).

Key corporate social obligation is vital in the travel industry area considering several factors. First, it promotes a sustainable tourist model. The tourism industry might get the sustainability of objections and moderate assets that draw in vacationers by carrying out capable practices, for example, diminishing energy and water utilization, taking out junk yield, and protecting regular living spaces (Textual Style & Lynes, 2018). Moreover, proactive corporate social obligation upgrades associations with nearby networks, representatives, and sightseers. Travel companies might develop trust and steadfastness and upgrade the general tourism insight for everybody by sponsorship of nearby organizations, ensuring good compensations, and working circumstances, and regarding social legacy (Madanaguli et al., 2022). SCSR eventually reinforces its business notoriety and requests to a growing segment of earth and socially mindful voyagers. Studies demonstrate that sightseers are keener on movement decisions that mirror their convictions, featuring the requirement for a vigorous SCSR plan as a powerful showcasing instrument (Alatawi et al., 2023; Horng et al., 2018; Shahzalal & Elgammal, 2023).

Vital corporate social responsibility is a moral need and an essential component for making progress in the travel industry area. Tourism companies can ensure the long-term sustainability of destinations, strengthen relationships with stakeholders, and boost brand reputations by incorporating social and environmental responsibility into their core business strategies. This will prompt a more capable and feasible tourism industry (Goffi et al., 2022).

2. Literature Review

2.1. Theoretical Foundation

The Sustainable Innovation Framework for Tourism Management integrates principles from the Diffusion of Innovation Theory (Gu et al., 2019) to drive the adoption of sustainable practices and innovative strategies within the tourism industry. Comprising core elements such as Sustainable Tourism Practices and Innovation in Tourism Management, the model delineates components like Awareness, Interest, Evaluation, Trial, and Adoption to guide the process (Stumpf et al., 2016). Leveraging the insights of diffusion theory, it underscores the importance of creating awareness, fostering interest, evaluating feasibility, implementing trials, and ultimately encouraging widespread adoption of sustainable innovation (Gellner, 2023). This coherent approach not only works with the comprehension of how novel thoughts spread inside the tourism industry but also accentuates the requirement for coordinated effort and ceaseless improvement. By lining up with ecological, social, and economic objectives, the system expects to support sustainability and seriousness, in this way driving positive change and accomplishing sustainable improvement goals in the tourism industry.

2.2. The Evolution of CSR in Tourism

The evolution of Corporate Social Responsibility (CSR) in the tourism industry has experienced a significant transformation, developed from its early stage to a mature and more effective stage inside the sector. The field of CSR in the tourism industry has shown big advancements in academia and industry as well.

This advancement is clear with a creating assortment of assessments that examine social and moral standards in the tourism industry (Wu et al., 2023). The improvement is perceived by a constant development in which speculative assessments have enlarged to wrap judicious and exploratory solicitations. According to Sanchez et al. (2022), this development indicates a developing research climate that is dynamically recognizing the complexity of CSR within the tourism industry. From a condition of calculated uncertainty to a more exact and logical examination of the effect of corporate social obligation (CSR) on advancing economic and mindful the travel industry rehearses, research on CSR in the travel industry has advanced.

2.2.1. Historical Overview of CSR in the Tourism Industry

The evaluation of the historical development of CS) in the tourism industry shows a development depicted by the consistently developing affirmation and joining of CSR thoughts into the utilitarian and crucial plans of the area. There has been a growing academic interest in the tourism industry's CSR since the middle of the 1990s. Accordingly, more examinations have been finished on the ecological and financial parts of the tourism industry tasks (Wu et al., 2023). This time saw the improvement of major hypotheses and examination into the job of CSR in alleviating the adverse consequences of the tourism industry. Critical revelations, for example, the Earth's Highest point in 1992, which underlined the sustainable tourism industry practices, affected this study (Sánchez et al., 2022). A correlation between the tourism industry improvement and social responsibility describes the sustainable foundation of CSR in the tourism industry. There is a rising focus on involving CSR as a fundamental instrument to deal with the tourism industry's viability and moral perspectives (Lopez et al., 2022).

2.3. The Core Elements of Strategic CSR

SCSR goes beyond conventional corporate charity and compliance by incorporating social, environmental, and economic considerations into a company's business strategy (Bhattacharyya, 2010). Vital CSR spins around emphatically impacting society while achieving business goals. This requires a proactive and thoroughly examined way to deal with CSR projects that line up with the organization's main goal and vision (Lopez et al., 2022). The significant parts integrate a pledge to endure through goals and the hypothesis of resources toward CSR drives that are crucial for the industry's fundamental targets. This, according to Camilleri (2021) and Heslin and Ochoa (2008), demonstrates the necessity of addressing current environmental and social issues as well as proactively anticipating upcoming challenges and opportunities that may have an impact on society. Important CSR necessitates a comprehensive perspective that considers the impact of business activities on various partners, such as employees, customers, networks, and the environment. As per Solangi and Siddiqui (2023), this technique guarantees that CSR drives add to the association's drawn-out development and the government assistance of society.

2.3.1. Integrating CSR into Business Strategy

Organizing CSR into the business method incorporates embedding social and ecological considerations into the business exercises and dynamic cycles. According to Alatawari et al. (2023), this integration guarantees that CSR initiatives directly contribute to the company's strategic objectives, thereby enhancing brand reputation, stakeholder relationships, and competitive advantage. Taking a strategic approach to CSR entails locating areas where the company's business interests and societal requirements meet, resulting in initiatives that create shared value for the company and society. For instance, by zeroing in on practical obtaining, an organization gets its store network and advances ecological stewardship and social improvement in its obtaining areas. Coordinating CSR with business techniques additionally implies including partners in the dynamic cycle, guaranteeing straightforwardness, and estimating the effect of CSR exercises to consistently improve and develop CSR rehearses in arrangement with business targets (Lopez et al., 2022).

2.3.2. Aligning CSR with Corporate Governance

The alignment of CSR with corporate governance is of the most extreme significance in laying out CSR as a fundamental part of corporate culture and functional systems (Lopez et al., 2022). Senior management and the board of directors must actively participate in formulating explicit CSR policies, establish CSR priorities, and enforce these policies throughout the company. Moreover, it includes carrying out responsibility measures, like CSR detailing and execution measurements, to direct the viability of CSR tries and their harmoniousness with the industry's moral standards and governance commitments (Koseoglu et al., 2021; Lopez et al., 2022). By coordinating corporate social obligation (CSR) with corporate administration, associations can lay out a firm system that incorporates CSR drives into their general corporate methodology and governance structure (Sánchez-Camacho et al., 2022).

2.4. Business Ethics in Tourism

The tourism industry is a critical monetary peculiarity with significant moral standards. It is essential to develop ethical guidelines and resolve ethical issues to guarantee that tourism has a positive impact on the communities and ecosystems it interacts with.

2.4.1. Developing and Communicating Ethical Standards

The foundation of moral benchmarks in the tourism industry area involves the plan of orders that exemplify the business' ethos and defy the eccentric difficulties innate to its exercises (Downs & Swienton, 2012). The dispersal of these benchmarks is fundamental to guarantee comprehension and consistency among every single included party. The industry's operational and policy decisions can be guided by ethical benchmarks (Ndlazi et al., 2023). These benchmarks, reflecting the aggregate upsides of the business and tackling the difficulties of the travel industry exercises. The explanation and declaration of these benchmarks are basic to accomplishing compatibility among all partners, including legislatures, undertakings, tourists, and neighborhood populaces (Amponsah et al., 2023).

The United Nations World Tourism Organization's (UNWTO) Worldwide Set of rules for the travel industry (GCET) remains a key system for moral and reasonable the travel industry, offering a thorough cluster of principles to control partners toward expanding the area's positive commitments while diminishing its unfriendly impacts (UNWTO, 1999). These ethical standards are the result of a comprehensive investigation, the active participation of stakeholders, and a comprehensive comprehension of tourism's sociocultural, economic, and ecological aspects. When these guidelines are sanctioned, their useful correspondence to all involved elements is basic, cultivating a widespread adherence to and commitment to moral lead inside the business. The determined checking and execution of the GCET are crucial for the development of a moral milieu in the domain of the travel industry, as highlighted by the World Committee on Tourism Ethics (WCTE) (UNWTO, 2020).

2.4.2. Managing Ethical Dilemmas in the Tourism Sector

Cultural, environmental, and economic factors are all intertwined with ethical considerations in the tourism industry. It is occupant upon the business to navigate this multi-layered moral landscape, which incorporates the objectives of ecological stewardship and social regard toward have networks. Sharma and Sodani (2023) highlight the meaning of partner responsibility in developing reasonable travel industry rehearses that blend social, monetary, and ecological interests, subsequently giving moral goals to the area's problems.

2.4.3. Ethical Foundations for Sustainable Tourism Management

The ethical standards behind the sustainable tourism industry underscore the meaning of participating in tourist activities that protect the integrity of the natural environment, encourage social legacy, and contribute benefits to networks. Ethical tourism management includes carrying out sustainable practices to relieve unfavorable consequences for the climate and society while upgrading the tourism industry's valuable commitments to preservation endeavors and local area advancement (Goffi et al., 2022). This incorporates the execution of proper waste management practices, the advancement of energy protection endeavors, the upgrade of neighborhood economies by using nearby items and governance, and the shielding of social and verifiable landmarks. In the tourism industry, moral issues envelop the basics of maintaining standards of decency and value in business techniques, guaranteeing impartial compensation, and laying out secure and regarded working conditions for tourists (Shahzalala & Elgammal, 2023). Organizations in the tourism industry area can advance the feasible improvement of their objections and work on the drawn-out productivity of the tourism industry and the prosperity of host networks by keeping these moral rules (Alatawari et al., 2023).

3. Methodology

3.1. Research Design

The methodology utilized in this chapter includes a brief review of existing literature on strategic corporate social obligation (SCSR) in the tourism industry. A systematic approach was utilized to recognize significant examinations (Kim, 2020), break down key ideas, and blend discoveries to give a careful comprehension of CSR rehearses in the tourism industry.

3.2. Data Collection Methods

Data collection essentially involved accessing academic databases, scholarly articles, and sources connected with CSR, the tourism industry, and corporate governance (Kallio et al., 2016). Significant articles, research papers, and reports were recognized and checked on to accumulate experiences on the combination of CSR standards in the tourism industry (Nanu et al., 2024).

3.3. Data Analysis Techniques

The data analysis process focused on combining data from the literature review to distinguish trends, difficulties, and best practices in SCSR execution inside the tourism industry (Whittemore & Knafl, 2005). Comparative analysis and thematic synthesis were used to extract key discoveries and suggestions for the tourism industry.

3.4. Limitations

It is vital to recognize the limitations of this methodology, which remember expected biases for the determination of literature, varieties in research techniques across studies, and the advancing idea of CSR rehearses in the tourism industry. The extent of the review may not envelop all new improvements in CSR and the tourism industry, featuring the requirement for additional exploration around here.

3.5. Ethical Considerations

Ethical considerations were central all through the process, guaranteeing legitimate reference of sources, regard for licensed innovation privileges, and adherence to scholarly honesty norms. The review was led with straightforwardness and meticulousness to keep up with the validity and unwavering quality of the data introduced in this chapter.

4. Discussion and Findings

4.1. Strategies for Building a Positive CSR Image

CSR addresses an independent business paradigm that enables an organization to be socially liable to itself, its partners, and people in general at large (Lincoln &

Diamond, 2023). Companies can become aware of their impact on all aspects of society, including the economic, social, and environmental realms, by adopting CSR (Rasyid, 2023). To develop a positive CSR notoriety, organizations must capably communicate their CSR tries, use CSR to reinforce their image picture, and produce associations inside the local area (Sharma et al., 2023).

4.2. Strategies for Ethical Management in Tourism

- **Sustainable Practices**: Taking precautions that are considerate of the environment to reduce the negative effects that tourism activities have on the environment.
- **Social Protection**: The obligation to defend the social uprightness of nearby social orders during the travel industry development.
- **Monetary Reasonableness**: The evenhanded designation of the travel industry's monetary profits among every single included partner.
- **Partner Coordinated Effort**: The dynamic support of all substances in consultative and dynamic systems to resolve moral issues by and large.

With regard to the previously mentioned systems, the travel industry's commitment to 10.4% of the worldwide gross domestic product and the arrangement of 319 million positions, likening to 10% of the all-out work in 2019, emphasizes the need for moral stewardship to safeguard the area's drawn-out practicality (WTTC, 2019).

4.3. Communicating CSR Initiatives to Stakeholders

The dissemination of CSR initiatives is crucial for cultivating a positive corporate image among stakeholders in business. The participation of stakeholders in a discourse that promotes transparency, trust, and cooperative effort is necessary for effective dissemination to go beyond the boundaries of straightforward information sharing (Le, 2023). Yang and Basile (2021) highlight the meaning of useful CSR correspondence, which applies a positive impact on hierarchical execution, especially when outer partners are fundamentally engaged with CSR exercises. The scattering system of CSR is multi-layered, including assorted stages and strategies to connect with different partner gatherings.

Social media, for instance, has emerged as an effective tool for increasing the visibility and authenticity of CSR communications and opening new avenues for stakeholder interaction. External stakeholders, such as non-profit organizations, can boost an organization's performance by participating in CSR activities (Sultan et al., 2024; Yang & Basile, 2021). This can increase the effectiveness of CSR communication.

4.4. Leveraging CSR for Brand Enhancement

CSR is more than just giving back to the community; it's a strategic tool that can make a big difference in how people think and feel about a company's brand. By synchronizing CSR methodologies with the basic beliefs and mission of the organization, organizations can produce a powerful, socially upright brand character that resounds with purchasers, financial backers, and other relevant partners.

According to Mondal (2023), the development of a formidable brand image through CSR initiatives necessitates articulating a distinct purpose and locating pertinent CSR initiatives. Customers are increasingly drawn to the ethical behavior of the businesses they do business within today's market. CSR drives that are carefully created and truly executed can result in uplifted client constancy, a more devoted labor force, and an upper hand in the business field. Studies demonstrate that when organizations capably benefit from their CSR exercises, they add to cultural and ecological flourishing as well as receive the benefits of escalated brand faithfulness and purchaser certainty (Mason et al., 2023).

4.5. The Role of CSR in Tourism Marketing

CSR has been incorporated as an essential component for the growth of several economic activities, and tourism is one of these industries that has incorporated CSR practices the most, both in the hotel industry and other businesses associated with other tourism departments. These practices have experienced undertakings or drives with an emphasis on bringing benefits both to the climate and to society (Ghaderi et al., 2019). As per Tripathi and Sharma (2023), a few worldwide organizations (Accor, Hilton, and Marriott Global) have progressively looked to lay out in their business strategies, the improvement of CSR rehearses. Community involvement and energy conservation are two examples of these practices. According to Annamalah et al. (2013), this involvement is because of the significant connection that exists between the local community and the tourism industry in the areas where these businesses are established. As a result, they also have a significant influence on the socioeconomic development of these areas.

At the point when we allude to corporate social responsibility, a few monetary areas have similar qualities as these practices; nonetheless, in the tourism industry area, there are two of these attributes. In a few places, the essential wellspring of monetary assets is through the tourism industry, and this area frequently has government intervention. Since locals will play a crucial role in the growth and success of the tourism industry, these two particulars point to the significance of CSR (Ahmad et al., 2023). For this accomplishment to be victorious, a blend of good relations between government, non-legislative associations, and occupants should be as one through legitimate organization, because without this comprehension between the groups, the tourism industry area keeps an eye on not find success over the long haul-term (Eichelberger et al., 2020). The branding component can make sense of the connection between CSR and support by businesses in the advancement of the tourism industry (Gursoy et al., 2019).

4.5.1. Utilizing CSR as a Marketing Tool

In recent years, researchers and professionals in the tourism industry have shown a lot of interest in the idea of brand advocacy of CSR (Choi et al., 2021; Wang & He, 2022). Integral to this idea, branding, and advertisement includes dynamic individual support of a brand. Significantly, it outperforms basic suggestions, addressing an enveloping part of support (Lowenstein, 2014). As brand advocates, sightseers intentionally and emphatically support a running brand to their informal organizations, partners, and families (Kumar & Kaushik, 2020). The research recommends that travel and tourism organizations' CSR activities can positively influence individual behavior, especially extra-role behavior (Baniya et al., 2019). Research investigating the crossing point of CSR and tourism behavior uncovers those tourists, going about as partners, well assess an association between the tourism industry and CSR initiatives, impacting their promotional goals (Zhang et al., 2022).

According to Sun et al. (2020), the social bond between an ethical organization and its stakeholders is strengthened by the additional societal support provided by its CSR strategy. According to Tuan et al. (2019), in addition to providing financial benefits, an organization's socially responsible behavior encourages tourists to participate in extra-curricular activities. All in all, tourists look to respond to the honorable goals of a moral association toward the local area through social corporate responsibility, laying out a positive connection between CSR and traveler brand promotion.

4.5.2. Consumer Perceptions and Preferences

Suryani (2008) says that customers perceive that an item enjoys benefits that are not quite the same as different items and that benefit makes a big difference to consumers, then, at that point, consumers will pick that item, even though the item is moderately like the others. Because of this, there is a belief that perception is more important than reality, and as a result, consumers' perceptions of the quality of a service play a major role in how they judge it (Sultan et al., 2024). As indicated by research by Gartner et al. (2020) connected with entertainment in the tourism industry, it is utilized to break down tourists' view of entertainment to decide significant elements considering their discernments and inclinations. This concentration additionally expresses that entertainment is vital to help possible maintainability and is vital for making worth, supportability, and coming up with esteem systems for progress and spotlight on the tourism industry.

As indicated by Surface (2023), consumer preference means inclinations, decisions, or something that consumers like, which can be framed from consumer understanding and memory through item discernments. Inclinations are what buyers think about with the goal that they decide the customer's buying choice interaction for an item. Similarly, research by Gartner et al. (2020) found that consumers can simultaneously develop both positive and negative attitudes toward online technologies like social media. This shows that buyer's preference to embrace online entertainment likewise includes web-based entertainment.

4.6. Case Studies and Best Practices

4.6.1. Examining Successful CSR Initiatives in Leading Tourism Businesses

Companies are adopting eco-tourism, green tourism, environmentally friendly travel, and alternative tourism in the tourism industry (Le Tan et al., 2023).

According to Youell (1998), the only way the tourism industry can thrive is to commit to maintaining the resources that sustain tourists. The tourism industry can act both as a driver of financial power as well as a danger to the climate and society (Chilufya et al., 2019). As a result, the tourism industry has increasingly adopted CSR initiatives to reduce negative effects (Han et al., 2020). According to Mihalic (2016), the tourism industry is expected to highlight ethical business practices like enhancing the quality of life for employees, supporting local communities, and protecting the environment. The pertinence of CSR rehearses has become more conspicuous because the business relies on neighborhood networks, human and normal assets, and the climate, alongside issues concerning the climate, basic liberties, and fair exchange (Hadj, 2020).

According to Frey and George (2010), CSR practices also aim to cut down on waste and make it easier to use limited natural resources sustainably. CSR in the tourism industry area has been expanding consideration in the past ten years (Hong et al., 2018; Putra et al., 2019). The sustainability of the tourism industry's objective assets is a worry for the tourism industry administrators (Luo et al., 2020). The growing awareness of environmental issues necessitates that the sector take responsibility for the consequences of its actions and contribute to sustainable development. By starting CSR, the travel industry firms can assist the business with chasing after financial development and upgrade the personal satisfaction of representatives, their families, and the neighborhood society overall.

4.6.2. Extracting Lessons and Principles for Implementation

The tourism industry is not an exception to the trend of CSR taking on an increasingly significant role across all sectors. In addition to improving the tourism industry's sustainability and competitiveness, CSR practices also benefit society and the environment. Understanding the sector's unique challenges and opportunities is necessary for extracting lessons and principles for the implementation of CSR in the tourism industry.

CSR in the tourism industry, right off the bat, ought to focus on the sustainable turn of events (Pereira et al., 2021). This involves advancing the travel industry practices that limit ecological effects, monitor regular assets, and save social legacy (Punzo et al., 2022). For example, drives like waste decrease, energy proficiency, and biodiversity protection can add to economic travel industry advancement. Further, commitment is vital for the smooth implementation of CSR in the tourism industry (Shaikh et al., 2022; Yasir et al., 2021). Attracting networks, management, NGOs, and other stakeholders develops normal data collection, mergers, and complete navigation (Henry, 2023). This incorporation ensures that initiatives for CSR enhance social outcomes while being aligned with local requirements and preferences. Besides, upgrading moral strategic policies is also crucial for CSR in the tourism industry. Fair dealing with employees, respect for human rights, and anti-corruption are a part of his (Hassim & Susetio, 2023). Additionally, effective posting and response are considered an important part of developing initiatives for CSR within the tourism industry (Ahmad et al., 2023).

Customer benefits and brand loyalty will also increase when efforts toward CSR are posted accurately (Lee & Chung, 2023). In addition, effective tourism policies and procedures can be achieved by training the tourists in cultural and behavioral sensitivity.

5. Conclusion

Briefly, this chapter sheds light on a brief review of SCSR in the tourism industry, marking its significance, enhancement, competence, performance, and ethical standards. To check the expectations of stakeholders and ensure a sustainable advantage, CSR in tourism should involve moral, social, environmental, and financial practices under procedures. Along with increasing interest in CSR, specifically in the tourism sector, exploration in this area is still lacking in comparison to other areas. Nevertheless, there is an affirmation of the importance of CSR in the future for the enhancement of brand reputation. The improvement of CSR in the tourism industry epitomizes a shift from conceptual haze to a more exact perception of its effect on advancing harmless to environment-friendly practices of the tourism industry. A more profound comprehension of the association between the tourism industry improvement and social obligation has arisen due to sustainable turns of events, with a rising accentuation on the essential utilization of CSR for upgrading sustainability and moral standards. As part of strategic CSR, businesses must incorporate CSR into their business strategy and corporate governance, uphold ethical principles for managing sustainable tourism, and align CSR initiatives with their mission and vision. Organizations can assess the effect that CSR has had on business performance and anticipate designs for the future with the assistance of performance measures and vision frameworks, taking into consideration pivotal free bearing and guaranteeing long-haul sustainability.

Moreover, concerning settling ethical issues and managing the moral norms of the tourism industry, moral standards and rules play a significant part. The development and scattering of moral norms, the governance of moral standards, and the execution of procedures for moral governance are important for advancing the tourism industry practices that are gainful to networks, ecological systems, and the tourism industry. The tourism industry discussion emphasizes the significance of CSR in promoting sustainable practices and enhancing brand reputation. Through productive correspondence of CSR drives, organizations can draw in assistants and assemble trust, at long last supporting their corporate picture. By using CSR for brand improvement, progressive qualities are adjusted to social prerequisites, making a persuading brand image that resounds with accomplices and clients the same. Also, the mix of CSR into business development shows procedures such as ways to deal with complexities as well as makes brand image among tourists, prompting broadened consistency and a positive brand image. In the tourism industry, consumer inclinations and perceptions play a huge part in simply deciding, featuring the meaning of moral practices and monetary benefits. By organizing their CSR initiatives under the values and preferences of their customers, organizations can increase their intensity and appeal to socially conscious tourists. Additionally, examining the successful CSR campaigns of tourism industry organizations provides significant knowledge and best practices for putting maintainable methodologies into place throughout the business.

Future tourism CSR trends will emphasize the increasing significance of technological innovation, stakeholder engagement, and environmentally friendly practices. Important opportunities for improvement in the tourism industry lie in using development to make sharper, more acceptable objections and experiences. The tourism industry can not only meet the changing needs of customers and stakeholders but also contribute to the long-term sustainability of the environment and society by embracing CSR principles and innovative solutions.

6. Future Trends and Opportunities

6.1. Emerging Trends in CSR for Tourism

Koch et al. (2020) tracked down that organizations' sustainable ways of behaving decidedly connect with consumer loyalty. According to Martinez and Rodriguez del Bosque (Chuah et al., 2023), consumers' identification with the company, trust, satisfaction, and loyalty increase when they perceive a high level of engagement from the company in these corporate and civic activities. Additionally, Nugroho et al. (2024) found that organizations' endeavors to accomplish something useful for society and partners can increase buyer brand inclination and dependability. Also, certain examinations have researched the overflow impact, showing that fulfillment with corporate, urban exercises during gatherings and shows can bring about objective connection and faithfulness among participants (Chubchuwong, 2019). Tuan (2018) found that when organizations effectively partake in corporate and community exercises, it emphatically impacts workers' authoritative citizenship conduct, which, thus, decidedly influences vacationers' citizenship conduct toward the climate. Nonetheless, Meuser and Smallfield, (2023) found that to affect workers' contribution to companies' endeavors to "accomplish something beneficial for society," specialists should think about both individual elements, like individual convictions, and gathering level variables, like the hierarchical environment, as these two variables have an intelligent relationship.

As the tourism industry objections depend vigorously on normal and legacy assets, include many partners, and have a complicated administration structure, the principal subjects in the writing survey were the travel industry arranging, strategy execution, dealing with administration issues, and safeguarding regular and legacy assets. Within a similar research area, some researchers considered the viewpoints of stakeholders. For instance, Nieforth et al. (2022) dissected partners' natural directions, and their examination accepted that partners' ecological perspectives can impact the course of managing the tourism industry. Meetings, overviews, and blended techniques survey the partners' insights (Stoffelen et al., 2020).

6.2. Opportunities for Growth and Innovation

The travel and tourism industry has been significantly altered by digitalization, making it a "smart" sector – that is, an innovative and technologically advanced sector that is fully integrated into the industry paradigm. As we head toward the tourism industry 4.0, in this manner, we inquire: what lies behind the articulation, and brilliant the travel industry? Femenia-Serra et al. (2019) highlight how the term "brilliant" addresses an at this point normal trendy expression used to depict the mechanical, financial, and social advances led by innovations that depend on sensors, Enormous Information, new types of networks and data trade (e.g., the IoT, IoS, remote correspondence or RFID, and close to handling correspondence or NFC), its importance intently matching the ability to conclude and reason in a keen manner. The integration of the physical and digital worlds is also referred to as "smart" in the context of physical structures like factories and homes (smart factory and smart home, respectively). Phones are becoming "smartphones," credit cards are becoming "smartcards, " and televisions are becoming "smart TVs," all of which share the characteristics of multi-functionality and the power of connectivity. In addition, the "smart economy" is supported by technologies that make it easier for people to work together and connect.

Further, the term "smart economy" has been utilized to recognize metropolitan settings that have embraced imaginative innovation to streamline the utilization of assets and to lean toward productive administration processes that go for the gold top-notch of life for the populace. At the end of the day, a "Smart City" is a city that unites innovation, government, and society, including six parts: shrewd economy, brilliant portability, brilliant climate, shrewd individuals, smart living, and shrewd administration (Lom et al. 2016). Concerning the tourism industry, "smart" is a term utilized for various devices, like utilizing Enormous Information to separate interest (division), embracing distributed computing as an outside memory bank in which to store information and data, or giving admittance to free wi-fi or sensors decisively positioned to let objects and physical, social, and administration (e.g., transportation) assets associate and speak with vacationers' cell phones inside the regional setting of locations.

Because tourism is a sector that features easily digitalized, information-rich value propositions that highlight the role played by new technologies, this sector lends itself well to the label "smart." Its mechanical development has been steady and critical (Buhalis & Regulation, 2008). As the travel industry objections depend vigorously on normal and legacy assets, include many partners, and have a complicated administration structure, the principal subjects in the writing survey were the travel industry arranging, strategy execution, dealing with administration issues, and safeguarding regular and legacy assets. Within a similar research area, some researchers considered the viewpoints of stakeholders. For instance, Nieforth et al. (2022) dissected partners' natural directions, and their examination accepted that partners' ecological perspectives can impact the course of managing the travel industry. Meetings, overviews, and blended techniques survey the partners' insights (Stoffelen et al., 2020).

References

Ahmad, N., Ahmad, A., & Siddique, I. (2023). Responsible tourism and hospitality: The intersection of altruistic values, human emotions, and corporate social responsibility. *Administrative Sciences, 13*(4), 105.

Alatawi, I. A., Ntim, C. G., Zras, A., & Elmagrhi, M. H. (2023). CSR, financial and non-financial performance in the tourism sector: A systematic literature review and future research agenda. *International Review of Financial Analysis, 89*, 1–25.

Amponsah, E., Takyi, S. A., Asibey, M. O., & Amponsah, O. (2023). Achieving sustainable cities: Analysis of the factors that influence compliance with telecommunication masts siting standards in Ghana. *Urban, Planning and Transport Research, 11*(1), 2159511. https://doi.org/10.1080/21650020.2022.2159511

Annamalah, S., Paraman, P., Ahmed, S., Dass, R., Sentosa, I., Pertheban, T. R., Shamsudin, F., Kadir, B., Aravindan, K. L., Raman, M., Chee Hoo, W., & Singh, P. (2023). The role of open innovation and a normalizing mechanism of social capital in the tourism industry. *Journal of Open Innovation: Technology, Market, and Complexity, 9*(2), 100056.

Baniya, R., Thapa, B., & Kim, M. -S. (2019). Corporate social responsibility among travel and tour operators in Nepal. *Sustainability, 11*(10), 2771.

Bhattacharyya, S. S. (2010). Exploring the concept of strategic corporate social responsibility for sustainable development. *Business Strategy and the Environment, 19*(7), 401–416.

Buhalis D, & Law, R. (2008). Twenty years on and 10 years after the internet: The state of tourism research. *Tourism Management, 29*(4), 609–623. https://doi.org/10.1016/j.tourman.2008.01.005

Camilleri, M. A. (2021). The market for socially responsible investing: A review of the developments. *Social Responsibility Journal, 17*(3), 412–428.

Chilufya, A., Hughes, E., & Scheyvens, R. (2019). Tourists and community development: Corporate social responsibility or tourist social responsibility? *Journal of Sustainable Tourism, 27*(10), 1513–1529.

Choi, Y., Kroff, M. W., & Kim, J. (2021). Developing brand advocacy through brand activities on Facebook. *Journal of Consumer Marketing, 38*(3), 328–338.

Chuah, S. H. W., El-Manstrly, D., Tseng, M. L., & Ramayah, T. (2020). Sustaining customer engagement behavior through corporate social responsibility: The roles of environmental concern and green trust. *Journal of Cleaner Production, 262*, 121348.

Chubchuwong, M. (2019). The impact of CSR satisfaction on destination loyalty: A study of MICE travelers in Thailand. *Asia Pacific Journal of Tourism Research, 24*(2), 168–179.

Coles, T., Fenclova, E., & Dinan, C. (2013). Tourism and corporate social responsibility: A critical review and research agenda. In *Tourism management perspectives* (Vol. 6, pp. 122–141). https://doi.org/10.1016/j.tmp.2013.02.001

Downs, J. U., & Swienton, A. R. (2012). Ethics codes in other organizations: Structures and enforcement. In *Ethics in forensic science* (pp. 155–199). Academic Press.

Eichelberger, S., Peters, M., Pikkemaat, B., & Chan, C. S. (2020). Entrepreneurial ecosystems in smart cities for tourism development: From stakeholder perceptions to regional tourism policy implications. *Journal of Hospitality and Tourism Management, 45*, 319–329.

Font, X., & Lynes, J. (2018). Corporate social responsibility in tourism and hospitality. *Journal of Sustainable Tourism, 26*(7), 1027–1042. https://doi.org/10.1080/09669582.2018.1488856

Frey, N., & George, R. (2010). Responsible tourism management: The missing link between business owners' attitudes and behaviour in the Cape Town tourism industry. *Tourism Management, 31*(5), 621–628. https://doi.org/10.1016/j.tourman.2009.06.017

Femenia-Serra, F., Neuhofer, B., & Ivars-Baidal, J. A. (2019). Towards a conceptualisation of smart tourists and their role within the smart destination scenario. *Service Industries Journal, 39*(2), 109–133. https://doi.org/10.1080/02642069.2018.1508458

Gartner, S., Nicholson, A., & Christou, E. (2020). Munich Personal RePEc Archive Tourism marketing and distribution through social media: Assessing business economic performance tourism marketing and distribution through social media: Assessing business economic performance. *Journal of Tourism Development & Hospitality Management, 17*(2). https://mpra.ub.uni-muenchen.de/99194/1/MPRA_paper_99194.pdf

Gellner, C. (2023). Building innovation: The role of apprenticeship training in knowledge diffusion within firms. *International Interdisciplinary Business Economics Advancement Journal, 4*(12), 1–6.

Ghaderi, Z., Mirzapour, M., Henderson, J. C., & Richardson, S. (2019). Corporate social responsibility and hotel performance: A view from Tehran, Iran. *Tourism Management Perspectives, 29*, 41–47. https://doi.org/10.1016/j.tmp.2018.10.007

Gu, D., Khan, S., Khan, I. U., & Khan, S. U. (2019). Understanding mobile tourism shopping in Pakistan: An integrating framework of innovation diffusion theory and technology acceptance model. *Mobile Information Systems, 2019*(1), 1490617.

Gursoy, D., Boğan, E., Dedeoğlu, B. B., & Çalışkan, C. (2019). Residents perceptions of hotels corporate social responsibility initiatives and its impact on residents sentiments to community and support for additional tourism development. *Journal of Hospitality and Tourism Management, 39*, 117–128. https://doi.org/10.1016/j.jhtm.2019.03.005

Goffi, G., Masiero, L., & Pencarelli, T. (2022). Corporate social responsibility and performances of firms operating in the tourism and hospitality industry. *TQM Journal, 34*(6), 1626–1647. https://doi.org/10.1108/TQM-06-2021-0166

Hadj, T. B. (2020). Effects of corporate social responsibility towards stakeholders and environmental management on responsible innovation and competitiveness. *Journal of Cleaner Production, 250*, 119490.

Han, S., Li, G., Lubrano, M., & Xun, Z. (2020). Lie of the weak: Inconsistent corporate social responsibility activities of Chinese zombie firms. *Journal of Cleaner Production, 253*, 119858.

Hassim, J. Z., & Susetio, W. (2023). Integrating governance and sustainability in sports tourism. In *International conference on "changing of law: Business law, local wisdom and tourism industry" (ICCLB 2023)* (pp. 912–928). Atlantis Press.

Hatipoglu, B., Ertuna, B., & Salman, D. (2019). Corporate social responsibility in tourism as a tool for sustainable development: An evaluation from a community perspective. *International Journal of Contemporary Hospitality Management, 31*(6), 2358–2375. https://doi.org/10.1108/IJCHM-05-2018-0448

Henry, L. A. (2023). Navigating disruptive times: How cross-sector partnerships in a development context built resilience during the COVID-19 pandemic outbreak. *Business & Society*, 00076503231169478.

Heslin, P. A., & Ochoa, J. D. (2008). Understanding and developing strategic corporate social responsibility. *Organizational Dynamics, 37*(2), 125–144. https://doi.org/10.1016/j.orgdyn.2008.02.002

Hong, S., Yoon, H. J., & Kim, H. J. (2018). CSR in the tourism industry area has been expanding consideration in the past ten years. *Journal of Travel & Tourism Marketing, 35*(3), 301–313.

Horng, J. S., Hsu, H., & Tsai, C. Y. (2018). An assessment model of corporate social responsibility practice in the tourism industry. *Journal of Sustainable Tourism, 26*(7), 1085–1104.

Kallio, H., Pietilä, A. M., Johnson, M., & Kangasniemi, M. (2016). Systematic methodological review: Developing a framework for a qualitative semi-structured interview guide. *Journal of Advanced Nursing, 72*(12), 2954–2965.

Koch, J., Gerdt, S. O., & Schewe, G. (2020). Determinants of sustainable behavior of firms and the consequences for customer satisfaction in hospitality. *International Journal of Hospitality Management, 89*, 102515.

Koseoglu, M. A., Rahimi, R., Okumus, F., & Liu, J. (2021). Corporate social responsibility and organizational ethics in the hospitality industry. *Journal of Business Ethics, 170*(1), 45–60.

Kim, M. (2020). A systematic literature review of the personal value orientation construct in hospitality and tourism literature. *International Journal of Hospitality Management, 89*, 102572.

Kumar, V., & Kaushik, A. K. (2020). Does experience affect engagement? Role of destination brand engagement in developing brand advocacy and revisit intentions. *Journal of Travel & Tourism Marketing, 37*(3), 332–346.

Le, T. T. (2023). Corporate social responsibility and SMEs' performance: Mediating role of corporate image, corporate reputation and customer loyalty. *International Journal of Emerging Markets, 18*(10), 4565–4590.

Le Tan, T., Tuong, N. C., Nguyet, P. H., Man, L. M., Nhi, H. T. L., & Van, N. T. (2021). Factors affecting the implementation of Green tourism in Da Nang City. *International Journal of Community Service & Engagement, 2*(4), 157–177.

Lee, A., & Chung, T. L. D. (2023). Transparency in corporate social responsibility communication on social media. *International Journal of Retail & Distribution Management, 51*(5), 590–610.

Lincoln, A. A., & Diamond, B. (2023). Contribution of sustainable development goals and corporate social responsibility initiatives of multinational enterprises (MNEs) to social development in Nigeria: A critical assessment of the different parties and the dynamic involved in mandating CSR to identify best practices for developing nations. In *The Elgar companion to corporate social responsibility and the sustainable development goals* (pp. 190–220). Edward Elgar Publishing.

Lom, M., Pribyl, O., & Svitek, M. (2016). Industry 4.0 as a part of smart cities. In *Smart cities symposium Prague (SCSP)* (pp. 1–6). IEEE.

Lopez, B., Rangel, C., & Fernández, M. (2022). The impact of corporate social responsibility strategy on the management and governance axis for sustainable growth. *Journal of Business Research, 150*, 690–698. https://doi.org/10.1016/j.jbusres.2022.06.025

Lowenstein, M. (2014). Customer advocacy, bonding, endorsement, recommendation, and influence: What's the difference? Retrieved August 21, 2021, from https://customerthink.com/customer-advocacy-bonding-endorsement-recommendation-andinfluence-whats-the-difference/

Luo, W., Tang, P., Jiang, L., & Su, M. M. (2020). Influencing mechanism of tourist social responsibility awareness on environmentally responsible behavior. *Journal of Cleaner Production, 271*, 122565.

Madanaguli, A., Srivastava, S., Ferraris, A., & Dhir, A. (2022). Corporate social responsibility and sustainability in the tourism sector: A systematic literature review and future outlook. *Sustainable Development, 30*(3), 447–461. https://doi.org/10.1002/sd.2258

Mason, A., Spencer, E., Barnett, K., & Bouchie, J. (2023). Examining the prominence and congruence of organizational corporate social responsibility (CSR) communication in medical tourism provider websites. *Journal of Hospitality and Tourism Insights, 6*(1), 1–17. https://doi.org/10.1108/JHTI-06-2021-0136

Meuser, J. D., & Smallfield, J. (2023). Servant leadership: The missing community component. *Business Horizons, 66*(2), 251–264.

Mihalic, T. (2016). Sustainable-responsible tourism discourse – Towards 'responsustable' tourism. *Journal of Cleaner Production, 111*, 461–470.

Mondal, M. (2023). *Building a strong brand image through thoughtful CSR activities.*

Nanu, L., Rahman, I., Ali, F., & Martin, D. S. (2024). Enhancing the hospitality experience: A systematic review of 22 years of physical environment research. *International Journal of Hospitality Management, 119*, 103692.

Ndlazi, S. E., Ogunsola, S. A., Dlamini, B. I., & Nhleko, M. A. N. (2023). Evaluating small, Medium and micro-enterprises' ethical management practises to ensure efficient business decision-making in the eThekwini municipal area. *Open Access Library Journal, 10*(12), 1–18.

Nieforth, L. O., Wahab, A. H. A., Sabbaghi, A., Wadsworth, S. M., Foti, D., & O'Haire, M. E. (2022). Quantifying the emotional experiences of partners of veterans with PTSD service dogs using ecological momentary assessment. *Complementary Therapies in Clinical Practice, 48*, 101590.

Nugroho, D. P., Hsu, Y., Hartauer, C., & Hartauer, A. (2024). Investigating the interconnection between environmental, social, and governance (ESG), and corporate social responsibility (CSR) strategies: An examination of the influence on consumer behavior. *Sustainability, 16*(2), 614.

Pereira, V., Silva, G. M., & Dias, Á. (2021). Sustainability practices in hospitality: Case study of a luxury hotel in Arrábida Natural Park. *Sustainability, 13*(6), 3164.

Punzo, G., Trunfio, M., Castellano, R., & Buonocore, M. (2022). A multi-modelling approach for assessing sustainable tourism. *Social Indicators Research, 163*(3), 1399–1443.

Putra, N., Rawi, S., Amin, M., Kusrini, E., Kosasih, E. A., & Mahlia, T. M. I. (2019). Preparation of beeswax/multi-walled carbon nanotubes as novel shape-stable nanocomposite phase-change material for thermal energy storage. *Journal of Energy Storage, 21*, 32–39.

Rasyid, A. (2023). The role of corporate social responsibility of implementing company business. *Infokum, 11*(5), 69–78.

Sánchez-Camacho, C., Carranza, R., Martín-Consuegra, D., & Díaz, E. (2022). Evolution, trends and future research lines in corporate social responsibility and tourism: A bibliometric analysis and science mapping. *Sustainable Development, 30*(3), 462–476. https://doi.org/10.1002/sd.2260

Shahzalal, M., & Elgammal, I. (2023). Stakeholders' perception of accessible tourism implementation based on corporate sustainability and responsibility: A SEM-based investigation. *Tourism Review, 78*(3), 986–1003.

Shaikh, E., Brahmi, M., Thang, P. C., Watto, W. A., Trang, T. T. N., & Loan, N. T. (2022). Should I stay or should I go? Explaining the turnover intentions with corporate social responsibility (CSR), organizational identification and organizational commitment. *Sustainability, 14*(10), 6030.

Sharma, A., Choudhury, M., Agarwal, S., Sharma, R., & Sharma, R. (2023). Corporate social responsibility and roles of developers for sustainability in companies. In *The Route towards global sustainability: Challenges and management practices* (pp. 313–332). Springer.

Sharma, A., & Sodani, P. (2023). *Ethics in tourism: Responsibility toward balancing sustainability*. Springer.

Sultan, M. F., Shaikh, S. K., & Tunio, M. N. (2024). CSR activities as a neutralizer: Halo effect of CSR for Asian companies. In *Strategies and approaches of corporate social responsibility toward multinational enterprises* (pp. 176–183). IGI Global.

Sultan, M. F., Tunio, M. N., Shaikh, S. K., & Shaikh, E. (2024). Strategic impact of corporate social responsibility: A perspective from the hospitality industry. In *Strategies and approaches of corporate social responsibility toward multinational enterprises* (pp. 23–33). IGI Global.

Sun, H., Rabbani, M. R., Ahmad, N., Sial, M. S., Cheng, G., Zia-Ud-Din, M., & Fu, Q. (2020). CSR, co-creation and green consumer loyalty: Are green banking initiatives important? A moderated mediation approach from an emerging economy. *Sustainability, 12*(24), 10688.

Surface, D. L. (2023). *Essays in Green marketing: Corporate social responsibility strategies, competitive advantages and consumer discernment.* Doctoral Dissertation, University of Massachusetts Lowell.

Suryani, T. (2008). *Perilaku Konsumen: Impilkasi pada Strategi Pemasaran* (1st ed.). Graha Ilmu.

Stoffelen, A., Adiyia, B., Vanneste, D., & Kotze, N. (2020). Post-apartheid local sustainable development through tourism: An analysis of policy perceptions among 'responsible' tourism stakeholders around Pilanesberg National Park, South Africa. *Journal of Sustainable Tourism, 28*(3), 414–432.

Stumpf, T. S., Sandstrom, J., & Swanger, N. (2016). Bridging the gap: Grounded theory method, theory development, and sustainable tourism research. *Journal of Sustainable Tourism, 24*(12), 1691–1708.

Solangi, A., & Siddiqui, D. A. (2023). The complementary role of organizational culture in the effect of different factors on employee's corporate social responsibility in Pakistan. *SSRN Electronic Journal.* 10.2139/ssrn.4432199

Textual Style and Lynes. (2018). *The complete guide to academic writing.* Oxford University Press.

Tingchi Liu, M., Anthony Wong, I., Rongwei, C., & Tseng, T. H. (2014). Do perceived CSR initiatives enhance customer preference and loyalty in casinos? *International Journal of Contemporary Hospitality Management, 26*(7), 1024–1045.

Tripathi, S., & Sharma, D. (2023). Green marketing: Sustainable strategies for success. In *Climate change management and social innovations for sustainable global organization* (pp. 76–92). IGI Global.

Tuan, L. T., Rajendran, D., Rowley, C., & Khai, D. C. (2019). Customer value co-creation in the business-to-business tourism context: The roles of corporate social responsibility and customer empowering behaviors. *Journal of Hospitality & Tourism Management, 39,* 137–149. https://doi.org/10.1016/j.jhtm.2019.04.002

United Nations World Tourism Organization (UNWTO). (2020). *Framework convention on tourism ethics.* https://www.unwto.org/ethics-convention

Wang, X. -X., & He, A. -Z. (2022). The impact of retailers' sustainable development on consumer advocacy: A chain mediation model investigation. *Journal of Retailing & Consumer Services, 64,* 102818. https://doi.org/10.1016/j.jretconser.2021.102818

Whittemore, R., & Knafl, K. (2005). The integrative review: Updated methodology. *Journal of Advanced Nursing, 52*(5), 546–553.

World Travel and Tourism Council. (WTTC). (2019). *Economic impact reports.* https://wttc.org/research/economic-impact#:~=WTTC's%20latest%20annual%20research%20shows,1.4%25%20below%20the%202019%20level

Wu, M. Y., Wang, Y., Li, Q., Wu, X., & Ma, S. (2023). The community social responsibility of rural small tourism enterprises: Scale development and validation. *Journal of Travel Research.* https://doi.org/10.1177/00472875231204183.

Yang, J., & Basile, K. (2021). Communicating corporate social responsibility: External stakeholder involvement, productivity and firm performance. *Journal of Business Ethics, 178,* 501–517.

Yasir, M., Majid, A., Yasir, M., Qudratullah, H., Ullah, R., & Khattak, A. (2021). Participation of hotel managers in CSR activities in developing countries: A defining role of CSR orientation, CSR competencies, and CSR commitment. *Corporate Social Responsibility and Environmental Management, 28*(1), 239–250.

Youell, R. (1998). *Tourism: An introduction.* Addison Wesley Longman Ltd.

Zhang, H., Cheng, Z., & Chen, X. (2022). How destination social responsibility affects tourist citizenship behavior at cultural heritage sites? Mediating roles of destination reputation and destination identification. *Sustainability, 14*(11), 6772.

Chapter 17

Sustainable Tourism: Integrating Social Responsibility for Enhanced Organizational Performance Content

Syed Rizwan Qadri, Ulfat Andrabi, Priyanka Chhibber and Mudasir Ahmad Dar

Lovely Professional University, India

Abstract

Purpose: This chapter examines the role of corporate social responsibility (CSR) in tourism operations, focusing on its influence on financial performance, social well-being, and environmental sustainability. This chapter aims to fill gaps in the literature by investigating the relationship between CSR dimensions and financial performance in tourism organizations, as well as the social and environmental impacts of integrating CSR principles into tourism operations.

Design/methodology/approach: This chapter employs a comprehensive literature review to explore the historical background of CSR, its conceptual framework, and its application in the tourism industry. It examines the various dimensions of CSR and their potential effects on financial performance, social well-being, and environmental sustainability in tourism operations.

Findings: The findings suggest that CSR initiatives in tourism operations can lead to improved financial performance through factors such as increased sales, cost savings, and enhanced market value. Furthermore, CSR practices contribute to social well-being by creating job opportunities, supporting local communities, and preserving cultural heritage. Additionally, CSR activities promote environmental sustainability by reducing

Corporate Social Responsibility, Corporate Governance and Business Ethics in Tourism Management: A Business Strategy for Sustainable Organizational Performance, 251–264

Copyright © 2025 by Syed Rizwan Qadri, Ulfat Andrabi, Priyanka Chhibber and Mudasir Ahmad Dar

Published under exclusive licence by Emerald Publishing Limited

doi:10.1108/978-1-83608-704-520241017

resource consumption, conserving biodiversity, and mitigating the negative impacts of tourism on ecosystems.

Originality/value: This chapter contributes to the literature by providing insights into the relationship between CSR and financial performance in tourism organizations, as well as the social and environmental impacts of CSR integration in the tourism industry. The findings highlight the importance of incorporating CSR principles into tourism operations to promote sustainable development and responsible tourism practices.

Keywords: Sustainability; tourism; corporate social responsibility; financial performance; organizational performance

Introduction

There is growing consensus that businesses should prioritize social and environmental responsibilities alongside economic and financial aims, while also considering the requirements and concerns of both external and internal stakeholders (Dahlsrud, 2008). Carroll (1999) stated that CSR includes legal, economic, discretionary, and ethical considerations. Economic duties are the cornerstone and the major concern of a firm. Without satisfying these fiscal obligations, completing the remaining responsibilities becomes difficult. Carroll further emphasized that managers are hesitant to adopt CSR projects unless they see a positive financial return. The critical inquiry focuses on establishing whether there is a positive association between CSR activity and financial performance. There has been a great deal of academic study and significant interest in investigating the impact and correlation between CSR and firm performance (FP) (Endrikat et al., 2014; Friede et al., 2015; Hang et al., 2019; Margolis & Walsh, 2003; Orlitzky et al., 2003; Wang et al., 2016). Engaging in CSR initiatives entails utilizing resources and considering the concerns of stakeholders beyond just shareholders. CSR research in tourism and hospitality has increased significantly in the past two decades (Coles et al., 2013). According to Font and Lynes (2018), there have been over 350 papers on CSR in tourism, with more than two-thirds published within the last seven years. Dodds and Kuehnel (2010) note that most CSR research focuses on hospitality operations. Several studies examined the impact of CSR on financial performance in tourism and hospitality. Although there is significant literature on this association, certain study gaps have been identified. CSR research in the tourist and hospitality sectors has grown significantly over the last 20 years (Coles et al., 2013). Font and Lynes (2018) discovered that over 350 papers on CSR in tourism have been published, with more than two-thirds emerging within the last seven years. However, Dodds and Kuehnel (2010) pointed out that CSR research has primarily focused on hospitality businesses.

While various studies have investigated the relationship between CSR and financial performance (FP) in tourism and hospitality, there are significant gaps in the literature that need to be filled. While previous studies have focused on various areas of tourism and hospitality such as hotels, guesthouses, restaurants, casinos, ski resorts, and airlines, there has been little emphasis on tour operators (TOs) thus far. Tour operators have a substantial impact on worldwide visitor movements (Andriotis, 2003), and their actions are critical in defining the tourism sector's sustainability (Van Wijk & Person, 2006, p. 381). Furthermore, tour operators are important stakeholders in a variety of sectors within the tourism and hospitality industries. Tour operators own, manage, or organize a variety of tourism-related businesses and operations, such as hotels, restaurants, tour guides, travel agencies, and transportation companies. Furthermore, studies on the relationship between CSR and financial performance (FP) in tourism and hospitality, which use primary data, have generally focused on individual countries and specific industries, primarily hotels. However, a full study with worldwide scope has yet to be conducted.

Literature Review

The environmental movement that gained traction in the 1970s laid the groundwork for the concept of sustainability. The International Union for the Conservation of Nature and Natural Resources (IUCN) formally launched the concept of sustainable development in 1980 with its World Conservation Strategy. The Brundtland Commission Report of 1987 defined sustainable development as "development that meets the needs of the present without compromising the ability of future generations to meet their own needs" (WCED, 1987, p. 43). The Commission emphasized that sustainable development is not a static condition of balance, but rather a dynamic process of continuous change aimed at improving both current and future capacity to meet human needs and aspirations (WCED, 1987). The World Tourism Organisation (WTO, 2001) endorses the following paraphrased definition of sustainable development in the tourism industry: Sustainable development in tourism refers to the continued ability to meet current tourism requirements without jeopardizing future generations' ability to meet their own needs. Sustainable tourism development seeks to meet the requirements of existing tourists and host communities while also protecting and expanding prospects for the future. It is intended to guide the management of all resources to meet economic, social, and esthetic requirements while protecting cultural authenticity, critical ecological processes, biodiversity, and life support systems. Prosser (1994) determines four social forces driving the quest for sustainability in tourism: dissatisfaction with current offerings, increased awareness of the environment and appreciation for culture, recognition by destination and areas of their valuable but delicate resources, and changing viewpoints among developers and tour operators. Sustainability is largely regarded as a potential solution for tackling the issues posed by tourism's negative externalities while also assuring its long-term viability. Bramwell and Lane (1993) praise it as a positive way to reduce tensions and conflicts caused by the complex relationships between the tourism sector, tourists, the environment, and host communities. This approach seeks to ensure the long-term viability and integrity of both natural and human resources. Cater (1993) identifies three key goals for sustainable tourism: improving the host population's living conditions in the short and long term, meeting the increasing expectations of tourists, and protecting the natural environment to enable the achievement of the objectives. Farrell (1999) emphasizes the concept of the sustainability trinity, which aims for a seamless and transparent integration of the business, society, and environment. Sustainable development, sustainable tourism, and environmentally friendly development are frequently used interchangeably in the literature, but some researchers, such as Butler (1999) and Harris and Leiper (1995), have attempted to distinguish between them. "Sustainability" broadly refers to a state-focused idea that implies long-term living circumstances for future generations. "Sustainable development" is viewed as more process-oriented, with managed improvements aimed at improving conditions for people engaged. Similarly, sustainable tourism refers to any sort of tourism, whether traditional or alternative, that aligns with or contributes to sustainable development. It is vital to emphasize that development does not always imply "growth," but rather refers to the process of reaching certain social and economic goals, which may need stabilization, expansion, reduction, qualitative changes, or even the elimination of existing aspects (Liu & Jones, 1996). The emergence of sustainable development, sustainable tourism, and environmentally friendly practices in the tourism industry is strongly linked to CSR efforts. CSR in tourism refers to the ethical and sustainable methods used by tourism companies to reduce negative impacts on the environment, society, and local communities while increasing positive contributions. The incorporation of CSR concepts into tourism operations demonstrates a broader commitment to sustainable development goals set by the International Union for the Conservation of Nature and Natural Resources (IUCN) and the Brundtland Commission Report. By matching their strategy with sustainability principles, tourist organizations demonstrate their commitment to serving current needs without jeopardizing future generations' ability to meet their own. Companies in the tourism industry are encouraged to practice CSR by promoting environmental conservation, supporting local people, and respecting cultural heritage. This includes activities like lowering carbon emissions, funding community development projects, and fostering cultural awareness among tourists.

Concept of CSR and Historical Background

Howard Bowen first promoted CSR in his landmark 1953 book Social Responsibilities of the Businessman. According to Carroll and Shabana (2010), CSR started to emphasize accountability, responsiveness, and performance in the 1970s. CSR positions a business as socially conscious. Using corporate resources and discretionary business practices, corporate social responsibility aims to enhance community well-being (Philip & Nancy, 2017). As trade and economic systems become more integrated globally, concerns about CSR have grown in importance. These concerns have been centered around multinational corporations and the outcomes of their operations. Businesses are putting a lot of effort into their social responsibility initiatives, trying to meet stakeholder expectations, and ultimately aiming for sustainability and profitability. The need to disseminate information about CSR initiatives arose from efforts to change the attitudes of certain stakeholders and obtain favorable tax treatment. The requirement for information dissemination resulted in the requirement that CSR initiatives be reported in addition to the legally required financial reports that these companies must submit. Consequently, the significance of non-financial reporting matters, such as CSR reports, has equaled that of mandatory financial reporting.

If one were to summarize CSR, it would be described as the engagement of corporations, which are essential members of society, concerning their obligations concerning adherence to moral principles (Yuksel, 2009). "CSR is about how companies manage the business processes to produce an overall positive impact on society," according to one representative definition of the term. Conversely, it is claimed that CSR theories apply when an enterprise incorporates social demands into its strategies (Hamid, 2010). According to Pelit et al. (2009), common elements among definitions of CSR are practices, strategies, and initiatives meant to mitigate the detrimental effects that businesses have on society, ranging from R&D to post-sale services. Policies, practices, and other measures can occasionally limit a company's ability to operate in favor of social concerns, or they may even require a company to act in a way that advances society on an economic, environmental, social, or cultural level. For some, the realization that trade could be used to satisfy the needs of others in addition to their own needs, in addition to the traditional way of life of production, was brought about by industrialization. This trend began at the end of the 1800s and resulted in the establishment of the foundations for awareness and responsibility (Yuksel, 2009).

A dynamic economic cycle that began in the 1900s came to an end when the New York Stock Exchange crashed in 1929. When the number of jobless persons rose sharply and their purchasing power declined, an economic depression spread throughout the world's economies. Businesses of all sizes were shutting down if they were not fortunate enough or powerful enough to take a defensive stance. According to Adam Smith's Wealth of Nations study, during those years, American corporations were expanding both numerically and in size, but they did not address environmental concerns or social demands. Following a sequence of subsequent social and economic developments, corporations had to deal with the effects of their operations on society on several fronts. The idea of social responsibility, which originated in Europe, found a home in North America. In terms of the concept of social responsibility's emergence, Howard Bowen is crucial. His research, "Social Responsibilities of Businessmen," establishes the theoretical framework for social responsibility and lays the groundwork for the concept of social responsibility (Jamal & Stronza, 2009).

CSR and Tourism

A substantial industry with room to grow, tourism generates profits that can be utilized to further the development of a nation (Kapoor & Jain, 2024). In the tourism sector, CSR is crucial because it gives companies the chance to improve local communities and the environment. Environmental conservation initiatives including cutting carbon emissions, cutting waste production, and protecting natural habitats are a part of CSR in the tourism industry (Bowen, 1953). Eco-friendly measures that tourism businesses can take include encouraging water conservation, using renewable energy sources, and supporting regional biodiversity initiatives. Businesses that implement sustainable practices help to preserve natural resources for the benefit of future generations while also reducing their environmental impact (Golja & Nizic, 2010). Moreover, CSR in tourism encompasses social responsibility toward local communities in addition to environmental concerns. Although tourism frequently boosts an area's economy, it can also cause problems like cultural eroding, the uprooting of indigenous communities, and the exploitation of local labor. Conscientious tourism organizations interact with nearby communities, honor their cultural legacy, and put locals' welfare first (Stefanikova & Rypakova, 2015). This can involve taking steps like encouraging cultural exchange programs, supporting community development initiatives, and hiring locally. Positive relationships with host communities are key to tourism businesses developing a more sustainable and inclusive industry that benefits both locals and tourists (Kasemsap, 2018).

Additionally, CSR in the tourism sector enhances the industry's overall reputation and businesses' ability to compete. Tourists are looking for businesses that exhibit sustainable practices and ethical business practices as they are growing more aware of the impact of their travels (Khan et al., 2021). Tourism companies can increase brand loyalty and gain a competitive edge in the market by attracting environmentally and socially conscious customers by adhering to CSR principles. Furthermore, through better resource management, increased operational efficiency, and decreased regulatory risks, CSR initiatives can result in cost savings (Malik et al., 2021). In the end, incorporating CSR into business plans helps local communities and the environment while also providing tourism businesses with long-term financial benefits. CSR in tourism includes ethical issues about human rights and cultural sensitivity in addition to environmental and social aspects. Sometimes, tourism unintentionally aids in the exploitation or commercialization of local cultures (Koutra, 2013). As a result, ethical travel agencies place a high value on cultural sensitivity and work to advance genuine cultural encounters that honor the customs, beliefs, and practices of the host communities. This may entail working with regional cultural organizations, lending support to initiatives to preserve cultural assets, and teaching visitors the value of respecting and celebrating diversity in culture (Lee et al., 2012). Tourism businesses can enhance the travel experience for all parties involved by fostering mutual understanding and appreciation between locals and visitors through the integration of cultural responsibility into their operations (Mowforth & Munt, 2009).

Moreover, tourism-related CSR programs frequently involve charitable endeavors meant to alleviate socioeconomic difficulties in the destinations. Particularly in rural or marginalized communities, tourism has the power to reduce poverty and promote economic growth (Wernerfelt, 1984). To empower locals and enhance their quality of life, CSR programs may involve investments in small business development, infrastructure, healthcare, and education. Tourism companies can create shared value a situation in which social progress and economic prosperity coexist by funding community-based initiatives (Frederick, 1994). Encouraging resilience and inclusive growth helps the communities themselves as well as the long-term sustainability of tourist destinations. In the end, the tourism sector's ability to grow and adapt to global issues like socioeconomic inequality, cultural homogenization, and climate change depends on its ability to incorporate CSR principles. In addition to reducing negative effects, ethical tourism practices open doors for constructive change and long-term growth (Elkington, 1999). Tourism businesses can show their dedication to moral principles, improve their reputation, and benefit the planet and human race by adopting CSR. Businesses, governments, local communities, and tourists working together can make the tourism industry a potent force for good, ensuring that destinations prosper while protecting their natural and cultural heritage for future generations to enjoy (Nassani et al., 2022). Implementing CSR principles in the tourism industry can have a substantial impact on a company's financial performance. While there may be early expenses associated with implementing sustainable activities, such as adopting eco-friendly technologies or sponsoring local community projects, the long-term advantages can exceed them. For example, lowering energy usage through sustainable methods not only benefits the environment but also saves money on power bills for tourism enterprises. Furthermore, CSR programs frequently attract ecologically and socially conscientious customers willing to pay a premium for products and services provided by responsible companies. This can lead to expanded income streams and profitability for tourism companies that value CSR (Wong et al., 2020; Zaragoza-Sáez et al., 2023). CSR activities in the tourism industry help to improve social performance by building positive relationships with local communities and stakeholders. Tourism enterprises exhibit their social responsibility by participating in community development projects, contributing to cultural preservation efforts, and investing in education and healthcare infrastructure (Uyar et al., 2020; Weaver et al., 2007). Positive partnerships with host communities not only improve the company's overall reputation but also foster more goodwill and trust among local citizens. This, in turn, can lead to a supportive community that is more willing to engage with the tourism sector, resulting in smoother operations and fewer disagreements. Furthermore, CSR activities that prioritize fair labor standards and promote local employment opportunities can improve social justice and employee well-being, hence increasing organizational performance. In addition, incorporating CSR principles into tourism operations improves environmental performance by promoting sustainable resource management and conservation initiatives. To reduce their environmental impact, tourism companies should embrace eco-friendly measures such as trash reduction, water conservation, and habitat protection. These projects not only promote environmental sustainability but also serve to offset the harmful effects of tourism activities on fragile ecosystems and biodiversity. Furthermore, adopting sustainable tourism practices can assist tourism organizations in complying with environmental rules, avoiding costly fines, and mitigating reputational concerns related to environmental deterioration (Scheyvens, 2016; Stoddard et al., 2012). Tourism organizations that prioritize environmental stewardship can increase their competitiveness and appeal to environmentally concerned travelers looking for eco-friendly places and experiences. CSR initiatives are critical to improving organizational performance in the tourism business. Tourism organizations that incorporate CSR concepts into their operations can increase financial success, develop social relationships, and promote environmental sustainability. Adopting CSR promotes not only the company's financial line, but also the well-being of local communities, the protection of natural resources, and the long-term viability of tourist attractions. Finally, by prioritizing ethical standards and responsible business behavior, tourist organizations can provide shared value for stakeholders while maintaining the industry's long-term growth and success in a continuously changing global landscape.

Research Methodology

The successful implementation of sustainable tourism, which prioritizes the integration of ethical behavior to enhance organizational efficiency, necessitates a complete approach. There are usually multiple important steps in the process. First, it starts by carefully evaluating the organization's present procedures and the way they affect the social, environmental, and financial facets of the business. This evaluation lays the groundwork for creating sustainable initiatives and aids in identifying areas that require improvement. Second, to make certain their sustainability initiatives are in line with the requirements and expectations of everyone concerned, organizations must also involve stakeholders, including local communities, governmental bodies, non-governmental organizations, and travelers themselves. Third, a well-defined and feasible sustainability plan with precise objectives, deadlines, and goals should be created. Concerns including waste reduction, community involvement, managing resources, and cultural preservation should all be covered in this strategy. Fourth, in order to enable staff members and community members to actively engage in sustainable tourism projects, organizations need to make investments in training and development programs. To ensure continuous improvement, it is imperative to conduct continual evaluation, monitoring, and adaptation in order to identify obstacles, measure progress, and make required adjustments. By using this approach, businesses may successfully incorporate social obligation into their daily operations, improving both their performance and the sustainability of the travel and tourism sector as a whole.

Research Questions

R1. How do dimensions of Corporate Social Responsibility (CSR) influence the financial performance of tourism organizations?

R2. What are the social and environmental impacts of integrating CSR principles into tourism operations?

Effect of CSR Dimension

Impacts on Immediate Financial Gain

Berman et al. (1999) found that CSR dimensions have varying effects on short-term profitability, with favorable benefits from dimensions such as employee relations and product quality, but small effects from other CSR dimensions. However, they failed to provide a full theoretical reason for these different consequences, attributing some of the results to the use of various industry datasets (Berman et al., 1999). As a result, based on the dominant neoclassical economic perspective, a primary theoretical stance in contemporary discourse, it is proposed that each of the five dimensions of CSR (employee relations, product quality, community relations, environmental issues, and diversity issues) contribute positively to immediate financial gain (Brammer & Millington, 2008; McWilliams & Siegel, 2000). In the words of Brammer and Millington (2008), substantial CSR involvement can boost enterprises' short-term profitability by lowering operational expenses and increasing sales. For example, studies have found that business programs aimed at enhancing employee relations can lead to increased firm efficiency. This is due to the implementation of innovative human resource methods that allow businesses to increase productivity, reduce turnover rates, minimize absenteeism, and/or increase organizational engagement within their personnel (Berman et al., 1999). Concerning the product dimension, favorable consumer perceptions of product quality are predicted to contribute to increased sales for enterprises, eventually leading to an improvement in firm profitability (Waddock & Graves, 1997). Concerning the product dimension, favorable consumer perceptions of product quality are predicted to contribute to increased sales for enterprises, eventually leading to an improvement in firm profitability (Waddock & Graves, 1997). On the contrary, failing to maintain high product quality through irresponsible corporate practices might result in decreased consumer loyalty or more legal action, potentially lowering a company's profitability (Berman et al., 1999). In terms of environmental considerations, organizations that implement proactive environmental policies are expected to have increased profitability as a result of decreased regulatory compliance costs and improved operational efficiencies (Russo & Fouts, 1997). As a result, Russo and Fouts (1997) established a favorable relationship between high corporate environmental performance and company profitability, as measured by Return on Assets. Furthermore, in terms of the remaining two dimensions, corporate community relations activities may result in advantageous tax measures or reduced municipal regulations, allowing businesses to reduce operational costs (Waddock & Graves, 1997). Similarly, business support for women and minorities would boost profits by expanding the market, increasing productivity, and reducing costs (Robinson & Dechant, 1997).

Impacts on How the Market Assesses the Potential Profitability in the Future

Hillman and Keim (2001) and Kacperczyk (2009) showed that each dimension of CSR could have a different impact on future profitability. However, their findings are inconclusive: whereas Kacperczyk (2009) discovered that three of the five characteristics (natural environment, diversity, and community ties) had a favorable impact on future profitability, Hillman and Keim (2001) only identified a positive effect from community relations. Alternative researchers, on the other hand, have used the resource-based approach to justify the positive association between each facet of CSR and market-driven financial performance (Hull & Rothenberg, 2008;

McWilliams & Siegel, 2001; McWilliams et al., 2006). According to this viewpoint, varied and immovable business resources are required to develop a long-term competitive advantage (Barney, 1991). According to studies, CSR initiatives, particularly those that address all five dimensions, help to create a variety of non-transferable resources, such as highly skilled job seekers (Backhaus et al., 2002), corporate reputation (Brammer & Millington, 2005), and positive consumer perceptions of companies (Sen & Bhattacharya, 2001). As a result, cultivating these intangible assets enhances investors' expectations of a company's future profitability, increasing its market value (Luo & Bhattacharya, 2006). Research suggests that each CSR dimension contributes to commercial value by creating intangible resources (Becker & Gerhart, 1996; Brammer & Millington, 2008). Becker and Gerhart (1996) found consistent evidence that sophisticated human resource management strategies improve market-based financial performance. According to Berman et al. (1999), positive consumer evaluations of product quality might impact investors' perceptions of a company's market value. Brammer and Millington (2008) proved that significant community involvement resulted in higher market value. As previously stated, Kacperczyk (2009) proposed that business initiatives including the natural environment, diversity, and community interactions resulted in positive long-term financial performance as evaluated by market indices. Drawing on the resource-based perspective, this study claims that each of the five CSR characteristics contributes independently to future profitability.

Social and Environmental Impact of CSR in the Tourism Industry

Implementing CSR in tourism operations can have a variety of social benefits. According to Garay and Font (2012), CSR programs can improve the well-being of local communities by creating job opportunities, supporting local businesses, and investing in community development projects. This can lead to improved socioeconomic situations for people at tourist sites. Furthermore, Zhao et al., 2021 emphasize that by engaging in CSR practices such as promoting cultural heritage preservation and respecting local customs and traditions, tourism operators may develop greater cultural appreciation and understanding among tourists. Furthermore, incorporating CSR principles into tourism operations has the potential to improve environmental sustainability. Tourism businesses can reduce their environmental impact by using eco-friendly practices including energy and water conservation, waste minimization, and biodiversity conservation. Hall (2010) found that sustainable tourism practices are critical for conserving natural resources and protecting vulnerable ecosystems. Furthermore, initiatives such as carbon offset programs and the usage of renewable energy sources can assist reduce the carbon footprint associated with tourism activities, as noted by Gössling et al. (2013). Furthermore, CSR incorporation into tourism activities can boost destination attractiveness and competitiveness. According to Han et al. (2015), travelers are increasingly looking for authentic and sustainable travel experiences. As a result, tourism companies that demonstrate a commitment to CSR principles may gain a competitive advantage by recruiting ecologically and socially conscious visitors. Furthermore, good environmental and social consequences can help to improve destination branding and reputation, as observed by Nyantakyi et al. (2023), resulting in improved visitor numbers and income generation for tourist locations. In conclusion, incorporating CSR principles into tourism operations can have a significant social and environmental impact. Tourism businesses can contribute to the well-being of local communities and the protection of natural resources by encouraging community development, preserving cultural heritage, and implementing sustainable practices, as well as increasing destination competitiveness and attractiveness in the global tourism market.

Conclusion

In conclusion, incorporating CSR concepts into tourism operations provides several benefits to both communities and the environment. Prioritizing sustainable practices allows tourism stakeholders to strengthen local communities through job development, capacity-building programs, and cultural heritage preservation. This promotes social cohesion and economic resilience, ultimately boosting the well-being of citizens in tourist areas. Furthermore, CSR actions in tourism have a significant impact on environmental protection and resource management. Efforts to cut carbon emissions, save water, and reduce waste help to preserve natural ecosystems and biodiversity. Sustainable tourism practices not only reduce the environmental impact of tourism but also improve ecosystem resilience to climate change, assuring the long-term viability of tourist sites. Furthermore, responsible tourism experiences have the potential to educate and inspire travelers, raising awareness about environmental and social issues. Tourists learn more about local traditions, environmental conservation, and community development activities through immersive cultural encounters and educational programs. This transformative learning experience inspires travelers to adopt more sustainable behaviors and support responsible tourism practices even after they return home, thus contributing to the global sustainability agenda. Overall, incorporating CSR concepts into tourist operations is critical to encouraging inclusive growth, environmental stewardship, and responsible tourism practices that benefit both current and future generations.

References

Andriotis, K. (2003). Tourism in crete: A form of modernisation. *Current Issues in Tourism*, 6(1), 23–53.
Bowen, H. R. (1953). *Social responsibility of the businessman.* Harpers and Brothers.
Barney, J. (1991). Firm resources and sustained competitive advantage. *Journal of Management*, 17(1), 99–120.
Backhaus, K. B., Stone, B. A., & Heiner, K. (2002). Exploringthe relationship between corporate social performance and employer attractiveness. *Business & Society*, 41(3), 292–318.
Bramwell, B. (1998). Selecting policy instruments for sustainable tourism. In W. F. Theobald (Ed.), *Global tourism* (pp. 361–79). Butterworth-Heinemann.
Byrd, E. T., & Canziani, B. (2014). Tourism, cultural heritage, and the impact of sustainability. *Journal of Heritage Tourism*, 9(2), 103–115.

Butler, R. W. (1999). Sustainable tourism: A state-of-the-art review. *Tourism Geographies, 1*(1), 7–25.

Carroll, A. B. (1991). The pyramid of corporate social responsibility: Toward the moral management of organizational stakeholders. *Business Horizons, 34*(4), 39–48.

Cater, E. (1993). Ecotourism in the third world: Problems for sustainable tourism development. *Tourism Management, 14*(2), 85–90.

de Grosbois, D. (2012). Corporate social responsibility reporting by the global hotel industry: Commitment, initiatives, and performance. *International Journal of Hospitality Management, 31*, 896–905.

de Grosbois, D. (2015). Corporate social responsibility reporting in the cruise tourism industry: A performance evaluation using a new institutional theory-based model. *Journal of Sustainable Tourism, 24*(2), 245–269.

Dahlsrud, A. (2008). How corporate social responsibility is defined: An analysis of 37 definitions. *Corporate Social Responsibility and Environmental Management, 15*(1), 1–13.

Endrikat, J., Guenther, E., & Hoppe, H. (2014). Making sense of conflicting empirical findings: A meta-analytic review of the relationship between corporate environmental and financial performance. *European Management Journal, 32*(5), 735–751.

Elkington, J. (1999). *Cannibals with forks: The triple bottom line of 21st-century business.* Capston Publishing.

Farrell, B. H. (1999). Conventional or sustainable tourism? No room for choice. *Tourism Management, 20*(2), 189–191.

Friede, G., Busch, T., & Bassen, A. (2015). ESG and financial performance: Aggregated evidence from more than 2000 empirical studies. *Journal of sustainable Finance & Investment, 5*(4), 210–233.

Frederick, W. C. (1994). From CSR1 to CSR2: The maturing of business-and-society thought. *Business & Society, 33*(2), 150–164.

Garay, L., & Font, X. (2012). Doing good to do well? Corporate social responsibility reasons, practices and impacts in small and medium accommodation enterprises. *International Journal of Hospitality Management, 31*(2), 329–337.

Goeldner, C. R., & Ritchie, J. R. B. (2011). *Tourism: Principles, practices, philosophies* (12th ed.). John Wiley & Sons.

Golja, T., & Nizic, M. K. (2010). Corporate social responsibility in tourism—The most popular tourism destinations in Croatia: Comparative analysis. *Management: Journal of Contemporary Management Issues, 15*(2), 107–121.

Hamid, M. A. (2010). *Social science research network.* Retrieved October 7, 2015, from http://papers.ssrn.com/

İs'te Kobi. (n.d.). Retrieved November 6, 2015, from http://www.istekobi.com.tr

Hang, M., Geyer-Klingeberg, J., & Rathgeber, A. W. (2019). It is merely a matter of time: A meta-analysis of the causality between environmental performance and financial performance. *Business Strategy and the Environment, 28*(2), 257–273.

Harris, R., & Leiper, N. (Eds.). (1995). *Sustainable tourism: An Australian perspective* (pp. xxxiii+–156pp).

Hull, C. E., & Rothenberg, S. (2008). Firm performance: The interactions of corporate social performance with innovation and industry differentiation. *Strategic Management Journal, 29*(7), 781–789.

Hall, C. M., Scott, D., & Gössling, S. (2013). The primacy of climate change for sustainable international tourism. *Sustainable Development, 21*(2), 112–121.

Jamal, T. B., & Stronza, A. (2009). Collaboration theory and tourism practice in protected areas: Stakeholders, structuring and sustainability. *Journal of Sustainable Tourism, 17*(2), 169–189.

Kapoor, D., & Jain, A. (2024). Sustainable tourism and its future research directions: A bibliometric analysis of twenty-five years of research. *Tourism Review*, *79*(3), 541–567.

Kasemsap, K. (2018). Encouraging corporate social responsibility and sustainable tourism development in global tourism. In *Operations and service management: Concepts, methodologies, tools, and applications* (pp. 1028–1056). IGI Global.

Khan, M. I., Khalid, S., Zaman, U., José, A. E., & Ferreira, P. (2021). Green paradox in emerging tourism supply chains: Achieving green consumption behavior through strategic green marketing orientation, brand social responsibility, and green image. *International Journal of Environmental Research and Public Health*, *18*(18), 9626.

Koutra, C. (2013). *More than simply corporate social responsibility: Implications of corporate social responsibility for tourism development and poverty reduced in less developed countries: A political economy perspective*. Nova Science.

Lee, C. -K., Song, H. -J., Lee, H. -M., Lee, S., & Bernhard, B. J. (2013). The impact of CSR on casino employees' organizational trust, job satisfaction, and customer orientation: An empirical examination of responsible gambling strategies. *International Journal of Hospitality Management*, *33*, 406–415.

Malik, S. Y., Hayat Mughal, Y., Azam, T., Cao, Y., Wan, Z., Zhu, H., & Thurasamy, R. (2021). Corporate social responsibility, green human resources management, and sustainable performance: Is organizational citizenship behavior towards environment the missing link? *Sustainability*, *13*(3), 1044.

Mowforth, M., & Munt, I. (2009). *Tourism and sustainability: Development, globalization and new tourism in the third world*. Routledge.

Margolis, J. D., Elfenbein, H. A., & Walsh, J. P. (2003). Does it pay to be good... and does it matter? A meta-analysis of the relationship between corporate social and financial performance. *And does it matter*.

McWilliams, A., & Siegel, D. (2001). Corporate social responsibility: A theory of the firm perspective. *Academy of Management Review*, *26*(1), 117–127.

Nassani, A. A., Yousaf, Z., Radulescu, M., & Haffar, M. (2022). Environmental performance through environmental resources conservation efforts: Does corporate social responsibility authenticity act as mediator? *Sustainability*, *14*(4), 2330.

Nyantakyi, G., Atta Sarpong, F., Adu Sarfo, P., Uchenwoke Ogochukwu, N., & Coleman, W. (2023). A boost for performance or a sense of corporate social responsibility? A bibliometric analysis on sustainability reporting and firm performance research (2000–2022). *Cogent Business & Management*, *10*(2), 2220513.

Orlitzky, M., Schmidt, F. L., & Rynes, S. L. (2003). Corporate social and financial performance: A meta-analysis. *Organization studies*, *24*(3), 403–441.

Pelit, E., Keles, Y., & Cakır, M. (2009). Otel İşletmelerinde Sosyal Sorumluluk Uygulamalarının Belirlenmesine Yonelik Bir Araştırma. *Yonetim ve Ekonomi*, *16*(2), 1–30.

Prosser, M. (1994). A phenomenographic study of students' intuitive and conceptual understanding of certain electrical phenomena. *Instructional Science*, *22*(3), 189–205.

Robinson, G., & Dechant, K. (1997). Building a business case for diversity. *Academy of Management Perspectives*, *11*(3), 21–31.

Scheyvens, R., Egan, S., & Pickering, T. (2016). Tourism and poverty reduction: Issues for small island states. *Journal of Sustainable Tourism*, *24*(4), 477–497.

Stefanikova, Ľ., Rypakova, M., & Moravcikova, K. (2015). The impact of competitive intelligence on sustainable growth of the enterprises. *Procedia Economics and Finance*, *26*, 209–214.

Stoddard, J. E., Pollard, C. E., & Evans, M. R. (2012). The triple bottom line: A framework for sustainable tourism development. *International Journal of Hospitality & Tourism Administration*, *13*(3), 233–258.

Tsai, H., Tsang, N. K. F., & Cheng, S. K. Y. (2012). Hotel employees' perceptions of corporate social responsibility: The case of Hong Kong. *International Journal of Hospitality Management*, *31*(4), 1143–1154.

Uyar, A., Kilic, M., Koseoglu, M. A., Kuzey, C., & Karaman, A. S. (2020). The link among board characteristics, corporate social responsibility performance, and financial performance: Evidence from the hospitality and tourism industry. *Tourism Management Perspectives*, *35*, 100714.

WCED. (1987). *Our common future*. Oxford University Press.

Weaver, D. B., & Lawton, L. J. (2007). Twenty years on the state of contemporary ecotourism research. *Tourism Management*, *28*(5), 1168–1179.

Wernerfelt, B. (1984). A resource-based view of the firm. *Strategic Management Journal*, *5*(2), 171–180.

Wong, A. K. F., Kim, S., & Lee, S. (2022). The evolution, progress, and the future of corporate social responsibility: Comprehensive review of hospitality and tourism articles. *International Journal of Hospitality & Tourism Administration*, *23*(1), 1–33.

Yuksel, M. (2009). *Kurumsal Sosyal Sorumluluk Kapsamında Derecelendirilmeye Tabi Tutulan İsletmelerin Finansal Gostergeleri Uzerine Bir Arastırma*. Yuksek Lisans Tezi. Dumlupınar Universitesi Sosyal Bilimler Enstitusu, Kutahya.

Zaragoza-Sáez, P. C., Claver-Cortés, E., Marco-Lajara, B., & Úbeda-García, M. (2023). Corporate social responsibility and strategic knowledge management as mediators between sustainable intangible capital and hotel performance. *Journal of Sustainable Tourism*, *31*(4), 908–930.

Zhao, F., Kusi, M., Chen, Y., Hu, W., Ahmed, F., & Sukamani, D. (2021). Influencing mechanism of green human resource management and corporate social responsibility on organizational sustainable performance. *Sustainability*, *13*(16), 8875.